DATE DUE

MY 08 8		
OCT 1 3 '93		
RT'D MAY 05		
NOV 0 9 '95		
RT'D OCT 22 95		
SEP 3 0 2008		
RECEIVED		
AUG 2 1 2008		
GAYLORD		PRINTED IN U.S.A.

Yale Historical Publications
Miscellany, 105

Mirror to the Son of Heaven

Wei Cheng at the Court of T'ang T'ai-tsung

Howard J. Wechsler

Yale University Press   New Haven and London   1974

Designed by John O.C. McCrillis
and set in Baskerville type.
Printed in the United States of America by
The Murray Printing Co., Forge Village, Massachusetts.

Published in Great Britain, Europe, and Africa by
Yale University Press, Ltd., London.
Distributed in Latin America by Kaiman & Polon,
Inc., New York City; in Australasia and Southeast
Asia by John Wiley & Sons Australasia Pty. Ltd.,
Sydney; in India by UBS Publishers' Distributors Pvt.,
Ltd., Delhi; in Japan by John Weatherhill, Inc., Tokyo.

To my parents
Melvin and Gertrude Wechsler

One may use bronze as a mirror to straighten one's clothes and cap; antiquity as a mirror to understand the rise and fall of states; a man as a mirror to correct one's judgment. We have always maintained these three mirrors. . . . Now that Wei Cheng is gone, one of those mirrors has disappeared.

T'ai-tsung speaking after the death of Wei Cheng

Contents

Acknowledgments

It is always a pleasure to be able to thank those who have helped make a difficult task easier, doubly so when one's debt of gratitude extends to so many teachers, colleagues, and friends. Foremost among these is Arthur Frederick Wright, Charles Seymour Professor of History at Yale University, who in 1965 first suggested that I look into Wei Cheng as a possible topic for a doctoral dissertation and, as director of the dissertation during the period 1966–70, was unstinting of his time and energies in providing me with incisive counsel and encouragement. I am also indebted to several scholars in the United States and abroad who offered helpful advice regarding matters both substantive and technical during the course of my work: Li Shu-t'ung of Taiwan Normal University; Nunome Chōfū of Osaka University; Denis Twitchett of Cambridge University; Tonami Mamoru of Kobe University; Mou Jun-sun of the Chinese University of Hong Kong; Mao Han-kuang of Academia Sinica, Republic of China; Li T'ien-yi, formerly of Yale University, now of Ohio State University; James T. C. Liu of Princeton University; Nathan Sivin of the Massachusetts Institute of Technology; and Ernst Wolff of the University of Illinois, Urbana-Champaign. Richard Harris, former Far Eastern correspondent of the London *Times,* furnished me with crucial leads relating to Wei Cheng's role in the Cultural Revolution, which I was able to follow through at the Library of the American Consulate-General of Hong Kong by means of the kind offices of a former colleague at Yale, Norman Tolman, then Cultural Attaché. I would also like especially to thank the staff and librarians of Academia Sinica, Nankang, Taiwan, and the Research Institute for Humanistic Studies of Kyoto University for the great kindness they showed a neophyte researcher.

Robert Somers of Yale University, Lloyd Eastman and Bennett Hill of the University of Illinois, Urbana-Champaign, and Jack Dull of the University of Washington each expended considerable time and effort reading the manuscript at various stages of preparation in its entirety and offering trenchant criticism and advice on ways to improve it. Lily Hwa, a graduate student in the Department of History at the University of Illinois, proved resourceful in helping to revise the translations that make up a considerable portion of this volume.

Dissertation research was carried out under two awards: a Foreign Area Fellowship for study in Taiwan, during 1966–67, sponsored by the American Council of Learned Societies and the Social Science Research Council, and a Fulbright-Hays Graduate Study Fellowship for research in Japan, 1967–68, provided by the United States Department of Health, Education, and Welfare. A major portion of the dissertation was written during 1968–69 at Yale University under a second Foreign Area Fellowship grant. The Center for Asian Studies and the Research Board of the University of Illinois, Urbana-Champaign, provided funds for research, travel, and clerical assistance while the manuscript underwent revision. I am deeply grateful to these organizations for their financial assistance and support.

A special vote of thanks is owed Mrs. Barbara Thayer, who typed successive drafts of the manuscript with uncommon geniality and precision, and Duncan Streeter, who generously gave of his time in proofing the text.

Last but not least I would like to express my appreciation to the faculty and staff of the Center for Asian Studies of the University of Illinois, whose unflagging good spirits did much to buoy my own during times of frustration and self-doubt.

Abbreviations

Ch'enS   *Ch'en-shu*, compiled 629–36 by Yao Ssu-lien et al.

CKCY   *Chen-kuan cheng-yao*, compiled ca. 707–09 by Wu Ching.

CTS   *Chiu T'ang-shu*, compiled 940–45 by Liu Hsü et al.

CTShih   *Ch'üan T'ang-shih*, compiled 1707 by Ts'ao Yin et al.

CTW   *Ch'üan T'ang-wen*, compiled 1814 by Tung Kao et al.

CYCCC   *Ta-T'ang ch'uang-yeh ch'i-chü-chu*, compiled prior to 627 by Wen Ta-ya.

HL   *Wei Cheng-kung chien hsü-lu*, compiled ca. 1330–33 by Chai Ssu-chung.

HS   *Han-shu*, compiled 58–76 by Pan Ku.

HTS   *Hsin T'ang-shu*, compiled 1043–60 by Ou-yang Hsiu et al.

KSSI   *Wei Wen-chen kung ku-shih shih-i*, compiled and annotated by Wang Hsien-kung, 1883.

LS   *Liang-shu*, compiled 629–36 by Yao Ssu-lien et al.

PCh'iS   *Pei Ch'i-shu*, compiled 629–36 by Li Pai-yao et al.

PS   *Pei-shih*, compiled 630–50 by Li Yen-shou.

SC   *Shih-chi*, compiled 104–87 B.C. by Ssu-ma Ch'ien.

SKCSTM   *Ssu-k'u ch'üan-shu tsung-mu*, compiled 1782 by Chi Yün et al.

SPTK   *Ssu-pu ts'ung-k'an.*

SuiS   *Sui-shu*, compiled 629–36 by Wei Cheng et al.

SungS   *Sung-shih*, compiled 1343–45 by T'o T'o et al.

TCTC   *Tzu-chih t'ung-chien*, compiled 1084 by Ssu-ma Kuang.

TFYK   *Ts'e-fu yüan-kuei*, compiled 1005–13 by Wang Ch'in-jo et al.

THY   *T'ang hui-yao*, compiled 961 by Wang P'u.

TTLT   *Ta-T'ang liu-tien*, attributed to T'ang Hsüan-tsung, compiled ca. 739.

WCKCL   *Wei Cheng-kung chien-lu chiao-chu*, compiled prior to 702 by Wang Fang-ch'ing and annotated by Wang Hsien-kung, 1883.

WCKWC   *Wei Cheng-kung wen-chi*, compiled by Wang Hao, 1879–92. and annotated by Wang Hsien-ch'ien, 1883.

WS   *Wei-shu*, compiled 551–54 by Wei Shou.

Full references for the above are given in the bibliography.

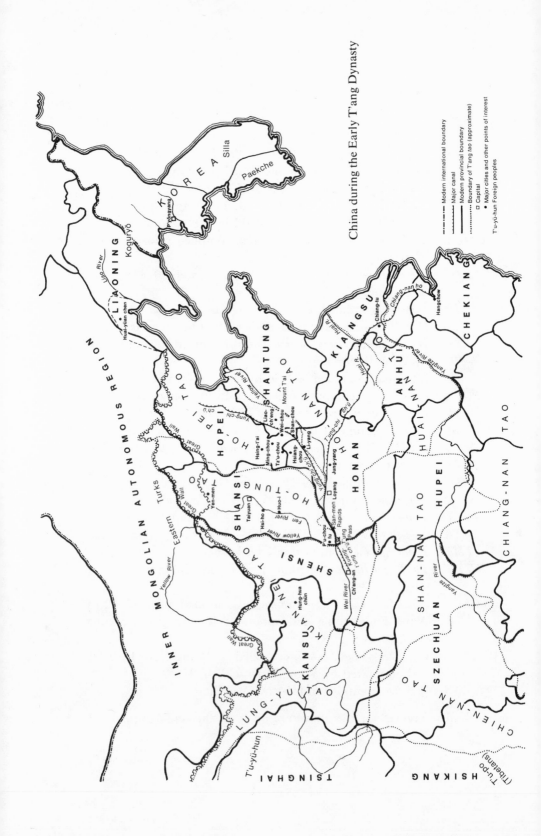

China during the Early T'ang Dynasty

- · — · · — Modern international boundary
- ———— Major canal
- ———— Modern provincial boundary
- · · · · · · · · · Boundary of T'ang tao (approximate)
- □ Capital
- ● Major cities and other points of interest
- T'u-yü-hun Foreign peoples

KOREA

Silla

Paekche

P'yŏngyang

Koguryŏ

LIAONING

Liao River

Huai-yüan chen

INNER MONGOLIAN AUTONOMOUS REGION

Turks

Eastern Turks

Yellow River

Great Wall

Great Wall

HO-PEI TAO

SHANTUNG

Yellow River

Yung-chi ch'ü

Mount T'ai

HO-NAN TAO

Hsing-t'ai

Ming-chou

Liao-ch'eng

Wei-chou

Shan-chou

T'zu-chou

Hsiang-chou

Li-yang

HO-TUNG TAO

Yen-men

Yen-men Pass

T'ai-yüan

Fen River

Hsi-ho

Huai-i

Pu-chou

San-men Rapids

San-men Loyang

Kuang-t'ung Rapids

Jung-yang

Pien-chü

Yellow River

T'ung-chi ch'ü

HONAN

Chiang-tu

KIANGSU

Huai R.

Huai River

Chiang-nan ho

Hangchow

CHEKIANG

ANHUI

HUAI-NAN TAO

SHENSI TAO

Wei River

Ch'ang-an T'ung Pass

KUAN-NEI TAO

Hung-hua chen

Great Wall

LUNG-YU TAO

T'u-yü-hun

TSINGHAI

HSIKANG

T'u-po (Tibetans)

SZECHUAN TAO

Yangtze River

CHIEN-NAN TAO

SHAN-NAN TAO

HUPEI

Yangtze River

CHIANG-NAN TAO

Introduction

China boasts the longest continuous tradition of monarchy and bureaucracy in the world. Not surprisingly, therefore, the ruler-minister
(*chün-ch'en*) relationship has furnished Chinese history with one of its
dominant motifs. As early as the fourth century B.C., the Confucian
Analects (*Lun-yü*) was already prescribing standards of conduct for the
model minister in the service of his prince, but for the earliest example
of the ideal ruler-minister relationship we must go back even further in
time, to the shadowy and mythological beginnings of Chinese history
and the culture-heroes Yao and Shun in the third millenium B.C.
Following Yao and Shun come ruler-minister pairs nearly as distinguished but historically more verifiable: King Wu of Chou and the
Duke of Chou in the twelfth century B.C., Duke Huan of Ch'i and
Kuan Chung in the seventh century B.C., Han Kao-tsu and Chang
Liang in the third century B.C., Liu Pei of Shu Han and Chu-ko Liang
in the third century A.D., to mention the most notable examples down
to the time of the Three Kingdoms and the Period of Disunion (220–
589). In the T'ang dynasty (618–907) perhaps the classic case of a ruler-
minister relationship in the grand Chinese tradition was that between
the second emperor, T'ai-tsung, and his minister Wei Cheng (580–643).

   T'ai-tsung's reign (627–49), named *Chen-kuan* ("True Vision") on
the first day (January 23) of the lunar year 627, was itself one of China's
most resplendent eras, distinguished by beneficent government, material
prosperity, and the reassertion of Chinese control over a good portion
of Asia. It was so exceptional, in fact, that the Chinese have revered it
with a special complimentary designation, *Chen-kuan chih chih* or the
"good rule of the Chen-kuan reign." The *Chen-kuan chih chih* came
to serve as a model of administration for rulers of later ages, among
them such diverse personalities as the Mongol Kubilai Khan, the
shogun Tokugawa Ieyasu of Japan, and the Ch'ien-lung Emperor of
the Ch'ing dynasty. Wei Cheng, who served at T'ai-tsung's side for
seventeen of his twenty-three years on the throne, is widely viewed as

1

having been a prime motive force behind the success of the Chen-kuan period. This alone might provide sufficient justification for a study of his life and career. Yet Wei is of interest for a number of other reasons, chief among them being his status in China as a forceful symbol of bureaucratic power and of the civil, prudential counterweight to imperial grandeur and might.

The struggle for power between sovereign and official is as old as the institution of monarchy itself. In bureaucratic polities, Eisenstadt points out,[1] the political struggle is generally waged on two levels. On the first level it is waged between the political elite (emperors, kings, and bureaucrats) on the one hand, and hereditary-ascriptive groups (e.g., the landed aristocracy) or occupational groups (e.g., the merchants) on the other, to determine the scope of bureaucratic and centralized political activity. Here, sovereign and official usually share similar goals, especially the maintenance of a strongly centralized political structure in the face of feudal or other centrifugal tendencies. On the second level the political struggle is waged *within* the framework of the central political structure among the bureaucracy, the ruler, his relatives and close associates, religious and military elites, and the like, to decide who will exploit this structure, who will dominate the major bureaucratic and advisory positions, and who will formulate the major domestic and foreign policies. Here, the official competes both with his sovereign and other power groups for a larger piece of the power pie.

The struggle on this second level, particularly the attempts made both by the Chinese ruler and his officials to enhance their own power and prestige and maximize their own political autonomy at the expense of the other, provides a focal point for our examination of the relationship between Wei Cheng and T'ang T'ai-tsung. In China, as in other bureaucratic polities, such a struggle often revolved around the question of who possessed the greater political legitimacy. The ultimate political authority of the Chinese ruler, or Son of Heaven (*t'ien-tzu*), derived from a belief, embodied in the Mandate of Heaven (*t'ien-ming*) concept, that his surpassing wisdom and exemplary virtue had prompted Heaven to confer upon him (and his descendants) a divine mandate to rule the

---

[1]S. N. Eisenstadt, "Political Struggle in Bureaucratic Societies," *World Politics,* 9 (1956–57), 22–25.

land. Chinese officials naturally took steps to counter this powerful imperial legitimating ideology, stressing that the Mandate was merely provisional and could be revoked from the morally bankrupt as readily as it had been conferred on the worthy. At the same time they attempted to gain a controlling influence over the ruler by appealing to Confucian scripture, which, they claimed, sanctioned their all-pervading administrative, advisory, and ethical responsibilities in government. The considerable charisma accruing to Chinese officialdom as a result of its intense campaign of self-legitimation, combined with the monopoly it exerted on the country's administrative skills and the professional traditions and morale it developed with time, came to pose a challenge to the supremacy of imperial authority. To check increasing bureaucratic autonomy, Chinese rulers resorted to various practices, among them the institutionalization of bureaucratic regulative mechanisms such as the censorate and the creation of "inner courts" made up of imperial family members, relatives, and eunuchs, to compete with "outer courts" of regularly constituted officials.[2] The Chinese monarch, Joseph Levenson has noted, needed his Confucian officials "to make good his centralization; then, in turn, to protect it, he had to restrain their ominous appetites."[3]

In this eternal power struggle, whether the pendulum swung in favor of the sovereign or his officials was largely a function of specific personalities and events, although it may be noted in general that the bureaucracy became increasingly subordinate to the throne from the Sung dynasty (960–1279) onward, when the supreme power of the ruler received both Confucian and institutional underpinnings. During the last three Chinese dynasties, the Yüan (1279–1368), Ming (1368–1644), and Ch'ing (1644–1911), particularly during the Ming, few officials dared challenge their ruler's authority, and then only at the peril of their lives. Indeed, forced kow-tows, public beatings with heavy clubs, secret tortures whose effects were even ghastlier, and numerous other routine applications of terror by the throne, bludgeoned most of the bureaucracy into a meek passivity.[4]

[2]On the above themes, see ibid., pp. 20–22, and idem, *The Political Systems of Empires* (Glencoe, Ill., 1963), pp. 132–40, 159–72.

[3]*Confucian China and Its Modern Fate*, vol. 2, *The Problem of Monarchical Decay* (Berkeley, 1968), p. 49. On the theme of monarchic-bureaucratic tensions, see pp. 25ff.

[4]See F. W. Mote, "The Growth of Chinese Despotism: A Critique of Wittfogel's Theory of Oriental Despotism as Applied to China," *Oriens Extremus*, 8 (1961), 11–31.

The early T'ang, however, was a far different time, marked by an impressive degree of official participation in decision making and official freedom to criticize the throne, more, perhaps, than during most other periods in Chinese history. T'ai-tsung's reign, particularly, is famed as a time of bureaucratic self-confidence without parallel in China. Wei Cheng was the focus and ultimately the symbol of this self-confidence. It is difficult to conceive of any Ming official who would have dared address his own sovereign with Wei Cheng's temerity. Wei took literally the Confucian dictum that a minister was duty-bound to rectify his prince, never hesitating to denounce any aspect of T'ai-tsung's behavior that displeased him or to resist any of the emperor's policies he believed detrimental to the interests of the state. We were reminded of this aspect of Wei's political personality as recently as 1966 when, during the turmoil of the Cultural Revolution in the People's Republic of China, talk of the "Wei Cheng spirit" of open political opposition—in this case, opposition to Mao Tse-tung and his policies—briefly filled the air at Communist Party meetings and brought forth loud hurrahs or bitter denunciations from the opposing sides.[5]

Perhaps more than any other of his early T'ang colleagues, Wei Cheng represents the return of the Confucian civil official to the halls of government following an eclipse of more than three centuries. The Period of Disunion, during which China had been divided between semi-"barbarian" regimes in the north and Chinese colonial regimes in the south, had been a time of endemic interracial violence, a renascent feudalism presided over by warriors and a privileged aristocracy, and incessant internecine struggles for power. Confucianism had given way to Taoism and Buddhism as the primary religious and philosophical interests of a demoralized official class. Even during the first years of the recentralizing Sui dynasty (589–618), real Confucians were still almost completely absent from court.[6] Consequently, much of Wei Cheng's career during the early T'ang was spent lending renewed authority to the Confucian doctrine that government was a joint enterprise of the ruler and his civil officials and defining the roles and responsibilities of these officials vis-à-vis the throne. His jealous and unflagging guardianship of bureaucratic prerogatives against

    [5]See below, pp. 206–10.
    [6]Arthur F. Wright, "T'ang T'ai-tsung and Buddhism," in *Perspectives on the T'ang*, Arthur F. Wright and Denis Twitchett, eds. (New Haven, 1973), p. 241.

imperial encroachment and against challenges from other power groups—the imperial family, its relatives by marriage, the clergy, the eunuchs—helped to ensure during the early T'ang the primacy of civil officials as imperial advisers and as high-level policy makers. Wei's devotion to officialdom's cause earned him a lofty place in the pantheon of Confucian worthies and the encomiums of successive generations of Confucian admirers and mythologizers.

Which brings us to yet another reason why Wei Cheng is of historical interest—as a case study in the pervasiveness of myth in Chinese history. Indeed, myth occupies a central place in this study of Wei and his relationship to Emperor T'ai-tsung, for myths have colored our attitudes toward both these towering figures. Traditionally, Wei is portrayed as a model Confucian minister, a paragon of wisdom, and a personification of moral excellence. His biographers show him adhering precisely to many of the patterns of protocol and conduct prescribed for the model minister in the Confucian *Analects*. At the same time, they have screened from their accounts aspects of his career that did not fit the mold of the model minister. This was a common practice in Chinese historiography, which was designed above all to teach moral lessons, lessons that could be conveyed most clearly by the judicious selection of materials and the coloring of narrative for effect. Because Wei's biographers were Confucian literati themselves and thus sympathetic toward his efforts to enhance the power and prestige of their class, they regarded his role with much favor. There was a natural tendency on their part to suggest that Wei was one of the key reasons for the great success of the Chen-kuan period.

The Wei Cheng myth, seductive as it was to generations of Chinese bureaucrats, is, naturally, partly fiction. We must therefore apply a bit of chiaroscuro to the excessively schematized line portrait of Wei that adoring Confucians have transmitted to us through the ages. When this is done, we discover that Wei's rise to eminence was not untouched by a certain amount of opportunism and ruthlessness and that his subsequent performance as a minister was, naturally, less than perfect. Even more important, we find that Wei's much-praised influence over T'ai-tsung and, consequently, his contributions to the Chen-kuan period have been considerably exaggerated. Although this influence appears to have been strong at the beginning of T'ai-tsung's reign, it waned appreciably within a few years, by which time the emperor began to act with greater independence and to chart his own course, ignoring much of Wei's advice on substantive policy matters and leaving that disgruntled minister stranded in his wake. Wei then became bitter and morose and hypercritical of T'ai-tsung's administrative performance. In all probability he died believing that he had been, all in all, a political failure. Nevertheless, the Confucians have celebrated him as a great hero.

Perhaps the Wei Cheng myth would not have been so potent had it not been intimately associated with an even more powerful myth surrounding T'ai-tsung himself. To a substantial degree, T'ai-tsung's impressive stature in Chinese history derives from his putative role as the mastermind behind the uprising which led to the establishment of his house. Despite the fact that chronologically he followed his father to the throne, traditional Chinese historians have regarded him as the T'ang "founder," a view, tenaciously persisting to modern times, that is reflected in several biographies of the emperor published in China, Japan, and the West during our own century.[7] A major thesis of this study is that T'ai-tsung was the architect of his own founding-ruler myth.

According to traditional Chinese belief, because of the great store of morality and virtue possessed by a founding ruler, Heaven transfers to him a Mandate to govern in place of the corrupt last ruler of a defunct dynasty. Arthur Wright has catalogued the numerous evil qualities traditionally associated with the stereotyped "bad last" ruler in Chinese history.[8] Conversely, founding rulers have generally been viewed in a similarly stereotyped "good first" ruler fashion. The fame of such epic personalities as Kings Wen and Wu of the Chou, Kao-tsu of the Former Han, Kuang-wu of the Later Han, derives in large measure from their status as founding rulers. Moreover, the administrative reforms, institutional improvements, and economic advances that usually accompany the formation of new dynasties naturally reflect credit on the advisers and counselors of dynastic founders. It is by no means coin-

[7]See, for example, Li T'ang, *T'ang T'ai-tsung* (Hong Kong, 1963); Yüan Ting-chi, *T'ang T'ai-tsung* (Peking, 1963); Seike Eizaburō, *Tō no Taisō* [T'ang T'ai-tsung] (Tokyo, 1934); C. P. Fitzgerald, *Son of Heaven: A Biography of Li Shih-min, Founder of the T'ang Dynasty* (Cambridge, 1933).

[8]Arthur F. Wright, "Sui Yang-ti: Personality and Stereotype," in *The Confucian Persuasion*, Arthur F. Wright, ed. (Stanford, 1960), pp. 47–76.

cidental that so many of the ministers who have enjoyed the greatest esteem among Chinese historians and historical commentators—among them the Duke of Chou, Chang Liang, Chu-ko Liang—served founding rulers. In the same manner, Wei Cheng, a beneficiary of the traditional view that T'ai-tsung was the T'ang founder, for centuries has basked in the reflected glow of the myths surrounding his own prince.

A final reason why Wei elicits the historian's interest is that his life serves as an excellent *point d'appui* for an examination of the exciting and tumultuous transition period between the end of the Sui dynasty and the close of the formative years of the T'ang. Indeed, Wei participated in or was an eyewitness to virtually all of the most momentous events of the time: the late Sui civil wars; the long campaigns of the T'ang against rival aspirants to the Mandate; the struggle for the succession between T'ai-tsung and his elder brother, the crown prince; the T'ang conquest of the nomadic Turks and much of Central Asia; and the impressive reforms and improvements made in Chinese government during the Chen-kuan period.

Considering Wei Cheng's substantial reputation as a statesman and political symbol and the relatively large body of his surviving writings, surprisingly little attention has been devoted to him in China and Japan, not to mention the West. To this day no sustained analytical treatment of his life and career has appeared in any language; an annotated edition of his biographies and writings of late Ch'ing date, a few short Chinese and Japanese articles in this century,[9] and a recent master's thesis largely done in traditional Chinese style complete the skimpy list of modern Wei Cheng scholarship.[10] Unfortunately, too, the early T'ang period as a whole has been sorely neglected by Western scholars despite a recent upsurge in T'ang studies. It is to be hoped, then, that the present volume will contribute toward a better understanding not only of the political career and thought of one of China's foremost Confucian heroes but also of early T'ang political history and of the political process in pre-modern China in general.

---

[9] As this volume went to press, yet another short, general study on Wei Cheng appeared: Maeno Naoaki, "Gi Chō—iki ni kanjita jinsei" [Wei Cheng—A Deeply Felt Life], *Rekishi to jimbutsu* [History and Historical Personalities], 11 (special expanded ed., Nov., 1973), 82–93.

[10] Ch'en Ch'eng-chen, "Wei Cheng yü Chen-kuan chih chih" [Wei Cheng and the Chen-kuan chih chih] (M.A. thesis, College of Chinese Culture [Chung-kuo wen-hua hsüeh-yüan], 1967).

CHAPTER 1

The Rise to Power of the T'ang Dynasty:
A Reassessment

The traditional interpretation of the founding of the T'ang, which holds that T'ai-tsung rather than his father, Kao-tsu, was the genius behind the revolt that eventuated in the establishment of the dynasty, was given final form in the tenth and eleventh centuries with the compilation of two Standard, or canonical, dynastic histories (*cheng-shih*). The first of these, the *Old T'ang History* (*Chiu T'ang-shu*) of 945, states, "At this time, because Sui rule had already come to an end, T'ai-tsung secretly planned the righteous uprising."[1] The second, the *New T'ang History* (*Hsin T'ang-shu*), completed in 1060, notes, "When Kao-tsu first rose in Taiyuan, it was not his own idea; rather the affair originated with T'ai-tsung."[2] Perpetuating the view of the Standard Histories was the great Sung historian Ssu-ma Kuang, who, in his monumental chronicle, the *Comprehensive Mirror for Aid in Government* (*Tzu-chih t'ung-chien*) of 1084, concluded, "The emperor's raising of troops in Chin-yang was entirely planned by the Prince of Ch'in (T'ai-tsung)" and "Kao-tsu obtained the empire entirely because of T'ai-tsung's merit."[3] Until a short time ago this traditional view of early T'ang history received almost universal credence.

Recently, though, a small group of revisionists led by the Chinese scholars Lo Hsiang-lin and Li Shu-t'ung have reassessed the roles played in the T'ang founding by the first and second emperors.[4] They have reinterpreted data in the T'ang Standard Histories, relying chiefly

[1] *CTS* 2.2.
[2] *HTS* 2.4b.
[3] *TCTC* ch. 190, p. 5957; ch. 191, p. 6012.
[4] See Lo Hsiang-lin, *T'ang-tai wen-hua shih* [A Cultural History of the T'ang Dynasty] (Taipei, 1955), chap. 1; Li Shu-t'ung, *T'ang-shih k'ao-pien* [An Examination of T'ang History] (Taipei, 1965), pp. 1–42, 43–98, 276–309. The chapter by Lo was originally published

on information culled from their biographical sections (*lieh-chuan*), and have also made important use of an early seventh-century source almost totally ignored by the traditionalists, the *Diary of the Founding of the Great T'ang Dynasty* (*Ta-T'ang ch'uang-yeh ch'i-chü-chu*) by Wen Ta-ya. They have, in short, essentially rewritten the history of the period. The arguments presented in this chapter are to a substantial degree based on their impressively detailed researches as well as on my own more recent excursions through early T'ang history.

THE DECLINE OF THE SUI AND THE RISE OF LI YÜAN

The Sui dynasty (589–618), predecessor of the T'ang, came to power when its founder, Wen-ti, usurped the throne of the Northern Chou, last of the regimes that had dominated North China during the Period of Disunion. Eight years later Wen-ti toppled the southern house of Ch'en, brought to an end the political and cultural fragmentation that had plagued China for close to four centuries, and launched its Second Empire. But Wen-ti's triumph was ephemeral, and within two generations his dynasty also lay in ruins.

At first there was little to portend that the Sui would be so short-lived. Wen-ti reestablished a highly centralized government marked by an impressive level of administrative rationality. Many of the emperor's officials were recruited by means of the newly revived civil service examinations, which were designed to reward merit over hereditary privilege. A magnificent capital of unprecedented scale—almost six miles east to west and more than five miles north to south—and aptly named Ta-hsing-ch'eng, or "Great Revival City," was constructed southeast of the old Han capital, Ch'ang-an, on the site of modern Sian. Reimposition of the "equal-field" land-tenure system of the Northern Dynasties, combined with the development of new and more efficient methods of tax collection, swelled the national revenues. Grain shipments to the food-poor capital region were facilitated by the construction of a canal (the Kuang-t'ung ch'ü) linking Ta-hsing-ch'eng with the fertile plain lying to the east, beyond the T'ung Pass. A variety of state, prefectural, and village granaries were built to combat famine. The border defense along the northern frontier was substantially rein-

as an article in 1936; those by Li were originally published as articles in the 1950s and early 1960s.

forced by massively repairing, rebuilding, and extending the Great Wall. Neighboring tribes and states were weakened as a result of the vigorous foreign policies Wen-ti pursued on the diplomatic and military fronts. Lastly, Wen-ti began the difficult task of uniting the many disparate political, ethnic, and cultural groups that had developed during the Period of Disunion under successive alien regimes in the north and Chinese royal houses in the south.[5] By the time of his death in 604, the first Sui emperor had wrought what must have seemed a miracle to most of his subjects: China was united, peaceful, and prosperous for the first time in centuries.[6]

The reign of Wen-ti's son, Yang-ti, also began promisingly enough.[7] Yang-ti continued to improve Sui administration, promulgated a new code of laws less stringent than his father's, expanded the state system of education and civil service examinations (it was during Yang-ti's time that the famous *chin-shih* examination originated), and sponsored a revival of Confucian learning. On the foreign front, he briefly extended Sui suzerainty over the Eastern Turks to the north of China and manipulated the Western Turks, those in the region west of the Jade Gate and north of the Tarim Basin, to China's advantage. He drove the T'u-yü-hun from their homeland in modern Tsinghai province and opened relations with Japan. Great amounts of tribute from the Sui's Central Asian vassals poured into Ta-hsing-ch'eng along the silk routes, which were the links between China and West Asia and, beyond it, Europe.

In the end, if we are to believe accounts in the Sui Standard History, the *Sui-shu,* Yang-ti's program of public works, carried out on a gigantic scale, brought disaster to the dynasty. During the period 605–10 the second Sui emperor constructed an eastern capital (*tung-tu*) at Loyang in northern Honan, roughly half the size of Ta-hsing-ch'eng, and expanded upon his father's work on the Great Wall. He had a series of

---

[5]See Arthur F. Wright, "The Formation of Sui Ideology, 581–604," in *Chinese Thought and Institutions,* John K. Fairbank, ed. (Chicago, 1957), pp. 71–104.

[6]Two recent studies that stress the accomplishments of Sui Wen-ti are T'ang Ch'eng-yeh, *Sui Wen-ti cheng-chih shih-kung chih yen-chiu* [The Political Achievements of Sui Wen-ti] (Taipei, 1967), and Arthur F. Wright, "The Sui Dynasty," in the forthcoming *Cambridge History of China.*

[7]The following material relating to Sui Yang-ti is largely based on Woodbridge Bingham, *The Founding of the T'ang Dynasty: The Fall of Sui and the Rise of T'ang* (Baltimore, 1941; reprint 1970), pp. 1–59, and Wright, "The Sui Dynasty."

canals hundreds of miles in length redredged or constructed anew, linking Loyang first with the Huai and Yangtze River valleys (via the T'ung-chi ch'ü) and then with the region further south terminating at modern Hangchow (via the Chiang-nan ho). Following the completion of the T'ung-chi canal, the emperor set sail aboard a "dragon boat" for Chiang-tu (modern Yangchow), his "river capital" near the Yangtze, leading a flotilla of vessels stretching in close file for more than sixty miles. The longest of all Yang-ti's canals (the Yung-chi ch'ü) linked Loyang with the region around modern Peking. Hundreds of thousands of laborers were conscripted for these vast undertakings, great numbers of whom perished, and the economic resources of the newly united country were strained to the breaking point.

For these "excesses" Yang-ti has earned the opprobrium of countless Chinese commentators, who have damned him with a stereotyped portrayal as a "bad last" ruler. Yet in so doing they have largely ignored his many positive contributions to the consolidation of the Sui. To cite just two examples, the canals he built brought the Sui into easy communication with most of the major food-producing regions of China; and the elaborately mounted imperial progresses he made over their waters were in many respects a continuation by other means of his father's efforts to weld together the highly heterogeneous peoples of late sixth-century and early seventh-century China. Étienne Balazs has justly called Yang-ti the real founder of the Second Empire because he integrated the southeast into the rest of the country for the first time since the Han.[8]

Unfortunately, following upon the completion of many of his most ambitious public works, and before the peasantry had time to recover from oppressive levies of forced labor and taxes, Yang-ti began the first of three disastrous campaigns to conquer Koguryŏ, a kingdom located east of the Liao River on the northern half of the Korean peninsula. The first campaign of 611–12 proved unsuccessful for two major reasons: a great flood in the lower Yellow River valley that caused heavy desertions in the Sui ranks among men from the affected region, and the failure of Sui forces to reach the Koguryŏ capital before the onset of winter. Nevertheless, Yang-ti proceeded with his second and equally disappointing Koguryŏ campaign of 613, levying new taxes

[8]Étienne Balazs, "L'Oeuvre des Souei: L'Unification," in *Histoire et institutions de la Chine ancienne*, by Henri Maspero and Etienne Balazs (Paris, 1967), p. 165.

and conscripting more men. Widely scattered revolts now erupted across China, the most serious of which took place in Honan province led by the Sui president of the Board of Rites (*li-pu shang-shu*), Yang Hsüan-kan.[9] It was quickly crushed by the government.

Beginning in 614, as Yang-ti embarked upon yet another attempt to take Koguryŏ, rebellion began to engulf the entire country. Desertions in the Sui ranks became rife, supplies for the army failed to reach their destinations, and Sui military power rapidly ebbed. Late in 615 China's "barbarian" neighbors to the north, the Eastern Turks, weakened the emperor's prestige still further by surrounding him at the town of Yen-men in northern Shansi while he was inspecting fortifications along the Great Wall. Yang-ti was forced to endure the embarrassment of being detained at Yen-men for a full month before the Turkish siege was broken by Sui reinforcements.

Following his return to Ta-hsing-ch'eng from Yen-men, the growing threat of civil disturbance and the continued inability of Sui armies to restore order prompted the emperor to sail south to Chiang-tu. Thereafter he remained in seclusion, isolated from the news of his crumbling empire, immobilized by self-doubt. The resulting political vacuum was increasingly filled by other men: Sui local officials, commanders of local military elites (*hao-chieh*), "bandit" (*tsei*) chiefs, and rebel leaders. Early in 618 Yang-ti was assassinated at his Yangtze capital by one of his own officials, Yü-wen Hua-chi. By this time, however, he had already been demoted to the status of "retired emperor" (*t'ai-shang huang*) by the rebel conqueror of Ta-hsing-ch'eng, the Duke of T'ang, Li Yüan (the given name of T'ang Kao-tsu), who would shortly establish a dynasty that came to rival the Han in extent and splendor.

Like the majority of dynastic founders before and after him, Li Yüan was of noble lineage. His ancestors, members of the northwestern aristocracy centered in Shensi and Kansu, occupied prominent offices in successive semi-"barbarian" regimes in North China from the time of the Northern Wei dynasty; some scholars have even hypothesized that the Li-T'ang house was itself originally "barbarian."[10] What is clear,

[9]For a study of Yang Hsüan-kan's revolt, see Nunome Chōfū, "Yō Genkan no hanran" [The Revolt of Yang Hsüan-kan], *Ritsumeikan bungaku* [Ritsumeikan University Journal of Cultural Sciences], 236 (1965), 1–30.

[10]While it is clear that Li Yüan's immediate paternal forebears came from Lung-hsi, modern Kansu province, the more remote origins—both geographical and racial—of the Li-T'ang house have been hotly argued since the 1930s by Liu P'an-sui, Ch'en Yin-k'o

at any rate, is that the first T'ang emperor was at least half non-Chinese, for his mother, née Tu-ku, was of noble Hsien-pei stock. At the beginning of the Northern Chou dynasty, Li Yüan's grandfather was posthumously ennobled Duke of T'ang principality, a title that was first passed on to Li Yüan's father and then on to Li Yüan at the age of six in the year 574. Since his mother was the sister of Sui Wen-ti's consort, in his youth Li Yüan was a frequent guest at the Sui imperial palace.

While still in his teens, Li Yüan embarked upon his official career as one of the elite palace guard (ch'ien-niu pei-shen). His relationship by marriage to Emperor Wen brought him rapid promotion, and soon he was enjoying high office in the provincial bureaucracy. Under Emperor Yang, Li Yüan was summoned back to the imperial palace first as the assistant director of the Department of Imperial Domestic Service (tien-nei shao-chien) and later as the vice-president of the Court of Imperial Insignia (wei-wei shao-ch'ing). In 613, during Yang-ti's second campaign against Koguryŏ, he was put in charge of transporting provisions at the Huai-yüan garrison (chen) in modern Liaoning province.

A turning point in Li Yüan's career came this same year with the eruption of Yang Hsüan-kan's revolt at Li-yang in northern Honan. According to one source, when Yang was preparing to revolt, his brothers fled to Honan from the ranks of the Sui expeditionary army in Liaoning; it was Li Yüan who first discovered and reported these defections to Yang-ti.[11] The emperor then appointed Li Yüan garrison commander (liu-shou) of Hung-hua commandery (chün) at modern Ch'ing-yang in the easternmost part of Kansu province, and ordered that all armies "to the right of the Pass" (kuan-yu, the region to the west of the T'ung Pass, comprising modern Shensi and eastern Kansu provinces) were to be placed under his command in order to resist the rebels.

As a result of steadily deteriorating conditions throughout the country, from this time forward Li Yüan held posts exclusively in the Sui military hierarchy. During the period 615 to 616 he destroyed two "bandit" organizations in southern Shansi and successfully opposed Turkish incursions into the northern portion of the province. By 616 Sui control of the central Shansi region had become seriously weakened as a result

---

Kanei Yukitada, Chu Hsi-tsu, Wang T'ung-ling, and Ts'en Chung-mien, among others. The debate continues.

[11] HTS 1.1b.

of the defeat of imperial forces in Taiyuan by the "bandit" Chen Ti-erh and a force of followers said to have numbered one hundred thousand men. When Li Yüan crushed Chen less than a year later, he was awarded the post of garrison commander (*liu-shou*) of Taiyuan (*T'ai-yüan fu*), with headquarters at the town of Chin-yang. As Bingham has observed, this new appointment, made some months after Yang-ti had sailed into splendid isolation at Chiang-tu, may merely have reflected the considerable de facto power Li Yüan already wielded in the region.[12]

Despite this promotion, Li Yüan's position under the Sui was actually quite insecure. About the year 614 a ballad of enigmatic wording had gained currency among the people predicting that the next person to occupy the throne would be surnamed Li, a name as common in China as Smith and Jones in our country. The ballad helped to launch or advance precipitately the careers of other rebels surnamed Li, such as Li Mi and Li Kuei.[13] At the same time, it made Yang-ti paranoiacally suspicious of all those in his employ bearing the tainted surname, a condition most notably illustrated by his execution of thirty-two members of the clan of Li Hun, including that hapless official. Li Yüan well knew that there was a distinct possibility he would soon suffer a similar fate.

THE T'ANG UPRISING—VARIATIONS ON A THEME

It is at this point that the traditional and revisionist accounts of the T'ang founding part company. According to the traditional and widely accepted version of events based on the T'ang Standard Histories and the *Comprehensive Mirror*,[14] when Li Yüan became the garrison commander of Taiyuan, his second son, Li Shih-min (the later T'ai-tsung), by himself conceived of a revolt intended to sweep away the already moribund Sui and establish the Li-T'ang house in its place. Shih-min, the traditional accounts say, first discussed plans for such an undertaking with the former prefect (*ling*) of Taiyuan, Liu Wen-ching, who had been clapped into prison at Chin-yang because he was related by marriage to the anti-Sui rebel Li Mi. Liu energetically encouraged

---

[12] *The Founding of the T'ang Dynasty*, pp. 79–80.

[13] Woodbridge Bingham, "The Rise of Li in a Ballad Prophecy," *Journal of the American Oriental Society*, 61 (1941), 272–73; *TCTC* ch. 183, p. 5709; ch. 184, pp. 5745–46.

[14] The major accounts of the T'ang uprising and the campaign to take the Sui capital are in *CTS* 1.2b–4b, 2.1b–3b, 57.6–8b; *HTS* 1.2b–5, 2.1b–2b, 88.1–3; *TCTC* ch. 183, pp. 5728–35; ch. 184, pp. 5737–61.

Shih-min in his plans. But the latter, fearing that the elder Li would be too timid to second the venture and would thus pose an obstacle to the revolt, decided he would have to force his father's hand. He therefore engaged the aid of Li Yüan's old friend, P'ei Chi, then the assistant superintendent (*fu-chien*) of the Sui palace at Chin-yang. P'ei secretly sent ladies from the palace harem for Li Yüan's private enjoyment without informing him of their origin. When Li Yüan belatedly discovered that he had unknowingly been compromised, he realized that it would only be a matter of time before Yang-ti learned of his crime and ordered his execution. Therefore, early in the fifth month of 617 he reluctantly assented to raising the banner of revolt. Li Yüan's first and fourth sons, Li Chien-ch'eng and Li Yüan-chi,[15] were then summoned from southern Shansi to Chin-yang and the creation of a "righteous army" of revolt was begun.

The revolt, however, could not get under way until a serious obstacle had been removed. At the time Yang-ti appointed Li Yüan garrison commander of Taiyuan, he had also sent two deputies, Wang Wei and Kao Chün-ya, to serve under him. Li Yüan now became fearful that they would report the troop buildup to Chiang-tu. Thus, according to the traditional accounts, he summoned both deputies to audience, where they were seized by troops led by Li Shih-min, imprisoned, and executed shortly thereafter. In the subsequent T'ang campaign to conquer the Sui capital, we are also told, Li Yüan relied most heavily on the talents of Shih-min, who more than anyone else contributed the leadership and strategy which led to the T'ang triumph.

The traditional accounts portray Shih-min, who at the time of the revolt was about seventeen years of age,[16] as a brilliant military com-

---

[15]Li Yüan's third son, Li Hsüan-pa, had died earlier.

[16]The large amount of conflicting data regarding Shih-min's birthdate and his age at the time of the Taiyuan revolt is discussed by Bingham, *The Founding of the T'ang Dynasty*, p. 49, n.79; Nunome Chōfū, "Tensaku jōshō, Sentōdō daikōdai shōshorei, Shin Ō Seimin—sokuimae no Tō no Taisō" [Supreme Commander of Heavenly Strategy, President of the Department of Affairs of State of the Shan-tung Circuit Grand Field Office, the Prince of Ch'in, Shih-min—Prior to His Accession as T'ang T'ai-tsung], *Ritsumeikan bungaku* [Ritsumei-kan University Journal of Cultural Sciences], 255 (1966), 5–7; and Ma Ch'i-hua, "Chen-kuan cheng-lun" [Commentary on the Politics of the Chen-kuan Period], *Kuo-li cheng-chih ta-hsüeh hsüeh-pao* [National Chengchi University Journal], 1 (1960), 270–71. Nunome arrives at a birthdate of the first month of solar 599 (lunar 598), Ma at a birthdate of 600. This would make Shih-min eighteen years of age and seventeen years of age, respectively, at the time of the Taiyuan revolt. Because Shih-min himself once observed (*HTS* 102.6b) that he was seventeen years old (eighteen *sui*) when the revolt took place, I am inclined to accept a birth-

mander, physically powerful and intensely charismatic. On the other hand, they depict Li Yüan, then about fifty-one, as a doddering and spineless old man, buffeted about by events over which he had no control, an unwilling pawn in the hand of his wily son, Shih-min. The following, from C. P. Fitzgerald's 1933 monograph, *Son of Heaven: A Biography of Li Shih-min, The Founder of the T'ang Dynasty*, admirably sums up the view of Li Yüan's qualities that has persisted for more than a millenium: "Li Yüan, duke of T'ang, was an easygoing aristocrat, not remarkably intelligent, a weak character. He lacked tenacity, foresight and resolution. Had he not been the father of Shih-min there was no man living in China less likely to win his way to the throne."[17]

There is, however, another portrait of Li Yüan contained in Wen Ta-ya's *Diary of the Founding of the Great T'ang Dynasty*, compiled sometime during the period 617 to 626, that sharply contrasts with the above. Wen Ta-ya's Li Yüan is a great archer: "Whenever he sighted a running animal or a flying bird he shot without missing the mark."[18] He overwhelms his adversaries with dazzling displays of his martial power and swaggering bravado in the face of danger.[19] He is so adept at employing military strategies against his enemies that even the fierce Eastern Turks are loath to face him on the battlefield.[20] Wen Ta-ya's Li Yüan—a man of powerful ambition, inexhaustible energy, and indomitable will—emerges as the real leader of the Taiyuan uprising and the victorious T'ang campaign to conquer the Sui capital.

Wen shows that long before the T'ang uprising in the fifth month of 617, Li Yüan had already begun to dream of replacing the Sui. As we have seen, in 616 Li Yüan, Duke of T'ang, was assigned to combat "banditry" in Taiyuan, which was the site of his nominal fief. Now, Wen notes, Li Yüan came to view the coincidence of his fief and place of assignment as a propitious sign from Heaven.[21] Early in 617, still some

---

date of 600.

[17]P. 32.

[18]*CYCCC* 1.2b.

[19]Ibid. 1.2b, 4–4b.

[20]Ibid. 1.3.

[21]Ibid. 1.1–1b. The passage in question appears to contain an allusion to the "Li Ballad." The text says: "Thinking that the common people of Taiyuan were the 'old folk' of T'ao T'ang, and [that the area for which] he had received his pacification commission did not exceed his own [nominal] fief, the emperor [Kao-tsu] was secretly joyous." The way in which the "Li Ballad" alludes to T'ao T'ang (the culture-hero Yao) is discussed by Bingham, "The Rise of Li," 277.

months before the Taiyuan uprising, Wen records the following comment made by Li Yüan to his son Shih-min: "The allotted time of the
Sui is about over, [but] our house will continue to respond to auspicious
omens from Heaven. If we have not raised troops at this early time, it is
because you and your brothers have not yet assembled [your forces]."[22]
It is thus apparent that sometime before the T'ang revolt Li Yüan had
already become convinced that he was destined to inherit the Mandate,
a conviction reinforced by the "Li Ballad," which, Wen informs us,
was sung by young and old on the streets of Chin-yang. On one occasion
Li Yüan even remarked, "I ought to rise up [and march] one thousand
li to fulfill that prophecy!"[23]

The *Diary* also casts doubt on Shih-min's contributions to the Taiyuan
revolt. First, it makes no mention of his direct participation in the
seizure of Wang Wei and Kao Chün-ya, noting instead that the troops
which seized Li Yüan's deputies came from an army nominally under
Shih-min's command but actually led by other generals.[24] Second,
whereas the *Old T'ang History* describes only Shih-min's role in the
pacification of Hsi-ho prefecture (located just to the southwest of
Taiyuan) shortly following the T'ang revolt, the *Diary* shows that Shih-
min's elder brother Chien-ch'eng joined with him in the venture and
deserved equal credit.[25] The *Diary* serves to deflate Shih-min's reputation still further. According to the T'ang Standard Histories, it was
Shih-min who in 615 devised the strategy at Yen-men that freed Yang-
ti from the Turkish siege. Shih-min's activities at this frontier town
have traditionally marked his debut in Chinese historical records. Yet
the *Diary* makes no mention of his role at Yen-men, recording only
that Li Yüan led the army that helped free the Sui emperor.[26]

Significantly, the revisionists' contention that long before the Taiyuan
uprising Li Yüan had decided to turn against the Sui is supported by
various biographies in the T'ang Standard Histories. The biographies

[22]*CYCCC* 1.5. At this time Kao-tsu's sons, Li Chien-ch'eng and Li Yüan-chi, were still in
southern Shansi.
[23]Ibid. 1.15b.
[24]Ibid. 1.9b. This episode is corroborated in *HTS* 90.1.
[25]*CTS* 1.3; *CYCCC* 1.16b.
[26]*CTS* 2.1b; *HTS* 2.1–1b; *CYCCC* 1.1b; Bingham, *The Founding of the T'ang Dynasty*, p. 49,
n. 82. Actually, both these versions of the Yen-men incident may be incorrect. The biographies of Hsiao Yü, *CTS* 63.5b and *HTS* 101.1b, note that the Sui I-ch'eng Princess, wife of
Shih-pi Qaghan, leader of the Turks, persuaded her husband to lift the siege.

of Li Ching in the *Old* and *New T'ang History* record that in 616, when Li Yüan was made assistant to the deputy prefect (*ch'eng*) of Ma-i commandery, Li Ching noticed that Li Yüan "had ambitions to conquer the empire (*yu ssu-fang chih chih*)." He even set out to report this information to Yang-ti but found progress impossible because the roads were blocked.[27] The *Old T'ang History* biography of Liu Wen-ching, the official with whom Shih-min is said to have first plotted the T'ang revolt, records that the following year, when Li Yüan became garrison commander of Taiyuan, Liu similarly observed that the former had designs on the empire.[28] Moreover, it is clear that about the same time no fewer than four of Li Yüan's subordinates—Hsü Shih-hsü, T'ang Chien, Wu Shih-huo, and Ts'ui Shan-wei—were all exhorting him to revolt.[29] The *Old T'ang History* biography of Wu Shih-huo notes that when Li Yüan became garrison commander and the empire was daily falling into greater disorder, Wu secretly advised him to raise troops and presented him with lucky charms and treatises on military strategy. "Please do not say anything more," Li Yüan replied. "Books on military strategy are forbidden, yet you still bring them to me, so I well understand your meaning. [In the future] we will grow rich together."[30] Yet another piece of evidence comes from the *Old T'ang History* biography of Yü-wen Shih-chi, younger brother of Yü-wen Hua-chi, Yang-ti's assassin. Shih-chi had once served under Li Yüan when the latter was in the Sui employ at Ta-hsing-ch'eng. When Shih-chi surrendered to the T'ang early in 619 following his brother's death, Li Yüan, who had already ascended the throne, turned to P'ei Chi and observed, "It has already been six or seven years since this person and I discussed the taking of the empire. Those like you all came after him."[31]

It thus seems apparent that long before Shih-min allegedly precipitated the Taiyuan uprising, Li Yüan was already envisioning the succession of the Li-T'ang house to the Mandate and was under great pressure from numerous quarters to raise a standard of revolt. It is hardly likely, then, that Shih-min single-handedly forced his father to take up arms against the Sui or even that he was the most significant contributor to this decision.

[27]*CTS* 67.1b; *HTS* 93.1–1b.

[28]*CTS* 57.6.

[29]See, respectively, *CTS* 57.14, 58.1b, 58.12b; *HTS* 91.14b.

[30]*CTS* 58.12b. This story also appears in the *P'an-lung-t'ai pei* of Li Ch'iao (644–713); *CTW* 249. 7b–8. Wu Shih-huo was the father of the later Empress Wu.

[31]*CTS* 63.16.

Moreover, other bits of evidence widely scattered throughout the T'ang Standard Histories and the *Comprehensive Mirror* suggest, like Wen Ta-ya's narrative, that once the decision to revolt had been made Li Yüan had more than ample ability and strength to lead the T'ang forces to victory. It is said, for example, that the first T'ang emperor won his wife's hand in an archery contest by hitting the eyes of two peacocks painted on two gates with just two shots.[32] In a furious battle against bandit forces in Shansi, while loosening a quiver of seventy arrows, he is reported to have killed seventy men, then to have built a mound of their bodies and prudently retrieved the arrows for reuse.[33] Even if these stories are partly apocryphal, we know that prior to his appointment as garrison commander, Li Yüan had amassed a splendid record of successes on the battlefields of Shansi against both "bandit" marauders and the Eastern Turks. Furthermore, at the time of the T'ang revolt, Li Yüan seems still to have been quite vigorous of body, for although he was already past fifty, he is said to have fathered at least seventeen of his twenty-two sons *after* he became emperor![34]

THE ORIGINS OF THE CONFLICTING VIEWS

The conflicting narratives we have examined surrounding the launching of the T'ang dynasty give rise to two obvious questions: (1) why are the versions contained in the Standard Histories and Wen Ta-ya's *Diary* so much at variance? and (2) why are there so many internal contradictions within the Standard Histories themselves? The answers to these questions are to a large extent related to the manner in which these records were compiled.

At the very outset, it should be mentioned that Wen's *Diary* is a very special source for the Sui-T'ang transition period, owing primarily to the author's intimate association with the T'ang rebel movement. Wen's native place (*pen-kuan*) was Taiyuan. Sometime prior to Li Yüan's assignment there as garrison commander, Wen resigned his post as a Sui official and returned home. Subsequently, he joined Li Yüan's staff as a secretary (*chi-shih ts'an-chün*) and accompanied the

[32]Ibid. 51.3.
[33]*HTS* 1.2. Tuan Ch'eng-shih, *Yu-yang tsa-tsu* (853; *Ts'ung-shu chi-ch'eng* ed., 1937), ch. 1, p. 1, records the number of dead as eighty.
[34]*TCTC* ch. 190, pp. 5957-58, and note of Hu San-hsing.

T'ang leader on the campaign from Chin-yang to Ta-hsing-ch'eng.[35] His *Diary*, covering a period of 357 days from the Taiyuan uprising to Li Yüan's enthronement in the Sui capital, thus represents nothing less than an eyewitness account of the T'ang founding.

Overwhelmingly, the evidence suggests that Wen's work is genuine and that it was written shortly after the events it narrates. Judging by the official titles which precede Wen's name in various notices of the *Diary* still extant, it was first compiled during 617–18; a later version was probably made sometime during Kao-tsu's reign, 618–26. This view is reinforced by the existence of the titles of what may have been earlier versions of the work: the *Record of the Great Chancellor Prince of T'ang and His Officials (Ta-ch'eng-hsiang T'ang-wang kuan-shu chi)* in two *chüan*, and *Record of the Kingly Enterprise of the Present Ruler (Chin-shang wang-yeh chi)* in six *chüan*. Great Chancellor Prince of T'ang is a title Li Yüan held during the last Sui reign, I-ning (617–18), presided over by a Sui puppet emperor he had placed on the throne. The *Diary*'s avoidance of T'ang taboo names, references to the second Sui emperor by his post-humous name, Yang-ti, and to Shih-min as Prince of Ch'in, a title he held after the beginning of 618, demonstrate that Wen's final version of his text was not completed until sometime after the founding of the T'ang. The work is mentioned in the *Conspectus of History (Shih-t'ung)* of Liu Chih-chi, written in 710, and is included in the "Monograph on Literature" *(ching-chi chih* and *i-wen chih)* of the *Old* and *New T'ang History*, each of which was based on catalogues of books held in the Imperial Library dating from the K'ai-yüan period (713–41).[36] From all this we may conclude that the *Diary* was not a forgery of later date.

It has been pointed out, moreover, that the *Diary* may well contain an objective treatment of Shih-min's role in the establishment of his house. First, it was probably written prior to Shih-min's assassination of his elder brother, the crown prince Chien-ch'eng, and his usurpation of the throne in 626,[37] thus before any need arose for him to alter the historical records in such a way as to lend legitimacy to his rule. Second,

[35]*CTS* 61.1–1b.

[36]Liu Chih-chi, *Shih-t'ung* [Conspectus of History] (710; Shanghai, 1928), p. 47; Woodbridge Bingham, "Wen Ta-ya: The First Recorder of T'ang History," *Journal of the American Oriental Society*, 57 (1937), 372–73; Fukui Shigemasa, "Ō Tō sōgyō kikyochū kō" [A Study of the Diary of the Founding of the T'ang Dynasty], *Shikan*, 63–64 (1961), 83–88; Lo Hsiang-lin, *T'ang-tai wen-hua shih*, pp. 1–3.

[37]See below, pp. 67–77.

on the eve of the assassination plot against Chien-ch'eng, Shih-min ordered the author of the *Diary*, Wen Ta-ya, then his own subordinate, to garrison his base at Loyang on the northeastern plain, and sent him secret messages there.[38] Had Shih-min read Wen's *Diary* (a point to be raised again shortly) and had Wen's judgment of him therein been unduly harsh, it is hardly likely that he would have demonstrated such confidence in Wen.

The present title appended to Wen Ta-ya's work, *Ta-T'ang ch'uang-yeh ch'i-chü-chu*, makes it the only example surviving in its entirety of the T'ang "diary of activity and repose" (*ch'i-chü-chu*) genre. During the T'ang such diaries were compiled four times a year (once each season) from daily records of the emperor's actions and words,[39] and served as raw materials for two other kinds of historical compilations, the "veritable records" (*shih-lu*) and "dynastic history" (*kuo-shih*). Yet Wen's *Diary* differs from orthodox examples of *ch'i-chü-chu* in that it was privately rather than officially compiled and covers a period of time completely anteceding the inauguration of the dynasty. Perhaps because of this, it was not kept at the History Office (*shih-kuan*) with all the other records of its kind but was included as a separate title in the Imperial Library. This is probably how it was able to survive the conflagration during the An Lu-shan rebellion of 755–56, which destroyed 3,682 *chüan* of diaries and numerous other records stored in the History Office.[40]

The complex process by which the T'ang Standard Histories were compiled has been traced in some detail by Pulleyblank and Rotours, among others.[41] Simply speaking, it is apparent that the *Old T'ang History* narration of the T'ang founding was ultimately based on the *Kao-tsu Veritable Records* (*Kao-tsu shih-lu*) and *T'ai-tsung Veritable Records* (*T'ai-tsung shih-lu*).[42] The *New T'ang History* represents a revision of the

[38]*CTS* 61.1b; *HTS* 91.1b.

[39]Chu Hsi-tsu, "Han-T'ang-Sung ch'i-chü-chu k'ao" [A Study of the Diaries of Activity and Repose of the Han, T'ang, and Sung Dynasties], *Kuo-hsüeh chi-k'an* [Journal of Sinological Studies, Peking National University], 2 (1930), 634.

[40]*THY* ch. 63, p. 1095; letter from Denis Twitchett to Robert Somers, 29 September 1970, used by permission of the recipient.

[41]See E. G. Pulleyblank, "The Tzyjyh Tongjiann Kaoyih and the Sources for the History of the Period 730–763," *Bulletin of the School of Oriental and African Studies*, 13 (1950–51), 448–57; Robert des Rotours, *Le traité des examens* (Paris, 1932), pp. 56–71.

[42]Chao I, *Nien-erh-shih cha-chi* [Detailed Notes on the Twenty-two Histories], 2 vols. (1795;

Old, making use of many materials unavailable at the time its predecessor was compiled. Yet these new materials relate chiefly to the
period after the An Lu-shan Rebellion, not to the early T'ang. The
Kao-tsu and *T'ai-tsung Veritable Records* thus provided both of the T'ang
Standard Histories with the bulk of their materials on the establishment of the dynasty.

Compilation of the *Kao-tsu Veritable Records,* which covered the period
618–26, and the first half of the *T'ai-tsung Veritable Records,* covering the
period 626–40, began sometime in the late 630s or early 640s. While the
compilation of these materials was proceeding, the ruler by custom did
not interfere in any way with the work of the historians lest he impair
their veracity. By the late 630s T'ai-tsung had been on the throne for
more than a decade and had achieved a remarkable record of accomplishment. Yet his murder of Crown Prince Chien-ch'eng and his
usurpation of the throne had sullied an otherwise exemplary reputation.
It seems, therefore, that he decided to influence the historical materials
surrounding his rise to power to make it appear that he, even more than
his father or elder brother, deserved to inherit the Mandate.

T'ai-tsung amply demonstrated his anxiety over his historical image
on various occasions. At such times he made it clear to the historians
who were compiling the records of his father's reign and of his own that
he was more than just routinely interested in the outcome of their
labors. About the year 641 he said to Ch'u Sui-liang:

"Since you recently have been an official in charge of recording the deeds
and actions of the emperor *(chih ch'i-chü),*[43] what kinds of affairs have you
recorded? Generally, is the ruler allowed to examine [the records] or not?
We wish to read these records so that We may take as a warning what they
consider to be Our successes and failures." Sui-liang replied: "The present
recording officials [correspond to] the ancient historians of the left and right.
In recording the ruler's words and actions, good and evil must be written

Taipei, 1965), vol. 1, ch. 16, pp. 214–16. The veritable records were, of course, utilized by
Wei Shu, compiler of the *T'ang-shu,* a dynastic history covering the period 618 to the mid-
eighth century that was for the most part incorporated verbatim into the *Old T'ang History;*
see Pulleyblank, "The Tzyjyh Tongjiann Kaoyih." Ssu-ma Kuang quotes from both the
Kao-tsu and *T'ai-tsung Veritable Records* in his *k'ao-i,* or "investigations of discrepancies" sections, now usually interspersed throughout the text of the *Comprehensive Mirror.*

[43]Robert des Rotours, *Traité des fonctionnaires et traité de l'armée,* 2 vols. (Leiden, 1947), 1: 153,
notes that the *chih ch'i-chü* designation meant that the holder occupied the posts either of
grand secretary of the Chancellery or remonstrating counselor. Ch'u was appointed remonstrating counselor in 641; *CTS* 80.1b.

down so that the ruler will not act improperly. I have never heard that rulers could themselves examine the histories [of their reigns]." T'ai-tsung said: "If We have bad points, must you record them?" Sui-liang replied: "I have heard that 'it is better to fulfill the duty of one's office than an obligation towards one's ruler.'[44] My duty in office is to uphold the brush, so how could I not record them?"[45]

On yet another occasion T'ai-tsung approached Fang Hsüan-ling, an official in charge of supervising the compilation of dynastic history, and said:

"When We read the histories of former dynasties, [the way in which] they 'distinguish the good so as to make it bad for the evil'[46] is sufficient to provide Us with a warning for the future. [Thus] We do not know why since ancient times rulers have not been allowed personally to read the dynastic history (kuo-shih) of their reigns." [Fang] replied: "Since the dynastic history must record good and evil so that the ruler will not act improperly, [the compilers] fear that they will offend him. Therefore, he may not see them." T'ai-tsung said: "Our reasoning is quite different than that of the men of old. If We now wish to read the dynastic history, it is because if there are good deeds [recorded therein] they need not be discussed, but if there are faults, We wish to use them as a mirror-warning by which to improve Ourself. You are to compile the records and present them."[47]

At this time the remonstrating counselor (chien-i ta-fu) Chu Tzu-she vehemently protested T'ai-tsung's attempt to inspect the records. Ssu-ma Kuang laconically records only that "the emperor did not pay heed," and that he ordered Fang Hsüan-ling and his fellow historians, Hsü Ching-tsung and others, to edit the dynastic history into chronicle (pien-nien) form, the results of which were the Kao-tsu and T'ai-tsung Veritable Records.[48] It is apparent, then, that during the period of their

[44]From the Tso-chuan, Duke Chao, 20th year; see James Legge, The Chinese Classics, 2nd ed. rev., 5 vols. (Hong Kong, 1961), vol. 5, The Ch'un Ts'ew with the Tso Chuen, p. 684.

[45]CKCY 7.7b–8. The CKCY gives the year of this episode as 639. THY ch. 63, p. 1102 and TFYK 554.25b both place it in 642. Ch'u Sui-liang's biography in CTS 80.1b–2 gives the year 641. For a related episode, see CKCY 6.18b–19. The CKCY has been the subject of a master's thesis; George Winston Lewis, "The Cheng-kuan Cheng-yao: A Source for the Study of Early T'ang Government" (University of Hong Kong, 1962).

[46]Legge, The Chinese Classics, vol. 3, The Shoo King, p. 573.

[47]CKCY 7.8–8b; see also TCTC ch. 197, p. 6203; THY ch. 63, p. 1103.

[48]TCTC ch. 197, p. 6203; CKCY 7.8b; THY ch. 63, p. 1102. The sources do not agree on the year is which this episode occurred. The biography of Chu Tzu-she, CTS 189A.10b, lists the year of his death as 641.

compilation both the dynastic history and veritable records received
T'ai-tsung's strong editorial influence. Yet when the veritable records
were finally completed and presented to the emperor in the seventh
month of 643, they evidently still were not written in a manner calculated to please him. On the contrary, he claimed that he was unsatisfied
with the way in which events surrounding his assassination of the crown
prince were narrated:

Long ago, when the Duke of Chou killed [his brothers] Kuan[-shu] and
Ts'ai[-shu] the House of Chou was made peaceful, and when Chi-yu
poisoned [his elder brother] Shu-ya the state of Lu was made tranquil. My
action was as righteous as theirs because it has brought security to the state
and benefit to all the people. Why then do the historians obscure [this fact]
with their brushes? They should delete their embellishments and write a
true account of the affair.[49]

Although the emperor ordered that the historians rectify their narrative concerning the circumstances surrounding Chien-ch'eng's death,
probably far more than just these sections were altered at the time.

Ironically, Wei Cheng's concern that history record the truth may
have prompted him to become an unwitting accomplice in T'ai-tsung's
efforts to tamper with the record. Wei, who by this time had achieved
a substantial reputation in his own right as a historian, sent a memorial
to the throne applauding T'ai-tsung's emendation order. At first glance
this may seem a rather strange mode of behavior for an official renowned for his fearless and forthright opposition to all irregularities in
his prince's conduct. However, the reason Wei gave in his memorial for
supporting T'ai-tsung's action—that the purpose of history was to
condemn evil and to encourage good and that if the narratives of the
period were "not written truthfully" (shu pu i shih), then posterity would
have no way of learning from the past[50]—suggests that he may not have
been in full possession of all the facts regarding the case. Certainly, it
is difficult to believe that he was consciously advocating that his fellow
historians falsify their accounts simply to conceal the darker aspects of
T'ai-tsung's rise to power and thereby to enhance his place in history.

One historian, however, who may have been persuaded by the emperor to do exactly this was a chief compiler of dynastic history and

[49]CKCY 7.8b; see also TCTC ch. 197, p. 6203.
[50]CKCY 7.9. For a discussion of Wei's historiographical beliefs, see below, pp. 138–39.

veritable records for the reigns of Kao-tsu and T'ai-tsung, Hsü Ching-tsung (592–672).[51] Hsü had been a colleague of Wei Cheng's at the camp of the rebel Li Mi during the last years of the Sui, and would, long after Wei's death, gain a dubious reputation as the chief hatchet man of Empress Wu. Hsü was notorious for his avarice, even betrothing, it is said, one of his own daughters to the son of the Man "barbarian" chief, Feng Ang, in return for a considerable amount of gold and other valuables.[52] But even more important for the present discussion, Hsü was an unscrupulous historian, numerous instances in which he distorted his records having been well documented.[53] At T'ai-tsung's behest, and provided with sufficient means to make it worth his while, it seems possible that Hsü might have made his accounts appear as if T'ai-tsung alone had masterminded the Taiyuan revolt. When work was begun on compiling the dynastic history of the early T'ang, of the four key people involved in the revolt according to the traditional narratives—Kao-tsu, T'ai-tsung, Liu Wen-ching, and P'ei Chi—only T'ai-tsung was still alive.[54] Moreover, Hsü's penchant for dissembling was apparent at least to the third T'ang emperor, Kao-tsung, who in 673 read accounts of his predecessors' reigns that had been written in large part by Hsü, found several passages he knew to be false, and ordered them corrected.[55] Kao-tsung was evidently unaware of the real story of the Taiyuan uprising and of the exaggerated accounts of T'ai-tsung's contributions to the founding of the dynasty. So, although

[51]The exact nature of Hsü Ching-tsung's contributions to the *Kao-tsu* and *T'ai-tsung Veritable Records* remains unclear, but there is no doubt that they were quite extensive. The *New T'ang History* "Monograph on Literature" (*HTS* 58.11b) notes that Ching Po compiled, Fang Hsüan-ling supervised, and Hsü Ching-tsung revised the *Kao-tsu Veritable Records*. The veritable records for T'ai-tsung's reign up to 640, known as the *Chin-shang shih-lu*, are listed as having been compiled by Ching Po and Ku Yin and supervised by Fang Hsüan-ling; *HTS* 58.11b–12. But there are several other places where Hsü is listed as a contributor to the work; see *THY* ch. 63, p. 1092 and Li Shu-t'ung, *T'ang shih k'ao-pien*, p. 30. Even more intriguing is the information provided by the Sung scholar Ch'en Chen-sun. He notes that title pages of his own editions of the *Kao-tsu* and *T'ai-tsung Veritable Records* list Hsü Ching-tsung alone as having received the order to compile them, although he concludes that this information is probably false; *Chih-chai shu-lu chieh-t'i* [Annotated Catalogue of the Chih Library] (ca. 1235; *Ts'ung-shu chi-ch'eng* ed., 1937), ch. 4, p. 117.

[52]*CTS* 82.2b.

[53]A long list of historical falsifications perpetrated by Hsü appears in his biographies, *CTS* 82.3b–4 and *HTS* 223A.3b–4, and also in *THY* ch. 63, pp. 1093–94. See also Chao I, *Nien-erh-shih cha-chi*, vol. 1, ch. 16, p. 211, and Pulleyblank, "The Tzyjyh Tongjiann Kaoyih," 451.

[54]Li Shu-t'ung, *T'ang-shih k'ao-pien*, p. 31.

[55]*THY* ch. 63, p. 1093; *TCTC* ch. 202, p. 6371.

certain offending sections in the historical records were changed at his order, probably only the most blatant errors were corrected, since it was not known precisely which passages had been emended by Hsü, then dead.

Moreover, it is apparent that Hsü Ching-tsung, or whoever else lent a hand in falsifying the dynastic history and veritable records, could not deal effectively with all the material that eventually comprised the narration of events surrounding the T'ang uprising and its aftermath in the two T'ang Standard Histories and their intermediate compilations, thus giving rise to numerous internal contradictions in the texts. Already by the eleventh century Ssu-ma Kuang was noting in his work entitled *Investigations of Discrepancies (K'ao-i)* inconsistencies and outright contradictions he had encountered in his sources for the early T'ang period while compiling the *Comprehensive Mirror*. He perceived, for example, that T'ai-tsung's contributions to the Taiyuan uprising and Ta-hsing-ch'eng campaign had been exaggerated at the expense of the crown prince and partially took account of this fact in compiling his own narrative.[56] But although he occasionally made use of information culled from Wen Ta-ya's *Diary*, he apparently failed to be persuaded by its central thesis and chose to perpetuate the traditional interpretation of the T'ang founding.

Despite evidence to the effect that T'ai-tsung altered the historical records in his own favor, a few nagging questions remain. Because Wen's *Diary* is biased in favor of Kao-tsu,[57] who is portrayed virtually without fault, it may be that the version of events recorded in it are as distorted as those in the Standard Histories. If the *Diary* was written during Kao-tsu's reign, what would have been more natural than to glorify the record of a "good first" emperor? Since Li Chien-ch'eng was the T'ang heir at the time the *Diary* was compiled, is it possible that Wen Ta-ya exaggerated his role in the Taiyuan uprising and its aftermath so that he would compare favorably with Shih-min? It seems strange that T'ai-tsung failed to suppress the *Diary* even after he began to take a supervisory role in the compilation of the dynastic history and veritable records. Did he underestimate the *Diary*'s threat to his his-

[56]See *TCTC* ch. 184, p. 5738.

[57]This bias has been noted by several scholars. See Ssu-ma Kuang's note in *TCTC* ch. 184, p. 5737; Bingham, *The Founding of the T'ang Dynasty*, p. 120; Fukui, "Ō Tō sōgyō kikyochū kō," 86–87; Nunome, "Tensaku jōshō," 3, 13.

torical image because only the dynastic history and veritable records were intended to be transmitt to posterity? Did he never himself read the *Diary* since it was a short, private account of the founding of his house, and so remain completely ignorant of its content and the necessity for its destruction? All these questions, unhappily, remain unresolved.

LI YÜAN REHABILITATED

The above imponderables cannot, of course, negate the impressive body of evidence in the T'ang Standard Histories we have already reviewed supporting Wen Ta-ya's contention that Li Yüan himself conceived and led the Taiyuan revolt. Nor did Li Yüan's role in the founding of the T'ang dynasty simply end here. On the contrary, the strong qualities of leadership he evinced at the very outset of his revolt continued greatly to benefit the T'ang cause even afterwards. A strong case, I believe, can be made that Li Yüan made a substantial contribution first to the capture of the Sui capital at Ta-hsing-ch'eng and later to the pacification and unification of the entire country under T'ang rule.

Particularly impressive, it seems to me, was Li Yüan's ability to parry successive challenges to his power from various quarters. Initially, the gravest of these challenges came from the Eastern Turks, the effective rulers of northern Asia, who controlled territory north of the Great Wall stretching from modern Liaoning province to western Mongolia. Seeing profit in a weak and divided China, the Turks had compelled many anti-Sui rebels in North China to declare themselves Turkish vassals and had provided them with soldiers, arms, and precious horses for their campaigns.[58] Shortly after Li Yüan executed his deputies Wang Wei and Kao Chün-ya in the fifth month of 617, the Turks invaded the Taiyuan region and jolted the T'ang camp by advancing as far as the walls of Chin-yang before retreating. Clearly, it would have been arrant folly for Li Yüan to quit Taiyuan—a major bastion of defense against the Turks—on a campaign to conquer China without first reaching an accommodation with them. He therefore sent a letter to the Turkish qaghan, Shih-pi, professing a desire to save the

---

[58]According to *HTS* 215A.6 and Tu Yu, *T'ung-tien* [Comprehensive Statutes] (801; Taipei, 1966), ch. 197, p. 1069a, numbering among these rebels were Hsüeh Chü, Li Kuei, Liu Wu-chou, Liang Shih-tu, Wang Shih-ch'ung, Tou Chien-te, and Kao K'ai-tao.

Sui and, to that end, offering to restore harmonious relations with the Turks. The proposal was sweetened with the promise that if Shih-pi allied with Li Yüan, all the booty to be gained from the campaigns against the rebels would be turned over to the qaghan.[59]

The letter was very respectful in tone, and when it was completed Li Yüan affixed to it the character *ch'i*, "communication from inferior to superior," a move ethnocentric Chinese commentators have taken to mean that Li, like his rivals for the Mandate, had for the sake of expediency decided to become a Turkish vassal. Recently, some controversy has arisen as to whether this was indeed the result.[60] What is significant, however, is that the maneuver succeeded in its objective. It created a rapprochement between the T'ang and the Turks that worked to Li Yüan's advantage and allowed him a crucial breathing spell during which he was able to strengthen his forces and plan the strategy of his advance.

With the Turkish threat out of the way for the moment at least, Li Yüan could turn to the task of military organization, which he completed in the sixth month. The executive and administrative arm of this organization was known as the Administration of the Grand General (*ta-chiang-chün fu*) and was staffed largely by incumbent or former Sui military and civil officials working or residing in the Taiyuan vicinity. The T'ang army was initially recruited and supplied by the efforts of these men. In the building of his army, Li Yüan appears to have made excellent use of the Sui militia organization (*ying-yang fu*) in Taiyuan. Since several members of the Administration of the Grand General were officers in the Sui militia, they simply transferred militia troops to Li Yüan's command, thereby swelling his ranks.[61] P'ei Chi, the assistant superintendent of the Sui palace at Chin-yang, provided the T'ang forces with abundant supplies of grain and armor from the palace storehouses.

[59]*CYCCC* 1.11b–12.

[60]Opposing views on this question are found in Ch'en Yin-k'o, "Lun T'ang Kao-tsu ch'eng-ch'en yü T'u-chüeh shih" [On T'ang Kao-tsu Calling Himself a Subject of the Turks], *Ling-nan hsüeh-pao*, 11 (1951), 1–9; Li Shu-t'ung, *T'ang-shih k'ao-pien*, pp. 214–46, and idem, "Tsai-pien T'ang Kao-tsu ch'eng-ch'en yü T'u-chüeh shih" [A Further Examination of T'ang Kao-tsu Calling Himself a Subject of the Turks], *Ta-lu tsa-chih* [The Continent], 37 (1968), 248–66.

[61]Nunome Chōfū, "Ri En shūdan no kōzō" [The Structure of Li Yüan's Organization], *Ritsumeikan bungaku* [Ritsumeikan University Journal of Cultural Sciences], 243 (1965), 27–29. The rebels Liang Shih-tu and Li Kuei probably profited in similar fashion from their connections with the Sui militia; see *TCTC* ch. 183, p. 5718, and ch. 184, p. 5745.

The first major military objective of Li Yüan was the Sui capital, about three hundred and fifteen miles as the crow flies to the southwest of Taiyuan, for which he set out in the seventh month, marching down the Fen River valley toward the T'ung Pass, the gateway to Shensi. The capture of Ta-hsing-ch'eng was important for two reasons. Politically, it represented a symbol of dynastic legitimacy—the passing of the Mandate from the Sui to the T'ang. Strategically, it commanded the Shensi plain, which Li Yüan, like other dynastic founders before him— Ch'in Shih-huang-ti, Han Kao-tsu, and Sui Wen-ti—planned to use as a springboard for the conquest of all China.

At Huo-i, a town in the southern Fen River valley, Li Yüan met with yet another major threat to his advance. He had called a halt at Huo-i because of strong Sui resistance and torrential late summer rains. While waiting for the weather to clear, he received a message from Li Mi, the powerful Honan rebel leader and fellow beneficiary of the "Li Ballad," proposing an alliance with the T'ang. Li Yüan suspected that Li Mi would pose a formidable obstacle if he became aware of his plans to take Ta-hsing-ch'eng.[62] He therefore wrote a polite but deceptive letter to his rival in which he portrayed himself as a loyal subject of the Sui who had raised an army only to reestablish order and disclaimed any ambition other than that of being left with his noble title, Duke of T'ang. At the same time he encouraged Li Mi in his own efforts to topple the Sui: "Heaven has created the common people, who need a shepherd. Now, who else is that shepherd if not you!"[63] Whether Li Mi was reassured by the letter or preoccupied by troubles in his own camp,[64] we do not know. In any event, he allowed Li Yüan to march on Ta-hsing-ch'eng without hindrance—a move he subsequently came to regret.

When the rains let up in the eighth month, the T'ang army was able to overcome Sui resistance at Huo-i and move on. During the battle of Huo-i, Li Yüan, it is said, contributed to the defeat of the Sui forces by circulating the rumor that their commander had been killed, thus throwing them into full rout.[65] P'u-chou fu, a town in southern Shansi

[62]Li Mi certainly realized the strategic importance of capturing the capital region in any campaign to win the empire. He had so advised Yang Hsüan-kan after the former had revolted against the Sui, and had long been encouraged to capture the capital by his own officials; see CTS 53.2 and TCTC ch. 183, p. 5735.

[63]TCTC ch. 184, p. 5743.

[64]See below, p. 51.

[65]CYCCC 2.15.

that controlled access to the T'ung Pass and, beyond it, the Shensi plain, was taken by T'ang forces in the ninth month of 617, largely, it appears, by the planning of Li Yüan.[66] Perhaps one of the reasons for these early T'ang successes was the high morale among the T'ang troops, for Li Yüan speedily rewarded all those meritorious in battle regardless of their rank.[67]

The T'ang campaign to conquer Ta-hsing-ch'eng has been described in some detail elsewhere and need not be elaborated here.[68] It is worth mentioning, however, that, judging from Wen Ta-ya's *Diary*, Shih-min appears to have contributed no more to its capture than his elder brother Chien-ch'eng, perhaps even less. All during the march on the capital the two brothers were almost invariably appointed to military duties with comparable responsibilities. For example, both shared in the initial planning of strategy for the battle of Huo-i, and both led troops to surround Ta-hsing-ch'eng.[69] Even more important, when the city finally fell to the T'ang, troops under the command of Chien-ch'eng's subordinate, Lei Yung-chi, were first to breach its walls.[70] The notion, sedulously propagated by the T'ang Standard Histories and *Comprehensive Mirror*, that Shih-min almost single-handedly brought about a victorious conclusion to the Ta-hsing-ch'eng campaign, must now be laid to rest.

Once inside the Sui capital, Li Yüan established a grandson of Yang-ti as a puppet emperor. Yet never for a moment was there any doubt that he would himself shortly assume the imperial mantle: he had already begun acting and speaking like Han Kao-tsu after that dynastic founder marched through the T'ung Pass,[71] and was assuming the highest official and noble titles in the land preparatory to his accession. On the twentieth day of the fifth month, 618 (June 18, 618), the first anniversary by the Chinese calendar of the seizure of the Sui deputies Wang Wei and Kao Chün-ya and the effective beginning of the

[66]Ibid. 2.21–21b.

[67]Ibid. 2.15b–16.

[68]See, especially, Bingham's account in *The Founding of the T'ang Dynasty*, pp. 95–104 and the author's treatment, "Kao-tsu the Founder," in the forthcoming *Cambridge History of China* volume on the T'ang dynasty.

[69]See *CYCCC* 2.13–15, 21–25b; Lo Hsiang-lin, *T'ang-tai wen-hua shih*, p. 17; Li Shu-t'ung, *T'ang-shih k'ao-pien*, p. 283.

[70]*CYCCC* 2.27; Li Shu-t'ung, *T'ang-shih k'ao-pien*, pp. 279–80; Lo Hsiang-lin, *T'ang-tai wen-hua shih*, p. 19.

[71]Fukui, "Ō Tō sōgyō kikyochū kō," 88–89.

Taiyuan revolt, Li Yüan mounted the throne amid great pomp and ceremony.

Immediately following his accession, Kao-tsu (as we will hereafter refer to him) appointed his eldest son, Chien-ch'eng, as the T'ang heir, named his second son, Shih-min, Prince of Ch'in, and his fourth son, Yüan-chi, Prince of Ch'i. The T'ang capital was established at Ta-hsing-ch'eng and renamed Ch'ang-an, a self-conscious act linking the T'ang to the last great Chinese empire of Han.

If important questions have arisen concerning the nature of Shih-min's role in launching the T'ang, there is nevertheless wide agreement that after the dynasty was formally proclaimed, Shih-min made major contributions toward the strengthening of T'ang military power and the destruction of rival contenders for the empire. Between 618 and 622, the Prince of Ch'in was almost constantly in the field as commander-in-chief (*yüan-shuai*) of numerous T'ang armies-on-campaign (*hsing-chün*) that were raised piecemeal to combat "rebel" groups. His defeat of Hsüeh Jen-kuo in the northwest and, especially, Tou Chien-te and Wang Shih-ch'ung on the northeastern plain,[72] virtually assured the reunification of China by the T'ang.

Because Kao-tsu led no troops in the field after the capture of the Sui capital, Shih-min's role in the T'ang pacification effort during the next several years greatly overshadowed his father's. It has thus not been sufficiently appreciated that Kao-tsu's political and military strategies designed to secure the allegiance of various power groups throughout the country effectively complemented Shih-min's military campaigns and thus greatly accelerated the T'ang reunification.

China in the year 618 was a patchwork of contending authorities, great and small. Hundreds of "rebel" and "bandit" organizations had occupied territory of varying size and had established at least rudimentary governments to administer them. Many areas continued to remain under the jurisdiction of Sui civil and military officials who hoped to be confirmed in their power by a new dynasty. In still other localities, leaders among the gentry had raised private armies to oppose civil strife and were filling with varying degrees of success the administrative vacuum left by the fall of the Sui. All of these areas had to be brought under T'ang control, by military means if necessary, but preferably by persuasion.

[72]See below, pp. 64–66.

To this end, Kao-tsu promoted a three-pronged policy of amnesty, appointment, and reward to persuade his adversaries to capitulate. Those who voluntarily surrendered with their armies and territories as well as many of those defeated on the battlefield were spared their lives. The followers of those who for one reason or another were executed were usually pardoned. Important "rebel" leaders were allowed to incorporate their forces into the T'ang military as whole units remaining under their personal command,[73] thus increasing their willingness to fight for the T'ang. Incumbent Sui local officials were often reconfirmed in their posts, and "bandit" or "rebel" leaders in control of given localities were often appointed to govern the identical areas as T'ang prefects.[74] At court, the surname Li, which Kao-tsu liberally bestowed on important rebels, conferred high prestige on them, and granted them such privileges as being honored above officials of equal rank.[75] Frequently, the emperor generously rewarded former foes and granted them high noble titles. The considerable number of voluntary surrenders to the T'ang and the few instances of revolt by those who had surrendered suggest that, beyond purely military considerations, Kao-tsu's policies were effective in rallying support for his regime over much of the country.

By early 624, Kao-tsu's pacification policies, combined with the military campaigns led by Shih-min and other T'ang generals, brought disorder within the Great Wall to an end for the first time in a decade. The emperor now proclaimed a great amnesty and joyfully declared that China was once more at peace.

Although the evidence presented in this chapter has undercut some of the foundations upon which Li Shih-min's historical reputation rests, the view that he was one of China's more extraordinary rulers remains unassailable. Yet he did not, it seems, possess the prescience and almost superhuman qualities the traditional narratives of the founding of his house have attributed to him. In toppling him from the "founding ruler" pedestal he has occupied for so long, we place him in a more accurate perspective not only in relation to his father, Kao-tsu, but also in relation to his courtiers, among whom stood Wei Cheng.

[73]See *CYCCC* 2.16; 2.23.

[74]See *TCTC* ch. 185, pp. 5796, 5805; ch. 186, pp. 5807, 5808, 5827; ch. 187, pp. 5852, 5863, 5869; ch. 189, pp. 5921, 5929; ch. 190, p. 5944; *CTS* 57.17, 69.13b; *CYCCC* 2.19b.

[75]See *CTS* 1.9, 1.10, 1.10b, 1.11, for the cases of Hsü Shih-chi, Lo I, Liu Hsiao-chen, Tu Fu-wei, Kao K'ai-tao, and Hu Ta-en. *TCTC* ch. 187, p. 5840, lists special privileges accorded those with the Li surname.

CHAPTER 2

Searching for a Master: Wei Cheng's Early Life and Career (580-618)

André Maurois has described the development of personality as "the successive deposits left by Time on a central kernel constituted by heredity, environment, and childhood."[1] Unfortunately, we find ourselves largely uninformed or uncertain regarding all three constituents of Wei Cheng's "central kernel." Because the T'ang Standard Histories and other sources for Wei's life are primarily interested in limning his public career, they inform us only meagerly about his activities prior to his thirty-seventh year, at which time he first entered the political arena. Even afterward they provide information on his private life—marriage, the birth of children, and the like—only in passing or not at all. We thus learn almost nothing about his formative years, the period of his early maturity, or his immediate surroundings all during this time.

WEI CHENG'S CLAN

Even Wei's ancestry and native place are subjects of dispute.[2] The biography of Wei's father, Wei Chang-hsien, in the *Northern Dynasties History* (*Pei-shih*) records that he belonged to the same clan as Wei Shou (506–72), historian-official under the Northern Wei (386–534), Eastern Wei (534–50), and Northern Ch'i (550–77) dynasties.[3] Wei Shou's clan, a noble lineage that traced its origins back to the beginning of the Former Han, had furnished officials for several dynasties during

[1]"The Ethics of Biography," in *Biography as an Art, Selected Criticism 1560–1960,* James L. Clifford, ed. (New York, 1962), p. 172.

[2]References to Wei's ancestry and native place are discussed in *WCLC* 1b–2, and Kao Pu-ying, *T'ang-Sung-wen chü-yao* [Selections from T'ang and Sung Literature], 2 vols. (Peking, 1963), 1:1–2.

[3]*PS* 56.18. Wei Shou's biographies are in *PS* 56.1–18 and *PCh'iS* 37.1–14b. His autobiography is in *WS* 104.1–7b.

the disunion period. Its seat was Chü-lu county (*hsien*), modern Hsing-t'ai in southwestern Hopei province.[4] Wei Shou's biography in the *Northern Dynasties History* more precisely gives his native place as Chü-lu, Hsia Ch'ü-yang.[5] Since the native place supplied for Wei Cheng in his biography in the *Old T'ang History* is Chü-lu, Ch'ü-ch'eng (Ch'ü-ch'eng is a variant of Ch'ü-yang),[6] this would appear to confirm his membership in Wei Shou's clan.

The great Chinese scholar Ch'en Yin-k'o, however, has argued against such a conclusion.[7] He points out that during the early T'ang it was still a common practice, a holdover from the Period of Disunion, for high-ranking bureaucrats to brag about or invent illustrious ancestries in order to enhance their social station at court. He further observes that the *Yüan-ho chün-hsien t'u-chih*, a gazetteer of late T'ang times, lists the location of Wei Shou's tomb as Chü-lu and notes that all the Wei clan members of the Northern Wei and Northern Ch'i dynasties, the "men of Chü-lu, Ch'ü-yang," were from this area.[8] On the other hand, the gazetteer places the tomb of Wei Cheng's father more than ninety miles to the southeast, in Shan prefecture near modern Ch'ing-feng.[9] Ch'en also cites the preface to a poem by the T'ang poet Kao Shih (d. 765) in which he writes of a trip he once took through Wei commandery, the site, he notes in passing, of Wei Cheng's home. During the early T'ang, Wei commandery was known as Hsiang prefecture (the site of Yeh, capital of the Eastern Wei and Northern Ch'i dynasties, modern Anyang in northern Honan province),[10] located approximately seventy miles to the south of Chü-lu. Matters are complicated still further by the notation in Wei Cheng's biography in the *New T'ang*

[4]See Lin Pao, *Yüan-ho hsing-tsuan* [Compendium of Surnames of the Yüan-ho Period] (preface 813; Chin-ling shu-chü ed., 1880), 8.8b–9b, and Ts'en Chung-mien, *Yüan-ho hsing-tsuan ssu-chiao-chi* [A Fourfold Collation of the Compendium of Surnames of the Yüan-ho Period], 3 vols. (Shanghai, 1948), 3:767–68.

[5]*PS* 56.1.

[6]*CTS* 71.1; *WCLC* 1b.

[7]Ch'en Yin-k'o, "Lun Sui-mo T'ang-ch'u so-wei 'Shan-tung hao-chieh' " [The So-called "Shan-tung hao-chieh" at the End of the Sui and Beginning of the T'ang Dynasty], *Ling-nan hsüeh-pao*, 12 (1952), 5, 8.

[8]See Li Chi-fu, comp., *Yüan-ho chün-hsien t'u-chih* [Geographical Gazetteer of Administrative Subdivisions of the Yüan-ho Period] (813–15; reproduction of *Chi-fu ts'ung-shu* ed., Taipei, 1965), 17.6.

[9]Ibid., 16.25.

[10]Ibid. 16.9b.

History that his native place was in Wei prefecture (modern Ta-ming),[11] situated more than sixty miles southeast of Chü-lu.

Fortunately, some light is shed on the thorny problem of Wei Cheng's native place by Wu Ching's *Essentials of Government of the Chen-kuan Period* (*Chen-kuan cheng-yao*), which was compiled about 707–09[12] and which thus contains the earliest published data on Wei's origins. Wu Ching notes that Wei's family was originally from Chü-lu but later moved south to Hsiang prefecture, Nei-huang county,[13] an intriguing possibility that is supported by several pieces of evidence. First, during Chen-kuan Wei received two titles of nobility, both of which directly link him to Chü-lu.[14] Second, when the T'ang turned to compiling the Standard Histories of its predecessors, Wei Cheng successfully fought against the compilation de novo of a history of the Northern Wei dynasty, a version of which had been compiled earlier by Wei Shou, thus ensuring that Shou's became canonical.[15] Third, upon his death Wei Cheng was awarded the same posthumous name as Wei Shou.[16] It is at least apparent that during Wei Cheng's own time the idea that he was related to the Chü-lu Wei clan was accepted by his contemporaries. Fourth, during the Eastern Wei and Northern Ch'i dynasties, Wei's father, whom we shall treat shortly, lived in the capital city of Yeh in Hsiang prefecture. It is possible that sometime during this period Wei Cheng's branch of the Wei clan moved to Hsiang prefecture from Chü-lu. Fifth, upon his death Wei also received the posthumous title of governor-general (*tu-tu*) of Hsiang prefecture.[17] All this suggests that Wei's family may indeed have been related to the Wei clan of Chü-lu

[11]*HTS* 97.1. The *New T'ang History* "Genealogical Table of Chief Ministers" (*tsai-hsiang shih-hsi piao; HTS* 72B. 24) gives Wei's native place as Kuan-t'ao county, which the *Yüan-ho chün-hsien t'u-chih*, 16.7–7b, also puts in Wei prefecture. It was located roughly fifty-five miles southeast of Chü-lu. Evidence of a perhaps more tenuous nature linking Wei to Kuan-t'ao is found in Wang T'ung's *Chung-shuo* [Discourses on the Mean] (ca. 618–26; *SPTK* ed., Shanghai, 1929), 4.4; on this point, see also Yoshikawa Tadao, "Bunchūshi kō—toku ni Tōkōshi o tegakari toshite" [A Study of Wen-chung-tzu—with Special Reference to Tung-kao-tzu], *Shirin*, 53 (1970), 252–53.

[12]See Harada Tanashige, "Jōkan seiyō no seiritsu" [The Formation of the *Chen-kuan cheng-yao*], *Shibun*, 22 (1958), 18–30.

[13]*CKCY* 2.5b.

[14]See *CTS* 71.2b; *HTS* 97.2.

[15]See below, p. 111.

[16]*WS* 56.16b; *CTS* 71.17b; *HTS* 97.14.

[17]*CTS* 71.17b; *HTS* 97.14.

and that sometime prior to Wei Cheng's birth they had moved from southern Hopei to northern Honan province.

Had Wei Cheng been a member of the Chü-lu Wei clan, its strong tradition of government service and, especially, historiographical endeavor would certainly have influenced him. Mention has already been made of Wei Shou's history of the Northern Wei dynasty, which was compiled under his direction during the period 551–54. Because of alleged deficiencies in Wei Shou's work, Sui Yang-ti later ordered another member of the Chü-lu Wei clan, Wei Tan, to revise it. Wei Tan's work is said to have differed from Wei Shou's on a number of points of interpretation, but while Shou's version was eventually accepted with some modifications as the Standard History of the Northern Wei, Tan's work is now almost entirely lost.[18]

Government service, and historiography in particular, was also prominent in the careers of members of Wei Cheng's immediate family. Wei's grandfather, Wei Yen, was a scholar who served as a secretary (*chi-shih ts'an-chün*) on the staffs of various nobles during the late years of the Northern Wei. Believing that a work known as the *Chin-shu*, a history of the Chin dynasty (265–419), but not the Standard History of the dynasty that later bore the same title, suffered a lack of uniformity because of the great number of compilers who had labored on it, Wei Yen attempted to correct its errors and unify its style. A transfer of posts, however, caused him to abandon his work on the history. During the reign of Emperor Hsiao-ming (rg. 516–28), he rose to the office of prefect (*tz'u-shih*).[19]

Wei Chang-hsien, Cheng's father, first studied for government service at Loyang but moved to Yeh after the capital was transferred there in 534 at the beginning of the Eastern Wei. It was at Yeh that Wei Chang-hsien obtained a *hsiu-ts'ai* degree in the renascent examination system. Under the Northern Ch'i dynasty, which succeeded the Eastern Wei at Yeh, Wei Chang-hsien continued the work begun by his father of revising the Chin history. This was, of course, a labor of filial piety in keeping with a venerable tradition dating back at least as far as the Han historians, Ssu-ma T'an and his son Ch'ien, and Pan Piao and his son

[18]*PS* 56.22–23b; *SKCSTM* 45.46–49; Chou I-liang, "Wei Shou chih shih-hsüeh" [Wei Shou's Historiography], *Yen-ching hsüeh-pao*, 18 (1935), 112–14.

[19]*PS* 56.19–19b. The "Genealogical Table of Chief Ministers," *HTS* 72B.24, mistakenly reverses the places of Wei's great-grandfather Chao and his grandfather Yen.

Ku. Wei Chang-hsien attained the office of prefect (*ling*) of T'un-liu (in modern Shansi province), but sometime during the period 570–75 he resigned this post because of illness and did not take up further employment during the Northern Ch'i. Using the pretext of poor health, Wei Chang-hsien continued to refuse office under the Northern Chou dynasty, which conquered the Northern Ch'i at Yeh during 576–77.[20] At the beginning of 580, when Wei Chang-hsien was well into his autumn years, Wei Cheng was born.

The strong scholastic tradition evidenced at least among Wei Cheng's immediate ancestors, combined with a revival of Confucian learning early in the Sui,[21] suggest that as a youth he was exposed to an extensive Confucian education. He is said to have been fond of studying and widely read, and his mastery of classical literature and history later in his life was certainly impressive. Yet Wei's formal schooling was suddenly interrupted, most likely before he had reached adolescence, by the death of his aged father. Reduced to impoverishment—Chinese Marxist historians view him as a member of the poor landlord class[22]—he eventually decided to leave home. It is apparent that the Chü-lu Wei clan itself either had not the financial wherewithal to help him continue his studies, or, if we accept the view of Ch'en Yin-k'o, had no reason to lend him financial assistance.

The Confucian Teacher Wang T'ung

Exactly what Wei Cheng did and where he went during his long peregrinations away from home remain a mystery. It is likely that by one means or another he attempted to continue his education, perhaps by attending a local school or by studying under a private teacher. We know of at least one Confucian scholar said to have taught Wei during this period. He is Wang T'ung (584?–617), also known posthumously as Wen-chung-tzu, or "Master Wen-chung." Most of what we know about Wang T'ung is contained in his biography, reputedly

---

[20]*PS* 56.19b–21b.

[21]See T'ang Ch'eng-yeh, *Sui Wen-ti*, pp. 209 ff., and Arthur F. Wright, "The Formation of Sui Ideology," p. 88.

[22]Wu Che and Yüan Ying-kuang, "T'ang-ch'u cheng-ch'üan yü cheng-cheng ti hsing wen-t'i" [Problems Concerning the Characteristics of Political Power and Political Strife in the Early T'ang], *Li-shih yen-chiu* (1964, no. 2), p. 113; Ch'i Ch'en-chün, "Shih-lun Sui ho T'ang-ch'u ti cheng-ch'üan" [An Examination of Political Power during the Sui and Early T'ang], *Li-shih yen-chiu* (1965, no. 1), p. 119.

written by the early T'ang official Tu Yen (d. 628) and included in a
work attributed to Wang, the *Discourses on the Mean (Chung-shuo)*.[23]
According to this biography, in 603, at the age of nineteen, Wang
journeyed to the court of Sui Wen-ti and presented him with a twelve-
point guide for ruling the empire. The emperor was pleased with Wang's
advice and desired to appoint him to office but later dropped the
matter after encountering stiff opposition among his own officials.
Wang then withdrew to Ho-fen, an area located between the Fen and
Yellow Rivers in southern Shansi, and there gave instruction to more
than one thousand students who flocked to him. Among them, it is said,
were Tu Yen, Li Ching, Fang Hsüan-ling, Wen Yen-po, and Wei
Cheng, all of whom later became important early T'ang bureaucrats.
As Wang's fame as a Confucian master spread, he repeatedly had to
decline summonses to the Sui court. Instead, he devoted his time to
teaching and writing in Ho-fen, where he died prematurely in 617.

Such a simple biographical sketch of Wang T'ung cannot begin to
suggest the storm of debate he has engendered among scholars during
the last thousand years.[24] Basically, the Wang T'ung controversy
revolves around three questions: the authorship of the works attributed
to him, his own historical reality, and the identities of his disciples.

All of the works allegedly written by Wang T'ung are now lost except
two, the *Primal Classic (Yüan-ching)*, a chronicle covering the period 290–
589 that is modelled on the *Spring and Autumn Annals (Ch'un-ch'iu)*,
and the aforementioned *Discourses on the Mean*, in which Wen-chung-
tzu and his "disciples," Wei Cheng among them, engage in philosophical discourses in the manner of the *Analects*. So derivative is the *Discourses on the Mean*, in fact, that several sections have been lifted verbatim
from the *Analects*. Yet the *Discourses on the Mean* has been criticized as
philosophically shallow by comparison, and Wen-chung-tzu is sometimes linked to eminent men who died before his time or with events
that occurred after his death. Errors and anachronisms have been detected as well in Tu Yen's biography of Wang. Some scholars have

[23]Wang T'ung, *Chung-shuo*, 10.6–9b; see also *CTW* 135.18b–23.

[24]It is impossible in such limited space to list the scores of commentators who have dis-
cussed the Wang T'ung problem. The two most detailed Chinese explorations are Wang
Ying-lung, *Wen-chung-tzu k'ao-hsin-lu* [Records Concerning the Existence of Wen-chung-tzu]
(Shanghai, 1934), and Wang Li-chung, *Wen-chung-tzu chen-wei hui-k'ao* [An Examination of
the Truths and Falsehoods Surrounding Wen-chung-tzu] (Changsha, 1938). The best
Japanese treatment is Yoshikawa, "Bunchūshi kō."

therefore concluded that Wang T'ung's "works" are either partly or entirely Sung dynasty forgeries.

The *Discourses on the Mean,* at least, does not seem to be a forgery of late date, since by the middle T'ang period it was already being quoted or mentioned by title in various places.[25] After Wang's death his words were probably gathered together by his disciples in the time-honored Chinese fashion, and then gradually shaped (and added to) by his brothers, sons, and grandsons to produce the present text.[26] Ssu-ma Kuang praised the work, but he, like others, suspected that heavy-handed efforts had been made by Wang's relatives to exaggerate his fame and following beyond all reality.[27] Presumably, this would explain some of the historically more dubious passages scattered throughout the text.

Another source of puzzlement is the absence of a biography of Wang T'ung in the "Confucian scholars" (*ju-lin*) section of the *Sui History (Sui-shu)* despite Wang's reputed fame late in that dynasty. Since Wang T'ung's alleged disciple, Wei Cheng, supervised the compilation of the *Sui History,*[28] this omission is all the more startling. Neither is there any mention of Wang in Wei Cheng's biographies or in the biographies of any of the other early T'ang statesmen said to have been his disciples. For these and other reasons the early Sung scholar Sung Hsien was moved to exclaim, "Wen-chung-tzu is an invention of later men; there was no such person!"[29] an audacious charge that neverthe-less exerted a strong influence on commentators of later ages.

There can be little doubt that Wang T'ung actually lived. The biographies of Wang Chi in the *Old* and *New T'ang History* note, respectively, that the "eminent Confucian" (*ming-ju*) and "great

---

[25]See Wang Ying-lung, *Wen-chung-tzu,* pp. 69–70, and Wang Li-chung, *Wen-chung-tzu,* p. 16.

[26]Jung Chao-tsu, "Mu-fang K'ung-tzu ti Wang T'ung" [Wang T'ung, Imitator of Con-fucius], *Ling-nan hsüeh-pao,* 6 (1941), 7–10 (I am indebted to Professor Jack Dull for this reference); Hsiao Kung-ch'üan, *Chung-kuo cheng-chih ssu-hsiang shih* [A History of Chinese Political Thought], 2 vols. (Chungking, 1945, and Shanghai, 1946), vol. 2, chap. 12; Wang Li-chung, *Wen-chung-tzu,* pp. 30–33.

[27]Ssu-ma Kuang, "Wen-chung-tzu pu-chuan" [Supplement to the Biography of Wen-chung-tzu], in *Sung-wen chien* [Mirror of Sung Literature], Lü Tsu-ch'ien, comp. (Wan-yu wen-k'u ed., Shanghai, 1936), ch. 149, p. 1980.

[28]See below, pp. 112–13.

[29]Quoted in Chu I-tsun (1629–1709), *Ching-i k'ao* [Examination of Interpretations of the Classics] (Che-chiang shu-chü ed., 1897), 279.3.

Confucian" (*ta-ju*) of the late Sui period, Wang T'ung, was Chi's elder
brother;[30] the biography of Wang Po in the *Old T'ang History* briefly
sketches the career of his grandfather T'ung at the end of the Sui,
including his writing of the *Primal Classic* and the *Discourses on the Mean*;[31]
the biographies of Wang Chih in both T'ang Standard Histories record
that the "great Confucian" Wen-chung-tzu was his ancestor five
generations removed.[32] Moreover, several sources of T'ang date affirm
the reality of Wang T'ung's existence.[33]

If Wang T'ung was a real person and, as the biographies of his
relatives note, an eminent Confucian of late Sui times, why is there so
little further mention of him in the Standard Histories? Some scholars,
noting the rather shallow philosophical substance of the works attributed to Wang, have theorized that Wei Cheng could not in all good
conscience have included the biography of such a mediocre teacher in
the *Sui History*, even if the latter had been his master.[34] Yet there is
evidence suggesting an equally plausible reason for the absence of
Wang's biography in the Standard Histories—a political falling out
between Wang's friend and alleged biographer, Tu Yen, and a powerful
early T'ang official, Chang-sun Wu-chi, who was also T'ai-tsung's
brother-in-law. It appears that at some intermediate stage in the
compilation of the Sui or T'ang Standard Histories a biography had
been devoted to Wang T'ung. The biography of Wang Chi in the
Old T'ang History says of his elder brother T'ung: "During the Ta-yeh
reign of the Sui he was an eminent Confucian called Wen-chung-tzu.
He has his own biography (*tzu yu chuan*)."[35] And in a letter written by
one of T'ung's sons, Wang Fu-chih,[36] we learn that a split occurred
between Tu Yen and Chang-sun Wu-chi sometime during the late
620s. Some scholars have doubted Fu-chih's assertion, but his account
is corroborated at the end of Tu Yen's own biography in the *Old T'ang
History*, presumably a more reliable source, which says, "formerly, [Tu]

[30]*CTS* 192.2–2b; *HTS* 196.1b.

[31]*CTS* 190A.22b–23.

[32]Ibid. 163.10b; *HTS* 164.17.

[33]See Wang Ying-lung, *Wen-chung-tzu*, pp. 1–27, and Wang Li-chung, *Wen-chung-tzu*, pp.
1–11.

[34]See, for example, the theory of Wang Chih-ch'ang, *Ch'ing-hsüeh chai-chi* (n.p., 1895),
18.20b–21; Ch'en Ch'eng-chen, "Wen-chung-tzu hsin-k'ao" [A New Examination of Wen-
chung-tzu], *Ta-lu tsa-chih* [The Continent], 36 (1968), 25, echoes Wang's conclusion.

[35]*CTS* 192.2–2b.

[36]See Wang T'ung, *Chung-shuo*, 10.11b; *CTW* 161.2b–3.

was not on friendly terms with [Chang-sun] Wu-chi."[37] Chang-sun Wu-chi, the most influential of all Chen-kuan officials, may have been able to gain revenge by having Tu's biography of Wang and all mention of the philosopher cut out of the *Sui History* and also out of the T'ang dynastic history and veritable records for the reigns of Kao-tsu and T'ai-tsung, all of which were being compiled during the height of Chang-sun Wu-chi's career. Such a possibility is supported by information provided by the late twelfth-century writer, Ch'ao Kung-wu, that a work called the *Sui-T'ang t'ung-lu,* since lost, claimed that Wang T'ung's biography had indeed been deleted by the historians.[38]

Turning to the question of Wang T'ung's disciples, we discover that Wang appears to have been much younger than some of his students and that there is little agreement among scholars as to their true identities. According to Tu Yen's biography of Wang, he was born in the year 584. This makes him approximately four years younger than Wei Cheng and more than ten years younger than some of the other "disciples" listed in Wang's biography by Tu Yen. The question is, could Wang have established master-disciple relationships with men so much older than himself? At least one scholar, Jung Chao-tsu, is not disturbed by the discrepancy in ages, noting that Tu Yen's biography of Wang also mentions that when Wang first became a tutor at the age of fourteen (!), his first student was a white-haired old man. On the other hand, Jung cautions that we need not believe that all those who are depicted sitting at the feet of Wen-chung-tzu in the *Discourses on the Mean* were actually his disciples. He argues from the evidence that the greater proportion of them, including Wei Cheng, probably were not in a strict sense disciples but may nevertheless have studied with the master for various periods.[39]

Had Wang T'ung instructed Wei Cheng for any substantial length of time, we might expect that he would have exerted some influence on Wei's thought. Although he does not directly link Wei with Wang, Mou Jun-sun has suggested that at the very least the two shared a common ideology. He shows that both Wang in the *Discourses on the Mean* and Wei in his introductions (*hsü*) and discussions (*lun*) in the Standard

[37]*CTS* 66.14b. See also Jung Chao-tsu, "Wang T'ung," 7, for a recent summary of the evidence related to this problem.

[38]*Chao-te hsien-sheng chün-chai tu-shu chih* (1819 ed.), 10.15b.

[39]Jung, "Wang T'ung," 5–6. A similar conclusion is reached by Yoshikawa, "Bunchūshi kō," 248–53.

Histories of the Liang, Ch'en, and Sui dynasties are highly critical of the elegant literary style which flourished during the Southern Dynasties and Sui, and hypothesizes that the tendency of Wei and other early T'ang dynasty statesmen from North China to link literary decadence with dynastic decline may have been derived from Wang T'ung and the ideological tradition he represented.[40]

There are other points of agreement between ideas ascribed to Wen-chung-tzu in the *Discourses on the Mean* and those later espoused by Wei Cheng at T'ai-tsung's court: opposition to the extravagance of the elaborate Feng and Shan rites; advocacy of punishment in certain cases to supplement rule by moral suasion; the need for rulers to accept remonstrance and the obligation of loyal officials to offer it; antipathy toward excessive activity on the part of rulers—"those who love activity meet with many calamities"—and advocacy of non-activity (*wu-wei*); and the importance of requiring moral virtue as well as administrative talent in those filling office.[41] On the other hand, there are some important dissimilarities as well. Wen-chung-tzu's emphasis on the role played by rites and music in ordering the state goes far beyond anything we encounter in Wei's writings, and his call for the reestablishment of the "feudal" (*feng-chien*) system to prolong the life of dynasties,[42] as we shall soon see, was antithetical to Wei's own views on the matter.

In conclusion, judging from the evidence at hand, it is conceivable that sometime between 605 and 617 Wei Cheng journeyed to southern Shansi and attended lectures given by the Confucian teacher Wang T'ung. He may even have spent some time studying with Wang and have been influenced by elements of his philosophy, thin as this philosophy may seem to us in retrospect. But if so, just how long he remained at Wang's side and to what degree his own thought was actually shaped by the master remain unclear.

A TAOIST INTERLUDE

Wei's biographies make no reference whatsoever to his studies under

[40]Mou Jun-sun, "T'ang-ch'u nan-pei hsüeh-jen lun-hsüeh chih i-ch'ü chih ch'i ying-hsiang" [The Differences of Academic Approach between the Northern and Southern Scholars in the Early T'ang Period and Their Influence], *Hsiang-kang chung-wen ta-hsüeh Chung-kuo wen-hua yen-chiu-so hsüeh-pao* [The Journal of the Institute of Chinese Studies of the Chinese University of Hong Kong], 1 (1968), 57–60.

[41]See Wang T'ung, *Chung-shuo*, 1.4b; 3.6; 5.3; 5.6; 5.7 and 9.4b; and 5.6b, respectively.

[42]See Sa Meng-wu, *Chung-kuo cheng-chih ssu-hsiang shih* [A History of Chinese Political Thought] (Taipei, 1969), p. 293.

Wang T'ung. Rather, they note that sometime after leaving home he entered the Taoist priesthood. The *New T'ang History* biography of Wei, as well as a work included in the massive Taoist repository, the *Tao-tsang,* both date this event during the Sui disorders;[43] there was thus ample time for Wei to have continued his Confucian studies under Wang T'ung or some other tutor. It is possible, but by no means certain, that one of Wei's literary compositions, "*Fu* on a Cypress in a Taoist Monastery" (*Tao-kuan nei po-shu fu*), was written during his Taoist interlude.[44] Writers of Chinese fiction, ever eager to seize upon the more colorful components of their subjects' personalities, have played up Wei's relationship with Taoism. In the *Romances of the Sui and T'ang* (*Sui-T'ang yen-i*), for example, he appears in the guise of a Taoist hermit.[45] Yet the Sung compilers of Wei's *New T'ang History* biography note that he only "pretended" (*wei*) to be a Taoist. This use of the character *wei* was surely prompted by the compilers' Neo-Confucian displeasure over the fact that such a celebrated Confucian personage as Wei Cheng had once worn the robes of a Taoist priest.

On the other hand, since there is rather little in Wei's family background or in his philosophical thought to link him with Taoism,[46] perhaps the interpretation of the *New T'ang History* is not far from the truth. Actually, Wei's decision to become a Taoist priest may merely have been a prudent way of coping with the times. In the last years of the Sui, the northeastern plain, comprising modern Hopei, Honan, and Shantung provinces, was the scene of great turmoil. For years the region had been ravaged in quick succession by flood, famine, drought, and pestilence, and now, to compound the misery, it had become a center for military conscription and heavy requisitioning of supplies for Yang-ti's Koguryŏ campaigns. Deteriorating economic conditions at home soon forced many of the northeastern conscripts to desert, and the region soon became infested with "bandit" and rebel groups.[47] Masquerading as a Taoist may have provided Wei Cheng with a convenient method of avoiding conscription, corvée, or political involvement with any number of dissident leaders operating in the Honan-

[43]*HTS* 97.1; Chang T'ien-yü, *Hsüan p'in-lu* [Classified Record of Taoists], in *Tao-tsang* [The Taoist Repository] (reproduction of 1445 ed.; Taipei, 1962), *han* 63, *ts'e* 558, 4.8.

[44]For a discussion of this work, see below, pp. 116–17.

[45]See below, pp. 203–05.

[46]For a discussion of possible Taoist themes in Wei's writings, see below, pp. 170–71.

[47]See Bingham, *The Founding of the T'ang Dynasty,* chapters 5 and 6, appendices D and E, and map IIa.

Hopei region at the time. That membership in the Taoist priesthood conferred some immunity against harassment or even a quasi-privileged status during the late Sui and early T'ang is suggested by the following incident. In 626, when Li Shih-min urgently required the services of two former subordinates who had been cashiered by his father, they were able to reenter his camp by disguising themselves as Taoists.[48]

THE REBELS YÜAN PAO-TSANG AND LI MI

We do not know how long Wei wore his Taoist robes or to what monastery, if any, he retired. What is clear, at any rate, is that he soon grew weary of concealing himself under the cloak of religion from the hurly-burly of the late Sui and made a decision to participate actively in the political and military events of the time. Late in 617, the last year of the Sui, Wei underwent a complete reversal of roles: from a Taoist recluse to a member on the staffs of two anti-Sui rebels. Nor should this surprise us, for the role of Taoist priest was basically ill-suited to Wei's personality, one of the most salient characteristics of which was a driving ambition (ta-chih).[49] As we shall soon see, Wei's intense desire to succeed and to exert a dominant influence at various centers of power dictated all of the roles he would play during his subsequent political career.

Naturally, Wei's decision to join the rebels took into consideration not only his personal ambition but the range of roles available to him under existing conditions in China. By the late Sui the civil official and his writing brush had been replaced by the warrior with bow and halberd as the symbol of authority throughout most of the country. The value of a Confucian education, with its emphasis on the literary, the art of government, and social ethics, had declined. Power in the late Sui was generally obtained through military accomplishment. Wei had not received any education consonant with this end, yet he was perspicacious enough to perceive that the skills which his Confucian education had conferred on him were not altogether useless. Some of the more successful rebels against the Sui were beginning to style themselves "emperor" or were using other equally audacious titles, and were creating courts and elaborate bureaucracies to lend some credence to

---

[48]CTS 66.2b, 68.5. See below, p. 74.

[49]See ibid. 71.1; HTS 97.1; TCTC ch. 184, p. 5751; Liu Su, Ta-T'ang hsin-yü [New Anecdotes of the Great T'ang Dynasty], (807; Pai-hai ed., Pai-pu ts'ung-shu chi-ch'eng, Taipei, 1957), 11.2.

their claims. These would-be Sons of Heaven required scribes to record their "imperial" annals, secretaries to aid them in drafting "edicts" and diplomatic correspondence, and, perhaps most of all, advisers to offer sage counsel on the best means of winning the empire. It was with all this in mind that Wei now began, as his biographies put it, "to focus his attention on theories of the Vertical and Horizontal Alliances" (*tsung-heng chih shuo*),[50] strategies dating from the Warring States period for conquering and governing the empire during a time of disorder, i.e., *Realpolitik*. He then began to search for a worthy master to whom he might offer his services and knowledge.

In the ninth month of 617, three months after Li Yüan took up arms against the Sui in Taiyuan, Wei apparently found his man—the former assistant to the deputy prefect (*ch'eng*) of Wu-yang commandery (southern Hopei), Yüan Pao-tsang.[51] Wei served Yüan as a secretary-envoy (*hsing-jen*),[52] whose task it was to help recruit soldiers by writing tracts outlining the crimes of the Sui and explaining the reasons why Yüan had turned against the dynasty. A key factor in Wei's decision to serve Yüan may well have been that the latter had decided to join forces with yet another rebel, Li Mi, and was now raising troops on his behalf. As Bingham observes, by this time Li Mi had become one of the strongest contenders for the throne, both ideologically, because he possessed the magical Li surname, and strategically, because he occupied an extensive and rich area on the northeastern plain centering around, but not including, the great city of Loyang.[53] This was, of course, some months before Li Yüan's triumphant entrance into Ta-hsing-ch'eng drastically altered the configurations of power in North China, and most signs were still pointing to the probability that Li Mi and not Li Yüan would inherit the Mandate of Heaven. If Wei Cheng was seeking a place in history, Li Mi was certainly the man to follow.

In return for the troops Yüan Pao-tsang brought with him, Li Mi appointed him commander-in-chief (*tsung-kuan*) of Wei prefecture. There is some confusion concerning exactly how Wei Cheng secured a position of Li's staff. According to his biographies in the T'ang Standard

[50]*CTS* 71.1.

[51]Since Wu-yang was in Wei prefecture (*TCTC* ch. 186, p. 5800, note of Hu San-hsing; *Yüan-ho chün-hsien t'u-chih*, 16.8), Wei Cheng's native place according to his *New T'ang History* biography, he may have been previously acquainted with Yüan.

[52]See *CTS* 62.9b and *TFYK* 126.11.

[53]Bingham, *The Founding of the T'ang Dynasty*, pp. 67–69.

Histories, while Yüan was raising troops for Li Mi the latter read Wei's tracts and admired his work. He then summoned Wei to an audience and appointed him to office.[54] The version in the *Comprehensive Mirror* is slightly different; it records that after Yüan had gone over to Li with his newly raised army, receiving as a consequence both honorary and noble titles, he sent Wei to express his gratitude to Li, and that it was then that Wei received the appointment.[55] Whichever the case, Wei's duties under Li Mi appear to have substantially duplicated those with which he had been charged earlier under Yüan Pao-tsang.

Soon after Wei's arrival at Li's camp, the rebel's forces, led by Yüan Pao-tsang and other generals, attacked and occupied the granary town of Li-yang on the Yung-chi Canal in northern Honan, one of the richest prizes on the northeastern plain. Although the region had recently suffered great floods and Yang-ti had ordered that the granaries be opened to the people, Sui officials there had dragged their feet, and many of the populace had starved to death. Upon taking the town, Li quickly threw open the granaries and distributed grain freely. The strategem paid off handsomely, for in a short while he was able to recruit from among the people in the area an army said to have numbered over 200,000 men, which then comprised the strongest force in all China.[56] A month later he made his unsuccessful bid to ally himself with Li Yüan and divide the Sui empire between them.

Li Mi spent the remainder of 617 and most of 618 locked in battle with the Sui general Wang Shih-ch'ung, whom Yang-ti had sent to the northeastern plain to protect his eastern capital at Loyang from rebel forces. Although Li was often victorious, he failed to break Wang's military might or to capture Loyang. Nevertheless, by the beginning of 618 almost all the rest of Honan had fallen to him except one commandery, which, despite repeated attempts to take it, had remained beyond his grasp. This was Jung-yang,[57] whose incumbent prefect,

[54]*CTS* 71.1; *HTS* 97.1.

[55]*TCTC* ch. 184, p. 5751.

[56]*CTS* 67.15 and Liu Su, *Ta-T'ang hsin-yü*, 7.13–13b both record that the general Hsü Shih-chi (Li Shih-chi) occupied Li-yang at Li Mi's command. They also note that at this time tens of thousands of starving people came to Li-yang from all parts of the empire, and that among them was Wei Cheng. Ssu-ma Kuang, however, discounts this version on the grounds that by this time Wei had already joined Li Mi's retinue; *TCTC* ch. 184, p. 5752, *k'ao-i* section.

[57]By coincidence, sometime during the period 605–17, Li Yüan had been the prefect (*t'ai-shou*) of Jung-yang; *HTS* 1.1b.

Yang Ch'ing, waited inside its walled capital. Sometime during the spring of 618, Li had Wei Cheng write a long letter entreating Yang to end his resistance,[58] a document of some interest since it not only is the earliest extant example of Wei's writing, but also represents a tool of psychological persuasion commonly used by military leaders of the Sui-T'ang transition period against their rivals.

Like much of Wei's later literary efforts, and in typical Chinese fashion, the letter is elaborately embroidered with literary and historical allusions. Ultimately, though, these do little to mask the speciousness of the letter's central argument. Wei attempts to convince Yang Ch'ing to abandon the cause of Yang-ti and join Li Mi on the grounds that Yang was unrelated to the Sui imperial house and therefore owed it no special allegiance. Yet we discover a far different story in the biography of Yang Ch'ing's father, where we learn that the father was a paternal relative of the Yang-Sui family.[59] Some excerpts from the letter follow:

Many years have passed since the suspicious and wild one [i.e., Yang-ti] came to the throne. He has fleeced the common people and poisoned the empire. Despite his extravagance in constructing beautiful palaces and terraces, he has not yet reached the limits of his arrogance and wastefulness. Despite his recklessness in making hillocks of distillery grains and ponds of wine, he does not consider this profligate. He has, moreover, neglected the remonstrances of loyal officials and followed the advice of his concubines, slain the loyal and good and levied taxes without cease. That is why like a porcupine raising his quills and like a leopard changing his spots we are together raising the righteous banners of revolt and eliminating his tyranny. . . .

The Viscount of Wei was the elder brother of Chou ["bad last" ruler of the Shang]; their relationship was really very close. Hsiang Po was the uncle of Chi [ruler of the Western Ch'u]; their relationship was not remote. But [the Viscount of Wei] left Ch'ao-ko [a capital of the Shang dynasty] and lived in [the domains of the] Chou. [Hsiang Po] turned his back on the Western Ch'u and went over to the Han. Was it that they felt no affection for their ancestral temples or for their kin? No, it was because they knew that the precious tripod [political power] was going to be transferred, and that the

[58]From the letter's contents, it is likely that it was written before the news of Yang-ti's assassination reached the Loyang region in the fifth month of 618; see *TCTC* ch. 185, p. 5791.

[59]According to *SuiS* 43.1, Yang Ch'ing's grandfather, Yang Yüan-sun, was raised by the family of his mother, surnamed Kuo. When the Northern Chou came to power, Yang Yüan-sun was living in Yeh, the capital of its rival, the Northern Ch'i. Since the Yang family was also related to the Northern Chou royal house, Yang Yüan-sun feared for his life. He thus discarded his real surname and adopted that of his mother. When the Sui came to power, the surname probably reverted to Yang.

position of the divine vessel [the throne] would change first; that the river banks had been broken and could not be shored up; that the trees had been toppled and could not be supported. They were the so-called omniscient men and clear-sighted *chün-tzu* [morally superior men].

The house of your ancestors was in Shan-tung, their original name was Kuo, and they were not of the Yang clan. It is only because your ancestors aided the rise of the Sui that they received considerable merit, subsequently obtained important positions, and were placed on the list of remote relatives [of the imperial house]. [Your relationship to the Sui is like that of] Lo Ching and Han Kao[-tsu, who] were not actually relatives, and Lü Pu and Tung Cho, [who] were not really kin. Your situation is not like "the orchid that sighs when the iris burns" [i.e., when one feels empathy for another because of close familial relationships] . . . .

By yourself you occupy an isolated city cut off for a thousand *li*. If you calculate the extent of your provisions, they will barely be sufficient for a month or more. Your soldiers are exhausted and they are not more than a few hundred in number. How can you depend on them to resist me? . . .

Now my brave troops of one million are turning their horses eastward, only awaiting the destruction of Wang Shih-ch'ung before marching in that direction. Our scaling ladders will be raised high [everywhere in Jung-yang]. Our drums will beat and our horns will blare. I will laugh at the death of Kuo Shu [who died in vain; i.e., a senseless death like the one you are about to die] and will pity those still living in Hsiang-yang [attacked by Hsiang Yü; i.e., Jung-yang]. [If you do not surrender to me as did] I, the prefect of Nan-yang, [to Han Kao-tsu,] you will have no hopes for enfeoffment. [And like Li Ssu's] lament upon being executed [that he would not again be able to go out of] the eastern gate [of his native city] to hunt [with his son], it will be too late. Since I have such great regard for you, I have cut off a piece of silk with which to write this letter. I hope you will give it due consideration in order thereby to enhance your fortunes.[60]

Wei's letter (about twice as long again as the portions translated above), may have helped convince Yang Ch'ing to capitulate to Li Mi without a fight. Yang's biography, at any rate, laconically records only that "[after] receiving the letter, he surrendered."[61] Despite this success, or perhaps because of it, Wei grew restless at the prospect of continuing to serve Li Mi merely in the capacity of a secretary, for he wanted to put his knowledge of practical politics to good use and hoped to make

60 *WCKWC* ch. 3, pp. 32–33.
61 *SuiS* 43.3b.

Li Mi his instrument. His goal was to become Li's adviser, mastermind his conquest of the empire, and obtain high position under the new Son of Heaven. He therefore presented Li with a broad ten-point plan, the contents of which are unknown, but which undoubtedly outlined a method to defeat Li's rivals and win him the empire. Although Li is said to have admired Wei's plan, in the end he made no use of it.[62]

Beginning with the summer of 618, Li's military position began to change drastically. In the fifth month, upon learning of Yang-ti's assassination in Chiang-tu, Wang Shih-ch'ung placed a young grandson of the late emperor on the throne in Loyang as his puppet. Shortly afterwards, news reached the northeastern plain that forces led by the Sui regicide Yü-wen Hua-chi were moving north from Chiang-tu toward Li-yang, Li Mi's stronghold. The advisers of the new "emperor" in Loyang now formulated a plan to pardon Li Mi in return for his cooperation in opposing Yü-wen Hua-chi, hoping thereby to weaken and destroy both rebel leaders simultaneously. Li Mi accepted the offer of amnesty for at least two reasons. First, he had to defend his headquarters at Li-yang in any case, and second, he hoped to turn his détente with the Loyang administration to good advantage and eventually to eliminate his arch-rival, Wang Shih-ch'ung.

Just as those in Loyang had predicted, although Li routed Yü-wen Hua-chi in several engagements around Li-yang, he was unable to defeat him decisively and only succeeded in eroding much of his own power. Many of his best troops and horses perished and the strength of those who survived became exhausted. In the meantime, Wang Shih-ch'ung had built up an army of more than two hundred thousand men and twenty thousand horses. He had liberally rewarded his officers and troops and kept their weapons in excellent repair. Thus, full of confidence, in the ninth month of 618 he marched through the gates of the Eastern Capital and went out once more to engage Li Mi on the battlefield.

At the granary town of Lo-k'ou, a short distance to the east of Loyang, Li Mi called a council of his generals to ask their opinions on what strategy he should employ against Wang. A clear majority were in favor of taking the offensive despite Wang's numerical superiority,

[62]*CTS* 71.1.

cutting off his line of retreat to Loyang, and attacking the Eastern Capital. Li Mi accepted their counsel.

Wei Cheng, not a party to the above deliberations, opposed the plan of the generals. He was still smarting, however, from Li's refusal earlier to implement his ten-point plan and did not want directly to offer him further advice. Instead, he sought out one of Li's subordinates, the administrator-in-chief (*ch'ang-shih*) Cheng T'ing, and observed:

The Duke of Wei [Li Mi] has been repeatedly victorious, but many of his brave generals and valiant soldiers have been killed and wounded. Moreover, since the army does not have a [full] treasury, he has not been able to reward those meritorious [in battle], and they have become remiss. For these two reasons it will be difficult to engage the enemy. It would be better to dig moats, erect ramparts, and bide our time. In less than ten days or a month the provisions of the bandit [Wang Shih-ch'ung] will be exhausted. He will be unable to fight and will withdraw, and we will be able to pursue and attack him and gain a victory. Moreover, the food in the Eastern Capital is almost gone. Shih-ch'ung has run out of tactics and intends to fight to the death. It may be said that it is difficult to vanquish a desperate bandit. I [therefore] request that you act cautiously and not fight him.[63]

Cheng T'ing sniffed, "This is nothing but the typical talk of an old scholar." His face darkening with rage, Wei retorted, "This is an excellent scheme and a profound plan. How can you call it 'typical talk'?" He then withdrew in a huff.[64] Here we see an illustration of the age-old tension in China between the military establishment and the Confucians. The military was typically for strong, positive action designed to crush its adversaries. The Confucians were more likely to urge caution and patience and the postponement of military operations until all else had failed. Perhaps in the interim, they would argue, the enemy might weaken sufficiently so that he could be taken easily or would realize the superior morality of his opponent and thus capitulate without bloodshed. Although Wei's strategy would not prevail this time, even later, under T'ai-tsung, he would continue to advocate similar policies.

Shortly after this rebuff to Wei by Cheng T'ing, Li Mi's forces were decisively crushed by Wang Shih-ch'ung's army in a fierce battle near the granary town of Lou-k'ou. According to one account, one of Wang's

[63]Ibid. 71.1b; *TCTC* ch. 186, p. 5810.
[64]*CTS* 71.1b. *HTS* 97.1b says that Wei left without replying.

soldiers greatly resembled Li. Wang had this soldier trussed and bound and at the height of the fighting exhibited him to Li's forces, thus throwing them into great confusion. The tide of battle turned, and Li and the remnants of his men were forced to flee back to Lou-k'ou.[65] Li had now lost his bid to become the next emperor of China.

Ultimately, there were several reasons for Li's failure to gain the Mandate. Cohesion in his organization had been seriously weakened after a split developed between those elements who were dedicated to building a viable alternative government to the Sui and those who were interested merely in the rewards of plunder.[66] The granaries Li had captured were full, but, ironically, he had little money or silk with which to reward his officers and the bandit elements among his men.[67] A majority of his troops were from "east of the mountains" (shan-tung, i.e., east of the T'ai-hang mountains of modern Shansi province),[68] thus making it difficult for Li to plan a campaign against Ta-hsing-ch'eng, as his men were ill-disposed to move westward before they had occupied Loyang. The effect of these weaknesses was greatly intensified by mistakes in tactics Li had made against both Yü-wen Hua-chi and Wang Shih-ch'ung.[69]

Realizing that their situation was now hopeless, Li and his generals decided to "enter the Pass" and throw themselves upon the mercy of T'ang Kao-tsu. They reasoned that Li had not hindered the T'ang leader on his march to Ta-hsing-ch'eng and that by surrounding Loyang they had cut off Sui forces from the roads leading westward to the Sui capital; Kao-tsu would therefore be grateful to them.[70] They were no doubt also aware of the emperor's policy of leniency and generosity toward surrendered foes.

[65] TCTC ch. 186, p. 5811.

[66] Nunome Chōfū, "Zuimatsu no hanranki ni okeru Ri Mitsu no dōkō" [Li Mi's Rising in the Last Years of the Sui], Shigaku zasshi [Journal of Historical Studies], 74 (1965), 3, 26–28.

[67] TCTC ch. 186, p. 5808.

[68] SuiS 70.15b.

[69] For example, by the ninth month of 618 Wang was low on food and Li's army was short of clothing. Wang thus made a proposal to Li for an exchange of food for clothing. Li, who controlled all the granaries in the immediate vicinity, at first opposed Wang's plans. Others in his organization, however, hoping to reap profits from the resulting business transaction, eventually persuaded him to approve it. Although hundreds of people had daily fled to Li's camp from Loyang during the period of famine, the flow was reduced to a trickle once the city was furnished with grain; TCTC ch. 186, p. 5809.

[70] Ibid. ch. 186, p. 5813.

Wei Cheng, too, now decided to try his luck with the T'ang regime. His period of service under Li Mi had been singularly disappointing. He had sought to be much more than Li's secretary, but the strategies he had offered to help win him the empire had twice been spurned, and in the end Li himself had been defeated. On the other hand, by late 618 T'ang Kao-tsu had already enhanced his position as the legitimate successor to the Mandate by occupying the Sui capital. He had gone on to consolidate his power in southern Shensi and had already begun extending his control over other areas in northern China. Clearly, the T'ang star was in the ascendant, and Kao-tsu appeared to have a good chance of reuniting China and establishing a viable regime. Wei Cheng, now thirty-eight years old, was poised on the threshold of his middle years with a career sadly lacking in accomplishment. Surely he was painfully aware of Confucius' observation that "if a man has reached forty or fifty and nothing has been heard of him, then indeed there is no need to respect him."[71] Time was growing short, and if his political ambitions were not realized soon, he knew that they prdbably would never be realized at all. Thus, when on the eighth day of the tenth month, 618, Wei passed through the great gates of Ch'ang-an in the train of Li Mi and several thousands of his followers, his renewed hopes for success must have been mingled with great anxiety over what the future might bring.

[71]*Analects* 9.22. Arthur Waley, *The Analects of Confucius* (London, 1938), p. 143, slightly emended.

CHAPTER 3

Bobbing on the Waters: Wei Cheng at the Court of T'ang Kao-tsu (618-626)

Conditions were in a state of flux when Wei Cheng arrived in the T'ang capital. Kao-tsu had occupied the city for less than a year and was still faced with enormous problems of organization, the recruitment of personnel, and the raising of revenues to finance his civil and military operations. The emperor, moreover, had only recently begun to pacify the country, and his military position was still far from secure. During his reign, which he hopefully named *Wu-te* ("Military Virtue"), Kao-tsu's chief tasks were the development of a smooth-functioning administrative apparatus and the recentralization of political authority throughout China.

THE WU-TE GOVERNMENT AND BUREAUCRACY

One of the most important administrative problems the emperor and his advisers initially had to tackle was the rebuilding of the central government. Years of civil war and Yang-ti's withdrawal to Chiang-tu had left the Sui civil administration in Ta-hsing-ch'eng in a state of chaos. One source reports that when Kao-tsu set about reviving the bureaucracy, there was not even any paper available for the use of his officials.[1] Fortunately, the first T'ang emperor did not have to build his government from scratch, but instead found himself the beneficiary of a rich institutional legacy. Upon reuniting China three decades earlier, Sui Wen-ti had built his government out of institutions that had developed during the long Period of Disunion.[2] Kao-tsu was in turn able to select and adapt many of these same institutions to fit the requirements of his own regime.

[1] *THY* ch. 56, p. 961.
[2] See Ch'en Yin-k'o, *Sui-T'ang chih-tu yüan-yüan lüeh-lun kao* [Draft Outline of the Origin and Development of Sui and T'ang Institutions] (Chungking, 1944, and Shanghai, 1946).

To serve as the nucleus of the T'ang central government, the emperor adopted the Sui Three Department (san-sheng) system, made up of the Department of Affairs of State (shang-shu sheng) and its Six Boards (liu-pu) of Civil Appointments, Finance, Rites, War, Punishments, and Public Works; the Department of the Imperial Secretariat (chung-shu sheng); and the Department of the Imperial Chancellery (men-hsia sheng).[3] When the Sui fell from power this system had not yet developed fully, and the responsibilities of the Departments occasionally overlapped or were ill-defined. During the early T'ang period the Three Department system gradually underwent a process of rationalization, essentially completed by the middle years of T'ai-tsung's reign, after which time the division of powers among the Departments became fixed. Stated very simply, the Department of the Imperial Secretariat drafted imperial orders and edicts, the Department of the Imperial Chancellery reviewed and emended them, and the Department of Affairs of State implemented them through its various boards. During Wu-te, because the Three Department system did not always function efficiently, Kao-tsu would often issue orders and edicts himself, which, without going through the above machinery, still had the force of law.[4]

The highest officials of the Three Departments, that is, the two presidents of the Department of the Imperial Secretariat (chung-shu ling), the two presidents of the Department of the Imperial Chancellery (shih-chung), and the left and right vice-presidents of the Department of Affairs of State (shang-shu tso- and yu-p'u-yeh),[5] were designated regular chief ministers (cheng tsai-hsiang). The chief ministers met regularly among themselves and with the emperor to formulate state policy.

[3]The Departments were so designated beginning in the third month of 624; TCTC ch. 190, p. 5978. Prior to this time they had retained their Sui names.

[4]Sun Kuo-tung, "T'ang-tai san-sheng chih chih fa-chan yen-chiu" [The Development of the Three Department System of the T'ang Dynasty], Hsin-ya hsüeh-pao [New Asia Journal], 3 (1957), 20–21, 39–41.

[5]Generally, there was no president of the Department of Affairs of State (shang-shu ling). After the third year of Sui Yang-ti's reign (607), this office always remained unfilled, and after Li Shih-min was president of the Department from 618 to 626, the office remained vacant out of deference to him during most of the rest of the T'ang. See Yamazaki Hiroshi, "Zuichō kanryō no seikaku" [The Character of Bureaucracy in the Sui Dynasty], Tōkyō Kyōikudaigaku bungakubu kiyō, 6 (1956), 18, and Yen Keng-wang, T'ang p'u-shang-ch'eng-lang piao [Tables of High Officials in the Department of Affairs of State during the T'ang Dynasty], 4 vols. (Taipei, 1956), 1:15.

Subordinate to the Department of Affairs of State—the central executive power—were the nine Courts (*ssu*) and five Directorates (*chien*).[6] The Courts undertook much of the routine executive functions of government relating to imperial sacrifices, insignia and equipment, defense, agriculture, revenue, justice, and the like. The Directorates were also practical executive organs. They controlled, among other things, the imperial workshops, the imperial armory, and construction projects in the palace and in the capital.

Another important organ of state, independent of the Three Department system, was the Censorate (*yü-shih t'ai*). The most important duty of the censors was to supervise and discipline the bureaucracy. The censors were charged with reporting to the throne any instances of administrative malfeasance or misfeasance and were given the power to impeach offending officials.

As the basic unit of his provincial administration, Kao-tsu established prefectures (*chou*) to replace the old Sui system of commanderies (*chün*).[7] As in Sui times, counties (or subprefectures—*hsien*) were under the jurisdiction of the prefectures. Kao-tsu perpetuated the Sui program of administrative centralization by continuing its practice of placing the appointments of prefects (*tz'u-shih*) and subprefects (*hsien-ling*) under the Board of Civil Appointments in the capital.

To safeguard the T'ang realm along the frontiers and at other strategic points in the interior, Kao-tsu revived the Sui administrations of the commander-in-chief (*tsung-kuan fu*), later known as governments-general (*tu-tu fu*). These administrations exercised combined civil and military powers over their subordinate prefectures and resident populations. The emperor also divided Kuan-nei (Shensi), site of the T'ang capital as well as of its military headquarters, into twelve military districts (*chün-fu*) and garrisoned each with its own army (*chün*).[8]

---

[6]See Yen Keng-wang, "Lun T'ang-tai shang-shu sheng chih chih-ch'üan yü ti-wei" [On the Authority and Status of the Department of Affairs of State of the T'ang Dynasty], *Kuo-li chung-yang yen-chiu-yüan li-shih yü-yen yen-chiu-so chi-k'an* [Bulletin of the Institute of History and Philology, Academia Sinica], 24 (1953), 3–4. A revised version of this article is included in idem, *T'ang-shih yen-chiu ts'ung-k'ao* (Hong Kong, 1969), pp. 1–101.

[7]The Sui had employed the prefectural system during the period 589–607. In both the Sui and T'ang cases the changes in administrative subdivisions often related more to nomenclature than to the boundaries of the administrative subdivisions. The commandery system was later revived at various times under the T'ang.

[8]See Ts'en Chung-mien, *Fu-ping chih-tu yen-chiu* [A Study of the Militia System] (Shanghai, 1957), chapter 5, and T'ang Ch'ang-ju, *T'ang-shu ping-chih chien-cheng* [Commentary on and Corrections to the Military Monograph of the New T'ang History] (Peking, 1962), chapter 1.

The early T'ang law system was to a great extent modeled on that of the Sui. When Kao-tsu first ascended the throne he allowed most of the articles of the Sui K'ai-huang code—itself based in large part on the laws of the Wei, Chin, Liang, and Northern Ch'i dynasties—to continue in force. Although the following year the emperor empowered a commission to formulate a comprehensive code of T'ang administrative and penal law, this code, presented to the throne five years later, was still heavily influenced by that of K'ai-huang.[9]

It was one thing to piece together an efficient civil and military administration, but quite another to pay for it. Initially, Kao-tsu's regime was financed by what remained of the Sui treasury in Ch'ang-an and by loot obtained on campaign. But the Sui treasury and storehouses were already nearly empty when Kao-tsu entered Ta-hsing-ch'eng and became even further depleted following his presentation of generous rewards to surrendered rebels and veterans of the Taiyuan uprising.[10] As T'ang administrative control spread over China, a permanent source of revenue to finance the dynasty's expanding operations was urgently required. To meet this exigency, under laws of 619 and 624, Kao-tsu established a system of taxation, the tsu-yung-tiao, which was levied in grain, cloth, and labor-service. The tsu-yung-tiao was paid by adult cultivators on the basis of land distributed to them under the "equal-field" (chün-t'ien) system, which Kao-tsu established at the same time. Both the equal-field and tsu-yung-tiao were T'ang adaptations of land tenure and tax systems created under the Northern Dynasties. Although the equal-field system was once simply dismissed as an idealized scheme that was never put into practice, in recent years it has become increasingly apparent that in many areas in China proper and in the far northwest (western Kansu and Sinkiang provinces) it actually functioned more or less as prescribed in the T'ang statutes.[11]

In other moves to strengthen the economic position of the dynasty, Kao-tsu attempted to provide an adequate coinage[12] and continued the Sui policy of developing the waterworks.[13]

[9]Étienne Balazs, Le traité juridique du "Souei-chou" (Leiden, 1954), pp. 25–26, 208; TCTC ch. 190, p. 5982; THY ch. 39, p. 701.

[10]CTS 57.11b.

[11]See Denis Twitchett, Financial Administration Under the T'ang Dynasty, 2nd ed. (Cambridge, 1970), chaps. 1–2, and Mark Elvin, The Pattern of the Chinese Past (Stanford, 1973), pp. 59–63.

[12]TCTC ch. 189, p. 5924; THY ch. 89, pp. 1622–23; Twitchett, Financial Administration, pp. 69, 70.

[13]THY ch. 87, p. 1595.

Given the circumscribed area under T'ang control in the early years of the dynasty and its relatively modest administrative requirements, the Wu-te central bureaucracy was minuscule compared to the size attained by its counterparts later in the dynasty. Nevertheless, the emperor found it difficult to staff all the openings in his administration,[14] for many people evidently assumed that T'ang rule would not endure long and were afraid to serve the dynasty lest they be labelled traitors by some subsequent regime. It was for this reason that rebel leaders like Li Mi, who brought many of his staff members along with him, were so heartily welcomed by Kao-tsu, and also why talented men like Wei Cheng were able to find such ready employment in Ch'ang-an.

As an aid in recruiting bureaucrats, sometime prior to 622 Kao-tsu reintroduced the Sui civil service examination system.[15] He also reestablished three state schools in Ch'ang-an dating from Sui times designed to prepare future candidates for the examinations. These were the School of the Sons of State (*kuo-tzu hsüeh*), the Superior School (*t'ai-hsüeh*), and the School of the Four Gates (*ssu-men hsüeh*), initially attended by more than three hundred students drawn chiefly from among the sons of the imperial family and high court officials.[16]

In sharp contrast to later T'ang governments, Kao-tsu's administration at the highest levels appears to have operated on a relatively informal basis, a reflection of the existence of familial and strong personal relationships between the emperor and his key officials.[17] To ensure bureaucratic loyalty during a critical phase in the dynasty's development, the emperor staffed the highest echelons of his administration with old friends, veterans of the Taiyuan uprising and the Ta-hsing-ch'eng campaign, and relatives by blood or marriage. Eight out of his twelve chief ministers were related to the imperial house, and his high-ranking civil and military officials generally were former members of the Administration of the Grand General, Kao-tsu's military organization in Taiyuan.[18]

[14]See *TCTC* ch. 192, p. 6043.

[15]See Wang Ting-pao, *T'ang chih-yen* [Collected Anecdotes of the T'ang Dynasty] (ca. 955; Taipei, 1962), ch. 15, p. 159.

[16]*THY* ch. 35, p. 633; *TCTC* ch. 185, p. 5792.

[17]See, for example, *TCTC* ch. 185, p. 5794, where Kao-tsu and his old friend P'ei Chi sit on the same couch while conducting official business.

[18]Tsukiyama Chisaburō, *Tōdai seiji seido no kenkyū* [Studies on the Governmental System of the T'ang Dynasty] (Osaka, 1967), p. 29; Nunome Chōfū, "Tōchō sōgyōki no ichi kōsatsu" [A Study of the Founding Period of the T'ang Dynasty], *Tōyōshi kenkyū* [The Journal of Oriental Researches], 25 (1966), 3–15.

To a large extent, the Wu-te administration reflected a perpetuation of control by the ruling classes of the Northern Dynasties and Sui periods. Nunome Chōfū's study on the backgrounds of presidents and vice-presidents of the Three Departments and Six Boards during Wu-te shows that in a total of forty-five such officials, of forty-one for whom background data was available, four had fathers who had served in the Southern Dynasties of the Later Liang and Ch'en; all the rest either had fathers who served under the Northern Ch'i, Northern Chou, and Sui dynasties or had been Sui officials themselves. Thus, the establishment of the T'ang was not accompanied by any major change in the composition of the ruling class, much less by any social revolution.[19]

Chinese commentators, ancient and modern, have generally given Kao-tsu poor marks as an emperor.[20] Typically, they portray him as a hedonist who preferred lolling about the palace or pursuing pleasurable activities to the relatively unrewarding and burdensome task of administering the country. In some respects this view is justified. The emperor did enjoy the good life. Like most of the racially mixed northwestern aristocrats brought up amidst strong military traditions, he took great pleasure in the chase and always seemed to be commencing one costly hunting expedition or completing another. He relished the elaborate song and dance entertainments (we read of five hundred articles of clothing required for the costumes of the women entertainers alone at one performance) that were mounted upon his command at the Hsüan-wu Gate in the center of the northern wall of the palace city, even admiring one entertainer so much that he awarded him an official post.[21] As a result, very early in his reign puritanical Confucians were already clucking their disapproval and warning him that his behavior would have a dire effect on the future of his house.[22] As an administrator the emperor also had his failings. He was quick-tempered, often

[19]Nunome, "Tōchō sōgyōki," 15–33, esp. p. 32. See also Tsukiyama, *Tōdai seiji seido*, pp. 18–20. Among the many Marxist interpretations which oppose this view are those of Wu Che and Yüan Ying-kuang, "T'ang-ch'u cheng-ch'üan," and Ch'i Ch'en-chün, "Shih-lun Sui ho T'ang-ch'u ti cheng-ch'üan."

[20]See the remarks of the compilers of the *CTS*, 1.16b–17, and of Lü Ssu-mien, *Sui-T'ang-Wu-tai shih* [History of the Sui, T'ang, and Five Dynasties], 2 vols. (Shanghai, 1959), 1:74–76, for two examples.

[21]*TCTC* ch. 186, p. 5834. A protest against the appointment by the official Li Kang is found in his biography, *CTS* 62.3b–4.

[22]See the long remonstrance of Sun Fu-chia, *TCTC* ch. 185, pp. 5796–97.

meted out punishment too harshly or too hastily,[23] and occasionally exhibited great partiality toward certain of his subordinates.[24] He was also, as we shall soon see, susceptible to being manipulated by the women of his harem and the numerous gossip-mongerers of his court.

Despite these shortcomings, by most criteria Kao-tsu's reign was rich in accomplishment and by its conclusion the dynasty had been put on solid administrative, economic, and military foundations. Admittedly, the last of these achievements were owed largely to the efforts of Li Shih-min and other T'ang generals; but the less glamorous work of building the T'ang administration fell squarely on the shoulders of Kao-tsu and his advisers, who remodeled and improved, or, at the very least, revived a host of institutions and systems from earlier dynasties that became hallmarks of the T'ang age and, in many cases, of Chinese civilization down to the present century. In short, the father laid much of the groundwork for the brilliant reign of his son.[25]

Wei's Mission to the Northeast

It is quite possible that Wei Cheng already knew something of Kao-tsu's qualities when he arrived in Ch'ang-an. Whatever the case, he quickly assessed the character of the emperor and formulated a strategy by which to ingratiate himself with the throne and win an important place in the T'ang administration. At the time, Li Mi's old territory in the northeast had been reoccupied by one of his subordinates, Hsü Shih-chi. Wei, who was surely acquainted with Hsü, volunteered to journey to Hsü's headquarters at Li-yang to persuade him to surrender to the T'ang. Fortunately for Wei, his path had crossed that of the T'ang just at the moment when the dynasty was still young, when capable men were in great demand, and when upward mobility in the ranks came relatively easily. Kao-tsu was pleased by his plan, appointed him assistant in the Department of the Imperial Library (*pi-shu ch'eng*), a post of fifth degree, second class in the T'ang nine-degree, thirty-class

[23]See, for example, ibid. ch. 186, p. 5834; *CTS* 69.15b; *HTS* 94.11.

[24]For the case of Kao-tsu's execution of Liu Wen-ching at the instigation of his crony, P'ei Chi, see *TCTC* ch. 186, pp. 5861–62. The emperor's handling of this case has been almost universally condemned; see, for example, the commentary of the compilers of the *Old T'ang History, CTS* 1.17, and of Sun Fu, *T'ang-shih lun-tuan* [Opinions on T'ang History], (preface 1052; *Ts'ung-shu chi-ch'eng* ed., Shanghai, 1939), ch. 1, p. 2.

[25]On this theme, see Ma Ch'i-hua, "Chen-kuan cheng-lun," 255–57.

system of ranks, and sped him on his way. According to Ssu-ma Kuang, the entire period from Wei's arrival in the T'ang capital to his first appointment took barely a month.[26]

The mission to the northeast prompted Wei to write a "five word" poem of unknown date called "Setting Down Innermost Thoughts" (*Shu-huai*), in which he expressed his feelings upon undertaking the journey.[27] Although the poem is a single rhyme in Chinese, for the purpose of discussion I have divided it into five sections of four lines each.[28]

I   Since once again "the deer is pursued on the Central Plain,"[a]
    I fling down my writing brush to serve the chariots of war.
    Hitherto my strategies have not been successful,
    But my determination remains intact.

II With riding crop as a cane I pay a farewell call on the emperor,
    Then urge on my horse through the Pass.[b]
    I have requested reins with which to bind Nan-yüeh;[c]
    Resting on the rail of my chariot, I will subdue the eastern
        domain.

III Apprehensively I scale high peaks;
    Emerging and disappearing,[d] I gaze down upon the plains.

[a]I.e., the empire is in contention.
[b]I.e., the T'ung Pass, which leads from Shensi to Shansi and, beyond it, the northeastern plain.
[c]Although the literary allusion is to Vietnam, the character *yüeh* in Wei Cheng's poem unaccountably refers to the Chinese provinces of Kwangtung and Kwangsi.
[d]I have purposely left the subject of this phrase vague, as in the Chinese.

[26]*TCTC* ch. 186, p. 5823. See also *TFYK* 891.26–27. Oddly, Wei's two biographies note that after arriving in Ch'ang-an he received no recognition "for a long time"; *CTS* 71.1b; *HTS* 97.1b.

[27]The text of the poem is found in *CTShih, han* 1, *ts'e* 8, 6–6b, and *Wei Cheng-kung shih-chi* [Collected Poetry of Duke Wei of Cheng] (*Ts'ung-shu chi-ch'eng* ed., Shanghai, 1937), attached to the *WCKWC*, pp. 45–46.

[28]There is a rather large body of commentary on *Shu-huai*. I have depended heavily for my translation on a recent study by Hoshikawa Kiyotaka, "Gi Chō 'Jukkai' no shi to soji" [Wei Cheng's "Shu-huai" and the Ch'u-tz'u], *Shibun*, 27 (1960), 12–27, and also on Kanno Dōmei, *Tōshisen shōsetsu* [Detailed Commentary on the Anthology of T'ang Poetry], 2 vols. (Tokyo, 1930), 1:4–11. An old and poor translation of *Shu-huai* into French is found in M. J. L. d'Hervey-Saint-Denys, *Poésies de l'époque des Thang* (Paris, 1862), pp. 171–72.

A cold bird cries on an ancient tree;
A night monkey screams on a deserted mountain.

IV   I am pained by eyes that strain to see one thousand *li*,[e]
      And frightened by spirits that seek to return home nine times.[f]
      How can I not shrink from these difficulties?
      [It is because] I enjoy [the emperor's] profound favor as an envoy of
         state.

V   Chi Pu kept his promise;
      Hou Ying made good his vow.
      Living beings are inspired to acts of courage by the favor they
         receive;
      So as for merit and fame, who will again speak of them?

Not surprisingly, many of the literary and historical allusions in
Shu-huai are to the Han, the dynasty with which the T'ang founders so
strongly identified. In the first section of the piece Wei notes his earlier
failure to put his policies into practice under Li Mi; the "strategies"
mentioned are the same Horizontal and Vertical (*tsung-heng*) strategies
he had studied as a youth. The last two lines of the second section
contain allusions to two Han personages. The first, Chung Chün,[29]
upon being sent as an envoy to Nan-yüeh (Vietnam), requested that
his ruler, Han Wu-ti, provide him with long reins so that he might bind
the Vietnamese king and send him back to the Chinese capital. The
second, Li Sheng,[30] persuaded the Prince of Ch'i to declare his land
the "eastern domain" of Liu Pang (Han Kao-tsu) during the wars
attending the establishment of the Han, thereby gaining the land for
the Han founder by "resting on his chariot rail" rather than by
fighting for it—just as Wei hoped to do for T'ang Kao-tsu. In the third
section Wei evokes the rigors of the journey and the starkness of the
landscape. In the fourth the emphasis is on homesickness, a mood
achieved by calling upon lines in earlier Chinese poetry dealing with
the melancholia of traveling far from home. The last section contains
references to two stalwarts who were famous for keeping their word.

[e]I.e., one thousand *li* (roughly 330 miles) homeward.
[f]There is a Chinese belief that when a person is on the road he may dream that his spirit
goes back home nine times in one night.

---

[29]For his biography, see *HS* 64B.4b–8b.
[30]See *SC* 97.3–5.

The loyalty of Chi Pu, a subordinate of Hsiang Yü during the Ch'in-Han transition period, was so highly prized that there was a proverb in his native state of Ch'u that "One hundred catties of gold are not as valuable as a promise from Chi Pu."[31] During the Warring States period, the aged Hou Ying vowed that because he could not accompany his lord on campaign he would take his own life. Then, after waiting precisely the length of time he had calculated it would take his lord to arrive at the appointed battlefield, he committed suicide.[32] In the concluding two lines of his poem, Wei stresses—quite disingenuously—that he is undertaking the mission not in order to seek fame but rather to reciprocate the kindness shown him by Kao-tsu. Yet despite Wei's claim to the contrary, the motive for his mission is clear: the desire to prove his loyalty and utility to the T'ang and to reap the rewards that success would confer on him.

Upon arriving at Hsü's headquarters in Li-yang, Wei sent a message calling on Hsü to capitulate to the T'ang as his superior Li Mi had done earlier.[33] Hsü probably had been waiting for just such an opportunity and accepted the proposal with alacrity, surrendering with ten commanderies. A T'ang army led by Li Shen-t'ung, Kao-tsu's uncle, was soon sent to occupy Li-yang. The emperor then bestowed the imperial surname on Hsü, who now became Li Shih-chi,[34] and made him a commander-in-chief (*tsung-kuan*) of Li prefecture (in which Li-yang was situated).

Not content with just one success, early in 619 Wei persuaded yet another of Li Mi's former subordinates in the Li-yang region to throw his lot in with the T'ang. This time it was Wei's old boss, Yüan Pao-tsang, who had remained in his post as commander-in-chief of Wei prefecture in southern Hopei even after Li Mi's surrender to Kao-tsu. Wei made the short journey from Li-yang to Yüan's camp personally to advise him to go over to the T'ang. Since enemy forces led by the regicide Yü-wen Hua-chi had been besieging the capital of Wei prefecture for forty days, Yüan prudently decided to accept Wei's advice. Shortly thereafter, Li Shen-t'ung attacked Yü-wen Hua-chi, broke the

[31]*HS* 37.3b.

[32]See *SC* 77.2–5.

[33]For the text of this letter, see *WCKWC* ch. 3, pp. 31–32; *CTW* 141.6b–7.

[34]*CTS* 1.9. Hsü Shih-chi is often referred to in the T'ang sources as Li Chi, the character *shih* having become taboo by virtue of its association with Li Shih-min.

siege of Wei prefecture, and forced him to flee northeast to Liao-ch'eng (modern-day western Shantung).[35]

Wei Cheng remained at Li-yang all during the remainder of 619. The reason for this is nowhere revealed in the sources but was probably related to Li Mi's revolt against the T'ang at the beginning of the same year. Li had not found the T'ang court to his liking. Upon his arrival in Ch'ang-an, T'ang officials treated him stingily and withheld rations from his troops; later they slighted him and demanded bribes. Kao-tsu, as was his general policy, had treated Li with deference, presenting him with a patent of nobility and appointing him to office. But Li regarded one of his posts, that of president of the Court of Imperial Banquets (*kuang-lu ch'ing*), one of whose duties was to serve food to the emperor, as an insult.[36] He also resented the fact that those of his former subordinates who had surrendered to the T'ang earlier than he had been rewarded with higher offices.[37]

Growing to detest his situation in the capital, late in 618 Li requested that he be allowed to lead his forces to the northeastern plain to pacify holdouts against the T'ang who had formerly been under his command. Although the emperor was warned by his courtiers that once out of the reach of Ch'ang-an, Li would turn against the throne, he nonetheless granted the request, but with the stipulation that Li leave half of his army in the capital region and take only the remaining half with him. Li then set off on his way. Soon afterward, however, when one of Li's own subordinates reported that Li would definitely revolt, Kao-tsu reversed himself and ordered Li to leave all his troops behind and by himself return immediately to the capital. Li now feared for his life and took flight toward Li-yang, where he hoped to gain the aid of his old confederates in arms. Shortly after passing through Shan prefecture to the west of Loyang, he was attacked by pursuing T'ang troops, captured, and beheaded.[38]

Li Mi's revolt and his attempt to link up with former supporters

[35] *TCTC* ch. 187, pp. 5837–38. According to the biography of Yang Kung-jen, *CTS* 62.9b, at this time Wei Cheng advised Yüan Pao-tsang to seize Yang, who was occupying part of Wei prefecture on behalf of Yü-wen Hua-chi, and to send him to Ch'ang-an, probably as a gesture of goodwill to Kao-tsu. See also *TFYK* 126.11.

[36] *TCTC* ch. 186, pp. 5816, 5824.

[37] See Li Mi's tomb inscription by Wei Cheng, *WCKWC* ch. 3, p. 37.

[38] *TCTC* ch. 186, pp. 5830, 5832.

around Li-yang made it apparent to Kao-tsu that T'ang control in that area was not yet secure. Wei Cheng, who was a northeasterner, who had already proved his loyalty by persuading Li Shih-chi and Yüan Pao-tsang to surrender, and who had previously served as one of Li Mi's officials, was obviously the perfect choice to provide liaison between Ch'ang-an and the Li-yang region. It was probably for this reason that he was ordered to remain at Li-yang during 619. Unexpectedly, Wei's sojourn at that granary town would be far longer than either he or Kao-tsu thought.

ONCE AGAIN AMONG THE REBELS

Late in 619, about a year after Wei received his assignment at Li-yang, the Hopei rebel Tou Chien-te attacked and captured the town so swiftly that Li Shih-chi, Li Shen-t'ung, the T'ung-an Princess (Kao-tsu's sister), Wei Cheng, and other T'ang partisans were all taken captive.[39] Li Shih-chi escaped confinement early in 620 and the T'ung-an Princess was later repatriated, but Wei and the rest of the captives spent almost a year and a half in Tou's camp before being rescued.

At the time of Wei's capture, Tou had already been in revolt against the Sui for eight years. In 611 he had deserted Yang-ti's first expeditionary army against Koguryŏ and had followed his friend, Sun An-tsu, into hiding at Kao-chi-po on the Yung-chi Canal in western Shantung province, where they were soon joined by scores of other desperadoes. When Sun was later killed, Tou became their leader. By late 616 Tou and his followers, said to have numbered more than one hundred thousand, occupied territory from the lower Yellow River valley to northern Hopei. During 617–19 Tou continued to make territorial gains in the Hopei vicinity and before taking Li-yang had distinguished himself by slaying the regicide Yü-wen Hua-chi at Liao-ch'eng.[40]

During his captivity Wei Cheng served Tou as an official charged with recording the actions of the ruler (ch'i-chü she-jen) at Tou's capital in Ming prefecture in southern Hopei.[41] Although Tou set up the trappings of an imperial court in Ming prefecture, he led an austere life: he was a strict vegetarian, dressed his wife in simple style, and kept the

[39] Ibid. ch. 187, p. 5868.
[40] CTS 54.9–14b; HTS 85.8b–12b; also Bingham, The Founding of the T'ang Dynasty, pp. 40–41, 66–67.
[41] CTS 71.2b; HTS 97.1b.

number of his maidservants and harem women to a bare minimum. Tou was also a man of high principle. He treated his literati with deference and employed them judiciously. He freed many Sui officials at their own request and provided them with food and military escorts out of his domains. When Li Shih-chi escaped from his camp, Li's father was left behind; although many of Tou's men clamored for the father's death, Tou refused, observing that the son was guilty of no other crime than loyalty to the T'ang.[42] Thus, it seems possible that working under Tou was not an altogether distasteful experience for Wei. He shared many of Tou's values (especially frugality, judging by the style of life he was later to lead at T'ai-tsung's court) and must have approved of Tou's respectful attitude toward the literati class. None of Wei's own impressions of his sojourn with Tou has survived, however.

Wei finally regained his freedom after Tou went to the aid of another powerful T'ang foe, the former Sui guardian of Loyang, Wang Shih-ch'ung. Although Wang had become the undisputed master of Honan following his defeat of Li Mi late in 618, thereafter increasing pressure from T'ang armies caused him steadily to lose ground. By the middle of 620 he had been pushed back to the region immediately surrounding the former Sui Eastern Capital, and in the seventh month Kao-tsu ordered Li Shih-min to lead T'ang armies to crush him. In repeated skirmishes with Wang's forces, Shih-min's superior skill caused many of the rebel's generals to desert to the T'ang side, and by the eleventh month Wang's situation had become so desperate that he was forced to appeal to Tou Chien-te to help relieve him. Ironically, at the time, relations between the two rebels could hardly have been worse.[43] Nevertheless, the growing pressure exerted by Shih-min on Wang now forced Tou to reconsider matters. He knew that if the T'ang succeeded in destroying Wang's power, his own independence would surely be

[42]*CTS* 54.11b–14; *TCTC* ch. 188, p. 5876.

[43]Prior to his capture of Li-yang, Tou had been on good terms with Wang. But in the fourth month of 619, after Wang deposed the Sui puppet emperor he had previously established in Loyang and proclaimed himself "emperor of Cheng," Tou's attitude toward him cooled perceptibly and he assumed an imperial mantle of his own as "emperor of Hsia." Kao-tsu exacerbated the growing discord between his two enemies by sending an envoy to Tou's camp proposing an alliance between T'ang and Hsia. As a gesture of good faith, Tou allowed the T'ung-an Princess to return to Ch'ang-an. Angered by the détente between Kao-tsu and Tou, Wang invaded Tou's positions at Li-yang; Tou, in turn, countered by attacking Wang's territory to the northeast of Loyang. The two rebels then broke off relations entirely. See *TCTC* ch. 187, p. 5853, ch. 188, pp. 5889, 5896.

threatened. He thus answered Wang's plea for aid by agreeing personally to lead an army to rescue him.

By early 621 Wang had fallen back to a position inside the walls of
Loyang. His forces were greatly weakened and food was growing extremely scarce, but still Tou Chien-te did not appear. At the same
time, after hurling several futile assaults against the city, Shih-min's
men had become tired of fighting and some spoke of returning to
Ch'ang-an, thus giving rise to fears of mutiny in the T'ang camp. At
the end of the third month, however, Tou's land and river forces arrived
at a point near Loyang.

Shih-min's strategy was first to attack Tou, who had come a great
distance and possessed the stronger force, and face Wang only after his
ally had been vanquished. After two successive defeats by the T'ang
army, Tou began thinking of giving up his plans to aid Wang, but
Wang's envoys successfully bribed a group of Tou's generals into
persuading him to continue his efforts on Wang's behalf.[44] It was an
unfortunate choice, for early in the fifth month, in the midst of battle,
Tou was hit by a lance and captured shortly thereafter, along with
fifty thousand of his men. When four days later he was brought beneath
the walls of Loyang, Wang Shih-ch'ung had no other recourse but to
surrender. Contrary to Kao-tsu's general policy of leniency toward
surrendered foes, Wang was killed on his way into exile, and Tou was
sent to Ch'ang-an and beheaded in one of its marketplaces.

As soon as he was released from Tou's camp, Wei hurried back to
the T'ang capital where, probably much to his delight, the crown
prince Li Chien-ch'eng promptly recruited him as one of the two
librarians (hsien-ma) in his household. The new office, ranked fifth
degree, fourth class,[45] was even lower than Wei's post as assistant in
the Department of the Imperial Library, which he continued to hold
concurrently. But it at least meant that he would now serve the heir
apparent and with any luck might gain an important post in the central
government once Chien-ch'eng ascended the throne. Since Kao-tsu
was already in his mid-fifties, that time appeared to be not far off.
On the other hand, as far as Wei was concerned, the post of librarian
on the crown prince's staff, while well suited to his literary talents,
left much to be desired. Once again, just as he had under Li Mi, Wei

44Ibid. ch. 188, pp. 5913.
45TTLT 26.23.

wanted to play a far more influential role than his office nominally conferred on him. Although Wei was soon granted such an opportunity, at the same time he came perilously close to destroying his political career and, even, to forfeiting his life.

THE HSÜAN-WU GATE INCIDENT

The collective shout of joy in Ch'ang-an that had greeted the news of the great T'ang victory over Tou Chien-te and Wang Shih-ch'ung on the northeastern plain was soon stilled by an ominous development. For the fall of Loyang and the accompanying reduction of hostilities over much of North China had merely set the stage for yet another power struggle, this time within the T'ang house itself. Before it was brought to a bloody conclusion in front of the Hsüan-wu Gate in Ch'ang-an, the dynasty almost ended prematurely, the casualty of civil war. The adversaries in this struggle were Crown Prince Li Chien-ch'eng and his younger brother Li Yüan-chi, on the one hand, and on the other, Li Shih-min. Both Chien-ch'eng and Yüan-chi are portrayed in rather unflattering terms in the T'ang Standard Histories. If these accounts are taken at face value, the crown prince was surrounded by gamblers and vagabonds, and drank and hunted to excess. Yüan-chi was unmatched in arrogance and cruelty. He would order his servants and members of his retinue to don armor and attack and stab at one another in mock combat, many dying of wounds so inflicted Addicted to the hunt, during his innumerable hunting expeditions he would trample the fields of the common people and shoot at them, watching with glee as they dodged his arrows. Yet these unsympathetic portraits of Shih-min's brothers may well be the result both of the fact that they and not Shih-min were the victims at the Hsüan-wu Gate and of Shih-min's later emendation of the historical records.[46]

What appears to have caused the initial deterioration in relations between Shih-min and Chien-ch'eng was a sizable gap in their respective military reputations. With the capture of Tou Chien-te and Wang Shih-ch'ung, Shih-min capped a glorious career on the battlefield. The defeat of two of Kao-tsu's strongest rivals tipped the balance of power in North China in the emperor's favor and virtually guaranteed the eventual reunification of the country under T'ang leadership. Shih-

[46]Ssu-ma Kuang, for one, knew that the veritable records he had at his disposal were biased against the crown prince and Yüan-chi; see *TCTC* ch. 190, pp. 5959–60, *k'ao-i* section.

min thus became a T'ang hero. In recognition of his contributions (and perhaps to placate him as well), Kao-tsu established a special title for him, Supreme Commander of Heavenly Strategy (*t'ien-ts'e shang-chiang*), which raised his position above that of all the nobles in the the empire.[47] Shih-min then opened an Office of Heavenly Strategy (*t'ien-ts'e fu*). At the same time, the emperor appointed him to oversee civil and military matters in much of present-day Honan and Hopei provinces as president of the Department of Affairs of State of the Shan-tung Circuit Grand Field Office (*Shan-tung tao ta-hsing-t'ai shang-shu ling*), located at Loyang. The crown prince could only watch these developments in frustration.

Moreover, Shih-min's extended activities in the field following 618 enabled him to recruit from among the many subordinates of his defeated opponents a formidably gifted corps of officials to fill posts in his Prince of Ch'in Office (*Ch'in-wang fu*), Office of Heavenly Strategy, and the Shan-tung Circuit Grand Field Office.[48] The crown prince, stationed most of the time on the northern frontier, had little such opportunity to locate and recruit administrative talent, Wei Cheng having been a notable exception. Therefore, following the fall of Loyang, when Shih-min returned to the T'ang capital leading former subordinates of Tou Chien-te and Wang Shih-ch'ung behind him, Chien-ch'eng began to vie with his brother over the human spoils of war. Naturally, the crown prince represented the most attractive choice to many of those who had surrendered to the T'ang. Chien-ch'eng was in direct line for the throne, and if they served him well they could hope eventually to reach some of the most exalted offices in the land. On the other hand, many able men who would have been happy to serve under the crown prince never made it, but were diverted instead into Shih-min's camp by his sharp-eyed and fast-working recruiters.[49] The size and quality of Shih-min's staff gradually came to pose a challenge to the crown prince's power and prestige at court.

[47]Ibid. ch. 189, p. 5931. Ts'en Chung-mien, *T'ang-shih yü-shen* [Marginalia on T'ang History] (Shanghai, 1960), pp. 2–3, persuasively argues that the title should read *t'ien-ts'e shang-chiang-chün*. This is, in fact, the way the title appears in *HTS* 102.12.

[48]Nunome Chōfū, "Tensaku jōshō," 20–31, shows that despite several civil and military offices Shih-min nominally filled at this time, he controlled real power only in the above three organizations. The biographies of Fang Hsüan-ling (*CTS* 66.1b; *HTS* 96.1b) note his contributions to Shih-min's recruitment campaigns. See also Li Shu-t'ung, *T'ang-shih k'ao-pien*, p. 201.

[49]See, for example, the case of Tu Yen, *HTS* 96.9.

Shih-min also threatened Chien-ch'eng in other ways. For example, shortly after his promotion as Supreme General of Heavenly Strategy late in 621, Shih-min founded a new organization, the College of Literary Studies (*wen-hsüeh kuan*). The college was composed of eighteen scholars, who for the most part served concurrently in the other organizations under Shih-min's control. They were divided into three shifts of six men each who took meals together and who were at the beck and call of Shih-min at any time of the day or night, acting as his brain-trust and advising him on important matters of state.[50] The establishment of such a body may well have suggested to Chien-ch'eng that his brother had powerful aspirations to succeed to the throne.

It was not long before Chien-ch'eng began to counterattack. Joined by his younger brother Yüan-chi, he made efforts to reduce Shih-min's prestige at court, tarnish his image in Kao-tsu's eyes, and undermine the effectiveness of the powerful civil and military organizations under his control. Wei Cheng naturally had everything to gain from Chien-ch'eng's accession and had probably based all of his hopes for the future on it. He therefore worked assiduously to maintain the crown prince's preeminent position, and along with Wang Kuei—a former Sui official who had joined Chien-ch'eng's staff late in 617—became the crown prince's chief adviser in planning strategy against Shih-min. The two soon decided that the crown prince should try to achieve some incisive military victories of his own to offset the successes of his brother. They advised him to enter the battlefield against one of Tou Chien-te's former commanders, Liu Hei-t'a, who had risen against the T'ang in the seventh month of 621, after Tou's execution had created great consternation among his supporters. By the end of the year Liu and his men had defeated successive T'ang armies sent against them and had regained much of Tou's old territory in Hopei. Early in 622 Shih-min had administered a blow to Liu's cavalry and infantry and wiped out much of his military strength, but Liu and a small group of followers had been able to make their way northward to safety among the Eastern Turks.

By the end of 622 Liu had reoccupied much of southern Hopei, and

---

[50]*CTS* 72.19b. For a discussion of the Wen-hsüeh kuan and an examination of the backgrounds of the twenty men who eventually served on its staff, see Fukusawa Sōkichi, "Bungakukan gakushi ni tsuite" [The Scholars of the Wen-hsüeh kuan], *Kumamoto Daigaku kyōikugakubu kiyō* [Bulletin of the Faculty of Education, Kumamoto University], 1 (1953), 35–41.

it became apparent to all at court that Shih-min's failure to capture the rebel had been a costly blunder. It was at this point that Wang and Wei came forward, chiding Chien-ch'eng for his lack of military prestige and proposing that he succeed where Shih-min had failed and destroy Liu's power conclusively. The crown prince willingly accepted their counsel and, accompanied by both advisers, led his army out of Ch'ang-an, arriving in the middle of the last month of 622 at the capital of Wei prefecture, then under attack by Liu's forces. Before Chien-ch'eng entered into battle, Wei Cheng devised a plan of action which, characteristically, emphasized the utility of psychological persuasion in place of crude military force. Liu's army had previously lost its best fighting men and was now very weak, yet those remaining with Liu who wanted to desert him were prevented from doing so because the T'ang had sentenced all of them to death in absentia and held members of their families as hostages. Now, Wei promised, if Chien-ch'eng were publicly to declare an amnesty, free all the hostages, and send them back to their homes, Liu's following would speedily disintegrate and the revolt would be quelled. Accordingly, the crown prince released the prisoners and had them plead with their husbands and comrades to lay down their weapons and return to their villages. As Wei correctly predicted, most of Liu's men thereupon deserted; many even bound their superior officers and delivered them to the T'ang. Early in 623 one of Liu's officials seized him and turned him over to a subordinate of Chien-ch'eng. The crown prince then beheaded Liu and returned to Ch'ang-an in triumph.[51]

It appears that Chien-ch'eng and his supporter Yüan-chi moved on other fronts as well to deflate Shih-min. With bribes and favors they first won the support of Kao-tsu's concubines, who were naturally interested in consolidating the positions of their families with the next emperor. The concubines, it is said, then began maligning Shih-min in front of Kao-tsu and intriguing on behalf of Chien-ch'eng and Yüan-chi.[52] The brothers also attempted to reduce Shih-min's power in Ch'ang-an by having several of his staff there transferred to posts in the provinces.[53] By 624 matters had grown so alarming that one of Shih-min's subordinates who had recently been transferred out of his

[51]HTS 79.2–2b; TCTC ch. 190, pp. 5962–63.
[52]HTS 79.2b–3b; TCTC ch. 190, pp. 5958–59, ch. 191, pp. 5989–90.
[53]See HTS 90.8b, 96.6b; TCTC ch. 189, p. 5932.

service warned him that his "hands and arms were all being amputated" and that the rest of his body would not long go untouched either.[54] In the middle of the same year, Chien-ch'eng took steps to further enhance his power in Ch'ang-an by recruiting more than two thousand bravos into a private army and garrisoning them in the vicinity of the Ch'ang-lin Gate, which was located in his compound, the Eastern Palace; these soon became known as the Ch'ang-lin Troops (*Ch'ang-lin ping*).[55] In order to counter the advantages his brothers enjoyed in the capital, Shih-min was compelled to build a base of support for himself among the civil and military elite of the Loyang region.[56]

If we are to believe the accounts of the Standard Histories, Chien-ch'eng and Yüan-chi even went so far as to make attempts on Shih-min's life. They record that in the sixth month of 624 Yüan-chi advised the crown prince to get rid of Shih-min and that when Shih-min accompanied Kao-tsu to Yüan-chi's residence shortly afterwards, the latter placed one of his guards in a bedchamber and planned to have him stab Shih-min. Chien-ch'eng, however, intervened and stopped the planned attack. Soon afterwards the crown prince himself planned to use Turkish troops to attack the Western Palace, Shih-min's residence, until someone informed Kao-tsu. Two years later Chien-ch'eng invited Shih-min to his quarters late at night and poisoned his wine, causing Shih-min to become violently ill.[57] Whether all these events actually occurred or were partly or wholly the fabrications of the historians who were later charged by T'ai-tsung with emending the records surrounding the Hsüan-wu Gate incident, is difficult to determine.[58]

---

[54]*CTS* 68.10.

[55]*HTS* 79.3b–4; *TCTC* ch. 191, p. 5985.

[56]See Ch'en Yin-k'o, "Shan-tung hao-chieh," 6; Li Shu-t'ung, *T'ang-shih k'ao-pien*, pp. 134–35; Lo Hsiang-lin, *T'ang-tai wen-hua shih*, p. 7; Chang Ch'ün, *T'ang-shih* [History of the T'ang Dynasty], 2 vols. (Taipei, 1958, 1965), 1:11.

[57]See *HTS* 79.5; 79.8–8b; *TCTC* ch. 191, p. 5985.

[58]As Fu Lo-ch'eng has pointed out, it is unlikely at this time, considering the deterioration of relations between Chien-ch'eng and Shih-min, that Shih-min would have visited his brother's palace in the middle of the night or have been duped into drinking wine with him; "Hsüan-wu-men shih-pien chih yün-niang" [Incidents that Led to the Hsüan-wu Gate Coup d'Etat], *Wen-shih-che hsüeh-pao* [Bulletin of the College of Arts, National Taiwan University], 8 (1958), 179–80. See also the remarks of Nunome Chōfū, "Genmumon no hen" [The Hsüan-wu Gate Incident], *Ōsaka Daigaku kyōyōbu kenkyū shūroku* [Researches of the Department of Education, Osaka University], 16 (1968), 33–34. I find it difficult to agree with Li Shu-t'ung, *T'ang-shih k'ao-pien*, passim, that the crown prince never actually desired to harm Shih-min physically.

We can only speculate as well about the extent of Wei Cheng's participation in the attempts of Chien-ch'eng on Shih-min's life, granted they took place. Wei's biographies in the Standard Histories naturally offer no details concerning the matter, a not surprising fact given Wei's later role as model minister under T'ai-tsung and the general disposition of biographers to treat worthy subjects in the best possible light. Instead, they resort to euphemism and merely note that Wei "saw that the merit of the Prince of Ch'in was great and secretly advised the crown prince to make plans at an early time."[59]

Its appears that even Kao-tsu did not know for certain how closely Wei was connected with Chien-ch'eng's strategy against Shih-min. In the sixth month of 624 the emperor left the capital in charge of the crown prince and journeyed to his summer palace, about ninety miles north of Ch'ang-an, in the company of Shih-min and Yüan-chi. Soon afterward he was informed that Chien-ch'eng's subordinate, Yang Wen-kan, was raising troops on the crown prince's behalf to send to Ch'ang-an, presumably for use against Shin-min. When Kao-tsu summoned Yang, the latter was frightened into revolting and was beheaded by his own troops the following month.[60] Instead of punishing the crown prince, Kao-tsu took out his wrath on Chien-ch'eng's advisers, ordering that they, including Wei Cheng and Wang Kuei, be seized and put to death. But his anger soon cooled, and Wang Kuei and another of Chien-ch'eng's advisers, Wei T'ing, were instead exiled to a pestilential region in southwestern China (modern Hsikang province). Oddly enough, Wei Cheng escaped with only the loss of his office; the evidence linking him with the plot against Shih-min was apparently insufficient. It is said that when Wei, incredulous about his good fortune, inquired of fellow officials why he alone had been spared banishment, they were as bewildered as he and merely attributed it to the will of Heaven.[61]

Scholars have long debated over which of the two brothers, Chien-ch'eng or Shih-min, Kao-tsu really favored. Those who claim that the emperor wanted Shih-min to succeed him point to traditional accounts

[59]*HTS* 97.1b.

[60]Ibid. 79.4; *TCTC* ch. 191, pp. 5986–87. See Li Shu-t'ung, *T'ang-shih k'ao-pien,* pp. 99–117, 143–48, for his view that the crown prince was not involved in Yang's revolt and that he was falsely implicated by Tu Yen, a subordinate of Shih-min; cf. the rebuttal to this argument by Nunome, "Genmumon," 29–32.

[61]Liu Su, *Ta-T'ang hsin-yü,* 6.6–6b.

that state that as early as the Taiyuan uprising Kao-tsu offered the throne to Shih-min, who declined,[62] and that later, at the time of Yang Wen-kan's revolt, the emperor once again promised the throne to Shih-min, only to go back on his word a short time later.[63] Still other scholars claim that Kao-tsu consistently supported Chien-ch'eng against Shih-min,[64] and that the Standard History accounts of Kao-tsu's desire to change the succession in favor of Shih-min are mere fabrications, the result of T'ai-tsung's emendation of the historical records.[65]

On balance, the evidence points to the conclusion that after a prolonged period of vacillation, Kao-tsu was eventually won over to the side of his eldest son—primarily by the machinations of members of his own harem and a few high placed officials, notably Feng Te-i—and remained there till the Hsüan-wu Gate incident. Significantly, the emperor did not punish Chien-ch'eng for his implication in the Yang Wen-kan affair, but simply punished his advisers. Later, Kao-tsu, told that Shih-min was talking as if he would soon become emperor, swiftly summoned him to the palace and there angrily reprimanded him, saying, "Any emperor naturally has the Mandate of Heaven. It cannot be sought by cleverness or strength. How urgently you are seeking it!"[66] Moreover, Kao-tsu made no effort to counter the moves being made by Chien-ch'eng and Yüan-chi to reduce the size of, and thereby substantially weaken, Shih-min's staff, while at the same time increasing their own military power in the capital by such means as the Ch'ang-lin Troops. The two brothers arranged, with Kao-tsu's assent, to have Fang Hsüan-ling and Tu Ju-hui, two of Shih-min's key advisers, dismissed from his service.[67] They hired assassins to execute Shih-min's general Yü-ch'ih Ching-te and, having failed in this effort, subsequently slandered him in front of the emperor. The general was saved from execution only through Shih-min's last-minute intervention.[68] When the Eastern Turks invaded the border in 626, Kao-tsu, at the suggestion of Chien-ch'eng, assigned Yüan-chi to oppose them. Yüan-chi then

---

[62]See, for example, *TCTC* ch. 190, p. 5957, ch. 191, p. 6004.
[63]*HTS* 79.4b; *TCTC* ch. 191, p. 5987.
[64]Wan Chün, *T'ang T'ai-tsung* (Shanghai, 1955), p. 20.
[65]Li Shu-t'ung, *T'ang-shih k'ao-pien,* passim.
[66]*TCTC* ch. 191, p. 5990.
[67]*CTS* 66.2b; *HTS* 96.2.
[68]*CTS* 68.3b.

conscripted some of Shih-min's best commanders and troops for his campaign.[69] The crown prince and Yüan-chi also offered lavish bribes to Shih-min's officers in the hope of turning them against him.[70] None of these strategems was opposed by the emperor.

Although Fang Hsüan-ling and Tu Ju-hui had long urged Shih-min to strike a blow against his brothers before it was too late, he had been slow to formulate an offensive strategy. But all this changed at the beginning of the sixth month of 626 when, it is said, Shih-min discovered that his brothers were planning to murder him when (as was the custom) he went to see off Yüan-chi on his campaign against the Eastern Turks. Resolving to kill them first, Shih-min quickly summoned Fang and Tu, disguised as Taoist priests, to his camp in the capital to aid him in making plans. He also bribed Ch'ang Ho, the officer in charge of the central gate in the northern wall of Ch'ang-an, called the Hsüan-wu Gate, into following his orders.[71]

By the fourth day of the sixth month, the plans which had been painstakingly worked out by Fang, Tu, Chang-sun Wu-chi, Yü-ch'ih Ching-te, and Hou Chün-chi were complete. Before dawn on this day Shih-min led several of his most trusted followers to the Hsüan-wu Gate, which was now under his control.[72] At the same time, he sent another group of men, including criminals who had been released from the jails for just this purpose, to garrison the Fang-lin Gate, also located in the north wall of Ch'ang-an, just west of the palace city.[73] It was in the immediate vicinity of the Hsüan-wu Gate that Shih-min and his men ambushed and killed both Chien-ch'eng and Yüan-chi while the latter were on their way to an audience with Kao-tsu. As was expected, the armies of the two brothers soon mounted an offensive on the gate, but when the severed heads of their masters were exhibited to them, their effort abruptly collapsed. Shih-min was now in control of the capital.

[69] *TCTC* ch. 191, p. 6007.

[70] See, for example, *CTS* 68.3–3b and 68.11b.

[71] Ch'en Yin-k'o, *T'ang-tai cheng-chih shih shu-lun kao* [Draft Narrative of the Political History of the T'ang Dynasty] (Chungking, 1944), pp. 39–41; Woodbridge Bingham, "Li Shih-min's Coup in A.D. 626," *Journal of the American Oriental Society*, 70 (1950), 93. Ch'ang Ho was later rewarded for his efforts; see *TCTC* ch. 193, pp. 6064–65.

[72] The precise number of men in Shih-min's party at this time is unclear. The longest list of followers, *CTS* 2.10–10b, contains the names of twelve men. See the discussions of Lü Ssu-mien, *Sui-T'ang-Wu-tai shih*, 1:78, and Nunome, "Genmumon," 39.

[73] *HTS* 95.1b. What role this gate played in the Hsüan-wu Gate incident remains unclear. Woodbridge Bingham, in his article "Li Shih-min's Coup," makes no mention of it.

Shortly following the deaths of the two princes, Wei Cheng, who since the banishment of Wang Kuei and Wei T'ing was the only one of Chien-ch'eng's advisers remaining in the capital, was summoned into Shih-min's presence. "Why did you set my brother and me quarrelling?" Shih-min demanded of him. Wei calmly replied, "If the crown prince had earlier followed Cheng's advice, then he would not have perished in today's calamity."[74] This has suggested to most Chinese commentators that Wei had advised Chien-ch'eng not to provoke Shih-min to violence but that the crown prince had overruled him.[75] Yet considering Wei's great ambition and the future he had planned for himself upon Chien-ch'eng's accession, such an interpretation might well be mistaken. Wei's reply to Shih-min was, after all, rather ambiguous. It could just as easily have signified that his advice on how to deal more effectively with Shih-min had not been accepted by the crown prince, thereby leading to his death. What is important here, at any rate, is that for the first time Wei was striking the bold and independent stance he would take time and time again before Shih-min after the latter became emperor. What Shih-min really thought of Wei's reply is not known. Wei's *New T'ang History* biography notes simply that Shih-min "appreciated his frankness and bore him no malice."[76]

AFTERMATH OF THE INCIDENT

Three days after the events at the Hsüan-wu Gate, Shih-min was proclaimed crown prince and took over effective control of the government from his father. His chief supporters, men like Chang-sun Wu-chi, Fang Hsüan-ling, Tu Ju-hui, and Yü-ch'ih Ching-te, all moved into key posts in his new household at the Eastern Palace.

Since it was now obviously just a short time before he would replace Kao-tsu as emperor, Shih-min needed all the men of high caliber he could recruit to aid him in governing the empire. He also wanted to rally behind him the support of all officials, regardless of the candidates they had supported for the throne, and so put an end to prolonged political strife at court. Thus, much to the astonishment of practically

---

[74]*CTS* 71.2b; *HTS* 97.1b; also *TCTC* ch. 191, pp. 6013–14.

[75]See, for example, Wang Fu-chih (1619–92), *Tu T'ung-chien lun* [Essays on Reading the *Comprehensive Mirror*] (reproduction of the *Ch'uan-shan i-shu* ed., Taipei, 1965), 20.11b, and Li Shu-t'ung, *T'ang-shih k'ao-pien*, p. 141.

[76]*HTS* 97.1b–2.

everyone, Shih-min appointed Wei Cheng to the post of superintendent of accounts (*chan-shih chu-pu*) in his household, changing this shortly afterwards to remonstrating counselor (*chien-i ta-fu*).[77] In another conciliatory move, Wang Kuei and Wei T'ing were summoned back from exile and also made remonstrating counselors.[78]

On the day following the slaying of Chien-ch'eng and Yüan-chi, and even several times afterwards, Kao-tsu, at Shih-min's behest, announced amnesties for all the followers of the two brothers. Nevertheless, fearing for their lives, former supporters of the slain princes fled in great numbers from the capital to their homes on the northeastern plain, where, seething with anger and worried about their fate, they presented a serious potential danger to Shih-min and T'ang unity. Just a month after appointing Wei Cheng to office, then, Shih-min appointed him as an emissary to the northeast to reassure his brothers' former comrades that their lives were not in danger. Wei undoubtedly welcomed this assignment as a means of proving his loyalty to his new master. He was, furthermore, particularly well suited for the mission: he was himself a northeasterner, he had previously served the crown prince and was therefore presumably acquainted with many of the dissidents, and, finally, he was living proof of Shih-min's even-handed policy toward his former enemies.

The journey, which was of a few months' duration, took Wei at least as far as Tz'u prefecture in southern Hopei, some 350 miles east-northeast of Ch'ang-an. There he interceded on behalf of two former supporters of Chien-ch'eng and Yüan-chi who, despite the amnesties, were being sent in custody to the capital by an overzealous functionary.[79] We know little else about the mission, but the absence of further

---

[77]There are discrepancies in the sources concerning both the title of Wei Cheng's first office under Shih-min and the date on which he received the appointment. *TCTC* ch. 191, p. 6014, records that he was made a superintendent of accounts in the sixth month of 626, that is, shortly after the Hsüan-wu Gate incident. But *TCTC* ch. 191, p. 6017, lists Wei as a remonstrating counselor scarcely one month later. *CTS* 71.2b records that Wei was given the post of superintendent following the Hsüan-wu Gate incident and the post of remonstrating counselor when Shih-min ascended the throne in the eighth month. *HTS* 97.2 merely notes his appointment as remonstrating counselor when Shih-min became emperor. Wang Hsien-ch'ien, *WCLC* 6b, believes that Wei was made remonstrating counselor in the sixth month. I have here taken the position that Wei was appointed to both offices in rapid succession before Shih-min ascended the throne.

[78]*HTS* 98.1b, 15b.

[79]*CTS* 71.2b; *HTS* 97.2; *TFYK* 662.7b; *TCTC* ch. 191, p. 6017.

mention in the sources about discontent in the area suggests that Wei had achieved his goal.

By the time Wei returned to Ch'ang-an in the autumn of 626, Kao-tsu had already abdicated and assumed the title "retired emperor," and T'ai-tsung, Shih-min's temple name and the name by which we will hereafter refer to him, had succeeded to the throne. Although the sources indicate that the transfer of power was entirely voluntary on Kao-tsu's part and followed ancient ritual procedure, given the relationship between father and son prior to the Hsüan-wu Gate incident, it is more likely that T'ai-tsung compelled Kao-tsu to surrender the reins of power.

There was welcome news for Wei upon reaching the capital. T'ai-tsung had ennobled him as *hsien-nan* of Chü-lu. *Hsien-nan*, or "baron of a county," was the lowest title in the T'ang nobility, carrying with it the rank of fifth degree, third class, and income from the taxes of 300 families.[80] It was the first fruit of Wei's employment under his new master and a sign that his position, for the moment at least, was secure.

However, Wei still owed one last obiligation to the past. In the tenth month of 626 T'ai-tsung ordered the rehabilitation of the two brothers slain at the Hsüan-wu Gate; although they had previously been stripped of all honors and rank, they were now to be reburied with posthumous titles of nobility. Wei and his former colleague on the crown prince's staff, Wang Kuei, thought it incumbent upon them to petition the throne to allow them to accompany Chien-ch'eng's funeral cortege to the burial site. The emperor granted the request, at the same time ordering all those who had formerly served the two princes to do likewise.[81] Once this painful duty was out of the way, Wei was able to turn all of his attention to the future and to what would be the final chapter of his political career.

Soon Wei would emerge as one of the most prominent and respected statesmen in all the empire. Nevertheless, the political road he had travelled had been a difficult one and was already littered with debris from his two wrecked careers under Li Mi and Li Chien-ch'eng. He had served both men to the best of his abilities in the mistaken hope that each would one day become a Son of Heaven, but they had been defeated in turn, and his own burning ambitions had almost brought

[80]Robert des Rotours, *Traité des fonctionnaires*, 1: 44.
[81]*TCTC* ch. 192, p. 6024. The text of the petition is found in *WCKWC* ch. 2, p. 23.

him to ruin. It is testimony to Wei's considerable talents that he was able to survive all these setbacks virtually unscathed. As one of his eulogists, Lü Wen (772–811), once observed, Wei had the rare ability to "bob upon the waters and freely adapt to circumstances" (*shen-fou pien-t'ung*),[82] that is, to accommodate himself easily to the ups and downs of fortune. Lü might also have added that Wei had the good luck each time to emerge from adversity in an even stronger position than before.

[82]Yao Hsüan (968–1020), comp., *T'ang wen-ts'ui* (*SPTK* ed., Shanghai, 1929), 23.3b.

CHAPTER 4

T'ai-tsung and the Chen-kuan Bureaucracy and Government

During the thirteen hundred years that have elapsed since the end of Chen-kuan, Chinese commentators have been tireless in extolling the virtues of a period that, much to their sorrow, has had few equals in the long march of Chinese history. Although they have occasionally differed in their analyses, most of them, I suspect, would agree that T'ai-tsung's reign distinguished itself from a majority of the reigns of his predecessors and his successors in three important respects. First, China was ruled by a wise and responsible monarch who, during his first years on the throne in any case, embodied a number of cherished Confucian virtues, especially those of humility, frugality, and a willingness to be guided by the counsel of his ministers on important matters of state. Second, serving this monarch was a superb group of administratively gifted and public-spirited bureaucrats who worked together in great harmony and fully shared with the emperor—for at least a time—the burden of making policy. Third, under this enlightened leadership China was guided to unparalleled triumphs both at home and abroad. This chapter briefly examines in turn the key factors contributing to the greatness of the Chen-kuan period: the emperor, his bureaucracy (its composition and operation), and the programs and policies they devised and implemented.

EMPEROR T'AI-TSUNG

Even had he not benefited from the added lustre associated with his status as a founding ruler, T'ai-tsung possessed ample personal qualities and talents that by themselves would have assured him a place among the epic rulers of China. A youthful twenty-six when he came to power, he displayed a sharply inquisitive mind and vast quantities of energy:

he is said to have ordered officials of the fifth rank and above to sleep in shifts at their offices in the Departments of the Imperial Secretariat and Chancellery so that he could question them at any time on matters of state or administrative problems, and to have pasted memorials from his officials on the walls of his chambers so that he could read and ponder them during his comings and goings or well into the night.[1]

We know little of the emperor's upbringing and education. His mother, née Tou, younger sister of Sui Yang-ti's consort, died sometime before the Taiyuan uprising. The Li-T'ang house, like those of most of the racially mixed northern elite, was inclined toward Buddhism, especially on the maternal side. Some of T'ai-tsung's brothers bore Buddhist childhood names and one had even served for a time before his death as a Buddhist monk.[2] As a scion of a house with a strong military tradition, T'ai-tsung had from childhood been schooled in the art of war. When still in his teens he accompanied his father on his military assignments in Shansi, learned the ways of the nomadic peoples beyond the frontier, and became inured to the hardships of the campaign. He developed into a powerful archer and swordsman and a superb horseman—a match for any adversary. Although probably not the recipient of a strong literary education, once on the throne T'ai-tsung nevertheless engaged in those civil pursuits thought to befit a Chinese monarch: he wrote poetry and gained a substantial reputation as a calligrapher.[3] All this, though, did little to soften an imperial bearing born of long and arduous military training. He was easily provoked, at which times his face would turn purple with rage, inspiring fear and trepidation in all who were by his side.

Having been a military man for so much of his life, the emperor prized most in men the quality of unswerving loyalty. Following the Hsüan-wu Gate incident, T'ai-tsung pardoned those commanders in the retinues of the crown prince and Li Yüan-chi who led troops to attack his own forces on the grounds that they had faithfully served their superiors.[4] He decreed early in his reign that servants who informed on

[1] *THY* ch. 26, p. 507; *TCTC* ch. 192, p. 6026.

[2] See Arthur F. Wright, "T'ang T'ai-tsung and Buddhism," p. 241.

[3] His verses are collected in *CTShih, han* 1, *ts'e* 2. Samples of his calligraphy are believed to be extant; see Chen Tsu-lung, "On the 'Hot-Spring Inscription' Preserved by a Rubbing in the Bibliothèque Nationale at Paris," *T'oung Pao*, 46 (1958), 378–81.

[4] See *CTS* 69.9b for one example.

their masters would be executed.[5] He developed a morbid preoccupation with the assassination of Sui Yang-ti and on numerous occasions attacked those responsible for his death, charging them with the crime of disloyalty; in the end he had many of them exiled.[6] On the other hand, as we have already seen, he was more than willing to employ those who had served their masters faithfully, even when these masters had previously been his own sworn enemies.

For his time, T'ai-tsung appears to have been remarkably free of superstition. Shortly after taking the throne, when officials from various parts of the empire began reporting lucky and unlucky omens to him, he retorted that whether the dynasty prospered or declined depended on the quality of government and on the actions of men, not on mere portents.[7] Later, he ordered the elaborate capping ceremonies for his son, the crown prince Ch'eng-ch'ien, to be held at a time when it would not interfere with agricultural labor, although this date, he was advised, was inauspicious.[8] He even ridiculed previous sovereigns for believing sorcerers who had promised to prolong their lives with magic potions.[9] But even this enlightened attitude was only relative. On the eve of the Hsüan-wu Gate incident, for example, T'ai-tsung summoned a diviner to practice scapulimancy in order to predict the success or failure of his scheme against his brothers,[10] and late in his life, after suffering a prolonged illness, it is said that he began taking longevity potions made by an Indian magician that may actually have hastened his death.[11]

Perhaps one of the most salient aspects of the emperor's personality was his concern with the historical image he would bequeath to posterity. Chapter 1 treats T'ai-tsung's efforts to alter the historical narratives concerning the founding of the dynasty and the Hsüan-wu Gate incident to wipe away the odium of fratricide and imperial usurpation. Few Chinese monarchs have been oblivious of the court scribes at their side who recorded their every word and deed for the perusal of

[5] *TCTC* ch. 193, p. 6061.

[6] *CTS* 2.15–15b, 3.3b–4; *HTS* 2.6b; *TCTC* ch. 192, pp. 6054–55.

[7] *THY* ch. 28, p. 531; *TCTC* ch. 193, pp. 6056–57. See also *CKCY* 10.6b–7 for a related example.

[8] *CKCY* 8.2–2b.

[9] *CTS* 2.14.

[10] Ibid. 68.12b.

[11] Ibid. 3.19; *THY* ch. 82, p. 1522; *TCTC* ch. 200, p. 6303. Cf. the view of Chen Tsu-lung, "On the 'Hot-Spring Inscription,'" 386–87, that these accounts are false.

future generations, but T'ai-tsung seems to have been more conscious than most that he was an actor on a stage, that his speeches and gestures were being written down for all time, and that his total performance would be rated by the Confucian critic-historians of a succeeding dynasty who would compile the official history of his house. He thus developed into a shrewd and artful manipulator of his public image. It is for this reason that we occasionally receive the impression that the emperor's behavior and speeches were conditioned less by his own personal convictions than by his "feel" for his audience of officials and scribes and by his goal of enhancing his place in history.

How else are we to explain, to take one particularly vivid example, the histrionics T'ai-tsung exhibited in the year 628 upon the arrival of large swarms of locusts in the capital district? The emperor passed through the Hsüan-wu Gate and traversed the Forbidden Park (chin-yüan) to inspect personally the damage they had caused. Picking up a handful of the insects, he loudly cursed them, crying: "The people regard grain the same as life itself, yet you devour it. Better that you devour my own lungs and bowels!" He then raised his hand and was about to eat them but was restrained by his attendants, who warned that he might become ill. "Since We will suffer this calamity for the sake of the people," he majestically replied, "how can We avoid illness!" So saying, he calmly swallowed them.[12]

T'ai-tsung's concern for his image may also have contributed to the adoption, early in his reign, of a humble mien before his subordinates. Years of military training as a youth, he frequently explained, had ill-prepared him for the arduous tasks he now faced as ruler, and he had much to learn. He once remarked:

When We were young and fond of archery, We obtained ten excellent bows and thought none could be better. Recently, We showed them to a bowmaker, who said: "All are of poor quality." When We asked the reason, he replied: "The hearts of the wood are not straight, so their arteries and veins are all bad. Although the bows are strong, when you shoot the arrows they will not fly true." We began to realize that We were not yet clever at discriminating. We pacified the empire with bows and arrows but Our understanding even of these was still insufficient. How much the less can We know everything concerning the affairs of the empire![13]

[12] TCTC ch. 192, pp. 6053–54; CKCY 8.1b–2.
[13] TCTC ch. 192, p. 6034; also THY ch. 26, pp. 506–07.

The emperor thus often posed as a student before his own officials, earnestly seeking their criticism and counsel.

Such humility naturally delighted the Confucians of the court, as did the emperor's frequent declarations, particularly during his first years on the throne, that he would curtail large public works projects and other expenditures in order to reduce the corvée and tax burdens of his people. A few months after assuming power T'ai-tsung must have warmed the cockles of even the most critical of Confucian hearts with the following speech:

The ruler depends on the state and the state depends on the people. Oppressing the people to make them serve the ruler is like cutting one's flesh to fill one's stomach. The stomach is filled but the body is injured; the ruler is made wealthy but the state is destroyed. Therefore, when calamity strikes the ruler it comes not from outside but always from within himself. If he desires grandeur, then expenditures must be increased; if expenditures are increased, then taxes must be made heavier; if taxes are made heavier, then the people become resentful; if the people become resentful, then the state is in danger; if the state is in danger, then the ruler is lost. I often think of this and thus do not dare indulge my desires.[14]

As the following chapters will reveal, however, once state power had been consolidated and the boundaries of China broadly extended, T'ai-tsung, too, fell victim to the seductions of grand imperium: his earlier modesty gradually gave way to a swaggering arrogance and he became far less disposed to seek the frank counsel of his subordinates; at the same time, his initial policy of frugality and restrictions on corvée was replaced by a more expansive program of palace construction and renovation. Such a turn of events greatly dismayed the Confucians of his court, not the least among them Wei Cheng.

THE COMPOSITION OF T'AI-TSUNG'S BUREAUCRACY

One of the great sources of T'ai-tsung's strength during his reign was the superior quality of the bureaucracy gathered under his leadership. Gradually, he dismissed most of those men who had served his father and replaced them with men of his own choosing. Age may partly have been a consideration here,[15] for Kao-tsu's key officials were of his own generation and probably seemed too overbearing and stuffy for

14 *TCTC* ch. 192, p. 6026.
15 Nunome Chōfū, "Tōchō sōgyōki," 14–15.

the new emperor. Unlike his father, who had emphasized family relationships and prior records of loyal service as criteria for appointment to high-level posts in his administration, T'ai-tsung generally searched for the best men for each office regardless of background. He once wrote:

The enlightened ruler employs men in the manner of a skilled carpenter. If the wood is straight he uses it as a shaft for a cart; if it is crooked he uses it as a wheel. If it is long he uses it as a roof-beam; if it is short he uses it as a rafter. No matter whether crooked or straight, long or short, each has something that can be utilized. The enlightened ruler's employment of men is also like this. From the wise man he takes his plans; from the stupid man he takes his strength; from the brave man he takes his courage; from the coward he takes his caution. No matter whether wise, stupid, brave, or cowardly, each can be employed [according to his abilities]. Therefore, the skilled carpenter has no rejected materials and the enlightened ruler has no rejected officials.[16]

The emperor's selection of Wei Cheng, Wang Kuei, and Wei T'ing, all former advisers to Crown Prince Chien-ch'eng, certainly seems to have exemplified these principles. Indeed, veterans of the Prince of Ch'in Office were soon complaining that former members of the staffs of Chien-ch'eng and Yüan-chi had often received appointments prior to themselves in the new administration.[17] Nevertheless, those who had served T'ai-tsung in the various organs he controlled during Wu-te went on to constitute a majority of his high-level officials during Chen-kuan.

There were a number of other ways in which T'ai-tsung's bureaucracy differed from his father's. First, as a result of his more liberal recruitment policies he reduced the number of relatives of the imperial family at the top level of government. Second, likely as a direct result of these same recruitment policies, during Chen-kuan merit rather than pedigree became an increasingly important requirement for entrance into the bureaucratic ranks. During the Sui dynasty all of the eighteen officials occupying the posts of heads of the Three Departments had been the sons or grandsons of officials. But although this figure remained stable during Wu-te, by Chen-kuan times it had declined to eighty-eight percent. Similarly, during the Sui, eighty-nine percent of

[16]T'ang T'ai-tsung, Ti-fan [Plan for an Emperor] (648; Ts'ung-shu chi-ch'eng ed., Shanghai, 1937), ch. 2, pp. 15–16.
[17]CKCY 5.13b–14; TCTC ch. 192, pp. 6022–23.

the presidents (*shang-shu*) of the Six Boards had fathers and/or grand-fathers in officialdom. This figure decreased to around eighty-two percent during Wu-te and even more sharply to about seventy-three percent during Chen-kuan. In a much larger sampling of one hundred and five early T'ang officials filling the posts of left and right vice-presidents and assistants to the left and right vice-presidents (*shang-shu tso-* and *yu-ch'eng*) of the Department of Affairs of State, as well as those of the two presidents of the Departments of the Imperial Sec-retariat and Chancellery, and those of the presidents and vice-presidents (*shih-lang*) of the Six Boards—the most important executive and admin-istrative posts in the bureaucracy[18]—we find that during Wu-te almost ninety-two percent of this group had direct ancestors in official-dom, but that this figure dropped to only slightly more than seventy-two percent during Chen-kuan. (See Appendix I, Tables A, B, and C.) Since a large majority of Chen-kuan bureaucrats were still descendants of officials, T'ai-tsung's accession by no means propelled a new ruling class into power. But it is apparent that long before the so-called triumph of the examination system during the reign of Empress Wu (684–705), an increasing number of officials without strong official family backgrounds were moving into positions of importance in the T'ang bureaucracy.

In one respect, at least, T'ai-tsung's recruitment policies served to continue a trend begun by his father. During the Western Wei (535–51), Northern Chou (557–81), and Sui dynasties (589–618), political power in China had been concentrated in the hands of officials whose native places (*pen-kuan*) were located in what was then northwestern China, modern Shensi and Kansu provinces. During the Sui dynasty, for example, slightly more than seventy-two percent of the heads of the Three Departments had native places in the northwest. However, by Wu-te this figure had plummeted to a mere forty percent and during Chen-kuan even further to less than thirty percent. A similar but less marked shift away from the northwest also took place in the native places of the presidents of the Six Boards from Sui to early T'ang. (See Appendix I, Tables D and E.) Of T'ai-tsung's twenty-one chief ministers, moreover, only seven (33.3 percent) were from the north-west.[19] Thus, it can be seen that by the Chen-kuan era the geographical

---

[18]Virtually all of the early T'ang chief ministers (*tsai-hsiang*) were drawn from these ranks.

[19]Tsukiyama Chisaburō, *Tōdai seiji seido*, p. 41. Matsui Shūichi, "Tōdai zenki no kizoku"

center of gravity in the highest ranks of the T'ang civil bureaucracy had noticeably shifted away from the northwest.[20] This change also commenced decades earlier than the reign of Empress Wu, when many scholars believe the shift first occurred as the result of her ardent patronage of the examination system, which allegedly decreased the power of the entrenched northwestern aristocracy while opening a new avenue to officialdom for the literati of the northeastern plain and the south.[21]

The shift away from the northwest for the native places of high-ranking officials in the T'ang bureaucracy was related in large part to the nature of the T'ang conquest of the empire, which was, it might be argued, essentially a double seizure of the Chinese throne from strongholds located in the northeast, first by Kao-tsu from Taiyuan in 618 and then again by T'ai-tsung from Loyang in 626. As we have previously seen, many officials in Kao-tsu's military organization in Taiyuan, the Administration of the Grand General, were from Taiyuan and its immediate vicinity or from areas on the northeastern plain. These officials subsequently formed the nucleus of the Wu-te civil bureaucracy. We have also seen that during the founding period of the dynasty and Wu-te, T'ai-tsung recruited a large number of officials first from the Taiyuan region and then from the northeastern plain, especially during his campaigns of 621 against Tou Chien-te and Wang Shih-ch'ung. Eventually, T'ai-tsung's own military headquarters was established on the northeastern plain at Loyang. A considerable proportion of T'ai-tsung's followers were thus non-northwesterners, and when they entered the highest ranks of the Chen-kuan bureaucracy following his accession, they dramatically altered the ratio of northwestern to other elements in the government.

Wei Cheng's background was, in many respects, typical of that of high-level officials serving in the Chen-kuan bureaucracy. His native place was on the northeastern plain, and both his father and grand-

---

[Aristocracy of the Early T'ang], *Rekishi kyōiku* [The Teaching of History], 14 (May, 1966), 41, gives a figure of twenty-six chief ministers, of whom nine were from the northwest.

[20]On this point, see also Ts'en Chung-mien, *Sui-T'ang shih* [History of the Sui and T'ang Dynasties], (Peking, 1957), p. 181, and the anonymously written "Kuan-yü Sui-T'ang shih yen-chiu chung ti i-ko li-lun wen-t'i" [A Theoretical Problem in the Study of Sui and T'ang History], *Li-shih yen-chiu*, (1958, no. 12), p. 39.

[21]Such views may be found in, among others, Ch'en Yin-k'o, *T'ang-tai cheng-chih*, p. 14, and E. G. Pulleyblank, *The Background of the Rebellion of An Lu-shan* (London, 1955), pp. 47–48.

father had served in the provincial bureaucracy. Also, like many of his colleagues, Wei possessed a previous history of official service prior to joining the T'ang. But just what place did Wei Cheng occupy in relation to his colleagues in the early T'ang power structure?

Contrary to popular belief, Wei was neither the most influential nor the most trusted of T'ai-tsung's officials. Rather, these relationships were reserved for the emperor's "meritorious officials" (kung-ch'en) or "patriotic officials" (hsün-ch'en), men who had stood by him through every vicissitude in his career, had substantially aided his rise to power, and had, in turn, won his undying gratitude and trust.[22] The most prominent among these was Chang-sun Wu-chi (d. 659),[23] elder brother of T'ai-tsung's consort, who had been close to the emperor since their youth and had occupied a prominent place on T'ai-tsung's staff beginning with the Taiyuan uprising. Later, he helped mastermind T'ai-tsung's counterstrategy against his two brothers and was part of the group positioned at the Hsüan-wu Gate when they were slain. At the beginning of Chen-kuan he became right vice-president of the Department of Affairs of State, one of the most powerful posts in the administration. Although removed from this office in 628 after a charge against him that he wielded excessive power, he was allowed to retain his high rank. After 633 he served in the prestigious but largely honorary posts of director of public works (ssu-k'ung) and director of instruction (ssu-t'u), where he continued his role as a close adviser to the throne.

Second only to Chang-sun Wu-chi as T'ai-tsung's most trusted counselors were Fang Hsüan-ling (578–648)[24] and Tu Ju-hui (585–630),[25] two more "meritorious officials." Fang, a former Sui official, joined T'ai-tsung's retinue soon after the Taiyuan uprising and remained in his service all during the Wu-te period. When T'ai-tsung ascended the throne, Fang was made a president of the Department of the Imperial Secretariat and later the left vice-president of the Department of Affairs of State. Tu Ju-hui, another Sui official, abandoned his post after a short while and joined T'ai-tsung's Prince of Ch'in Office following the

[22]T'ai-tsung ennobled his "meritorious officials" as dukes and furnished them with the taxes of households on the land of their nominal fiefs; see *THY* ch. 45, p. 800. Wei Cheng, having been adviser to the crown prince Chien-ch'eng, was not honored with the "meritorious official" designation during his lifetime.

[23]Biographies: *CTS* 65.6b–17; *HTS* 105.1–6b.

[24]Biographies: *CTS* 66.1–10; *HTS* 96.1–6.

[25]Biographies: *CTS* 66.10–15; *HTS* 96.6–8.

fall of Ta-hsing-ch'eng. Early in Chen-kuan he served as president of
the Board of War. In 629 he was promoted to right vice-president in
the Department of Affairs of State, where Fang served as his colleague.
The two were superb administrators and set the tone of sober, efficient,
and fair government with which their names have become synonymous
in Chinese history. Unfortunately, Tu's death in 630 from an illness
cut short a promising career. Fang, however, continued as left vice-
president for a total of thirteen years—the longest tenure in a single
office of any of T'ai-tsung's chief ministers—and remained at the
emperor's side until his death in 648. Not only was Fang a fine administrator, he also appears to have been an eminently likable person who
made few enemies at court; he was devoid of envy, careful when giving
orders not to offend subordinates, and, above all, diplomatic. When
T'ai-tsung once asked what opinion Fang had of an official the emperor
had recently appointed to high office, he was told that Fang, who
evidently thought little of the new appointee, had commented on the
fineness of his beard but had added nothing further.

REGIONALISM AND FACTIONALISM

"Fang and Tu," as the Chinese fondly refer to them, traditionally
have been viewed as the embodiment of the immense esprit de corps
said to have characterized T'ai-tsung's bureaucracy. Yet, like its
counterparts in other times and places, this bureaucracy was susceptible
to the tensions, strains, and even outright conflicts that form an integral
part of the political process everywhere. A number of approaches have
been adopted to explain the basis of early T'ang political strife. Marxist
historians have emphasized the class struggle as a primary cause and
have laboriously attempted, with little success, to determine which
major political figures (including emperors) were representatives of
which classes during the period.[26] With few exceptions, their conclusions have been influenced more by the dictates of ideology than by
scholarly acumen.

[26]See the previously cited articles by Wu Che and Yüan Ying-kuang, Ch'i Ch'en-chün,
and the anonymously published article "Kuan-yü," all in issues of *Li-shih yen-chiu*; also
Wu Che, "Lun T'ang-tai ch'ien-ch'i t'ung-chih chieh-chi nei-pu tou-cheng yü chieh-chi
tou-cheng" [Class Conflict and Internal Conflict within the Ruling Class during the Early
T'ang Dynasty], *Hsin chien-she* (1962, no. 1), pp. 16–32; Yang Kuo-i, "Lüeh-lun 'Chen-kuan
chih chih' " [A Brief Discussion of the "Chen-kuan chih chih"], *Li-shih chiao-hsüeh* (1961, no.
10), pp. 20–24.

The most widely accepted theories by non-Marxist scholars are those of Ch'en Yin-k'o and Ku Chi-kuang, both of whom stress the role played by geography in engendering political tensions and factionalism at the early T'ang court.[27] According to Ch'en, political power during the early T'ang was contested by two rival regional "blocs." The first, the northwestern or Kuan-lung bloc (*Kuan-lung chi-t'uan*), to which the imperial Li-T'ang house belonged, was centered on the capital and the region comprising modern Shensi and Kansu provinces; it was comprised of the descendants of aristocratic families that had controlled power in China since the Western Wei, Northern Chou, and Sui dynasties. The second, or Shan-tung bloc (*Shan-tung chi-t'uan*), was centered on the northeastern plain in the region east of the T'ai-hang mountains (thus, *shan-tung*), comprising eastern Shansi, Honan, Hopei, and Shantung provinces; members of this bloc were predominantly literati of modest backgrounds, many of whom had entered officialdom via the examination system.

Ku, whose research deals primarily with Ho-pei *tao* (whose T'ang boundaries did not markedly differ from those of the modern province of the same name), suggests that from the very beginning of the T'ang the imperial house practiced a conscious policy of discrimination against the Hopei region, evidenced most notably by T'ai-tsung's failure to provide for its defense by neglecting to garrison it with troops during his reorganization and expansion of the militia system. As a result, Ku maintains, Hopei—which during most of the second half of the sixth century had been the heartland of the Northern Ch'i dynasty, proud paladin of Chinese culture in the "barbarian" North—gradually became alienated from the rest of the empire. As Ku points out, both Kao-tsu and T'ai-tsung, especially the latter, had good reason to fear the people of the northeastern plain. First, the northeasterners had held out the longest and had offered the fiercest armed resistance to T'ang authority during the wars of internal pacification early in the dynasty. Second, they were easily excited to rebellion, e.g., the rebellion of Liu Hei-t'a in the wake of the execution by the T'ang of Liu's superior

[27]Ch'en Yin-k'o, "Chi T'ang-tai chih Li Wu Wei Yang hun-yin chi-t'uan" [The Li, Wu, Wei, and Yang Marriage Blocs of the T'ang Dynasty], *Li-shih yen-chiu* (1954, no. 1), pp. 33–51; idem, *T'ang-tai cheng-chih*, pp. 19ff Ku Chi-kuang, "An-Shih luan ch'ien chih Ho-pei tao" [Ho-pei *tao* Prior to the An-shih Rebellions], *Yen-ching hsüeh-pao*, 19 (1936), 197–209; see also Pulleyblank, *Background*, pp. 75–77.

and Kao-tsu's rival contender for the Mandate, Tou Chien-te. Third, many of the confederates of T'ai-tsung's slain brothers were north-easterners who, following the Hsüan-wu Gate incident, fled back to their homes in the region and represented a potential disruptive force to the new regime. As we have seen, it was for this very reason that T'ai-tsung deputed Wei Cheng to journey to southern Hopei to soothe the dissidents.

Yet a further indication, Ku maintains, of T'ai-tsung's antipathy toward the northeastern plain was the attitude the emperor adopted toward certain northeastern aristocratic lineages—collectively known as the *ssu-hsing* (or "four [categories of] surnames")—a matter to which we must devote some attention, however brief. During the Period of Disunion, members of the *ssu-hsing* had in considerable numbers occupied the most powerful offices in the land and had obtained for their clans exalted reputations on a national level. By early T'ang times the *ssu-hsing* were no longer represented in any great number at the uppermost levels of the bureaucracy. But their punctilious use of Confucian etiquette and ceremony in all its nuances and their policy of endogamous marriage alliances had done much to perpetuate, at least on a regional level, the enormous prestige and influence they had enjoyed in their heyday, allowing them to spurn marriage offers from even the imperial Li-T'ang house, which they regarded with ill-concealed disdain as a relative parvenu.

In 632 T'ai-tsung, who is said to have become incensed over the arrogant boasting of the *ssu-hsing* and the exorbitant betrothal gifts they were demanding for granting outsiders the privilege of marrying with them, ordered a survey of the social status of all the clans in the empire. Doubtless, the emperor hoped that because few members of the *ssu-hsing* were serving in his bureaucracy or had served in his father's, their social status would have in the meantime declined precipitously. Such was not the case, however. When the survey was completed and presented to the throne in 638, and all the clans of the empire were divided into nine grades on the basis of the social prestige they enjoyed, the Ts'ui of Ch'ing-ho—one of the *ssu-hsing*—was ranked among the first grade clans while the imperial Li-T'ang clan found itself relegated to the status of a third grade clan, a reminder that social prestige, at least early in the T'ang, was not simply a function of bureaucratic power. Enraged by these findings, T'ai-tsung promptly instructed his officials to alter the work. In the final version of the survey, published with the title *Compendium of Clans (Shih-tsu chih)* later the same year, the Ts'ui clan had been demoted to the third grade while the imperial family and the houses of the emperor's mother and consort had been magically elevated to the first and second grades, respectively.[28]

T'ai-tsung's attempt to enhance the social position of the imperial house at the expense of the *ssu-hsing* appears on the whole to have been unsuccessful. That the Ts'ui clan had achieved the highest grade in the original version of the *Compendium of Clans,* even though it exercised practically no direct influence at the early T'ang court, was a sign that its prestige could not be tarnished by a relatively short period of political inactivity at the highest level. Conversely, the social position of the imperial house had also not increased radically after such a short period as the ruling power. T'ai-tsung's failure to legislate social status by imperial fiat is attested to by the fact that even after the *Compendium of Clans* was published, three of his most eminent ministers—Fang Hsüan-ling, Li Shih-chi, and Wei Cheng himself—all ardently sought and consummated marriages with *ssu-hsing* clans. These marriage alliances, it is said, served to perpetuate the reputations of the clans and to nullify whatever small gains the emperor had achieved by altering the survey.[29]

T'ai-tsung's emendation of the *Compendium of Clans* was clearly a blow aimed at the entrenched aristocratic lineages of the northeastern plain

[28]Narratives of the compilation of the Chen-kuan *Compendium of Clans* are found in *CKCY* 7.11–12b; *THY* ch. 36, p. 664; *TCTC* ch. 195, pp. 6135–36; and the biographies of Kao Shih-lien, *CTS* 65.3–4 and *HTS* 95.3–3b. There have been a number of studies devoted in whole or in part to the work, among them, Ts'en Chung-mien, "Chiao Chen-kuan shih-tsu-chih ts'an-chüan" [A Collation of Remnants of the Chen-kuan *Compendium of Clans*"], *Kuo-li Chung-shan ta-hsüeh yen-chiu-yüan wen-k'o yen-chiu-so li-shih-hsüeh-pu pien-chi* [Papers of the History Department of the Research Institute of the Graduate Faculty of Letters, National Sun Yat-sen University], 2 (1937), 315–30; Takeda Ryūji, "Jōkan shizokushi no hensan ni kansuru ichi kōsatsu" [A Study of the Compilation of the Chen-kuan *Compendium of Clans*], *Shigaku,* 25 (1952), 456–74; Ikeda On, "Tōchō shizokushi no ichi kōsatsu—iwayuru Tonkō meizokushi zankan o megutte" [A Study of the Compendia of Clans of the T'ang Dynasty with Special Reference to the *ming-tsu-chih* Remnants], *Hokkaidō Daigaku bungakubu kiyō* [Annual Report on Cultural Science, Faculty of Letters, Hokkaido University], 13 (1965), 1–64.

[29]*HTS* 95.4b. Much later in the dynasty, as a result of a complex of factors, the prestige of the four surname clans declined. But even in the ninth century the emperor Wen-tsung (rg. 827–40) could still lament (*HTS* 172.7): "In concluding marriage alliances among the people, it is not one's position in officialdom that counts but rather esteemed lineage. Our house has furnished emperors for two hundred years, but we still do not rank with the Ts'ui and Lu."

and an effort to bring the political status and social status of early T'ang power groups more nearly into alignment; it is difficult, however, to agree with Ku Chi-kuang that it was a reflection of the emperor's discriminatory attitude toward the entire region.[30] Rather, as we have seen, both the first and second T'ang emperors were very much beholden to the great plain east of the T'ung Pass, a region from which so many of their own staunchest supporters had been recruited. T'ai-tsung's political fortunes, particularly, were intimately bound up with the northeastern plain, where during much of Wu-te his military headquarters was located, and with the so-called Shan-tung military elite (*Shan-tung hao-chieh*), whose strong assistance he had received on the eve of the Hsüan-wu Gate incident. Indeed, in 626, when Kao-tsu, in an effort to keep his feuding sons physically separated as much as possible, made plans to return T'ai-tsung to his headquarters at Loyang, hundreds of miles from the capital, the crown prince and Yüan-chi were quick to complain that "The Prince of Ch'in's associates are all Shan-tung people," and that if he were allowed to proceed to Loyang he would never return to Ch'ang-an.[31] It is, perhaps, not entirely coincidental that Ch'ang Ho, commander of the guards at the Hsüan-wu Gate, whose bribing by T'ai-tsung enabled him to obtain a great victory over his brothers, was also a northeasterner.[32]

Mou Jun-sun's recent study on political tensions at the early T'ang court similarly stresses the role played by geography, but Mou seeks to explain these tensions in terms of attitudinal differences arising not between northeasterners and northwesterners but between northerners and southerners, the legacy, he believes, of centuries of political and cultural division between North and South China during the Period of Disunion.[33]

Whatever analytical framework one chooses to adopt to examine the

---

[30]On this point, see, among others, Ch'en Yin-k'o, "Hun-yin chi-t'uan," 34–35; Matsui Shūichi, "Sokuten Bukō no yōritsu o megutte" [The Establishment of Empress Wu Tse-t'ien], *Hokudai shigaku* [Journal of the Historical Association of Hokkaido University], 11 (1966), 6, and idem, "Tōdai zenki no kizoku," 41–42.

[31]*HTS* 79.5b; *TCTC* ch. 191, p. 6004.

[32]Ch'en Yin-k'o, *T'ang-tai cheng-chih*, p. 41; idem, "Shan-tung hao-chieh," 6–7.

[33]Mou Jun-sun, "T'ang-ch'u nan-pei hsüeh-jen," 50–86. Mou notes on the one hand the southern fondness for certain types of music ("sounds of destroyed states" according to the more stolid northerners), elegant and flowery literary styles, and Neo-Taoism, and on the other the strong northern antipathy to these "decadent" cultural influences because of the belief that they resulted in political enfeeblement.

early T'ang power structure, it is at least clear that both Kao-tsu and T'ai-tsung were keenly aware of the potential role geography could play in the formation of political blocs or factions (*tang*) and therefore acted in a rather even-handed manner toward representatives of all the geographical regions at their courts. This was, naturally, a prudent policy based on their overriding need to consolidate their power bases and to reward men of varied geographical backgrounds who had figured prominently in their rise to power. A good illustration of both emperors' attitudes toward the various regions is provided by their geographically diverse appointments to paired posts in the central bureaucracy—those of the left and right vice-presidents of the Department of Affairs of State and of the two presidents in each of the Departments of the Imperial Secretariat and Chancellery—which all during the period 618–49 tended to be "balanced" geographically among representatives of the northwest, northeast, and south. On the whole, however, there is little evidence to support the view that during the early T'ang the geographical origins of officials actually served to determine their political behavior. If we examine, for instance, the way in which officials responded to a wide range of political issues at the Chen-kuan court, we find that men from allegedly opposing Kuan-lung and Shan-tung blocs, as well as northerners and southerners, routinely joined on the same side of an issue to oppose members of their own blocs or regions on the other side. Perhaps even more important, members of opposing blocs and regions frequently recommended one another to the emperor for both employment and promotion. All this suggests that political relations between officials of opposing blocs and regions were more often characterized by cooperation than by hostility. Configurations of power at the early T'ang court cannot, then, be understood simply in terms of geography.[34]

Factionalism, when it did occur during the early T'ang, was most often related to the problem of the succession. Prior to the Hsüan-wu Gate incident, for example, the court was split between the supporters of Crown Prince Chien-ch'eng and Li Yüan-chi on the one side and Shih-min on the other. As we shall see in chapter 7, the court was once again rent asunder in 643 by the rivalry generated among three of T'ai-

[34]For a more detailed presentation of the foregoing analysis, see the author's essay, "Factionalism in Early T'ang Government," in *Perspectives on the T'ang*, Arthur F. Wright and Denis Twitchett, eds. (New Haven, 1973), pp. 87–120.

tsung's sons, Crown Prince Ch'eng-ch'ien, Li T'ai, and Li Chih, and their respective supporters. Significantly, however, each of the candidates in both these succession struggles was supported by officials of varying backgrounds.

A major figure in the succession dispute of 643 was the emperor's brother-in-law, Chang-sun Wu-chi, who, as we have already observed, was the most powerful Chen-kuan official. At a crucial moment in this dispute, Chang-sun Wu-chi persuaded T'ai-tsung not to withdraw his support of Li Chih in favor of another of his sons, thereby allowing Chih to succeed as the third T'ang emperor, known posthumously as Kao-tsung. Kao-tsung's weakness, evidenced most conspicuously after the rise to power of his wife, Empress Wu, may well have commended him to Chang-sun Wu-chi, who probably hoped to perpetuate his considerable political influence over a feeble successor to the throne.[35]

Another supporter of Kao-tsung, often cited as having occupied a commanding position in the early T'ang power structure, was Li Shih-chi (594–669), formerly the rebel Hsü Shih-chi. Early in 619 Wei Cheng persuaded Li to surrender his extensive territory on the northeastern plain to Kao-tsu. Li thereby won the gratitude of the Li-T'ang house and went on to serve it with distinction in a variety of posts, including that of president of the Board of War and chief minister. Li, however, continued to maintain a strong base of support among the military elite (*hao-chieh*) of the northeastern plain, and thus constituted a strong centrifugal power that could be turned against the dynasty.[36] During all his years on the throne, T'ai-tsung remained chary of Li's might, even devising on his deathbed a scheme by which Kao-tsung might test for a final time Li's loyalty to the throne. Had Li failed the test he would have been liquidated.[37]

To what extent men like Chang-sun Wu-chi and Li Shih-chi actually served as leaders of factions during the period Wei Cheng was in office remains unclear. But most evidence points to the conclusion that prior to the succession dispute of 643—the year of Wei's death—factions with

---

[35]See Sun Kuo-tung, "T'ang Chen-kuan Yung-hui chien tang-cheng ti shih-i" [An Explication of Factional Strife during the Period from Chen-kuan through Yung-hui of the T'ang], *Hsin-ya shu-yüan hsüeh-shu nien-k'an* [New Asia College Academic Annual], 7 (1965), 40–43.

[36]See Ch'en Yin-k'o, "Shan-tung hao-chieh," 7–8.

[37]*TCTC* ch. 199, pp. 6266–67. Li's biographies, *CTS* 67.13b and *HTS* 93.9b, record a slightly different version of the emperor's scheme.

identifiable leaders and followers had not yet emerged at T'ai-tsung's court. During this time political alliances appear to have been ephemeral, generated more by individual issues and personalities than by any individual factors—geographical or otherwise—productive of sustained political cohesion.[38]

Needless to say, however, T'ai-tsung was ever sensitive to the threat that regionalism and factionalism posed to the stability of his house. It was for this very reason that he found in Wei Cheng such a valuable servitor. Like his father before him, T'ai-tsung was able to utilize Wei, a northeasterner, as a loyal representative of central power to the elite of the northeastern plain, to help convince them that the dynasty was sensitive to their peculiar regional interests and to gain their allegiance, or, at the very least, to lessen their disaffection.[39] Moreover, Wei was so staunchly independent in all matters political and otherwise, that the emperor must have been convinced that he would never ally himself with any factions at court.

DECISION MAKING

When conflict did arise in the course of politics during Chen-kuan, it was resolved by a variety of deliberative and decision-making bodies. On the first and fifteenth days of each lunar month, all officials of the ninth rank and above, that is, all officials "within the current" (*liu-nei*), met with the emperor in special audience at the T'ai-chi Hall, situated in the southern portion of the palace city. To the east and west of the T'ai-chi Hall were two smaller council chambers (*shang-ko*). After the audience—essentially ceremonial in nature—was concluded, the emperor retired to one of these council chambers, where soon afterwards he would be joined by his chief ministers, other designated high-ranking officials, remonstrating officials (*chien-kuan*) charged with pointing out errors in their deliberations, and one scribe to make a record of the proceedings.[40] Since the meetings in the council chambers were shorn of elaborate ceremony, the atmosphere was far more intimate than at the preceding large audiences, and the attending officials could speak their minds with relative ease.

[38]See Wechsler, "Factionalism in Early T'ang Government."
[39]Ch'en Yin-k'o, "Shan-tung hao-chieh," 8–9.
[40]*TCTC* ch. 192, p. 6031, note of Ch'eng Ta-ch'ang; *THY* ch. 56, p. 961, note of Su Mien; Rotours, *Traité des fonctionnaires*, 1:161, n. 1.

The more regular type of audience for all officials of the fifth rank
and above and certain other designated officials below that rank, such
as remonstrating officials and scribes, was held at the Liang-i Hall,
located midway along the north-south axis of the palace city directly to
the north of the T'ai-chi Hall. These audiences were held daily at dawn
until 639, after which time, until the very last year of Chen-kuan, they
were held once every three days.[41] The meetings in the council chambers of the T'ai-chi Hall and at the Liang-i Hall, especially the former
because of their relative informality, were forums of discussion and
debate, many of which are recorded in the *Essentials of Government of
the Chen-kuan Period,* by Wu Ching, and also in Wang Fang-ch'ing's
Recorded Remonstrances of Duke Wei of Cheng (Wei Cheng-kung chien-lu),
a major source of materials on Wei Cheng.[42]

Another important deliberative body was the council of state at the
Hall of Government Affairs (*cheng-shih t'ang*), located during Chen-kuan
in the Department of the Imperial Chancellery.[43] Meetings here were
attended by the regular chief ministers: the two vice-presidents of the
Department of Affairs of State, the two presidents of the Department of
the Imperial Secretariat, and the two presidents of the Department of
the Imperial Chancellery. In addition, men occupying other posts in
the central government were from time to time given special titles
denoting that they too were to attend discussions of the council and thus
share with the chief ministers in the important task of formulating
policy.[44] In this way the regime was able to obtain the services in the
Hall of Government Affairs and elsewhere of officials whose knowledge
and talents were useful for policy making but who still occupied relatively
modest offices. It also appears to have been a method by which the
emperor could circumvent the power of his highest officials by appointing lower-ranking but more congenial men to advisory positions
of great importance.

[41] *THY* ch. 24, p. 455.

[42] See Appendix IIA.

[43] The Hall of Government Affairs was later moved to the Department of the Imperial
Secretariat. For a discussion of the operation of this body, see Sun Kuo-tung, "T'ang-tai
san-sheng chih," 56–60.

[44] These titles are discussed in ibid., 61–65. The practice of combining the deliberative
function of the chief ministers with other offices in the central government began during the
Sui dynasty; Chou Tao-chi, "T'ang-tai tsai-hsiang ming-ch'eng yü ch'i shih-ch'üan chih
yen-pien" [Changes in the Names and Real Power of the Chief Ministers of the T'ang
Dynasty], *Ta-lu tsa-chih* [The Continent], 16 (1958), 104.

Still other bodies were sometimes called upon to aid in the resolution of political questions. Among these were the so-called Eight Seats (*pa-tso*), composed of the two vice-presidents of the Department of Affairs of State and the presidents of the Six Boards, and the so-called One Hundred Officials (*pai-kuan*), composed of the leading members of the Three Departments, Six Boards, and nine Courts.

Once a decision regarding policy had been reached, the scene usually shifted to the Department of the Imperial Secretariat, where the grand secretaries (*chung-shu she-jen*) drafted an imperial edict (*chao*) or imperial order (*ch'ih*) embodying that decision. The draft would then be sent to the emperor for his examination and approval. If the imperial assent was received, the draft would again be sent to the Secretariat, where the grand secretaries would co-sign it and pass it along to the Department of the Imperial Chancellery for review. The grand secretaries of the Chancellery (*chi-shih-chung*) had the power of veto and could return any drafts of which they disapproved to the emperor with suggestions for amendments. If they approved the draft, they would memorialize the throne requesting that it be promulgated. The approved draft would then be forwarded to the Department of Affairs of State, which would assign it to one of its Six Boards for disposition.[45] Sun Kuo-tung points out that nominally no imperial edict or order had the force of law unless it had been approved by both the Secretariat and Chancellery, and that in the end even the Department of Affairs of State might veto an edict or order by ignoring its provisions and taking no action on it.[46] The early T'ang was obviously a time when regularly constituted officials were not mere rubber stamps of the monarchy but were men who actually possessed the power both to make and to break policy.

Naturally, in the last analysis, despite the elaborate legislative machinery described above, the final arbiter of political power during the early T'ang was the emperor, whose authority was theoretically absolute and unlimited. Yet, as we will see in the next chapter, determined and obstinate officials like Wei Cheng were on occasion able to thwart even

[45]Sun, "T'ang-tai san-sheng chih," 57.

[46]Ibid., 23. Such a complex legislative system was bound to be time-consuming. Thus, minor matters of state or important matters which had to be acted upon swiftly were often handled directly by the chief ministers at the Hall of Government Affairs. Since the membership of the council at the Hall comprised the heads of the Three Departments, this meant that once the council approved an order or edict, it did not have to be reviewed by the Chancellery but might be implemented immediately; Lo Hsiang-lin, *T'ang-tai wen-hua shih*, p. 36.

T'ai-tsung's expressed will by means of the co-signing and veto pro-
cedures that were built into the Three Department system.

PROGRAMS AND POLICIES

During much of his reign, T'ai-tsung and his officials concerned
themselves with administrative improvements, reorganization, and
reform. Early in the dynasty, Kao-tsu had doubled the number of prefectures in existence during the Sui (190) in order to reward his many
supporters with provincial posts. Thus, soon after mounting the throne,
his son embarked upon a program to reduce excessive administrative
subdivisions by combining prefectures on a wide scale. At the same time,
T'ai-tsung divided all of China proper into ten *tao*, or "circuits," which
were much later to develop into full-fledged provincial administrations.
The ten *tao* were Lung-yu and Kuan-nei in the northwest; Ho-tung,
Ho-pei, and Ho-nan in the northeast; Shan-nan, Huai-nan, and Chien-
nan in central China; and Chiang-nan and Ling-nan in the vast region
south of the Yangtze. No governors were at this time appointed to
administer the *tao*, but imperial commissioners (*shih*) were sent out to
them from time to time in exceptional circumstances as "trouble-
shooters."[47]

Because bribery had become a flagrant abuse during his father's
reign, T'ai-tsung quickly sought means to curb corruption in government, including the dispatching of subordinates with money to test the
incorruptibility of his officials. When this predictably brought about
howls of outrage from those affected, the emperor adopted the device of
rewarding before the entire court those found guilty of accepting bribes,
thus greatly humiliating them.[48] By such means even the routine practice of accepting gifts in return for favors during Chen-kuan appears
to have decreased.

An attempt was also made to upgrade the quality of the provincial
bureaucracy. For a long while prior to Chen-kuan many local offices had
been filled by former military men and metropolitan officials "exiled"
to the countryside as punishment. Naturally, local administration had
suffered as a consequence. To reverse this trend, T'ai-tsung began

[47] *TCTC* ch. 192, p. 6033; *THY* ch. 70, pp. 1231–32; Robert des Rotours, "Les grands
fonctionnaires des provinces en Chine sous les dynastie des T'ang," *T'oung Pao*, 25 (1927),
222.

[48] *TCTC* ch. 192, pp. 6029, 6032; ch. 193, p. 6062.

pasting the names of local officials on screens in his apartments and promoting or demoting them according to a merit system he devised. When this failed to bring about the desired result, he began personally selecting all prefects and charged his officials in the capital with recommending candidates to fill positions as subprefects.[49] In addition, special investigators were sent on circuit from time to time to investigate the conduct of local officials. During one such cleanup campaign, it is said, several thousands were punished for malfeasance, including seven who were executed.[50]

As the bureaucracy grew larger and more complex during Chen-kuan, so too did the civil service and educational systems that helped feed it. Examinations were held on an annual basis (with two exceptions), and degrees were awarded in increasing numbers; at least some of the candidates were interviewed by both T'ai-tsung and the crown prince.[51] The system of state schools in Ch'ang-an designed to turn out an elite group of candidates for the examinations was expanded. In 627 the emperor founded the Directorate of the State University (kuo-tzu chien), which was designed to supervise the curricula of the three schools set up earlier by his father as well as two others soon to be established by himself, both on Sui models: the School of Calligraphy (shu-hsüeh) in 628 and the School of Law (lü-hsüeh) in 632. Because of the specialized instruction they offered, both schools were open to the sons of low-ranking officials and commoners. The emperor also increased the capacity of the School of the Sons of State, the Superior School, and the School of the Four Gates, so that by 640 the number of their students had reached more than two thousand. Late in 626 a school for the sons of the imperial family and high-ranking officials was established at the College for the Development of Literature (hung-wen kuan), which took over some of the functions of the old College of Literary Studies that T'ai-tsung had founded while still Prince of Ch'in.[52] Another similar college, the College for the Veneration of Literature (ch'ung-wen kuan), was added in 639.

[49] THY ch. 68, p. 1197; TCTC ch. 193, p. 6061.

[50] THY ch. 78, p. 1419; TCTC ch. 198, p. 6234.

[51] See Ma Tuan-lin, comp., Wen-hsien t'ung-k'ao [Complete Examination of Documents and Compositions] (prior to 1319; reproduction of 1748 ed., Taipei, 1964), ch. 29, pp. 276–77; and Li Fang et al., comps., T'ai-p'ing yü-lan (983; SPTK ed., Taipei, 1967), 629.1.

[52] See Liu Po-chi, T'ang-tai cheng-chiao shih [History of Politics and Education during the T'ang Dynasty] (Taipei, 1958), pp. 92–96.

T'ai-tsung's interest in education was also reflected in the numerous scholarly projects completed under his sponsorship, many of the most important of which involved Wei Cheng (to be discussed later).

In the field of law, the trend during Chen-kuan was to ameliorate the severity of corporal punishment and, in some cases, to do away with it altogether. Beating on the back with bamboo rods was nominally discontinued (nevertheless, the sources reveal instances in which the bastinade was personally ordered by T'ai-tsung), and the cutting off of feet, a traditional form of punishment, was abolished and replaced by banishment.[53] The emperor furthermore commanded that criminals could be executed only after officials had memorialized him several times about their cases in order to avoid miscarriages of justice.[54] In 637 a legal commission headed by Fang Hsüan-ling presented to the throne a revised body of codified law, including a five-hundred article penal code (lü). This so-called Chen-kuan Code, which replaced that completed in 624, reduced the number of offenses carrying a penalty of death or banishment and decreased punishments for many lesser crimes as well.[55] At the same time, an extensively revised body of administrative law (ling and shih) was also put into force.

The Chen-kuan period also saw an expansion of the T'ang military apparatus. Earlier, Kao-tsu had established twelve military districts in Kuan-nei (Shensi) and had garrisoned each with an army. In 636 these were replaced by a total of 633 or 634 militia units called the Intrepid Militia (che-ch'ung fu) that were distributed more widely over North China (with the exception of Ho-pei tao, which appears to have received none). A large proportion of these militia units, numbering according to various accounts either 261 or 361, was established in Kuan-nei.[56]

On the economic front an earnest effort was made to improve the lot

[53]CTS 50.3–4b; TCTC ch. 193, p. 6083.

[54]According to this scheme, during the period immediately before the execution metropolitan officials were to memorialize five times and provincial officials three times; HTS 2.9; THY ch. 40, p. 718; CKCY 8.7. During the Sui, Wen-ti had inaugurated a similar practice; see Étienne Balazs, "L'Oeuvre des Souei," p. 162.

[55]TCTC ch. 194, p. 6126. Balazs, "L'Oeuvre des Souei," p. 162, notes that during K'ai-huang, Sui Wen-ti had done away with the most draconian of criminal penalities. However, harsh punishments had subsequently revived during the late Sui disorders.

[56]THY ch. 72, p. 1298; TCTC ch. 194, pp. 6124–25; T'ang Ch'ang-ju, T'ang-shu ping-chih chien-cheng, pp. 9–11; Lao Ching-yüan, "T'ang che-ch'ung fu k'ao" [A Study of the T'ang Intrepid Militia], in Erh-shih-wu shih pu-pien [Supplements to the Twenty-five Standard Histories], 6 vols. (1937; reprint Peking, 1957), 6: 7593.

of the peasant. As a result of the lingering effects of the late Sui disorders and successive natural disasters that plagued much of China early in the T'ang, grain prices remained at inflated levels even after T'ai-tsung's accession. In order to help reduce these prices, the emperor in 628 revived the practice of establishing relief granaries (*i-ts'ang*) on a wide scale to store grain against crop failure.[57] Early in his reign, T'ai-tsung also restricted government expenditures by severely curtailing construction of large public works, thereby reducing the tax and corvée loads of his subjects. By the early 630s, good weather, domestic peace, and sound fiscal management had brought about a reduction of grain prices to low levels.

THE RENEWAL OF EMPIRE

Perhaps the most dramatic achievement of all during the Chen-kuan period was not the result of any administrative policies or improvements undertaken by the government, but was rather the spectacular geographical expansion of Chinese power to a total area matched previously only by the great Han. This expansion began slowly, for at first T'ai-tsung was chary of indulging in foreign adventures. Animosities that had developed during the period preceding the Hsüan-wu Gate incident had not yet fully dissipated, and all of his military commanders could not yet be fully relied upon.[58] Moreover, officials like Wei Cheng were able to prevail upon the emperor not to wage war by arguing that certain regions of China had not completely recovered from the economic ravages of the recent civil strife and that conscripting troops from these regions would cause unbearable hardship among the peasantry. Soon, though, these purely economic arguments could no longer be justified, and T'ai-tsung began to revive Sui Yang-ti's dream of reestablishing a grand empire on the Han model.

At the time, the mightiest foe of the T'ang was still the Eastern Turks, who underscored their power just a few weeks after T'ai-tsung ascended the throne by invading Shensi in great numbers and advancing to the Pien Bridge on the Wei River, about thirteen miles northwest of Ch'ang-an, forcing T'ai-tsung to part with a large amount of treasure to secure their withdrawal.[59] The Turks, however, soon became

[57]See *CTS* 2.14b; *THT* ch. 88, pp. 1611–12; Twitchett, *Financial Administration*, p. 32.
[58]See Li Shu-t'ung, *T'ang-shih k'ao-pien*, pp. 253–59.
[59]See ibid., pp. 247–75. According to traditional accounts in *CTS* 2.11b and *TCTC* ch. 191,

wracked by a series of internal convulsions, culminating in 627 in the revolt of their subject tribes, the Hsüeh-yen-t'o, Pa-yeh-ku, and Uighurs (*Hui-ho*). Later the same year they suffered deep snows in which most of their livestock perished. By diplomatic ploys, T'ai-tsung succeeded in alienating Hsieh-li Qaghan from his nephew T'u-li, leader of several Turkish tribes, thereby further eroding Turkish power. The emperor then recognized the legitimacy of a leader elected by those tribes which had recently cast off Turkish control, causing new defections in Hsieh-li's ranks. (This policy of divide and conquer was a time-honored Chinese strategy against "barbarians," at least as old as the Former Han.) Late in 629 T'ai-tsung sent a force said to have numbered more than one hundred thousand against the qaghan at his headquarters south of the Gobi, which was taken with a great loss of Turkish life. On this occasion, Hsieh-li made good his escape, but he was captured the following year and sent to Ch'ang-an to live out the remainder of his days as a political hostage.[60]

T'ai-tsung also undertook diplomatic efforts to weaken the Western Turks, who, since their split from their Eastern brethren at the beginning of the Sui, controlled much of the vast region stretching from Kansu in the east to Sassanid Persia in the west, and from Kashmir in the south to the Altai mountains in the north. In 634 this empire was divided at the Ili River into eastern and western halves controlled by rival federations of tribes. By recognizing the legitimacy of first this khan, then that anti-khan, the emperor was able to exacerbate tribal discord still further. The Western Turk empire was eventually reunited by a chieftain who had received T'ai-tsung's backing and who then began sending tribute to Ch'ang-an as a symbol of his submission to China.[61]

The destruction of the Khanate of the Eastern Turks and the reduction to vassalage of the Western Turks were soon followed by T'ang

---

pp. 6019–20, T'ai-tsung was able to overwhelm the Turks and force them to sue for peace; they withdrew shortly after signing a treaty on the Pien Bridge. But information in Wang Tang, *T'ang yü-lin* [A Forest of Anecdotes of the T'ang Dynasty] (ca. 1100; Taipei, 1959), ch. 5, p. 152, that the emperor followed the advice of Li Ching to "empty out the storehouses" to bribe the Turks into retreating, and T'ai-tsung's reference in Li's biography (*HTS* 93.4) to his "humiliation at the Wei River" (*Wei-shui chih ch'ih*), suggest that the Turks, not the T'ang, had emerged victorious from the Wei River confrontation. The discrepancies in the sources may once more reflect T'ai-tsung's emendation of the historical records.

[60]*HTS* 215A.12–14. See also René Grousset, *L'Empire des steppes* (Paris, 1939), pp. 138–40.

[61]See Edouard Chavannes, *Documents sur les Tou-kiue (Turcs) Occidentaux* (Paris, 1900), pp. 20–60; Grousset, *L'Empire des steppes*, pp. 140–42.

military thrusts into the Tarim Basin region of Central Asia, known to the Chinese as the Western Regions (*Hsi-yü*). The Western Regions, once part of the Han Empire, now comprises modern Sinkiang province. Its thriving oasis-kingdoms, some of which were inhabited by Indo-European peoples, were important to the T'ang because they lay astride and controlled the "silk" routes over which envoys and merchants from Central Asia, Persia, and the East Roman Empire travelled to China to offer tribute and to trade. Inevitably, control of these routes became a cornerstone of T'ang foreign policy. The first oasis fell to T'ang forces in 640. This was Kao-ch'ang, located near modern Turfan in north-eastern Sinkiang. Karashahr (*Yen-ch'i*) to the southwest, was taken in 644, as was Kucha (*Chiu-tzu*), located still further west, later that year. Shortly before his death, T'ai-tsung was able to establish the "Four Garrisons" (*ssu-chen*) of Kucha, Kashgar (*Su-le*), Khotan (*Yü-t'ien*), and Toqmaq (*Sui-yeh*), manned by permanent contingents of Chinese troops, to control the entire Tarim Basin and part of modern Russian Turkestan.[62]

As neighboring states and tribes to the north and west of the T'ang fell one by one under its dominion, T'ai-tsung revived a dream that had obsessed Sui Yang-ti during his last years: the conquest of Koguryŏ. Late in 642, the king of Koguryŏ was slain by one of his ministers, Yŏn Kae-so-mun (Chinese name, Yüan Kai-su-wen), who then seized the reins of power and ruled as a dictator. A year later Koguryŏ attacked Silla (*Hsin-lo*), a T'ang vassal state on the southeastern portion of the Korean peninsula and then cut off the road upon which it sent tribute to Ch'ang-an. T'ai-tsung now had his excuse to attack the errant kingdom. Despite bitter opposition at court, he decided to lead troops personally against the dictator and make this area of Korea a part of the Chinese empire for the first time since the early fourth century. But although the emperor mounted two invasions of Liaotung (the western-most territory of Koguryŏ) in 645 and 647, he found it impossible to strike deep into the Korean peninsula or to capture its capital, only decimating his armies in the process.[63] He died before launching yet another campaign scheduled for the summer of 649, having found Koguryŏ to be as elusive an objective as had Sui Yang-ti.

Despite this setback late in Chen-kuan, T'ai-tsung's reign as a whole

---

[62]Ise Sentarō, *Chūgoku seiiki keieishi kenkyū* [A Study of the History of China's Administration of the Western Regions] (1955; 2nd ed., Tokyo, 1968), pp. 178–201.

[63]See *CTS* 199A.3b–9: *HTS* 220.3–12.

represents a high-water mark in Chinese history. Beneficent government, administrative reforms and improvements, ameliorated economic conditions, and the reestablishment of Chinese suzerainty over
much of Asia created a degree of national well-being unknown in China
since the Han and seldom thereafter. This is the way a half century
afterwards one Confucian writer idealized the Chen-kuan period:

Therefore, officials were all of their own accord honest and cautious in their
exercise of power. The families of the nobility and ranks of the great surnames
and local elite all feared [the emperor's] awesome power and restrained
themselves, not daring to encroach upon the common people. Merchants
travelling in the wilderness were never again robbed by bandits. The prisons
were always empty. Horses and cows roamed the open country. Doors were
not locked. Repeatedly there were abundant harvests and the price of grain
fell to three or four cash per *tou*. None who travelled from the capital to Ling-
piao [modern Kwangsi and Kwangtung] or from Shan-tung to the Ts'ang-hai
[i.e., down the eastern coast] had to carry provisions, but could obtain them
on the road. Upon entering villages "east of the mountains," those guests
who were passing through would be generously supplied and well treated,
and sometimes when they departed they would be presented with gifts. There
was nothing like this since antiquity.[64]

Naturally, these formulaic phrases, the conventions of Chinese historiography, present a far too rosy picture of the age. The T'ang Standard
Histories and other sources describe natural catastrophes, economic
disasters, civil disorders, and related problems that plagued China
during Chen-kuan as they did during all periods of Chinese history.
Yet, relatively speaking, these were indeed halcyon days, and generations of Confucian commentators have been generous in their praise of
them.

It is the general consensus of these commentators that the great
achievements witnessed during T'ai-tsung's reign were the result not
only of the emperor's personal talents and wisdom, considerable though
these were, but also of the sage counsel and unflagging support he
received from his devoted circle of ministers. One such minister generally singled out for special praise as having been a major contributor to
the "good rule of the Chen-kuan reign" was the very man the emperor had rescued from certain political oblivion, perhaps even death.
This was, of couse, Wei Cheng. The contention of the eleventh-century

[64]*CKCY* 1.22–22b.

scholar, Sun Fu, that T'ai-tsung's triumphs owed in great measure to his acceptance of Wei Cheng's counsel,[65] and the claim of the twelfth-century writer, Lü Tsu-ch'ien, that the *Chen-kuan chih chih* was brought about solely because Wei advised the emperor to put benevolence (*jen*) and righteousness (*i*) into practice,[66] reflect to a considerable degree the mainstream of traditional Chinese opinion regarding Wei's role in T'ang history. The following chapters, which treat Wei's rise to bureaucratic eminence, his political beliefs, and his contributions to his age, assess the validity of these traditional assumptions.

[65] *T'ang-shih lun-tuan,* 1.5b–6.
[66] *CKCY* 2.8.

CHAPTER 5

The Mirror Bright: Wei Cheng at T'ai-tsung's Court (626-635)

When we first encountered Wei, he had begun wandering over the countryside seeking initially to further his education, cut short by the death of his father, and then to secure religious protection from the fierce civil strife that had propelled the Sui into headlong decline. Sometime afterwards, having doffed his Taoist robes and arming himself with theories of *Realpolitik,* he had joined the military contests of the late Sui under the successive banners of the rebels Yüan Pao-tsang and Li Mi. Still later, during the early T'ang, he had helped formulate the political and military strategies by which Crown Prince Chien-ch'eng attempted to block T'ai-tsung's efforts to gain the succession. Now, with T'ai-tsung's victory an inescapable reality, Wei was compelled to adopt an entirely new role shaped by vastly altered conditions in China.

By 626 the dynasty was at peace. No longer were rebel movements a cause for alarm in Ch'ang-an, and long-standing frictions between opposing court groups had largely been terminated by the Hsüan-wu Gate incident and T'ai-tsung's generous policy of clemency toward his former enemies. The emperor was faced with new tasks that demanded a shift from the formulation of piecemeal military strategies to comprehensive civil policy making for a united empire. New tasks also faced the emperor's officials. Wei's early career had been as a military-political official. Now he had to assume the role of a civil official during a time of peace and institutional reform.

Happily, Wei found it easy to make this abrupt transition, since, as we have already observed, one of his strongest points was an ability to adapt readily to changing circumstances. Indeed, Wei's versatility was impressive even by the standards of the Confucians, who held up for emulation the ideal of a talented generalist who copes effortlessly with a wide range of problems and situations. Previously we saw Wei in the capacity of T'ai-tsung's envoy to the northeastern plain. During the next sixteen years Wei successively (often concurrently) assumed the roles of remonstrator, bibliographer, historian, jurist, compiler, ritualist, encyclopedist, poet, and tutor to the crown prince, in addition to his regular duties in various organs of the central government. Wei's rapid rise in T'ai-tsung's bureaucracy owed in no small measure to his remarkable virtuosity, which was amply demonstrated from his very first days at the Chen-kuan court.

Of course, it was also fortuitous that Wei crossed T'ai-tsung's path at the moment the emperor came to power. The young monarch was still inexperienced in governing and gratefully welcomed men of Wei's abilities. During his first months on the throne, T'ai-tsung would often summon his erstwhile enemy to his bedchamber and ply him with questions concerning the personalities and policies of former rulers, the world as the Chinese then knew it, and affairs of state in general. Wei was greatly impressed by this sign of the emperor's esteem and consequently exhausted himself in offering him sage counsel, writing, it is said, more than two hundred memorials dealing with various and sundry matters.[1]

Scaling the Bureaucratic Ladder

Although Wei's initial rank under T'ai-tsung as a remonstrating counselor—fifth degree, first class[2]—was fairly low, early in Chen-kuan the post acquired great importance. This was because the remonstrating counselors were given the right to co-sign orders and edicts passing through the Three Departments and thus maintained what amounted to a veto power over policy. Wei's use of this power at the end of 626, shortly after his appointment as remonstrating counselor, provides a striking example of the limits that could be placed on imperial power during the early T'ang.[3] At this time, on the advice of

[1] *CTS* 71.3b; *HTS* 97.2; *TFYK* 549.7b–8. Commentators have often claimed that Wei memorialized T'ai-tsung a total of two hundred times during his entire career, but as Wang Hsien-ch'ien correctly points out (*WCLC* 8), Wei already memorialized this many times early in his association with the emperor. Most of these memorials are apparently now lost.

[2] *TTLT* 8.19b–20. The rank was elevated to fourth degree, second class later in the dynasty; des Rotours, *Traité des fonctionnaires*, 1: 143, n. 3.

[3] Hu San-hsing, *TCTC* ch. 192, p. 6027, wonders if Wei Cheng, in the capacity of a remon-

the official Feng Te-i, the emperor had authorized the conscription into the army of all males in the adolescent (*chung-nan*) class aged eighteen to twenty-one *sui*.[4] Normally, only those who were twenty-one *sui* and above, in the full adult (*ting*) class, were liable to conscription. When the order was drafted Wei refused to co-sign it, raising strong objections:

I hear that if you drain a pond while fishing, you will indeed obtain fish, but the following year there will be no fish; and that if you burn the forests while hunting, you will indeed capture animals, but the following year there will be no animals. If those who are *chung-nan* and older are completely conscripted into the army, then how will we obtain taxes and corvée?[5]

Despite T'ai-tsung's repeated efforts to persuade Wei to co-sign the order, he remained adamant, and the emperor finally decided to abandon his scheme.

The privilege of co-signing edicts for remonstrating counselors was probably short-lived. But early in 627 the emperor began ordering remonstrating officials (*chien-kuan*), a generic term that included remonstrating counselors, to follow officials of the third rank and above when they entered the council chambers (*shang-ko*) for deliberations with the emperor and to criticize the proceedings when they felt some error had been committed.[6] Thus, throughout T'ai-tsung's reign, remonstrating counselors had a strong and independent, if largely negative, voice in the formulation of policy.[7]

---

strating counselor, could have been given the responsibility of co-signing edicts, which was normally reserved for the grand secretaries of both the Secretariat and Chancellery. Sun Kuo-tung replies that at this early date in the T'ang, when the functions of the Secretariat and Chancellery had not yet been fixed, the co-signing responsibility was exercised by various officials; "T'ang-tai san-sheng chih," 54.

[4]During the early T'ang, when a male reached the age of twenty-one *sui* he was classified as an adult, or *ting*. He was then entitled to a full allotment of land under the equal-field system, at the same time becoming liable to tax and labor service and also military conscription under the militia (*fu-ping*) system. The *chung-nan* class was comprised of males aged sixteen to twenty-one *sui*. *Chung-nan* were liable to miscellaneous labor and other special services but were not ordinarily liable to conscription into the militia. However, *chung-nan* eighteen *sui* and older received full allotments of land just as if they were *ting*; see *HTS* 51.2; *THY* ch. 85, p. 1555; Denis Twitchett, *Financial Administration*, pp. 25–26, 125. Since the *THY* (ch. 85, p. 1556) and the *CKCY* (2.37) make it clear that T'ai-tsung's order applied only to *chung-nan* eighteen *sui* and above, it is possible that Feng Te-i and the emperor felt that since these males received adult portions of land they should also shoulder adult obligations, such as militia service.

[5]*WCKCL* 1.3–3b.

[6]*TCTC* ch. 192, p. 6031.

[7]See Sun, "T'ang-tai san-sheng chih," 25.

Sometime during 626, probably soon after returning from his mission to the northeastern plain, Wei was promoted to right assistant in the Department of Affairs of State (*shang-shu yu-ch'eng*), with the rank fourth degree, second class; he continued concurrently to occupy the post of remonstrating counselor.[8] The Department was, early in the T'ang, by far the most powerful organ of government, controlling not only the Six Boards but also the nine Courts and five Directorates. The most important officials in the Department, the left and right vice-presidents, were also at this time the most prestigious officials in all the empire, an importance plainly reflected by their rank, the insignia they wore, and the deference paid them by the other chief ministers.[9] The assistants of the left and right were the second most important officials in the Department. Their responsibilities were to superintend the Department's internal affairs and, when necessary, to investigate and take disciplinary action against any official working there. The jurisdiction of the two assistants was divided; as right assistant, Wei's control extended over the Boards of War, Punishments, and Public Works.[10]

Yet Wei's duties were probably even broader than this. Although his superiors, the left and right vice-presidents, were supposed to supervise the activities of the Department, they actually had little time to devote to this responsibility. Early in the dynasty the vice-presidents were regular chief ministers and played key roles in the formulation of policy at court and at the Hall of Government Affairs. Since T'ai-tsung also delegated to them the additional time-consuming duties of recommending and recruiting officials for the bureaucracy, all routine matters in the Department were transferred to the two assistants.[11] Despite the great avalanche of work which descended on the Department during these years, Wei and his colleague, the left assistant Tai Chou, evidently were able to keep the bureaucratic machinery there functioning quite smoothly, for even years afterward their tenures in office were remembered with warm praise.[12]

In the autumn of 627 northern China was hit by an unseasonal frost that destroyed much of the harvest, already greatly diminished by

[8]*HTS* 97.2. The listing of Wei's office as left assistant in *CTS* 71.3b is erroneous; see *WCLC* 8. The exact date of Wei's appointment is unknown, but in *CTS* 2.13b he is already a right assistant in the ninth month of 627.

[9]Sun, "T'ang-tai san-sheng chih," 37.

[10]*HTS* 46.5; Sun, "T'ang-tai san-sheng chih," 31–32.

[11]Sun, "T'ang-tai san-sheng chih," 37–38.

[12]*CTS* 74.1b; *CKCY* 3.16; *CTW* 151.1b.

summer drought and insects. Accordingly, T'ai-tsung promulgated an edict in which he announced that imperial envoys would be sent out to the region of modern Shansi and Honan provinces along various routes to visit all the affected prefectures. The right assistant Wei Cheng is listed as one of these envoys, but we do not know to which route he was assigned. According to the edict, the emissaries were to determine how much of the population lacked grain and speedily memorialize the exact figures to the government so that it could proceed to offer relief.[13]

By early 629 Wei had once again been promoted, this time to the post of director of the Department of the Imperial Library (*pi-shu chien*), with the rank of third degree, second class. But more important, at the same time he received the special title *ts'an-yü ch'ao-cheng*, signifying that he could now participate in the deliberations of the council of state at the Hall of Government Affairs along with the regular chief ministers.[14]

During his tenure at the Imperial Library, Wei became involved in two major endeavors that did much to preserve and extend China's impressive heritage of scholarship and historiography. As director, Wei was in charge of the imperial archives, the largest and most comprehensive collection of written materials in the empire. The Sui had begun to recover, chiefly through purchases from private collections, some of the many works in the imperial collection that had been lost to fire and destruction during the Period of Disunion.[15] A good deal of their efforts was negated, however, by two crushing setbacks. During the T'ang siege of Loyang, Sui administrative and other records stored there were destroyed wholesale by the "rebel" Wang Shih-ch'ung, and, if this were not enough, eighty to ninety percent of the remaining Loyang records slipped beneath the water at the Sanmen Rapids on the Yellow River as the T'ang attempted to transport them to Ch'ang-an.[16] During Wu-te, Wei Cheng's predecessor at the Imperial Library, Ling-hu Te-fen, had begun to restore the collection, a task that Wei was left to finish. Soon after taking office he memorialized the throne suggesting that scholars be assigned to classify the holdings of the Imperial Library

[13]*CTS* 2.13b; *TFYK* 144.1b–2.

[14]The title *ts'an-yü ch'ao-cheng* was first employed in the case of Tu Yen, who in 627 was appointed president of the Board of Civil Appointments (*li-pu shang-shu*), a post which did not normally confer chief-minister status on its holder. Wei Cheng was the second T'ang official so designated.

[15]See Liu Po-chi, *T'ang-tai cheng-chiao shih*, pp. 108–09.

[16]*TCTC* ch. 189, p. 5916; *SuiS* 32.6b–7.

according to the Chinese four-part classification of literature (classics, history, philosophy, writings of individuals), and to produce definitive editions of various works, a project that was completed only after a number of years.[17]

About the same time Wei embarked upon an even more important scholarly undertaking as the general editor of the Standard Histories of no fewer than five former dynasties. During much of the Period of Disunion historiography had been sadly neglected. Historical sources gradually had become lost and scattered in the course of the destruction of successive regimes, a trend which, as we have just seen, continued during the civil wars of the late Sui and early T'ang. In 621 Kao-tsu was warned that materials for certain dynasties were already growing so scarce that it soon would become impossible to compile their histories. Late the next year, therefore, he announced the commencement of the largest historiographical project ever undertaken in China, before or since, which was intended to compile the histories of six dynasties—the Northern Wei, Liang, Ch'en, Northern Ch'i, Northern Chou, and Sui[18]—and appointed two or three officials, concurrently holding posts in the central government, to supervise the compilation of each. Wei Cheng, then assistant in the Department of the Imperial Library, was assigned as a supervisor of work on the *Ch'i-shih*, the history of the Northern Ch'i.[19] Because of bickering among the chief compilers and a general lack of coordination among the historians, the entire project was eventually abandoned.

In 629 T'ai-tsung resumed the historiographical project begun by his father at the urging, it is said, of Wei Cheng. At the same time, the emperor adopted Wei's suggestion that work not be continued on the compilation of the *Northern Wei History*, a version of which had earlier been completed by Wei Shou.[20] In order to avoid a repetition of the organizational problems that had beset the project under Kao-tsu, the emperor appointed Fang Hsüan-ling and Wei as supervisor and general editor, respectively, to control and coordinate the historians' work.[21] "What was to be included and excluded all depended on [Wei's] judg-

[17]*CTS* 71.4; *HTS* 97.15; *TFYK* 608.27b.
[18]Kao-tsu's edict is in *CTW* 2.12–13.
[19]*THY* ch. 63, p. 1090–91; *TFYK* 556.10b–11.
[20]*WCKCL* 5.8b; *HL* 2.2. Cf. the biography of Ling-hu Te-fen (*CTS* 73.12), which records that this decision was reached jointly by the compilers.
[21]*CTS* 73.12; *WCKCL* 5.9.

ment. His additions and deletions were numerous; they were [respectively] as brief and objective as possible."[22] This time the work, which occupied Wei's attention on and off for seven years, went far more smoothly. Annals and biographies of the histories of the Liang, Ch'en, Northern Ch'i, Northern Chou, and Sui dynasties were presented to the throne in the first month of 636.[23]

The project headed by Fang and Wei represented nothing less than a revolutionary development in Chinese historiography. Prior to the T'ang, Standard Histories were usually compiled by semi-professional historians who had access to materials in the imperial archives and to other official sources but who generally labored in a private capacity. The work of these historians was occasionally commissioned by the government; more often it was undertaken on their own initiative and only later awarded an official imprimatur. Under T'ai-tsung, however, a bureau of historiographers was especially established inside the palace city to compile the histories of former dynasties.[24] The writing of Standard Histories was thus brought under the supervision and control of the central government where it remained, with minor exceptions, down to the present century.

Beyond discharging his responsibilities as general editor of this grand historiographical project, Wei became the chief compiler of the Sui History,[25] personally contributing its "Monograph on Literature" (ching-chi chih),[26] as well as the prefaces (hsü) and discussions (lun) for its basic annals and biographies.[27] Compiling the Sui History must have been a great challenge, as materials for that dynasty were in particular disarray and there were many lacunae. To compensate for a lack of sufficient data on the dynasty, Wei and his associates were forced to ransack collections in private libraries and interview members of families

[22]WCKCL 5.9.

[23]CTS 3.6; THY ch. 63, p. 1091.

[24]See William Hung, "The T'ang Bureau of Historiography before 708," Harvard Journal of Asiatic Studies, 23 (1960–61), 93–107.

[25]For a history of the compilation of the Sui History, see SKCSTM 45.53–55b. Although Wei's name is attached to the work, other officials played important roles in its compilation, among them K'ung Ying-ta, Yen Shih-ku, and Hsü Ching-tsung.

[26]See SKCSTM 45.53b and Étienne Balazs, Le traité economique du "Souei-chou" (Leiden, 1953), pp. 6–7. The contents of the "Monograph" are analyzed by Balazs on pp. 303–07. Presumably Wei had become well acquainted with this body of literature as director of the Department of the Imperial Library.

[27]WCKCL 5.9; CTS 71.6.

with previous ties to the Sui—an attempt at oral history.[28] They even visited a Taoist magus famed for his memory in the hopes of supplementing their meager resources.[29]

Wei also contributed the general discussions (*tsung-lun*) for the basic annals sections of the Liang, Ch'en, and Northern Ch'i histories, and directed the compilations of all the monograph (*chih*) sections of the five histories then being compiled.[30] These were first published separately as the *Monographs of the Histories of the Five Dynasties* (*Wu-tai-shih chih*) early in Kao-tsung's reign.[31]

Although Wei's duties as director of the Department of the Imperial Library and editor of the historiographical project must have occupied a considerable amount of his attention, he appears to have found the time to accept still other weighty responsibilities from the emperor. One of these was the compilation of a work known as the *Essentials of Government from Divers Books* (*Ch'ün-shu chih-yao*), in fifty *chüan*, presented to the throne in 631, which contained selections from the classics, history, and philosophy illustrating extraordinary behavior on the part of a wide variety of people—good and bad rulers, loyal and disloyal ministers, virtuous women, scoundrels, and so on—from legendary antiquity up to the Chin dynasty.[32] If T'ai-tsung read the book daily, Wei promised in his preface to the work, it would be as if a fine mirror were forever hung in front of him by which he could guide his conduct.[33]

The same year in which the *Essentials of Government from Divers Books*

[28]*WCKCL* 4.4–4b; *HL* 1.17–17b.

[29]See the biographies of Sun Ssu-mo, *CTS* 191.9b and *HTS* 196.5b. They have been translated by Nathan Sivin, *Chinese Alchemy: Preliminary Studies* (Cambridge, Mass., 1968), pp. 81–144.

[30]*WCKCL* 5.9; *CTS* 71.6. Wei's name is appended to the "remarks of the historian" sections in *LS* 6.8, *Ch'enS* 7.7, and *PCh'iS* 8.17.

[31]*SKCSTM* 45.54b.

[32]*THY* ch. 36, p. 651. The work is also known as the *Ch'ün-shu cheng-yao* and *Ch'ün-shu li-yao*; see *WCKWC* 3, p. 29; Liu Su, *Ta-T'ang hsin-yü* 9.1–1b; and *CTW* 9.3b. The change of title appears to have occurred during the reign of the third T'ang emperor, Kao-tsung, whose taboo name was Chih; *Gunsho jiyō* [Ch'ün-shu chih-yao] (Tokyo, 1941), "kaisetsu" section, p. 1. The work is attributed to "Wei Cheng and others," and Wei contributed its preface, but the major portion was probably compiled by three other officials, of whom the most notable was Hsiao Te-yen; see the "t'i-yao" section, *Ch'ün-shu chih yao* (631; *Ts'ung-shu chi-ch'eng* ed., Shanghai, 1936), p. 1; Wang Ying-lin, comp. (1223–96), *Yü-hai* [The Sea of Jade] (Che-chiang shu-chü ed., 1883), 54.27b–28b; *KSSI* 1.29–29b. Of the original text, forty-seven *chüan* still survive in a number of editions, including one published in Japan in 1787.

[33]*WCKWC* ch. 3, p. 30.

was completed, T'ai-tsung decided to reconstruct a ceremonial building known as the *Ming-t'ang* ("Hall of Light"), which, as tradition has it, was first built by the culture-hero Shen Nung. The ancients had conceived of the *Ming-t'ang* as a cosmic house, a model of the Universe. T'ai-tsung's performance of ritual within the structure would have symbolized his great temporal power and his harmonious relationship with the forces of Nature.[34] Several officials, among them Wei Cheng, were charged with drawing up blueprints for its construction based on what was known about earlier designs. Since the hall had not been built for many centuries prior to the T'ang and concrete plans were lacking, Wei, like his colleagues, could only be rather vague about what precise form it should take: "I request that you erect a storied building of five halls, round above, square below. . . ."[35] In the end the project was abandoned, only to be revived again during the reigns of Kao-tsung and Empress Wu.

The following year, at T'ai-tsung's request, Wei compiled a work called *A Record of Good and Evil of Feudal Princes and Rulers since Antiquity* (*Tzu-ku chu-hou-wang shan-o lu*) in two *chüan*, which was intended to provide T'ai-tsung's sons with hortatory and minatory examples from China's long past to help guide them in their own conduct. It was far shorter and more limited in scope than the earlier *Essentials of Government from Divers Books*, but it must have contained a generous sampling of illustrations serving to underscore Wei's ideas on good government. Unfortunately, only the preface to the work now survives. Here Wei emphasizes his belief that human actions, not fate, ultimately determine the success or failure of any ruler.[36]

During the same period, Wei lent his hand to writing verses for the music played during the Sacrifice to Heaven, which T'ai-tsung performed on a round altar at the time of the winter solstice. The poems, probably of no great literary interest, still survive.[37]

Wei's labors on these numerous projects did not go unrewarded. In the fifth month of 632, after more than three years as director of the

---

[34]See William Edward Soothill, *The Hall of Light, A Study of Early Chinese Kingship* (London, 1951), and Arthur F. Wright's brief treatment of Sui Wen-ti's efforts to build a *Ming-t'ang* in "The Formation of Sui Ideology," p. 90.

[35]*WCKWC* ch. 2, p. 24; also *THY* ch. 11, pp. 271–72.

[36]*CKCY* 4.11b–13; *WCKWC* ch. 3, pp. 30–31; *HTS* 58.19, 59.2b.

[37]*THY* ch. 9A, p. 143. Wei's poetry is collected in the *Wei Cheng-kung shih-chi* and in *CTShih*, *han* 1, *ts'e* 8.

Department of the Imperial Library, he was promoted to the post of acting president of the Department of the Imperial Chancellery (*chien-chiao shih-chung*), with the rank second degree, first class. At the same time, his noble rank in Chü-lu was sharply increased to duke of a commandery (*chün-kung*), second degree, first class, with the revenues from two thousand families to nourish him in addition to his official salary.[38] Why Wei was only appointed acting president is unclear, but in the third month of 633, when his friend Wang Kuei was dismissed as one of the two presidents of the Chancellery for leaking confidential information, Wei was named to replace him.[39] As president, a post he served in until 636, Wei became one of the regular chief ministers.

If any further proof of Wei's administrative versatility was necessary, it came shortly after this new promotion. Because of legal intricacies, several cases had long clogged the agenda of the Department of Affairs of State. Hoping to rectify this situation, T'ai-tsung appointed Wei to render judgment on them. Although, as his biographies note, Wei was "not accustomed to legal practices, because he preserved the great principles and judged the cases by the circumstances (*ch'ing*, that is, human factors), everyone was pleased to submit [to his judgments]."[40]

WEI CHENG AS REMONSTRATOR

If you were to try to give water a flavor with water, who would care to partake of the result? If lutes were to be confined to one note, who would be able to listen to them? Such is the insufficiency of mere assent. (*Tso-chuan*, Duke Chao, 20th year)

From Wei's rapid rise up the T'ang bureaucratic ladder and the reliance T'ai-tsung placed on him in numerous areas of administration, the reader might well infer that he had entered into a deeply harmonious relationship with the emperor. Yet nothing could be further from the truth. Indeed, the tense confrontation between T'ai-tsung and Wei that took place immediately following the Hsüan-wu Gate incident was merely the first of many during what would be a frequently strained

---

[38]*HTS* 2.9b, 97.4; des Rotours, *Traité des fonctionnaires*, 1: 43. Although the *HTS* does not mention it, Wei was promoted to *chün-kung* of Chü-lu, the title Wei bears in his *Chiu-ch'eng-kung li-ch'üan ming* [Inscription on the Sweet Spring of the Chiu-ch'eng Palace] (632; reproduction of a stone rubbing of the original, Tokyo, 1966).

[39]*CTS* 71.5b; *HTS* 2.9b; *TCTC* ch. 194, p. 6102. Ssu-ma Kuang is wrong in still listing Wei as president of the Department of the Imperial Library.

[40]*CTS* 71.5b; *HTS* 97.5.

and stormy relationship, for Wei was as different from the emperor in personality and temperament as anyone could be.

Wei was not cast in a heroic mold. His physical appearance, as we learn in one of his biographies, was in no way more remarkable than that of an ordinary man.[41] He was, moreover, afflicted with an eye ailment, probably cataracts, which by the middle years of Chen-kuan was severely hampering his vision.[42] Almost twenty years T'ai-tsung's senior, his dry and humorless manner must have made him seem even older to the emperor. In addition to all of this, he was conspicuously frugal, even though successive high offices and titles of nobility gave him the wherewithal for a comfortable life, and was a stern moralist forever preaching the virtues of diligence and moderation in all things. He was, in fact, a living rebuke to every extravagance T'ai-tsung might conceive of.

Wei was also a man of unyielding principles and scorned those around him who based their attitudes on changing circumstances rather than on immutable norms. In his piece of rhyme-prose, "Fu On a Cypress in a Taoist Monastery," Wei depicts a tree whose development had been stunted by a dense overgrowth of vines and brambles. The fu is instructive because it deals with a quality Wei greatly admired and respected— steadfastness. While other varieties of trees and grasses bloomed with the spring rain and withered with the winter snow, he observed, only the cypress in the monastery garden did not change. In the spring it did not try to emulate the beauty of the peach and plum trees, and in the dead of winter, when the wind whirled and snow was everywhere, it watched the decline of all things without losing its greenness. "It still flourishes, standing alone and erect. Because its value lies in there being no change in its basic nature, it may be compared with a chün-tzu."[43]

Wei and the cypress are probably one and the same. His own worth as a minister, he believed, derived from his adherence to principles of government that were universally sound and that did not have to be altered to suit changing circumstances. At the same time, he often felt stifled at court by men of mediocre talents and weak convictions who ran with the times but who, nevertheless, often won T'ai-tsung's ear. These men are symbolized in his fu by the brambles that stunted the

[41]HTS 97.15.
[42]WCKCL 5.10b.
[43]WCKWC ch. 3, p. 39.

growth of the cypress and prevented it from reaching its full height and splendor.

Whereas Wei was steadfast to principle, T'ai-tsung cleaved only to those principles—and a changing lot they were—that contributed to the success of his administration and the glory of his house. He practiced frugality when the country was impoverished, but once China's economic health had been restored, he was eager to embark upon the construction of ornate palaces and public works. He eschewed foreign adventurism when China was militarily weak but later pursued policies of aggressive diplomacy and warfare to bring far-flung peoples under Chinese dominion. He paid lip service to the law but often tried to bend the law to serve his selfish interests. It was perhaps inevitable that the flexible and pragmatic T'ai-tsung and the narrow and rigidly principled Wei Cheng would repeatedly clash over questions of national policy, court affairs, and the emperor's personal conduct.

Despite his own ordinary appearance, Wei remained unawed by T'ai-tsung's imperial bearing and was completely unafraid of him. Wei's plucky defiance of the emperor was a consequence of the supreme confidence he placed in his own convictions, convictions that were in turn grounded on the lessons taught by China's most recent and vivid historical experience, the fall of the Sui dynasty. As Wei's "discussion" section for the Yang-ti Annals in the *Sui History* makes abundantly clear, he believed that Emperor Yang's two most unpardonable sins were excessive reliance on his own abilities and hyperactivity.[44] Emperor Yang had ignored the advice of his loyal officials and had charted his own course. He had been overambitious in undertaking grandiose public works projects and disastrous foreign military campaigns. He had thereby squandered the rich legacy bequeathed him by his father, the Sui founder, exhausted his political credit among the people, and been destroyed. Wei was deeply concerned that T'ai-tsung, the son of the T'ang founder, would ignore the lessons of history and repeat the mistakes of his Sui counterpart.

The Sui experience had taught Wei that the first priority of T'ai-tsung had to be the consolidation of T'ang power. (Although he makes no mention of it in any of his extant memorials, Wei surely knew that the great Han house had spent eighty years strengthening its defenses

---

[44]See *SuiS* 4.16b–18, "remarks of the historian" section.

and gathering its economic forces before embarking upon a program of military expansion.) Consolidation was for Wei not simply a military matter. Above all, it meant winning the allegiance of the people, who represented the proverbial water that either supported or capsized the ship of state. The people's allegiance would be gained only by sincerely attending to their livelihood; their livelihood would be improved only by returning China to prosperity; and prosperity would be regained only by healing the economic wounds of the past two decades with the soothing balm of tranquility. Frugality not prodigality, retrenchment not expansion, and peace not war—these had to be the policies of the time. And he, Wei Cheng, would act as a watchdog over the emperor, whose success or failure in implementing these policies would determine the fate of the fledgling dynasty.

Moreover, Wei was keenly aware that during the formative period of a dynasty precedents and patterns were set that would affect the tone and conduct of government for generations to come. During his own time, decisions that were being made regarding the legitimate bounds of imperial authority, the proper modes of imperial conduct, and the degree of civil official participation in policy making would furnish precepts for the remainder of the T'ang. If the dynasty were long to endure, he believed, imperial power had to be contained and the *chün-ch'en* (ruler-minister) system of shared authority in government, only recently restored after close to four centuries of rule by military might, terror, and inherited privilege, had to be vigorously reaffirmed.

Wei's chief weapon in his campaign to ensure the longevity of the T'ang was remonstrance. There is general agreement among Chinese commentators that Wei's most important and valuable role under T'ai-tsung was as a critic of imperial policy, a view summed up rather well in the words of the twelfth-century scholar Ts'ai K'an:

I have heard that a ruler who accepts remonstrance is a sage and that an official who offers remonstrance is loyal. Since the Three Dynasties [of Hsia, Shang, and Chou], as for rulers who accepted remonstrance none surpassed T'ang T'ai-tsung, and as for officials good at remonstrating none surpassed Wei Cheng. T'ai-tsung employed his extraordinary military genius to defeat the beleaguered Sui and to drive off all the bandits; the pacification of the empire was [thus] an insignificant affair. But the "good rule of the Chen-kuan reign" (*Chen-kuan chih chih*), which nearly matched that of [the golden age of the Chou kings] Ch'eng and K'ang, was not something T'ai-tsung could bring about all by himself. He was able to bring it about because of the power of Cheng's remonstrances.[45]

Admittedly, the materials on Wei now available to us are weighted in favor of his role as remonstrator. Because of such works as Wang Fang-ch'ing's *Recorded Remonstrances of Duke Wei of Cheng* we know far more about the motivations behind and contents of Wei's remonstrances than about any other of his numerous governmental activities. It is neverthe-less also clear that Wei's enormous aptitude and zeal as a remonstrator, which formed the basis of his fame even in his own time,[46] is precisely the reason why so many of his remonstrances were preserved following his death.

By early T'ang times remonstrance was a tradition already well over a millenium old.[47] In the *Analects*, Confucius rhetorically inquires, "How can he be said to be truly loyal, who refrains from admonishing the object of his loyalty?"[48] and warns that the wrong policies of rulers must be opposed by loyal officials or else their regimes will fall into ruin.[49] Mencius in his turn adds, "He who restrains his prince loves his prince."[50] The ancient Chinese chronicles are replete with examples of officials who bravely remonstrated with their princes, some of whom paid dearly for their efforts with their lives. At an early time, then, a pantheon of worthies famed for admonishing their sovereigns without regard for their own personal safety had been created in China that served to inspire later remonstrators like Wei Cheng.

During the Ch'in and Han, the practice of remonstrance was gradu-ally regularized and institutionalized; in both dynasties there were officials whose duty it was to criticize and protest, when necessary, their ruler's policies and personal behavior and to advise him on ways in which to better his government. During the T'ang, such officials were known as *chien-kuan,* or remonstrating officials. They were thirty-two in number (there may have been fewer remonstrating officials during Wei

---

[45] *Ting-chai chi* (n.p., 1897), 1.1.

[46] For example, see the appraisal of Wei's contemporary, Wang Kuei, *TCTC* ch. 193, p. 6084.

[47] On the practice of remonstrance, see Charles O. Hucker, "Confucianism and the Chinese Censorial System," in *Confucianism in Action,* David S. Nivison and Arthur F. Wright, eds. (Stanford, 1959), pp. 193ff.

[48] *Analects* 14.8. See Waley, *Analects,* p. 181.

[49] *Analects* 13.15 and 14.23; Waley, *Analects,* pp. 175, 186.

[50] *Mencius* 1.2. Legge, *The Chinese Classics,* vol. 2, *The Works of Mencius,* p. 161.

Cheng's time) and were divided equally between the Departments of the Imperial Secretariat and Chancellery.[51] The offering of remonstrance was not, however, a privilege limited solely to the remonstrating officials. Although Wei Cheng was a remonstrating counselor (one of the *chien-kuan* posts) during the period 626–29, even afterwards, in every post in which he served, he continued to send to the throne a continuous stream of pungent criticism.

Early in Chen-kuan, T'ai-tsung repeatedly called on his subordinates to criticize his rule, but even he must have been quite aghast at the uninhibited zeal with which Wei Cheng threw himself into the task. Wei's remonstrances—well-reasoned, to the point, and packed with appropriate classical and historical allusions for added potency—often produced a devastating effect on the emperor. The imperial visage would darken, and others at court would tremble in fear, but we are told that Wei always stood his ground and that T'ai-tsung, having publicly asked for these bitter pills of criticism, had to swallow them with as much grace as he could muster.

An interesting parallel might be drawn in this context between Wei Cheng and the type of bureaucrat Anthony Downs has dubbed "the zealot." According to Downs, zealots seek power not only for its own sake but also for the opportunity of putting into practice relatively narrowly conceived policies and concepts, what he calls their "sacred policies."[52] Downs' description of the zealot model fits Wei Cheng's bureaucratic personality astonishingly well:

[Zealots] are extraordinarily energetic and aggressive. These traits are evidenced by their willingness to promote their sacred policies in the face of seemingly overwhelming obstacles. Moreover, because they are "inner directed" in character, they continue to promote their own views even when most of their colleagues and associates—including their superiors—vehemently disagree with them. Many seem to relish conflict situations, even when vastly outnumbered. In fact, because of their "gadfly" roles in bureaus, many zealots develop an aggressive outspokenness that irritates most other types of officials. Finally, they are fanatically loyal to their sacred policies, which they

[51]Eugene Feifel, *Po Chü-i as a Censor* (The Hague, 1961), pp. 31–32, lists the titles and ranks of the various remonstrating officials. Although Feifel calls Po a "censor," it should be noted that Po filled the post of reminder of the left (*tso-shih-i*), and thus was one of the remonstrating officials rather than a member of the Censorate. See also Charles O. Hucker, *The Censorial System of Ming China* (Stanford, 1966), pp. 16–19.

[52]*Inside Bureaucracy* (Boston, 1967), p. 88.

promote at every opportunity, no matter what official position they occupy or what circumstances they are in.[53]

For Wei Cheng, dynastic consolidation and civil official preeminence in government were "sacred policies."

So anxious was Wei to begin plumping for these policies that he appears to have written the very first of his remonstrances to T'ai-tsung while still on the road during his mission to the northeastern plain late in 626. In it he warned the emperor not to postpone a previously announced decrease in taxes and corvée lest he forfeit the people's confidence.[54] Soon after Wei's second mission to the countryside, this one to offer relief after the frost of 627, he began to press the view that what the people needed most was a long period of tranquility in which to recover economically from the wounds of the past two decades. Stressing the need to maintain peace at all costs, he urged T'ai-tsung to refrain from triphammer responses to military threats and instead to seek alternate means of resolving differences with enemies of the throne both domestic and foreign.

Thus, when several reports arrived from Ling-nan (modern Kwangsi and Kwangtung provinces) late in 627 that the roads there had been cut off and that a former rebel of "barbarian" blood, Feng Ang, was again planning to revolt against the throne, Wei attempted to head off a military expedition T'ai-tsung began planning against Feng. In his remonstrance Wei pointed out that Ling-nan was far from Ch'ang-an and that transporting supplies for the army would be a serious problem. He maintained, too, that there were no clear signs that Feng actually planned to revolt and suggested that T'ai-tsung send a commission of inquiry instead of an army. The emperor took his advice.[55] When the T'ang envoys arrived, Feng sent a son back to Ch'ang-an with them to act as a hostage.[56] Wei was further vindicated some years afterwards when Feng visited the court himself and led troops for the T'ang against the rebellious Lao tribes of southern China.[57]

Similarly, in 627 when news reached Ch'ang-an that the Eastern Turks had been greatly weakened by natural calamities and revolts by subject tribes, Wei attempted to dissuade the emperor from heeding

[53]Ibid., p. 102.
[54]*WCKCL* 1.1–2b.
[55]Ibid. 1.7b–9b; *CKCY* 9.2–2b.
[56]*TCTC* ch. 192, pp. 6038–39; *TFYK* 164.17b.
[57]*TCTC* ch. 193, p. 6092.

the exhortations of his generals to attack them by predicting that Hsieh-li Qaghan, their leader, would soon be destroyed by his own folly:

Long ago, Marquis Wen of Chin asked Li K'o who among the Feudal Princes would perish first. K'o answered, "Wu will perish first." Marquis Wen inquired, "For what reason?" K'o replied, "Because when he fought he was repeatedly victorious. If one repeatedly fights the people grow exhausted. If there are repeated victories the ruler grows arrogant. When an arrogant ruler rules an exhausted people, how can he not perish? At the end of the Sui, when China was disordered, Hsieh-li relied upon his multitude to invade our land and even today has still not stopped. This is why he will be destroyed."[58]

On this occasion the emperor agreed with Wei. Nevertheless, at the end of 629 T'ai-tsung launched large-scale military expeditions that effectively destroyed the Eastern Turk Khanate. The court then began a long debate over the problem of how to dispose of the Turkish tribal remnants. The emperor eventually adopted the plan of Wen Yen-po to resettle the Turks inside the borders of China in the hopes that they would become farmers, absorb the civilizing influences of Chinese culture, and thus cease to menace the T'ang.[59] At the same time, he ignored Wei's warning that the Turks would constitute "a disease in the heart and belly of China" and that the T'ang was "raising a tiger to bequeath itself calamity."[60] Much to T'ai-tsung's regret, Wei's dire prediction came true scarcely nine years later, when one of the resettled Turks, the brother of T'u-li Qaghan, made an abortive attempt to revolt against the throne. T'ai-tsung then ordered the Turks speedily returned to their steppe homeland. By this time, though, the Hsüeh-yen-t'o, who had earlier succeeded in shaking off Turkish overlordship and had occupied much of their former masters' old territory, fiercely resisted their return, driving them back into China. T'ai-tsung eventually succeeded in resettling the Turks beyond the Great Wall, but not before he had ruefully recalled Wei Cheng's prophetic words of warning.[61]

The problem of imperial policy and its economic consequences for the peasantry rose once again in conjunction with tribute missions that were scheduled to pass through the northwestern portion of China in

[58] WCKCL 3.1b. CKCY 8.19 gives Marquis Wen of Wei instead of Chin.
[59] TCTC ch. 193, pp. 6075–77. See also THY ch. 73, pp. 1311–14; CKCY 9.14–17b.
[60] See Wei's remonstrance, WCKCL 2.8b–10b.
[61] TCTC ch. 195, pp. 6147, 6148–49.

630. Late that year the king of Kao-ch'ang, Ch'ü Wen-t'ai, and his consort planned to make a state visit and present tribute at the T'ang court.[62] Before their arrival, many other oasis-kingdoms of the Western Regions, whose nominal suzerains, the Western Turks, were being weakened by internal strife, also requested to send tribute to Ch'ang-an. The kingdoms were worried that if Kao-ch'ang alone sent tribute, China would favor it at their expense in future diplomatic relations. Pleased by the requests, the emperor appointed a "barbarian" in the employ of the T'ang, Ya-tan Ho-kan, to journey to each of the kingdoms and escort their tribute missions to court.

On the grounds that the people of the border districts through which the missions would pass could not bear the burden of supplying them, as was the custom, without compensation from the government, Wei objected to the plan. Abuses had occurred earlier, he noted in his remonstrance, when Kao-ch'ang sent tribute to court during Wu-te. The problem would surely be compounded now that many kingdoms were sending missions at the same time. As a solution, Wei suggested a practical but highly unorthodox alternative by which he rejected the typical Confucian bias against profit making. His plan was that the kingdoms not present tribute at court but instead be permitted to open trade fairs on the frontier so that the people might profit from them. T'ai-tsung accepted the recommendation and sent a messenger to instruct Ya-tan Ho-kan to return to Ch'ang-an.[63]

Economic arguments were also at the root of Wei's opposition to T'ai-tsung's decision to perform the Feng and Shan sacrifices. These sacrifices, performed on the summit and at the base of Mount T'ai, a high peak in central Shantung province, were a symbolic announcement to Heaven and Earth that the ruler's tasks on earth had been successfully accomplished. Because of their great ritual significance and the fear of most Chinese rulers that performing them would constitute an act of hubris, they had not been carried out since the heyday of Han power and self-confidence.[64] During the Wu-te period, Kao-tsu had refused the petitions of his officials to perform the Feng and Shan rites, as did T'ai-tsung in 630 and 631.[65] But the following year, when Fang

[62]*HTS* 221A.8b.
[63]*WCKCL* 1.14–14b; see also *CTS* 71.4; *TCTC* ch. 193, pp. 6083–84.
[64]See Edouard Chavannes, *Le T'ai chan* (Paris, 1910), pp. 16–21.
[65]*THY* ch. 7, pp. 79–80; *TCTC* ch. 193, pp. 6086, 6090; *CTS* 3.2b.

Hsüan-ling, Wang Kuei, and others reminded the emperor that the
Eastern Turks had been conquered and the harvests were increasing,
and again pressed him about the sacrifices, he finally consented. This
brought a swift rebuke from Wei Cheng:

Your Majesty's merit is indeed high, but the people do not yet receive your
benefits. Your virtue is indeed substantial, but it does not flow everywhere.
China is indeed at peace, but it does not yet serve you sufficiently. Distant
barbarians emulate us, but we cannot satisfy their requests. All kinds of
suspicious omens have arrived, but you have sought them too ardently. The
yearly harvests are abundant, but the granaries are still empty. This is why
I humbly consider that [the Feng and Shan] would be improper. I cannot
make a remote comparison, but let me take a man as an illustration. Today
there is a man who after continuously suffering a disease of ten years' duration
has been treated till almost cured. Now he is scarcely more than skin and
bones, barely alive. If you wanted him to carry a *shih* of rice on his back for
one hundred *li* in a day, it certainly would be impossible. The Sui disorder
was not merely one of ten years. Being a good doctor, Your Majesty has cured
that illness. But although we are already at peace, conditions are not yet
wholly satisfactory. I really doubt that you can announce your accomplishments to Heaven and Earth.[66]

This time T'ai-tsung was persuaded to call off the Feng and Shan,[67]
but further discussions were held on the rites in 637, and they were again
scheduled for 641. Wei appears to have continued his resistance to them
even then. On one occasion of unknown date, when T'ai-tsung again
raised the possibility of travelling to Mount T'ai, Wei caustically
observed:

[The success of] emperors and kings lies in their virtue and not in their
performance of the Feng and Shan. From the time of the [Sui] disorder, the
prefectures and counties around Mount T'ai were damaged most severely. If
your carriages were to travel there, you could not entirely be without servants
[from among the people]. This, then, would be laboring the common people
because of the Feng and Shan.[68]

---

[66] *WCKCL* 2.17–17b. See also *CTS* 71.16–16b; *THY* ch. 7, pp. 80–81; *TCTC* ch. 194, pp.
6093–94; *CKCY* 2.40b–41.

[67] There are two versions of what T'ai-tsung's attitude toward the Feng and Shan was at
this time: the first, that he did not want to perform the sacrifices but was being encouraged
by his officials to do so; the second, that he himself wanted to perform them; *TCTC* ch. 194,
p. 6094, *k'ao-i* section.

[68] *WCKCL* 4.19–19b; *HL* 1.26; *THY* ch. 7, p. 81.

The sighting of a comet in 641 was taken as an ill omen and the ceremonies were cancelled. Although rescheduled for 648 they were post-
poned once again, and T'ai-tsung ended his rule without performing
them.[69]

Superficially, Wei's opposition to the tribute missions from the
Western Regions oases and to the Feng and Shan sacrifices appears to
have been motivated by a traditional Confucian concern—the economic
hardships they would have posed for the common people. Yet it is
also significant that both the tribute missions and sacrifices, particularly
the latter, would have lent an enormous amount of prestige to the
throne and to T'ai-tsung himself. Perhaps at the bottom of Wei's
disapproval was a fear that both these events, had they taken place,
would have raised the position of the throne so far above that of the
bureaucracy that it would have become increasingly difficult for
subordinates to continue to exert a strong restraining influence over
the emperor.

Indeed, there are clear signs that by the early 630s Wei had already
become worried about what he viewed as a growing arrogance, laxity,
and moral turpitude in the emperor's behavior. By this time the borders
of China were secure and the country was tranquil. The Eastern Turks
had been reduced to impotence, relations with the Western Turks were
generally favorable, and T'ai-tsung had yet to begin his conquest of
the Tarim Basin region. The economy had improved markedly and the
storehouses were bursting with grain. Yet paradoxically, Wei believed,
just such conditions posed a grave threat to a ruler. History had repeatedly demonstrated that many monarchs had commenced their reigns
with great promise, only to lapse soon afterwards into a state of careless-
ness and neglect born of self-satisfaction. Destruction in such cases was
never far off. As it was written in the *Book of Odes (Shih-ching)*, "All are
[successful] at first, But few prove themselves to be so at the last."[70]
From this time forward, Wei's remonstrances indicate that he was
detecting signs that compared with the early years of Chen-kuan, T'ai-
tsung's administration, his relations with his officials, and his personal
conduct, all had begun to deteriorate.

Although initially T'ai-tsung had been modest in his tastes and had

[69] *TCTC* ch. 196, p. 6168, ch. 198, pp. 6245, 6248.

[70] Legge, *The Chinese Classics*, vol. 4, *The She King*, p. 505, slightly emended. On the use of
this theme in Wei's writings, see below, pp. 176–78.

eschewed large public works projects, all this changed with improvements in China's economic situation. Now he would often leave Ch'ang-an on long hunting expeditions or entertain his ministers in lavish style at the T'ai-chi Hall, where there would be elaborate entertainments and much drinking. In 631 the emperor embarked upon a prolonged period of palace renovation and reconstruction. First, he renovated and refurbished the Sui Jen-shou Palace and made it his summer retreat. Next, he made plans to reconstruct the huge Sui palace complex at Loyang. On this occasion, the president of the Board of Finance (*min-pu shang-shu*), Tai Chou, remonstrated, pointing out that the available labor force in the empire had already been depleted because of military requirements along the northern border in Shensi and the recent work on the Jen-shou Palace. He concluded that additional corvée would place too heavy a burden on the people. Nevertheless, T'ai-tsung ignored his counsel and proceeded apace with the reconstruction work.[71]

Even more disconcerting to Wei, it appeared that the emperor was no longer accepting with any equanimity the criticism of his officials. This message was brought home with particular force early in 632, when T'ai-tsung stormed out of court in a rage and returned to his chambers, crying, "I'm going to have to kill that old country bumpkin!" When Empress Chang-sun, T'ai-tsung's consort and devoted confidante, inquired why he had become so upset, he heatedly replied, "Wei Cheng is always insulting me at court!" This time, as on other occasions, the empress defended Wei for his uprightness and succeeded in dispelling her husband's wrath.[72]

Yet it was plain that although T'ai-tsung still occasionally paid lip service to the idea of remonstrance, he had begun to chafe at public disapproval of his administration; so much so, that when a local official in Honan, Huang-fu Te-tsan, sent in a memorial charging that, among other things, construction work on the Loyang palace was overworking the people and that taxes were too high, T'ai-tsung exploded in anger. He accused Huang-fu of slander and made plans to try him before the court. Naturally, Wei Cheng was at pains to uphold the right of all officials to remonstrate:

From ancient times memorials which have been presented to the throne for the most part have been provocative. If they had not been provocative, then

[71] *TCTC* ch. 193, p. 6088; *THY* ch. 30, p. 551.
[72] *TCTC* ch. 194, p. 6096; also *HL* 2.37.

they would not have aroused the ruler. This type of provocation resembles slander, but there is a saying that "A sage can select even the [good] words of a madman." Your Majesty should therefore select [his good words]. It would be improper to reprimand him.[73]

On this occasion Wei's soothing words persuaded T'ai-tsung to reward his critic rather than to punish him.

There were signs, too, that the emperor, compared to the early part of Chen-kuan, was no longer showing sufficient respect toward his officials and was denigrating their positions relative to other groups at court. In 632 T'ai-tsung was incensed to learn that members of the imperial harem had been moved out of a local official's residence upon the arrival of two court officials, Li Ching and Wang Kuei, who were then ensconced in their place. He immediately ordered that the local official who had perpetrated the offense be investigated for prosecution. Ever sensitive to imperial encroachment on the prerogatives of the official class, Wei Cheng interceded on behalf of the accused and persuaded the emperor to drop the whole matter. He noted in passing that Li and Wang were T'ai-tsung's highly trusted officials, while the harem ladies were no more than "sweeping servants" of the empress and that their respective positions could in no way merit comparison.[74] The next year Wei was again compelled to come forward to remonstrate against the emperor's order that another official be beaten with one hundred strokes of the bamboo and dismissed from office. The official, Hsüeh Jen-fang, had detained for questioning in a civil suit the father of one of T'ai-tsung's son's concubines. The son had then lodged a complaint against Hsüeh before the emperor. This case also ended in victory for Wei, after he warned T'ai-tsung about the evils of allowing relatives by marriage of the imperial house (wai-ch'i) to interfere with the law.[75]

There was also the troubling matter of T'ai-tsung's increasing disregard for the rules of Chinese etiquette (li). One of the gravest breaches of decorum by the emperor concerned a beautiful girl of fifteen or sixteen sui who had so caught his fancy that he made plans to make her his concubine. Possibly unknown to him, the girl had previously been betrothed to a commoner. The order to fetch the girl had

---

[73]WCKCL 1.13; also TCTC ch. 194, p. 6109.
[74]WCKCL 1.14b–16.
[75]Ibid. 2.3–4b.

already been given and the envoy was about to leave, when Wei Cheng rushed into the palace, crying:

Your Majesty is the parents of the people and you love the common folk as you do your own sons. You ought to worry about what worries them and be happy about what makes them happy. Since ancient times virtuous rulers have regarded the minds of the people as their own minds. Therefore, because the ruler lives in fine palaces he wants the people to have the security of roofbeams [above their heads]. Because he eats rich fare he wants the people to be without the miseries of hunger and cold. Because he desires imperial concubines he wants the people to know the joys of family life. This is the normal way of rulers of men. Now for a long time the daughter of the Cheng family has been betrothed to another, yet Your Majesty is taking her in disregard of this fact. If this be broadcast throughout the empire, would it be in accord with the morality of the parents of the people? What I have heard has perhaps not yet occurred, but I fear that [if it should] it would harm your great virtue and thus I dare not conceal my feelings. Because the ruler's actions must be recorded, I want you to consider the matter especially carefully.[76]

Playing on T'ai-tsung's concern over his historical image had the desired effect, for the emperor stopped the envoy and personally wrote an edict castigating himself.

In remonstrances of similar substance, Wei successfully protested against the emperor's decison to present one of his favorite daughters a larger wedding gift than he had given his own elder sister (who was higher in rank), and against T'ai-tsung's acceptance as tribute of two dancing girls sent by the kingdom of Silla.[77] Wei regarded both of these cases as serious breaches of etiquette.

If some of Wei's remonstrances involve what strikes us as relatively frivolous matters, we might remember that according to Confucian belief the ruler was an exemplar for his subjects and therefore had to be a paragon of wisdom and righteousness, and that it was incumbent upon all officials to assist their ruler in attaining the virtues of the sages of old. As far as Wei was concerned, no matter, however minor, which reflected badly on his prince could be allowed to pass without reproach.

[76]Ibid. 2.1b–2; see also *HTS* 97.3; *TCTC* ch. 194, pp. 6108–09. *CKCY* 2.34b dates this episode in the year 628, but as Wang Hsien-kung points out in *WCKCL* 2.2, by means of the titles of several officials mentioned in the text, the episode can be dated at about 634, the date given by the *TCTC*.

[77]*WCKCL* 1.16–17b; 2.23–23b.

SWEET SPRING AND SWEET DEW

The intense moral fervor and blunt manner with which Wei Cheng pursued his "sacred policies" did not endear him to all of his colleagues. There were those officials, perhaps veterans of the Prince of Ch'in Office, who resented seeing Wei, with his tainted record of service to the late crown prince, gain T'ai-tsung's favor and successive promotions. As early as 627, just after Wei assumed his post as right assistant in the Department of Affairs of State, his enemies were already beginning to make attempts to defame his character. At this time, some unknown official memorialized the throne claiming that Wei was practicing nepotism. The emperor duly appointed the president of the Censorate (*yü-shih ta-fu*), Wen Yen-po, to investigate the matter. Wen reported back that although the nepotism charge was basically unfounded, Wei was nevertheless somewhat incautious in his official conduct (*pu-neng shu hsing-chi*, "incapable of displaying proper formal behavior," i.e., neglectful of the niceties of form), and thus had become the object of suspicions and unfounded allegations on the part of his fellow officials; for this reason Wen recommended that Wei be reprimanded.[78] T'ai-tsung did not personally reprove Wei but sent Wen in his stead.

When next in the imperial presence a few days later, Wei proved to be sharply critical of T'ai-tsung's doubts regarding his behavior, warning the emperor that the flourishing or decay of a dynasty depended not on whether the ruler and minister acted with proper form but on whether their actions were right. When T'ai-tsung expressed regret over the incident and voiced the (perhaps not wholly sincere) hope that this would not prevent Wei from continuing to criticize his administration, Wei quickly assured him that he had nothing to fear and went on to press his view that rulers had to tolerate opposition from their subordinates or else face dire consequences:

"Because I devote myself to the state and act with rectitude, I dare not deceive you. But I hope that Your Majesty will enable me to be a good official rather than a loyal official." T'ai-tsung asked, "Are 'good' and 'loyal' any different?" [Wei] replied, "Good officials are those like Chi, Hsieh, and Kao Yao [ministers to the sage-emperor Shun]. Loyal officials are those like [Kuan] Lung-feng and Pi Kan [put to death for their opposition by, respectively, Chieh and Chou, 'bad last' rulers of the Hsia and

[78]*HTS* 97.2. Varying versions of Wen's report are given in other accounts.

Shang]. Good officials cause themselves to gain fine reputations, their rulers to gain illustrious names, their descendants to continue in their footsteps, and the good fortune [of the state] to be without limit. Loyal officials are themselves executed, causing their rulers to commit grave crimes and their states and families all to perish, leaving behind only their names. This is why I say that they are not at all alike."

To show Wei that he bore him no ill-feelings, the emperor rewarded him with one hundred rolls of silk.[79]

Later, sometime during his tenure as director of the Department of the Imperial Library (629–32), Wei was accused of the far more serious crime of plotting revolt against the throne. The different manner in which T'ai-tsung dealt with this accusation as compared with the way he dealt with the previous one reveals the extent to which he had in the meantime come to trust Wei. Upon receiving the accusation he cried, "Although Wei Cheng formerly was Our enemy, We selected and employed him because of his loyalty to those whom he served. Why then [does anyone] falsely create such slander?" He thereupon ordered the accuser beheaded without further inquiry.[80]

It is apparent, moreover, that despite the tension between emperor and minister that had arisen early in the 630s, both parties still hoped that a more harmonious relationship might be restored. One reflection of this hope can be seen in a composition now known as the "Inscription on the Sweet Spring of the Chiu-ch'eng Palace" (*Chiu-ch'eng-kung li-ch'üan ming*),[81] written by Wei in the summer of 632 when he accompanied T'ai-tsung on his annual summer retreat to the Chiu-ch'eng ("Nine Perfections") Palace, the renovated and renamed Jen-shou Palace of the Sui, nestled in the T'ien-t'ai Mountains about one

[79]*WCKCL* 5.1–2; see also *CKCY* 2.39–40; *CTS* 71.3b–4; *HTS* 97.2–2b; *TCTC* ch. 192, p. 6040; *THY* ch. 58, pp. 597–98. This is one of the most widely quoted of all of Wei Cheng's speeches. The *CKCY* is erroneous in placing this episode in the year 632.

[80]*CKCY* 6.18b; here Wei's accuser is not named. *WCKCL* 5.2b–3 and *HL* 1.29–29b note that someone named Huo Hsing-pin once accused Wei of involvement in a plot to revolt, prompting T'ai-tsung to accuse Huo of prevaricating and to order him sentenced for his crime. Although there is no internal evidence with which to date the episode, Wang Hsien-kung (*WCKCL* 5.3; *HL* 1.29b) suggests that the Huo Hsing-pin episode is identical to that recorded above. This seems likely, but in Harada Tanashige, *Jōkan seiyō teihon* [Authoritative Edition of the *Chen-kuan cheng-yao*] (Tokyo, 1962), pp. 193, 194, the two episodes are treated as completely independent. In Harada's version, however, the Huo Hsing-pin episode is dated 637 and Wei is listed as assistant in the Department of Affairs of State, a post he held between 627–29, thus making matters hopelessly confused.

[81]The complete text is found in *WCKWC* ch. 3, pp. 33–35.

hundred miles north of Ch'ang-an. The event that allegedly prompted
the work was the "discovery" by T'ai-tsung and Empress Chang-sun of
an underground spring on the palace grounds, where no water, it is said,
previously existed. T'ai-tsung then appointed Wei to commemorate the
occasion in writing.

The "Sweet Spring Inscription," the best known of Wei's literary
works, contains two sections: a long preface and a shorter formal text.
Wei begins the preface by extolling the cool and refreshing qualities that
made the Chiu-ch'eng Palace such a fine summer retreat, continuing
with extravagant praise for T'ai-tsung's many accomplishments since
coming to power, particularly his military conquests and his great
frugality—"he combs his hair with the wind and washes with the rain,"
etc. There follows upon this a description of the new palace with a
hyperbolic emphasis on the simple and unadorned style of the T'ang
reconstruction. In narrating the discovery of the spring, Wei describes
its virtues in rich detail:

Its clearness is like a mirror, its taste like sweet wine. . . . The transparent
waves billowing up from it can cleanse that which is defiled, can lead one to
nourish his correct nature, and can purify the spirit. It reflects the myriad
forms and waters the myriad things. With profound generosity it never dries
up, but flows continuously like the primeval swamp (*yüan-che*). Not only is
this the best of natural phenomena, it is also a spiritual treasure.[82]

There was a millenia-old tradition in China concerning the sweet
spring, suggesting that its discovery by the emperor and empress may
have been nothing more than a literary fiction. Like the fall of sweet
rain in season or the settling of sweet dew, the discovery of a sweet
spring was a sign that Heaven sent down when the governance of men
was just and the empire was harmonious.[83] Thus, as Wei points out in
the preface, the discovery of the spring was not just an accident:

The *Li-wei*[84] says: "If kings punish with death those who are truly criminal
and reward with gifts those who are truly meritorious, and behave according

[82]Ibid. ch. 3, p. 34.

[83]See, for example, *HS* 22.26–26b: "As the spirit (*shen*) glides, sweet dew falls and felicitous
clouds gather round." During the Ch'in dynasty, Shih-huang-ti built a Sweet Spring detached palace that was later rebuilt by Han Wu-ti. Perhaps one might note here that T'ai-
tsung and his empress are together alleged to have discovered the spring; thus the yin and
yang are in harmony.

[84]A work in three *chüan* allegedly annotated by Cheng Hsüan (127–200), but lost by the
time the *Sui-shu* "Monograph on Literature" was compiled; see *SuiS* 32.31.

to the code of etiquette (*li*), then a sweet spring will emerge from their palace halls." The *Ho-kuan-tzu*[85] says: "If a sage's virtue reaches Heaven above and Earth below, and reaches all things in between, then a sweet spring emerges. . . ."[86]

The formal text consists mainly of yet another paean to T'ai-tsung's accomplishments, favorably comparing the benefits he was bestowing on the Chinese people with those flowing from the sweet spring.

Having blocked the performance of the Feng and Shan sacrifices, Wei was now celebrating in literature what he had previously denied the emperor in the Feng and Shan ritual—an acknowledgment that T'ai-tsung had brought peace to the empire and that the people were content. Characteristically, however, he closed on a rather somber note. After praising his prince, he could not resist warning him against complacency and arrogance:

Occupying a high position, you must think of falling from it. Holding a full [vessel], guard against it overflowing. Think on this, rest your mind on this,[87] and you will forever be able to preserve good fortune.[88]

After Wei presented his composition, Ou-yang Hsün, one of the finest calligraphers of the age, copied the text, which was then inscribed on a stone monument more than three Chinese feet wide and more than seven Chinese feet high.[89] Rubbings from this monument are still extant and are employed as models by students of calligraphy in both China and Japan to this day.

In the same vein, later that summer, while feasting at the Chiu-ch'eng Palace, Wei extravagantly toasted T'ai-tsung's accomplishments and wisdom:

As for Your Majesty spreading a great transformation [over the people] and pacifying the empire, we may say that these achievements have already been completed. But I always notice that even during unusually auspicious times

[85]A largely Taoist work traditionally dating from late Chou times, but containing many additions of later date. It purports to represent the philosophy of a native of the state of Ch'u, of unknown name, who wore a cap made of pheasant feathers, thus giving rise to the name Ho-kuan-tzu, or "Feather-cap Master."

[86]*WCKWC* ch. 3, p. 34.

[87]*Nien tzu tsai tzu*; from "The Counsels of the Great Yü" (*Ta-Yü mo*) of the *Book of History*; Legge, *The Chinese Classics*, vol. 3, *The Shoo King*, p. 58.

[88]*WCKWC* ch. 3, p. 35.

[89]Wang Ch'ang, comp., *Chin-shih ts'ui-pien* [Collected Essays on Bronze and Stone Monuments] (1805; Shanghai, 1921), 43.5b.

you very urgently consider the possibilities of peril. From ancient times even the wisest of men do not surpass you in this.[90]

The emperor may well have been mollified by such efforts to regain his favor. A short time afterwards, at another banquet for his officials, he went out of his way to defend Wei against his detractors by observing: "People say that Cheng's behavior is rude. This really is not so. When We observe what he does, We only think of its attractiveness."[91] Two years later, the emperor once again demonstrated to the court that despite mounting disagreement between Wei and himself over his personal behavior and policy making, he still regarded Wei as a valued and loyal servitor of the throne. At this time the emperor was appointing a group of grand commissioners of promotion and demotion (ch'u-chih ta-shih) who were to go out on circuit and investigate the conduct of local officials. He could not find a sufficient number of qualified candidates for the job, however, and an opening remained in the circuit for the capital district. Accordingly, the left vice-president of the Department of Affairs of State, Li Ching, recommended Wei Cheng. T'ai-tsung, who had been preparing for another summer retreat at the Chiu-ch'eng Palace and had intended, as usual, to take Wei along with him, darkened and said:

Our wanting to go to the Chiu-ch'eng Palace is also not a trifling matter. Would you rather We send Wei Cheng [on circuit]? Whenever We travel, the reason We do not want to be separated from him is that he sees Our good and bad points and never keeps anything hidden from Us. Now if We follow your advice and appoint him to go, if We have faults, would you be able to correct them?

Consequently, he did not appoint Wei.[92]

Naturally, the emperor's support of Wei Cheng against his enemies was not completely altruistic. Wei was the kind of upright and sincere minister whose very proximity reflected well on any sovereign. He was a manifest symbol of T'ai-tsung's open quest for advice and criticism from his subordinates and could therefore be expected to help furnish the emperor with a good image for the Confucian historians. He could be counted upon to cast his critical eyes in all directions at court, and

[90] WCKCL 3.9.
[91] Ibid. 5.5b; also TCTC ch. 194, p. 6098.
[92] WCKCL 5.7; also TCTC ch. 194, p. 6105; THY ch. 78, p. 1419; HL 1.30b–31.

thus keep check not only on his prince but on his colleagues as well. His independent nature made it unlikely that he would ever ally with others for selfish ends. Finally, his untiring and efficient work in numerous areas of government made him invaluable during a time when T'ai-tsung had not yet become fully confident of his own administrative capabilities.

Yet, there was an inherent weakness in Wei's position at court. His place was predicated on the assumption that the emperor would continue to remain dependent on his subordinates, willing to accept their advice and criticism to the same extent that he had during his early years on the throne. As Wei already began to perceive early in the 630s (and it became even more obvious as time wore on), this was not to be the case. Sadly and ironically, like the careers of the many ill-fated men Wei was so fond of holding up to his prince as minatory examples, his own career at T'ai-tsung's court would not fare as well in the end as it had in the beginning.

CHAPTER 6

The Mirror Tarnished: Wei Cheng at T'ai-tsung's Court (635-642)

Despite Wei Cheng's advancing age (he was fifty-five years old in 635) and deteriorating state of health, the second half of his career with T'ai-tsung was nearly as crowded with promotions, rewards, and miscellaneous assignments as the first. Yet at the same time Wei was faced with the gnawing knowledge that his relationship with the emperor was continuing to worsen and that his influence over imperial policies was steadily waning. Contributing to this state of affairs were various factors. By the mid 630s, the form of the T'ang administrative system had become fairly stable. As the bureaucratic machinery began to function relatively smoothly and precedents were established, there was far less room for the kind of political maneuvering, such as the *chung-nan* veto, than had been possible for Wei to engage in earlier.[1] At the same time, T'ai-tsung was occupied far less with details of administration building and far more with policy making. He was more experienced, had a keener understanding of the political structure at his court and of the way of manipulating it, and so was increasingly able to act independently of his advisers. Equally important, T'ang power had by now been largely consolidated, and the empire was enjoying unparalleled prosperity. Whereas the ever-cautious Wei Cheng persisted in repeating ad nauseum the themes of frugality and peace, T'ai-tsung, exhilarated by the dynasty's economic recovery and the growth of its military might, was now intent on manifesting the glory of his house by means of public works and foreign conquest. In short, his goals and those of Wei Cheng had grown increasingly divergent.

[1]See Michel Crozier, *The Bureaucratic Phenomenon* (Chicago, 1964), chap. 6, for the hypothesis that bureaucratic power belongs to those officials capable of exerting discretion in areas of administrative uncertainty, and that routinization and bureaucratic formalization eliminate those areas of uncertainty.

135

One event which may have had a profound effect on the emperor and the style of his administration was the death of his father in the fifth month of 635. Following his abdication, Kao-tsu had become a retired monarch in fact as well as in name and, beginning in 629, had passed a cloistered life in the Ta-an Palace, to the west of the palace city.[2] There, on rare occasions, he would entertain T'ai-tsung, Empress Chang-sun, and various court officials. Very little is known of the relationship between Kao-tsu and T'ai-tsung during the period following 626, but there are signs that the ill will generated between father and son before the Hsüan-wu Gate incident was never completely dissipated. In 632 the examining censor (chien-ch'a yü-shih) Ma Chou observed that Kao-tsu's living quarters at the Ta-an Palace were cramped, and that although the palace was close to the emperor's residence, T'ai-tsung had not visited his father in quite some time. He also charged that when T'ai-tsung moved to his summer retreat at the Chiu-ch'eng Palace, he left his father behind to suffer the heat of Ch'ang-an.[3] Two years later, T'ai-tsung finally extended invitations to Kao-tsu to spend the summer at the Chiu-ch'eng Palace, but the former emperor excused himself on the pretext that it had once been the residence of Sui Wen-ti. T'ai-tsung then began construction on the Ta-ming Palace to the northeast of the palace city for his father to reside in, but Kao-tsu grew ill while it was under construction and died before setting foot in it.[4]

A further sign of T'ai-tsung's coolness toward his father was the modest scale of the tomb he constructed upon the latter's death. Following some lively debate at court concerning the size it should take,[5] Kao-tsu's tomb, known as the Hsien-ling and designed by the architect Yen Li-te, was constructed on a slightly elevated plateau about fifty feet high, some forty-three miles to the northeast of Ch'ang-an.[6] The unimposing elevation of the Hsien-ling would not have caused much

[2]THY ch. 30, p. 549. The Ta-an Palace had been Shih-min's residence during Wu-te. Also see Bingham, "Li Shih-min's Coup," 269.

[3]CTS 74.7–8; TCTC ch. 194, pp. 6094–95; THY ch. 30, p. 549.

[4]TCTC ch. 194, pp. 6106–07. See also Li Shu-t'ung, T'ang-shih k'ao-pien, pp. 164–65.

[5]See THY ch. 20, pp. 393–95.

[6]See Lin T'ung, T'ang Chao-ling shih-chi k'ao-lüeh [A Brief Investigation of the Stone Records of the T'ang Chao-ling] (1697; Ts'ung-shu chi-ch'eng ed., Shanghai, 1939), ch. 1, p. 4; Adachi Kiroku, Chōan shiseki no kenkyū [A Study of Ch'ang-an Historical Remains] (Tokyo, 1933), pp. 247–48 and end map; Shih Chang-ju, "Han-T'ang ti kuo-tu ling-mu yü chiang-yü" [Capitals, Tombs, and Frontiers in the Han and T'ang], Ta-lu tsa-chih [The Continent], 6 (1953), 247.

comment at court—after all, Kao-tsu had decreed that he and his successors were all to be buried in modest style[7]—had not T'ai-tsung been so unrestrained in the selection of a site for his own final resting place. This was a mountain almost one thousand feet high, located approximately fifty miles to the northwest of the capital. Here, a veritable tomb city, known as the Chao-ling and once again designed by Yen Li-te, soon took shape, coming eventually to contain the graves of the emperor and more than one hundred and sixty early T'ang personages: the empress, T'ai-tsung's sons and daughters, other members of the imperial family, and high civil and military officials of the Chenkuan period, including Wei Cheng.[8] Of all the T'ang imperial tombs, the Chao-ling was the most grandiose in conception.

The first occupant of the Chao-ling was T'ai-tsung's beloved consort, Empress Chang-sun, who died in the sixth month of 636. Since on a clear day from Ch'ang-an one could see the mountain on which the tomb was situated, the grieving emperor had a lookout tower constructed from which to view it. Shortly after the empress's interment, T'ai-tsung invited Wei Cheng to accompany him in ascending the tower. Wei viewed the vast discrepancy in scale between the Hsien-ling and the Chao-ling as a blatant expression of T'ai-tsung's unfilial attitude, which was a cardinal sin in Confucianism. Thus, upon reaching the top of the tower, he pretended that he could not make out the Chao-ling, using his old eye ailment as a pretext. In exasperation, T'ai-tsung finally pointed out the Chao-ling to him, at which point Wei craftily exclaimed, "Ah, that is the Chao-ling. . . . I thought Your Majesty was viewing the Hsien-ling. If that is the Chao-ling, I certainly can see it!" Upon hearing these words, it is said, T'ai-tsung shed tears and had the tower destroyed.[9]

Kao-tsu's death, then, was probably a source of relief to his son; while alive, the father was an ever-present reminder to the court of T'ai-tsung's role at the Hsüan-wu Gate, his usurpation of the throne, and the subsequent period of bitterness between the two. Moreover, the passing of both his father and his wife must have brought home to the emperor with great force the realization that the old guard had

---

[7]See *CTS* 63.2–2b.

[8]See Lin T'ung, *T'ang Chao-ling*, ch. 1, pp. 1–4; Adachi Kiroku, *Chōan shiseki*, pp. 249–55 and end map.

[9]*HTS* 97.5–5b; *TCTC* 194, p. 6123.

passed and that he was now, more than ever, "his own man." With this came an even further waning of official influence over the throne.

THE AUTUMN YEARS

If these developments served to diminish Wei Cheng's real power at court, the result was by no means apparent to the casual observer, since T'ai-tsung continued to promote his contentious minister and reward him generously for his services. Although the emperor was often at odds with Wei over matters of policy, he nevertheless seems to have considered it useful to keep Wei close by his side, probably reckoning that the political capital he would thereby gain among the Confucian literati at his court (and possibly among the Confucian historians of a later day) far outweighed the advantages of dismissing or demoting him.

In the first month of 636, Wei, along with Fang Hsüan-ling, presented the emperor with the completed annals and biographies for the five Standard Histories whose compilation they had directed since 629. It is clear from a reading of Wei's commentaries in the Liang, Ch'en, Northern Ch'i, and Sui histories that he believed the records compiled under his direction were intended not only to transmit an accurate account of past dynasties to future ages but also to provide a guide for T'ai-tsung's rule. For in them he continued to hammer away at his favorite themes: that warfare, even if it brought victory, was self-defeating;[10] that early rulers were industrious and frugal while their successors were indolent and allowed their passions free rein;[11] that when the influence of loyal Confucians in government waned, dynasties tended to decline;[12] and so on.

Michael C. Rogers has recently examined yet another Standard History compiled later in Chen-kuan, the Chin History (Chin-shu). According to Rogers, the compilers of the Chin History attempted to dissuade T'ai-tsung from pursuing his conquest of Koguryŏ by singling out Fu Chien (rg. 351–85) of the Former Ch'in dynasty and with prejudicial selection of facts, embellishment, and distortion, demonstrat-

---

[10]See, for example, Ch'enS 6.14b, where Wei uses the same quote he employed in attempting to prevent T'ai-tsung from attacking the Eastern Turks in 627 (see above, p. 122). For a fuller discussion of Wei's opposition to offensive warfare, see chapter 8.

[11]See, for example, PCh'iS 8.18.

[12]See, for example, SuiS 75.2b–3b.

ing how his warlike ambitions eventually destroyed his house.[13] Similarly, in his desire to draw strong object lessons from the past with which to instruct his prince, Wei Cheng frequently allowed his own moral concerns to distort his history. His view, for example, that the main flaws of Emperors Wu and Yüan of the Liang dynasty and Hou-chu of the Ch'en dynasty (all political failures) stemmed from their degenerate fondness of literary elegance, is patently absurd.[14] Nevertheless, Wei's historiographical work received high praise from his contemporaries.[15]

For his labors on the grand historiographical project Wei received a number of generous rewards: the honorary title *tso-kuang-lu ta-fu*, second degree, second class; the noble title *Cheng-kuo-kung*, Duke of Cheng principality, which was first degree, second class and just below the ranks of the imperial family members; and two thousand rolls of silk.[16] As duke of a principality, Wei now had at his disposal, in addition to his official salary and emoluments, the tax receipts of three thousand families.[17]

But the following month Wei went to the Liang-i Hall to request that he be released from his duties as president of the Chancellery, a post he had held since the third month of 633. He pointed out that the eye ailment he had long suffered from had lately worsened: "If daylight is even a bit obscured, I cannot see anything more than a few steps away. ... Now that the empire is at peace and able men are as numerous as trees [in a forest], there is no need for a sick man long to remain at the center of things."[18] He therefore asked to be released from his other responsibilities and to be given a post as minister without portfolio. In this way, he observed, he could continue to remain at T'ai-tsung's side and advise him on matters of state. Etiquette demanded that the emperor go through the motions of expressing reluctance at accepting the resignation of such a loyal and upright official:

Don't you see that while in a mine metal has no value? It is only when it is smelted and forged and made into an implement that people all value it. Now

---

[13]See Michael C. Rogers, *The Chronicle of Fu Chien: A Case of Exemplar History* (Berkeley, 1968), pp. 1–73, especially pp. 40–46.

[14]See Mou Jun-sun, "T'ang-ch'u nan-pei hsüeh-jen," 52–56.

[15]*CTS* 71.6.

[16]Ibid.; *WCKCL* 9.5b.

[17]des Rotours, *Traité des fonctionnaires*, 1:43.

[18]*WCKCL* 5.10b.

We liken Ourself to metal and regard you as a skilled workman who molds Us. Although you are ill you are not yet decrepit, so why do you want to resign?[19]

In the end, Wei prevailed—at least partially. In the sixth month T'ai-tsung appointed him to the honorary office of *t'e-chin*, second degree, first class. But the emperor does not seem to have altogether released him from his other duties, for at the same time Wei received the new title *chih men-hsia shih*, "in charge of the Department of the Imperial Chancellery," and another designation, *ch'ao-chang kuo-tien ts'an-i te-shih*, which may merely have carried with it fewer responsibilities than normal for a chief minister.[20] Moreover, because T'ai-tsung appointed no successor to Wei as president of the Chancellery, it may be that he continued to function there on a reduced schedule.

Wei's eye ailment did not prevent him from participating in or, at the very least, lending his name to a host of literary and scholarly projects undertaken during the second decade of T'ai-tsung's rule, some of the most important of which were designed to determine 'the form and content of T'ang ritual. Chinese ritual, or *li*, embraced the code of etiquette governing social relationships and also the religious ceremonial by which dynasties ordered themselves in relation to the cosmos. Although for the sake of expedience the rites of the Sui dynasty had remained in effect at the beginning of the T'ang, the need for a distinctive and orthodox T'ang ritual soon became obvious.[21] Consequently, T'ai-tsung ordered the scholars of his court to examine previous works on ritual as well as the lengthy commentaries that usually accompanied them, with the intention of formulating a ritual code for his own house. Fang Hsüan-ling and Wei Cheng once more were chosen to supervise the scholars' labors. In 636 the two presented the emperor with what became the basis of the T'ang ritual code, the so-called *New Rites (Hsin-li)* in 138 sections.[22]

Two years later Wei helped fix the regulations governing the wearing

[19]*HTS* 97.5; also *TFYK* 331.10.

[20]*TFYK* 331.10–10b; *TCTC* ch. 194, p. 6119; *CTW* 5.24–24b; Sun Kuo-tung, "T'ang-tai san-sheng chih," 61–63. Sun (p. 63) points out that Wei was the only official during the T'ang to receive the *ch'ao-chang kuo-tien ts'an-i te-shih* designation.

[21]See, for example, the circumstances surrounding the memorial of Wei T'ing, *HTS* 98.15b–16.

[22]*TCTC* ch. 194, p. 6127; *THY* ch. 37, p. 669, and note of Su Mien, pp. 669–70. This code was emended during Kao-tsung's reign.

of mourning (which in Confucian China was dependent on one's relationship to the deceased),[23] and compiled yet another work on ritual known as the *Categorized Rites (Lei-li)*.[24] The *Categorized Rites*, in twenty *chüan*, was based on the *Record of Rites (Li-chi)*, which during the Han dynasty had been designated as one of the five Confucian classics.[25] Wei's interest in the *Record of Rites* was probably prompted by its popularity as a subject on the civil service examinations.[26] With a view toward simplifying its study, he systematized its rather formless contents into topical categories and included the best of earlier exegeses on the text. Upon presenting the *Categorized Rites* to the throne, he was rewarded with a thousand rolls of silk. Copies were then distributed to the heir apparent and the imperial princes; another was stored in the imperial archives.[27] If Wei had hoped that his *Categorized Rites* would become the basis for the civil service examinations, he was disappointed. The text was not published during his lifetime, perhaps a result of opposition from among the more conservative Confucian scholars at court, who may have opposed sacrificing the form of such a venerable scripture on the altar of practicality, and from the emperor himself, who may have felt that Wei's reworking of the text had placed too many constraints on the scope of imperial activity. In the end, during the reign of T'ang Hsüan-tsung (rg. 713–56), all copies of the *Categorized Rites* were destroyed at the instigation of the minister Chang Yüeh.[28]

[23]*CKCY* 7.16b; *THY* ch. 37, p. 673. See also Fujikawa Masakazu, "Tōdai (Jōkanki) fukuki kaisei ni okeru ni san no dōkō" [Some Tendencies in the System of Clothing Regulations of the T'ang Dynasty (Chen-kuan Period)], *Hambun gakukai kaihō* [Bulletin of the Chinese Literature Society], 17 (1957), 29.

[24]The *Lei-li* is known by various other titles, including *Tai-shih li* (*CTW* 9.3) and *Tz'u Li-chi* (*HTS* 57.8b).

[25]According to Han tradition, the *Li-chi* contains notes on ritual made by the followers of Confucius' disciples, to whom the rituals were transmitted orally. These notes then passed through several hands, the last being those of Tai Sheng, who early in the first century B.C. edited them and produced a work in forty-nine sections that presently constitutes the *Li-chi*. See Ch'en Shou-yi, *Chinese Literature, A Historical Introduction* (New York, 1961), pp. 74–78.

[26]See R. P. Kramers, "Conservatism and the Transmission of the Confucian Canon: A T'ang Scholar's Complaint," *Journal of Oriental Studies* (University of Hong Kong), 2 (1955), 121.

[27]*CTS* 71.15b; *THY* ch. 36, p. 651; *TFYK* 606.14; *WCKCL* 5.15b–16b; *HL* 2.6–6b.

[28]*WCKCL* 5.16–16b, note of Wang Hsien-kung. Okazaki Fumio, "Gi Chō hyōden" [Commentary on the Biography of Wei Cheng], *Rekishi to chiri* [History and Geography], 33 (1934), 14; Kramers, "Conservatism," 121–22. Kramer's article treats the efforts of the scholar Yüan Hsing-ch'ung (653–729) to gain official recognition for his sub-commentary to the *Categorized Rites* in the face of opposition by Chang Yüeh.

Apart from his work on ritual, Wei's energies were also absorbed by a variety of other tasks. In 638 he composed a literary piece now known as the "Ti-chu Inscription" (*Ti-chu ming*), written, according to one account, to celebrate T'ai-tsung's "abundant virtue" (*sheng-te*). The text was inscribed on the great Ti-chu rock on the occasion of an imperial visit to the Sanmen Rapids on the Yellow River in modern Honan province. Only a few characters remain of the original text, which appears to have survived until sometime during the Sung dynasty.[29]

Wei was also one of several compilers of an encyclopedic work called the *Wen-ssu po-yao*, presented to T'ai-tsung in twelve hundred *chüan* in 641.[30] Its contents are not known but were doubtless far ranging. Despite the encyclopedia's huge size, it was decided in 701 that the work was still incomplete and twenty-six scholars were assigned to supply it with yet more material; new sections—on Buddhism, Taoism, genealogy, and cities—were then added.[31] By the fourteenth century only one *chüan* of the entire work still survived,[32] and today just the preface by one of its chief compilers, Kao Shih-lien, remains.[33]

The titles of three more works by Wei Cheng are recorded in the sources, although we know practically nothing about them or the dates when they were written. They are the *Lieh-nü chuan-lüeh* (*Concise Biographies of Virtuous Women*) in seven *chüan*,[34] representing a traditional Chinese biographical genre; the *Shih-wu ts'e* (*Questions on Current Political Affairs*) in five *chüan*,[35] probably a collection of examination answers designed for the use of aspiring civil service candidates; and the *Sui-ching lieh-chuan* in one *chüan*,[36] the subject matter of which is unclear.

BRICKBATS AND BRAMBLES

The rewards Wei received as the result of all these endeavors, the vast prestige lent him by his high rank and titles, and the economic security

[29]Li Fang et al., comps., *T'ai-p'ing yü-lan*, 590.2; Wang Ying-lin (1223–96), *T'ung-chien ti-li t'ung-i* [Comprehensive Explanations of Geography in the *Comprehensive Mirror*] (*Chin-tai mi-shu* ed. of Mao Chin, 1628–44; Shanghai, 1922), 5.8; *KSSI* 2.12–12b.

[30]See *THY* ch. 36, p. 656, for a list of its compilers.

[31]Ibid., p. 657.

[32]*SungS* 207.13.

[33]Included in *CTW* 134.19–22.

[34]*HTS* 58.21.

[35]Ibid. 60.20; *SungS* 205.23b lists the work in one *chüan*, perhaps all that remained of it.

[36]*SungS* 203.17b.

all this provided for him and his family did little to assuage a growing bitterness caused by the emperor's increasing refusal to accept his advice on substantive policy matters. It was by this time quite apparent that T'ai-tsung was no longer using as frequently as he had the mirror of counsel and warning that his minister was holding up to him. As a consequence, Wei's remonstrances and memorials to the throne became more sharply critical than ever before.

At the root of the problem were great changes that had come over T'ai-tsung's behavior, changes that convinced Wei Cheng more than ever that the emperor was marching along a path leading inexorably to destruction. Among T'ai-tsung's more serious faults was a recent tendency toward gross extravagance, reflected, among other things, in his construction of a new palace at Loyang, the Fei-shan. Thus, in the third month of 637, Wei sent a long message to the throne reminding the emperor that Yang-ti had used the wealth of the Sui to indulge his desires and had thereby brought calamity to the nation. Wei exhorted the emperor to return to simplicity:

Now you occupy all of [Yang-ti's] palaces and pavilions. You have completely appropriated all his exotic treasures and rare goods. You have all his concubines and women serving at your side. People in the Four Seas and Nine Continents have all become your slaves and handmaidens. If you are able to hold up as a mirror the reasons why he was destroyed and reflect upon the reasons why we gained [the empire]; keep alert day after day and never ease up even when you rest; burn the precious garments of the Lu-t'ai [the "Deer Terrace" where Chou, "bad last" ruler of Shang, kept his treasure], and destroy the spacious halls of the A-fang [a lavish palace built by Ch'in Shih-huang-ti, located slightly to the west of T'ang Ch'ang-an; it was destroyed by the rebel Hsiang Yü]; fear the danger and destruction [that comes of living] in lofty houses and give thought to living peacefully in humble palaces, then you will undergo a divine transformation and rule by non-activity (wu-wei). This is the highest virtue.

Wei then called upon the emperor to raze the Fei-shan Palace and issued a stern warning that unless he changed his ways he would encounter ruin. Nevertheless, T'ai-tsung completed the project.[37]

The memorial sparked by the construction of the Fei-shan Palace was merely the first of four long messages to come from Wei Cheng's brush in the year 637 that inundated T'ai-tsung in a torrent of advice and

[37] WCKWC ch. 1, pp. 1–2. See also CTS 71.7–7b; HTS 97.7b–8b; TCTC ch. 194, p. 6125.

sharp criticism. Because of their length and detail and the considerable intensity of feeling with which they were written, they indicate the degree to which Wei believed the emperor had by now strayed from the correct path of government. At the same time, they provide us with a veritable catalogue of elements in Wei's political philosophy.

In the second of these memorials, presented in the fourth month, Wei returned to some of his favorite themes:

I have heard that those who seek to make a tree larger must strengthen its roots; that those who wish to make water flow a long distance must dig out its source; that those who think of ways of bringing about the security of a state must develop their virtue and righteousness. If the source is not deep, yet to expect water that flows far; if the roots are not strong, yet to seek a tree that is large; if virtue is not substantial, yet to hope for good government in the state—even the most stupid person knows that this cannot be. How much more can an enlightened ruler not know this! The ruler sits upon a throne imbued with veneration and takes the entire country as his domain. He wants to be respected as high as highest Heaven and forever preserve his boundless blessings. If while in a position of security he does not think of peril (*chü an ssu wei*), if he does not abstain from extravagance by means of frugality, if his virtue is not made substantial or if his mind cannot overcome his desires, this is also like digging up the roots and seeking to grow a large tree, or blocking up the source and desiring far-flowing water.

He then went on to remind the emperor that "Those who have fine beginnings are many, but those who are able to attain successful conclusions are few," and proposed a ten-point guide for T'ai-tsung's conduct. The guide stresses the need for the emperor to curb his desires, exercise caution when undertaking important affairs, avoid arrogance, maintain an open mind in order to accept the opinions of his subordinates, reject the slander and falsehoods of others, and bestow both honors and punishments with impartiality.[38]

In the first part of the long third memorial written in the following month, Wei chided T'ai-tsung for punishing officials too harshly in the heat of anger and rewarding them too liberally when in a more favorable mood. This would never lead to good government, Wei warned, since it nullified the real goals of punishment and reward—the

[38] *WCKWC* ch. 1, pp. 2–3. See also *CKCY* 1.6–8; *CTS* 71.7b–9; *TCTC* ch. 194, p. 6128. A translation of this memorial into French is found in G. Margoulies, *Anthologie raisonée de la littérature chinoise* (Paris, 1948), pp. 217–18.

encouragement of good and the chastisement of evil. The second part of the memorial is of particular interest, since it provides us with what is perhaps the fullest exposition of Wei's consolidation themes:

But the reason the Sui had wealth and power and yet fell, was because they were hyperactive. The reason we are poor and yet peaceful, is because we are quiescent. Being quiescent, there is peace; being hyperactive, there is disorder. Everyone knows this; it is not hidden or difficult to see, not subtle or difficult to ascertain. But few follow the smooth and easy road and many follow the tracks of an overthrown cart [i.e., repeat a disastrous blunder]. Why is this? It is because when there is peace they do not think of peril; when there is order they do not think of disorder; when there is preservation they do not think of destruction.

Long ago, when the Sui were not yet in disorder, they naturally thought that there could be no disorder; when they had not yet been destroyed, they naturally thought that there could be no destruction. So their troops were always on the move and their corvée never ceased. Even when they were on the verge of final disgrace, they were still unaware of the causes of their own destruction. Is that not sad!

If you would mirror the beauty or ugliness of a form, you must go to still water. If you would mirror the security or danger of a state, you must seek out one that has been destroyed. The *Book of Odes* says, "The mirror of Yin is not far off; it lies in the age of Hsia."[39] It also says, "In hewing an axe-handle, in hewing an axe-handle, the pattern is not far off."[40] I hope that in your present actions you will regard the Sui as the mirror of Yin, and thereby deduce [the principles of] preservation and destruction, order and disorder. . . .

Reduce your numerous hunts, stop the manufacture of wasteful luxuries, dispense with matters that are not urgent, be cautious about prejudiced listening, draw near to those who are loyal, keep away from artful flatterers, shut out evil talk which pleases the ear, welcome the bitter taste of loyal advice. . . .

Now consolidating [the state] is easy, but winning it is what is really difficult. If you have been able to attain that which is difficult, how are you unable to preserve that which has been easy? The reasons for not preserving [the state] strongly enough are pride and extravagance, lewd and licentious

[39]This sentence is translated by James Legge, *The Chinese Classics*, vol. 4, *The She King*, p. 510, as "The beacon of Yin is not far-distant;—it is in the age of the [last] sovereign of Hëa." Yin is another name for the Shang dynasty.

[40]Ibid., p. 240, suggests that this may mean that "while there is a necessary and proper way for every thing, men need not go far to find out what it is."

behavior. Be careful in the end as you were in the beginning (*shen chung ju shih*). How can you not strive for this?[41]

After an imperial progress that T'ai-tsung made to Loyang in the seventh month of 637, there were great rains and flooding, and water inundated temples and homes, even entering the principal palace of the city; more than six thousand people are said to have lost their lives.[42] The Chinese regarded natural disasters of this magnitude as signs from Heaven that the sovereign had committed grave errors in his rule. The floods thus presented Wei with a convenient excuse for writing yet a fourth pungent memorial, part of which reads:

It has been more than ten years since Your Majesty came to the throne and peace returned. Your awesome power extends beyond the seas, the myriad nations come to pay court, the granaries daily grow fuller, and our territory daily broadens. But the Way and its power (*tao-te*) have not yet become substantial, and benevolence and righteousness are not yet far reaching. Why is this? It is because you have not yet employed sincerity and trust to the utmost in dealing with your subordinates, and because although there has been the diligence of an excellent beginning, we do not yet see the beauty of a successful conclusion. Such a state of affairs has developed gradually, not merely in one morning or one night. Earlier, at the beginning of Chen-kuan, you took good advice as a warning, and even after five or six years you still happily accepted remonstrance. But since that time you have gradually come to hate frank speech. Although sometimes you force yourself and are able to endure it, you are not as open minded as before. Outspoken officials tend to avoid you. The disciples of flattery are thus able to display their cleverness: they say that those who are of the same mind form factions; they say that those who accuse others are selfless; they say that strongly upright men are usurpers of authority; they say that those who give loyal counsel slander. . . . [So] upright men cannot reveal all that is on their minds and the great ministers cannot contend with [the flatterers and sycophants]. This is why your seeing and hearing have been confused, your great policies have been obstructed, and your virtue has been harmed.

The memorial continues with several historical and literary allusions, and encourages T'ai-tsung to distinguish between those at court who were truly loyal and those who were merely clever opportunists, and once having done so, to place complete confidence in the former.[43]

[41] *WCKWC* ch. 1, pp. 3–5. Also see *CKCY* 8.8–10b; *CTS* 71.9–11b; *HTS* 97.5b–7; *TCTC* ch. 195, pp. 6129–30.

[42] *TCTC* ch. 195, p. 6130.

[43] *WCKWC* ch. 1, pp. 5–7. See also *CKCY* 5.27–29; *CTS* 71.11b–14; *HTS* 97.8b–10; *TCTC*

As a sop to critics like Wei Cheng and as a sign of self-blame, T'ai-
tsung ordered that the small Ming-te Palace in Loyang as well as one
hall of the Fei-shan Palace be dismantled and the materials given to
families who had suffered from the flood.[44]

The four memorials of 637 must have singed the imperial ears, yet
Wei's criticism continued unabated. In the third month of 638, T'ai-
tsung celebrated the birth of a grandson with a banquet for his high-
ranking officials, during which he acclaimed the merits of Wei and
Fang Hsüan-ling and presented both of them with swords. But when he
was foolish enough to inquire of his guests how his present rule compared with that of his earlier years on the throne, Wei took the opportunity to drive his critical knife yet a bit deeper by commenting:

If we speak in terms of an enhancement of the imperial dignity [as demonstrated by] the coming of distant barbarians to pay tribute, the beginning of
Chen-kuan cannot be compared to the present. [But] if we speak in terms of
your virtue and righteousness thoroughly influencing the people so that they
joyfully obey you, the difference compared to the early years of Chen-kuan is
equally great. . . . Long ago, when the empire had not yet been pacified,
you always made righteousness and virtue your central concern. Now, thinking that the empire is without troubles, you have gradually become increasingly arrogant, wasteful, and self-satisfied. Therefore, although your achievements are great, in the end things are still not as good as in former times.[45]

Yet all of this was but a mere prelude to the longest and most im-
passioned of all of Wei Cheng's tirades against T'ai-tsung's behavior and
policies, which he delivered in the fifth month of the following year.
This memorial, as in the case of his fourth memorial of 637, was
prompted by calamities both natural and human: a drought of several
months' duration, a volcanic-like eruption in Shensi, and the attempted
assassination of the emperor by the younger brother of T'u-li Qaghan
of the Eastern Turks. When the emperor ordered his high officials to
criticize the faults of his rule reflected by these ill omens, Wei was more
then equal to the task. His memorial enumerates at length ten aspects
of T'ai-tsung's behavior and policies indicating that after an auspicious
beginning he was failing to guide his reign to a successful conclusion.
Here we see, for the most part, a repetition of Wei's earlier themes:

---

ch. 195, pp. 6130–31. The *CKCY* erroneously gives the date of this memorial as 636.
    [44]*HTS* 97.10; *TCTC* ch. 195, p. 6131.
    [45]*WCKCL* 1.23. See also *TCTC* ch. 195, p. 6137.

T'ai-tsung was seeking exotic goods from afar and manufacturing play-things for himself without end; he was overworking the people on construction projects for his private satisfaction; he was indulging petty men while becoming estranged from his loyal officials; he had become arrogant and was no longer following the advice of his subordinates; he was sending soldiers to foreign lands without cause and was bringing much suffering to the common people, and so on.[46] Upon receiving the memorial, T'ai-tsung duly rewarded Wei with ten catties of gold and two horses and made the hollow promise that he would change his ways.[47]

If we had only Wei Cheng's memorials of the late 630s to go by, we might well suppose that the T'ang administration had badly faltered, that scoundrels were in control of the government, that the emperor had become obsessed with fleshly satisfactions and led a dissolute life, that the populace was suffering under the grinding weight of corvée, and that T'ang armies were marching in every direction with the aim of bringing all of Asia under Chinese dominion. Actually, nothing of the sort had happened. Construction projects of some size were under way, especially in the Loyang area. The T'ang had attacked the T'u-yü-hun in the region of modern Tsinghai province and sent troops from time to time to help stabilize the political situation there. It had mounted a campaign against the T'u-po, a Tibetan people who were raiding Chinese territory in Chien-nan (modern Szechuan), and it had also begun pacifying the aboriginal Lao tribes of Shan-nan (modern Hupei and eastern Szechuan).

Yet the majority of T'ai-tsung's most dramatic and costly military offensives—against the several oases of the Tarim Basin, the Hsüeh-yen-t'o to the north of the Great Wall, and the kingdom of Koguryŏ—were still in the future. Most public works projects, especially palace con-struction, were also yet to come. Perhaps no imperial project would be able to compete in sheer wastefulness with the construction of the detached Hsiang-ch'eng Palace in the mountains to the southwest of Loyang, which between 640 and 641 entailed almost two million man-days of labor. Yet, when T'ai-tsung visited the site and found it uncomfortably hot and infested with poisonous snakes, in a fit

---

[46]*WCKWC* ch. 1, pp. 17–20. See also *CKCY* 10.13–17b; *HTS* 97.10–13; *TCTC* ch. 195, p. 6147.

[47]*HTS* 97.13; *TCTC* ch. 195, pp. 6147–48.

of pique he had its architect, Yen Li-te, demoted and the entire structure razed.[48] Moreover, the loss of humility and growing self-satisfaction that Wei Cheng had detected in the emperor during the 630s increased even more markedly during the following decade as Chinese armies swept over Central Asia. Now, T'ai-tsung began to dwell at length on his military achievements and on his view that he had surpassed other great rulers of China.[49] After one such self-congratulatory speech in 641, a grand secretary of the Department of the Imperial Chancellery, Chang Hsing-ch'eng, was moved to memorialize: "Yü [the Chinese culture-hero who drained the flood waters and founded the Hsia dynasty] did not brag, yet in the empire none compared with him. Your Majesty has swept away disorder and returned the empire to rectitude. All the officials are truly incapable of recognizing your brilliance, but you need not come to court to tell us about it!"[50]

From the foregoing we may conclude two things. First, by the late 630s Wei Cheng had become utterly disheartened by what he viewed as T'ai-tsung's failure to choose consolidation over expansion as a national priority and by his refusal to heed the admonitions of loyal courtiers like himself. He thus mounted an energetic and concentrated counter-offensive in the form of memorials and remonstrances in which he tended to exaggerate for effect the deterioration of conditions in government and the extent to which T'ai-tsung had exhausted the human and economic resources of the country. Second, in spite of such efforts, T'ai-tsung continued to pursue exactly those policies during the 640s which Wei had criticized most during the late 630s. It is thus apparent that by this time Wei had ceased to exert a strong restraining force on the emperor.

This was not always the case concerning less weighty issues, such as the code of etiquette (li), where Wei's influence remained relatively intact. Two examples will suffice here. Following the death of Empress Chang-sun, T'ai-tsung became enamored of the widow of his brother Yüan-chi, victim at the Hsüan-wu Gate. When the emperor announced his intention of making her his consort, Wei strongly protested, disparagingly comparing her to a princess of the house of the state of

[48]THY ch. 30, p. 560.
[49]See, for example, TCTC ch. 198, p. 6226, and note of Hu San-hsing.
[50]Ibid. ch. 196, pp. 6173-74.

Ch'in during the Spring and Autumn Period who in succession married two brothers of the royal family of Chin. The marriage was thereupon cancelled.[51] Later, Wei was able to persuade T'ai-tsung of the impropriety of sending envoys to purchase horses among the Western Turks too soon after sending another envoy with an imperial patent for the new Western Turk qaghan, arguing that the Turks would think the Chinese more interested in pursuing matters crassly commercial than diplomatic.[52]

On important matters of state, however, Wei's voice was seldom heeded, a point well illustrated by the case of the Central Asian oasis of Kao-ch'ang, which fell to T'ang forces in 640. When T'ai-tsung made plans to administer the territory with Chinese officials and to garrison it permanently with Chinese troops, Wei, as usual, protested the plans on economic grounds:

Now, if you regard [Kao-ch'ang's] territory as profitable and make it into prefectures and counties, you would always need more than one thousand troops to garrison and protect it. [The troops] would be replaced once every several years, but with each exchange some thirty or forty percent of those coming and going would die [from the rigors of the journey]. They would have to prepare clothing and supplies and part from their relatives. After ten years Lung-yu [modern Kansu, the area from which the replacements would presumably be conscripted] would be a wasteland. In the end, Your Majesty would not gain as much as a pinch of grain or a foot of cloth from Kao-ch'ang with which to aid China—as expressed in the saying "wasting the useful to serve the useless." I do not see how this can be.[53]

T'ai-tsung nevertheless spurned Wei's recommendation that Kao-ch'ang be allowed to preserve its independent status under the son of its late king, Ch'ü Wen-t'ai. Instead, he ordered that the son and his royal court be seized and sent to Ch'ang-an and that the territory of Kao-ch'ang, which the sources claim extended about two hundred and seventy miles east to west and about one hundred and seventy miles north to south, be annexed to China.[54]

---

[51]*HTS* 80.15b; *TCTC* ch. 198, p. 6249.

[52]*WCKCL* 1.25b–27; *CKCY* 2.32–32b; *TCTC* ch. 196, pp. 6168–69.

[53]*WCKCL* 2.14. See also *CKCY* 9.18–19b; *TCTC* ch. 195, pp. 6155–56. For a similar remonstrance against the annexation of Kao-ch'ang by Ch'u Sui-liang, see *TCTC* ch. 196, p. 6178. Both memorials are discussed in Ts'en Chung-mien, *Hsi T'u-chüeh shih-liao pu-ch'üeh chi k'ao-cheng* [Supplementation and Verification of Historical Materials on the Western Turks] (Shanghai, 1958), pp. 17–18.

[54]In 642, when the qaghan of the Western Turks began detaining Chinese envoys travelling

With the diminution of his power over the emperor during the 630s, Wei had begun to complain that T'ai-tsung was falling prey to sycophants and flatterers at his court who were leading him from the proper path of government. By 640 this theme began to occupy a central place in Wei's thoughts, as illustrated in two memorials he wrote during this year. In the first, he charged that T'ai-tsung was no longer placing a degree of trust in his high officials (such as himself, presumably) commensurate with their positions in the administration and that instead the emperor was surrounding himself with men of mediocre talents.[55] In the second, he cited numerous historical examples to drive home his point that when a ruler turned his back on good ministers he invariably came to a bad end. "Had Chieh of the Hsia dynasty not abandoned I Yin, and had the Hsiang family been favorable to Han Hsin, would regimes that were already established have been destroyed?"[56] He reminded T'ai-tsung of the reciprocal nature of the ruler-minister relationship by quoting, among others, the great Confucian philosopher Mencius:

When the prince regards his ministers as his hands and feet, his ministers regard their prince as their belly and heart; when he regards them as his dogs and horses, they regard him as any other man; when he regards them as the ground or as grass, they regard him as a robber and enemy.[57]

Finally, he took pains to stress the need for the sovereign to trust his subordinates, quoting from a source he knew well, the *Record of Rites*: "When the ruler is distrustful, the people are doubtful. When subordinates are not understood, the ruler must toil long. When ruler and subordinates mutually distrust one another, then it cannot be said that there is good government."[58]

Who, in Wei's eyes, were the men leading the emperor astray? We do not know for sure, but they were obviously rivals who had won T'ai-tsung's ear—the "brambles" Wei had alluded to in his "*Fu* on a Cypress in a Taoist Monastery." One such person may have been the

---

in Central Asia and invading the new Chinese prefectures set up at Kao-ch'ang, an independent kingdom of Kao-ch'ang could not, as before, act as a buffer between China and the Turks. T'ai-tsung now regretted not having accepted Wei Cheng's advice; see *TCTC* ch. 196, pp. 6178–79.

[55] *WCKWC* ch. 1, pp. 8–10. See also *CKCY* 3.17–20.

[56] *WCKWC* ch. 1, p. 11.

[57] Ibid., pp. 11–12. From *Mencius* 4.3; the translation by Legge, *The Chinese Classics*, vol. 2, *The Works of Mencius*, p. 318.

[58] *WCKWC* ch. 1, p. 13.

architect of the Chiu-ch'eng and Loyang Palaces, Chiang Hsing-pen. Chiang's *New T'ang History* biography notes that although he was an upright and conscientious official, Wei feared his growing influence over the emperor (undoubtedly in the area of capital construction) and attempted unsuccessfully to have him demoted.[59] An even more likely target of Wei's wrath was the one-time vice-president of the Censorate (*chih-shu shih-yü-shih*) Ch'üan Wan-chi, who had gained a dubious reputation in that capacity by falsely slandering several members of the court, including Wei Cheng.[60] In 631 Wei had charged Ch'üan and another censor, Li Jen-fa, with perpetrating injustices against innocent officials, and had also accused the emperor of encouraging their treachery so as to keep a tight rein on his bureaucrats. He even went so far as to extend a challenge to T'ai-tsung: "If matters have improved since you employed these two men, then I will be happy to be charged with disloyalty and suffer dismemberment!"[61] Later, under continued pressure from Wei and others, T'ai-tsung had Ch'üan demoted to a provincial post, only to allow him to return to the capital again in 637 as the left assistant in the Department of Affairs of State.[62] Such a development surely must have galled Wei.

It is even possible that Wei was shooting at far more prominent figures at court than either Chiang or Ch'üan, perhaps among them the pro-military elements who were urging the emperor on to greater territorial expansion or others advocating increased expenditures on a variety of "wasteful" projects. Certainly, as we have already seen, Wei's relationship with his colleagues was not universally harmonious. T'ang historians have concealed the names of eminent statesmen who wished Wei ill, for disclosure of such information might have reflected badly on those who otherwise made significant contributions to early T'ang history. So, we are only told that in 636 certain "powerful and esteemed" (*ch'üan-kuei*) officials attacked Wei, accusing him of pestering the throne with involved and repetitious memorials and treating the emperor as if he were a child.[63] Had we the names of such men, we

[59]See *HTS* 91.11b–12.

[60]*CTS* 185A.17b.

[61]*WCKCL* 1.18–19b; *CKCY* 2.38–39; *TCTC* ch. 193, p. 6088.

[62]See Yen Keng-wang, *T'ang p'u-shang-ch'eng-lang piao*, 1:24.

[63]*WCKCL* 5.2–2b; Harada Tanashige, *Jōkan seiyō teihon*, p. 194. I have been unable to locate this episode in the *Ssu-pu pei-yao* edition of the *CKCY*.

might understand far more than at present about the nature of political configurations and political intrigue at the Chen-kuan court.

Although until now the emperor had accepted Wei's criticisms with at least superficial equanimity and had even made a show of rewarding him for his troubles, it was also true that he had come greatly to resent Wei's incessant carping. A good indication of T'ai-tsung's real attitude toward Wei, which predictably does not appear in either of Wei's two biographies or in the *Essentials of Government of the Chen-kuan Period,* is revealed in an episode that occurred about 638 or 639. At this time Wei spread a rumor at court that the architect Chiang Hsing-pen had used an excessive amount of bronze in the construction of a building intended for imperial use. When T'ai-tsung heard about it, he confronted Wei and demanded to know why he had made such an accusation. After repeated questioning, Wei grudgingly answered that he had not intended a personal attack on Chiang but had merely wanted to criticize the emperor for his extravagance. T'ai-tsung was infuriated by this disclosure and immediately ordered an investigation into the affair. Later, in conversation with the vice-president of the Censorate, Tu Cheng-lun, he commented ominously:

Wei Cheng was not an official who righteously followed Our [Prince of Ch'in] Office, yet We selected him from the midst of criminals and gave him wealth and honor. Now when We question him, there are things he keeps hidden. When We serve Heaven We fear and respect It. When Wei Cheng serves Us he does not do so with complete honesty. . . . When We sent the censors to investigate him he was in quite a bad temper. If Our sons, when they remonstrated and argued with Us [like Wei Cheng], were to exhibit this kind of proud and rude behavior, they too would be put to death. Why should We be more considerate of him? From his manner, it is as if the country would no longer be orderly without him. Since ancient times rulers have had no Wei Cheng, yet they too were able to transform [the people]. So why do We now rely on Wei Cheng?[64]

Although the emperor eventually let the matter drop, his anger did not readily cool.

By the late 630s and early 640s, then, it is apparent that Wei Cheng's real influence at court had sunk to a low ebb. As a good Confucian he had assiduously followed the words of the great Sage concerning the

[64]*WCKCL* 5.11b–12; also *HL* 2.3b–4.

duty of the ideal minister to his prince: "How can he be said to be truly loyal, who refrains from admonishing the object of his loyalty?"[65] He had chided, ridiculed, and harangued T'ai-tsung with the aim of making him a model of rectitude and preventing the premature end of his house. But in so doing he had reaped the inevitable rewards of his behavior and had become a prickly thorn in the emperor's side. Such a plight had been foreseen centuries earlier by one of Confucius' foremost disciples, Tzu-yu, who had observed, "In the service of one's prince repeated scolding can only lead to loss of favour; in friendship, it can only lead to estrangement."[66] It was now Wei Cheng's turn to learn this very lesson.

[65]See chap. 5, n. 48.
[66]*Analects* 4.26; Waley, *Analects,* p. 106.

CHAPTER 7

The Mirror Lost: Wei Cheng's Last Months, His Death, and Its Aftermath (642-643)

Late in 642 Wei Cheng began serving in what was to be his last official post, that of grand tutor to the crown prince (*t'ai-tzu t'ai-shih*); concurrently he remained in nominal charge of the Department of the Imperial Chancellery. T'ai-tsung had first offered Wei his old position as right vice-president of the Department of Affairs of State, but Wei had refused.[1] At the time, the crown prince, Li Ch'eng-ch'ien, who had been designated heir shortly after T'ai-tsung came to power, was twenty-five years old. He suffered from a serious foot ailment, perhaps clubfoot or gout, but was apparently intelligent and capable, since upon reaching his maturity the emperor assigned him to oversee routine administrative matters and often left him in charge of the capital in his own absence.[2] Yet by the time he was twenty-two, the crown prince appeared to have developed a serious neurosis. He began rejecting his Chinese heritage, living in the style of a steppe nomad, speaking Turkish and clothing himself in Turkish fashion, while at the same time forcing thousands of his subordinates to sing, dance, and dress like Turks.[3] When officials at court began to criticize such unseemly behavior, he responded by making attempts on their lives, which, fortunately for him, remained undetected at the time.[4]

A Second Hsüan-wu Gate Incident?

Even before Ch'eng-ch'ien's excesses became the scandal of the court, T'ai-tsung began to show a marked preference for another of his sons,

[1]*CTS* 71.17; *HTS* 97.13b.

[2]See *CTS* 76.1b; *TCTC* ch. 193, p. 6078; ch.194, p. 6112.

[3]*CTS* 76.2–2b; *TCTC* ch. 196, pp. 6189–90. See also C. P. Fitzgerald, *Son of Heaven*, pp. 170–76.

[4]*TCTC* 196, pp. 6168, 6175.

the clever and ambitious Li T'ai. T'ai's biographies list him as the
fourth son of Empress Chang-sun, but there is some evidence to suggest
that he may in fact have been the son of a concubine.[5] The emperor's
partiality toward T'ai was first exhibited in 636, when his sons were
made hereditary governors-general (*tu-tu*) on the frontiers and T'ai
alone was allowed to remain in Ch'ang-an to construct a College of
Literary Studies (*wen-hsüeh kuan*) similar to the one his father had
founded years earlier as Prince of Ch'in. T'ai also built a luxurious
mansion in the capital, causing at least one official to memorialize on
his extravagance.[6]

T'ai soon became spoiled by such treatment and began to demand
greater deference from court officials. At the end of 636, someone,
perhaps at T'ai's own instigation, informed the emperor that high-
ranking officials were belittling his favorite. One of the targets of this
accusation was Wei Cheng.[7] T'ai-tsung then assembled his key ministers
and strongly rebuked them for not sufficiently respecting T'ai. Fang
Hsüan-ling and the others "trembled and perspired, and begged forgiveness," but Wei Cheng, undaunted, stepped forward to assert that the
officials had not disparaged T'ai but that on the contrary it was T'ai
who had not shown sufficient respect to the officials. "Moreover," he
continued, "Sui Kao-tsu [i.e., Wen-ti] did not understand propriety and
righteousness. He overindulged all his sons, causing them to act improperly. Before long they all committed offenses and were degraded.
He cannot be taken as a model and is unworthy of mention."[8]

Still, the emperor continued to indulge T'ai. Early in 642 he allowed
him to open a huge school and dormitory complex in Ch'ang-an, the

[5]*CTS* 76.7 and *HTS* 80.1 claim that T'ai was legitimate. Yet, strangely, he appears to have
been about the same age as or a bit older than Ch'eng-ch'ien, supposedly T'ai-tsung's eldest
son by the empress. *HTS* 80.8b notes that T'ai died at the age of thirty-four (35 *sui*), an event
the same source, 3.3b, places in the twelfth month of 652 (January, 653). This means that
T'ai was born sometime during 618. On the other hand, *CTS* 76.1b says that Ch'eng-ch'ien
was seven years old (8 *sui*) at the time T'ai-tsung assumed power in the eighth month of 626,
which would place his birth late in 618 or sometime during the first half of 619. On this
question, see also Ts'en Chung-mien, *T'ang-shih yü-shen*, pp. 10–11, and Matsui Shūichi,
"Sokuten Bukō," 16, n. 48. C. P. Fitzgerald, *The Empress Wu* (1956; reprint, London, 1968),
p. 215, n. 9, presents additional evidence against T'ai's legitimacy.

[6]*CTS* 76.7, 70.11b–12; *TCTC* ch. 194, p. 6119.

[7]*WCKCL* 1.19b; *TCTC* ch. 194, p. 6123; *CKCY* 2.44. The *CKCY* mistakenly refers to
another of the empress's sons in this episode.

[8]*WCKCL* 1.21; *CKCY* 2.44b.

gates and halls of which were so numerous that Ssu-ma Kuang compared them to a marketplace. Soon T'ai's monthly expenses had risen above even those of the crown prince.[9] Shortly afterwards, the emperor moved T'ai's lodgings to a hall situated nearer his own apartments than the Eastern Palace, residence of the crown prince. Wei Cheng, who at that time was not yet grand tutor to the crown prince but who since 636 had probably not harbored much affection for T'ai, strongly remonstrated against this blatant show of favoritism, ostensibly on the grounds that the hall had formerly been the residence of one of those slain at the Hsüan-wu Gate, Li Yüan-chi.[10] In this way he persuaded the emperor to return T'ai to his original quarters.

Despite this setback, T'ai remained convinced that the throne was not beyond his grasp and began gathering about him a group of young and discontented officials—several of them the sons or younger brothers of T'ai-tsung's key officials[11]—to support his candidacy.

In the meantime, Ch'eng-ch'ien's behavior had in no way improved and rumors began to fly at court that the succession would be changed. It was at this point, perhaps in a last ditch effort to reform his errant son, that T'ai-tsung chose the stern Wei Cheng to be his tutor "to end the doubts of the empire" over the succession.[12] There is also the possibility that the emperor had given up on Ch'eng-ch'ien and hoped that when he eventually fell, he would pull Wei Cheng down with him. Whatever the case, Wei, whose illness had somewhat worsened and who certainly did not want to become involved in a struggle between two imperial princes that might well develop into a repetition of the Hsüan-wu Gate incident, declined the post. T'ai-tsung would not hear of it:

Because the crown prince is the foundation of the state, he requires a tutor. Therefore, I am selecting someone loyal and upright to assist him. Long ago [King] Yu of the Chou dynasty [rg. 781–70 B.C.] and [Duke] Hsien of the state of Chin [Warring States Period] removed their legitimate sons and established the sons of concubines as their successors. If a state does this, that state will be endangered; if a house does this, that house will fall—like the case of the Han house [i.e., Kao-tsu] almost removing the crown prince.

[9] *TCTC* ch. 196, p. 6174. For Ch'u Sui-liang's memorial protesting this state of affairs, see *CTW* 149.14b–15.
[10] *WCKCL* 2.28–29. See also *CKCY* 6.19b–20; *TCTC* ch. 196, p. 6174.
[11] See Matsui, "Sokuten Bukō," 12.
[12] *TCTC* ch. 196, p. 6177.

Only when the aid of the Four Elders (*ssu-hao*) was relied upon did peace prevail. Now it is for this same reason that I am relying on you. I realize that you are ill, but you can still attend to these duties.[13]

Wei was thus prevailed upon to accept the assignment.

Had Wei lived long enough, he might possibly have had a salutary effect on Ch'eng-ch'ien, but his death snuffed out any hope of reforming the crown prince. Ch'eng-ch'ien soon became intimidated by T'ai's efforts to rally support around himself and made plans to kill both his brother and the emperor. When the plot was brought to light in the fourth month of 643, Ch'eng-ch'ien was swiftly demoted to commoner status. A short while later, after T'ai began to intrigue against another of T'ai-tsung's sons, Li Chih, a potential competitor for the throne, the emperor was reluctantly forced to demote his recent favorite.[14] The danger of armed conflict over the succession now subsided, and Li Chih eventually became emperor.

A Sturdy Bamboo Touched by Frost

By the beginning of 643, age and recent ailments had taken their toll of Wei Cheng and he became bedridden. T'ai-tsung now began sending messengers to his home to inquire solicitously after his health and to present him with medicines and rare delicacies to speed his recovery.[15] As was befitting Wei's station as a chief minister, the emperor and the crown prince Ch'eng-ch'ien often paid personal calls on him. At such times Wei would don his court robes and tie his girdle, thus conforming (or, his biographers would have us believe he was conforming) to a rule of etiquette for the model minister set forth in the *Analects*: "If he is ill and his prince comes to see him, he has himself laid with his head to the East with his Court robes thrown over him and his sash drawn across the bed."[16]

Realizing that Wei's days were numbered and that he would not have to bear the brunt of his criticisms much longer, T'ai-tsung began to bestow gifts and honors on his counselor in recognition of his long and

[13]*WCKCL* 5.19b; *HL* 2.8–8b.

[14]See *CTS* 76.2b–3, 9–10b; *TCTC* ch. 196, pp. 6189–92; ch. 197, 6195–96.

[15]*HTS* 97.14; *TCTC* ch. 196, p. 6183.

[16]*HTS* 97.14; *Analects* 10.13; Waley, *Analects*, p. 150. Legge, *The Chinese Classics*, vol. 1, *Confucian Analects*, p. 235, translates this passage as "made his court robes be spread over him, and drew his girdle across him."

faithful service. First he sent a mattress and cotton coverlet, an austere gift in keeping with Wei's frugal tastes.[17] Then he donated a formal reception hall for Wei's home built from materials he originally intended to use in the construction of a small pavilion for himself.[18] Wei's residence was situated in the wealthy and fashionable Yung-hsing quarter of Ch'ang-an,[19] just east of the imperial city, but it is said that he had no formal reception hall, perhaps in keeping with Confucius' dictum that the superior man did not demand comfort in his home.[20] The new hall was completed in a scant five days.

The last honor T'ai-tsung bestowed on Wei was the best of all—the betrothal of his sixteenth daughter, the Heng-shan Princess, to Wei's eldest son, Wei Shu-yü.[21] On his final visit to his minister's home, the emperor brought his daughter along to be presented to her future father-in-law. But when T'ai-tsung asked Wei whether he was strong enough to receive the princess, the minister was already too feeble to reply. The next morning, on the seventeenth day of the first month (February 11), 643, Wei died at the age of sixty-three.[22]

As a sign of respect for his departed servant, T'ai-tsung closed the court for the unusually long period of five days and ordered princes of the blood and civil and military officials of the ninth degree and above all to mourn him.[23] At the same time he bestowed upon Wei the post-

[17]*HTS* 97.14; *TCTC* ch. 196, p. 6176.

[18]*CTS* 71.17–17b; *HTS* 97.14; *TCTC* ch. 196, p. 6176; *CKCY* 6.5b; *WCKCL* 5.21b–22; *HL* 2.10. The discrepancy in dating this episode arising out of accounts in the *TCTC* and Wei Cheng's two biographies is discussed in *WCKCL* 5.22, note of Wang Hsien-kung.

[19]Wei Shu (d. 757), *Liang-ching hsin-chi* [New Records of the Two Capitals] (*Nan-ching cha-chi* ed., Taipei, 1963), p. 11.

[20]*Analects* 1.14; Waley, *Analects*, p. 87. Since, according to the *Liang-ching hsin-chi*, Wei Cheng's house had formerly been owned by Yü-wen K'ai, the chief architect of the Sui capital, it is unlikely that it originally had no formal reception hall. It is also worth remarking that upon the passing of Wen Yen-po, T'ai-tsung also presented his family with a reception hall; *HTS* 91.2b. It is possible that more form than substance was involved in this act. Conflicting accounts of the fate that befell Wei's house after his death are discussed in Ch'eng Ta-ch'ang, *K'ao-ku pien* [Investigations of Antiquity] (1181; *Ts'ung-shu chi-ch'eng* ed., Shanghai, 1939), ch. 8, p. 65, and Feifel, *Po Chü-i*, p. 91.

[21]*HTS* 97.14; *TCTC* ch. 196, p. 6184. Wang Hsien-ch'ien, *WCLC* 48b–49, quoting from the eighteenth-century writer Ch'ien Ta-hsin, shows that during Kao-tsung's time the Heng-shan Princess was retitled the Hsin-ch'eng Princess, the name by which she is most usually referred to in the sources. She was a daughter of Empress Chang-sun. See also the note of Lü Ssu-mien, *Sui-T'ang-Wu-tai shih,* 1:128.

[22]*CTS* 3.13b, 71.17b; *HTS* 2.15, 97.14.

[23]*HTS* 97.14; *WCKCL* 5.23; *HL* 2.10b.

humous name Wen-cheng, "refined and pure." A two-character post-humous name was a special distinction.[24]

Then the emperor began making plans to hold an elaborate state funeral for Wei, replete with a large feathered canopy over the carriage carrying his coffin, drums and pipes, and forty men wielding swords marching in procession. Wei's two biographies tell us that his widow complained to T'ai-tsung about the proposed funeral, maintaining that since her husband had lived a frugal and simple existence he would not have wanted such extravagant ceremonies in his honor. T'ai-tsung is said to have complied with her wishes.[25] Yet an equally dependable source notes that the only concession the emperor made was to allow a simple hearse, free from excessive ornamentation; the rest of the funeral was carried out as previously planned.[26] After all, T'ai-tsung had intended the rites to enhance not just the image of the loyal servant but the image of the master as well.

On the day of the funeral, metropolitan officials, both civil and military, escorted Wei's body to a point just beyond the K'ai-yüan Gate, the northernmost of the three gates in the west wall of the outer city. From there it was borne to the Chao-ling, T'ai-tsung's great tomb complex northwest of Ch'ang-an, to be interred. The location of Wei's tomb at the Chao-ling is noteworthy. It was not included in the main area on the east side of the complex, where T'ai-tsung, Empress Chang-sun, and such chief ministers as Chang-sun Wu-chi and Fang Hsüan-ling, were all buried. Rather, it was placed well off to the west, on the far side of a small hill.[27] Wei was thus relatively isolated from the tombs of his colleagues, a fitting symbolic reminder, perhaps, of his solitary position at court when he was alive.

The emperor did not personally take part in the funeral ceremonies but watched from a lookout tower located somewhere in the imperial

[24]See *THY* ch. 80, p. 1479, and note of Su Mien, pp. 1477–79.

[25]*CTS* 71.17b; *HTS* 97.14b. Very little concerning Wei's family appears in the sources. His wife, née P'ei, appears to have been a member of the Ho-tung branch of the clan; *WCLC* 50b. There were four sons and at least one daughter, who, sometime after 633, married the fourteenth son of Kao-tsu, Li Yüan-kuei; *CKCY* 5.13; *THY* ch. 5, p. 55; *HL* 2.31–31b.

[26]*WCKCL* 5.23–23b. The form of this ceremonial appears to have been standardized early in the T'ang; see the cases of the generals Li Ching (d. 649) and Yü-ch'ih Ching-te (d. 658); *CTS* 58.11b–12 and *WCLC* 50–50b.

[27]See map 18 in Adachi Kiroku, *Chōan shiseki*, opposite p. 254.

park.[28] He did, however, compose the funeral dirges and write the eulogy for Wei's gravestone, for which he also supplied the calligraphy. When the stone was placed on exhibition at one of the northern gates of Ch'ang-an, it is said that officials and commoners vied with one another in copying it. "Horses and carriages clogged the roads, and every day there were several thousands of people."[29] The gravestone does not survive, but we still have a poem which T'ai-tsung wrote while viewing the funeral procession:

> Gold-saddled horses assemble at the palace gates;
> Imperial carriages roll toward the Shang-lin.[a]
> In the outer suburbs there is the sadness of a new parting;
> At the river bridge[b] I cannot see you off as before.
>
> A sorrowful sun glimmers on a mountain peak, then sinks;
> A melancholy cloud trails your hearse, then veers off.
> Mournful flutes wail briefly, wail long;
> Sad banners now unfold, now furl once more.
>
> How deep are my feelings of longing!
> Waves of tears splash down in vain.
> My friend of old is no more;
> With whom shall I together spend a fragrant spring?[30]

After the procession had passed beyond the suburbs of Ch'ang-an, T'ai-tsung returned to court to render his speech describing Wei Cheng as the mirror with which he corrected his judgment and which he had now lost.[31]

[a]The Shang-lin was originally the hunting park of Ch'in Shih-huang-ti. It was a large area southwest of the Ch'in capital, and was thus north-northwest of T'ang Ch'ang-an, on the road to the Chao-ling. See Yves Hervouet, *Un poète cour sous les Han: Sseu-ma Siang-ju* (Paris, 1964), pp. 222–24.

[b]The Wei River bridge north of the city is undoubtedly meant here. It was the scene of many farewells when, according to custom, officials or travelers were seen off on their way northward.

---

[28]*WCKCL* 5.23b; *HL* 2.11. Again, this appears to have been a standard early T'ang practice; see *CTS* 67.15, where Kao-tsung observes the funeral ceremonies of Li Shih-chi from a watchtower.

[29]*TFYK* 40.17b.

[30]*WCKCL* 5.24; *HL* 2.11.

[31]*HTS* 97.14b; also *CTS* 71.18; *TCTC* ch. 196, p. 6184. See the frontispiece of the present study.

Shortly before his death, Wei had begun to write a final memorial to the emperor that remained in draft form. Hearing of its existence, T'ai-tsung had a messenger fetch it from Wei's house. Its theme was one Wei had stressed frequently during his last years:

Among all things under Heaven there are the good and the evil. If you employ good men the state will be at peace. If you employ evil men the state will be in disorder. Among high officials there are those you love and those you hate. You see only faults in those you hate and only good points in those you love. You ought to be meticulously careful concerning those you love and hate. If you love someone and understand his faults, if you hate someone and understand his good points, if you do away with evil men without hesitation and employ the worthy without suspicion, then [the state] will flourish.[32]

About a month after Wei's funeral, T'ai-tsung ordered that twenty-four early T'ang "meritorious officials" were to be immortalized in painting and that the portraits of each were to be placed in a chamber called the Ling-yen-ko, located in the northeastern section of the palace city. Most of the men so designated had joined the T'ang uprising during its initial stages in Taiyuan or had served T'ai-tsung in his Prince of Ch'in Office, and thus were pillars of the Li-T'ang house and of T'ai-tsung's regime in particular. Yet T'ai-tsung also magnanimously included Wei Cheng, despite his tardy arrival on the scene.[33] The portraits, rendered by the artist Yen Li-pen, brother of the architect Li-te, faced north in the Ling-yen-ko, the direction their subjects had faced at imperial audiences.[34] T'ai-tsung himself composed a panegyric for each and Ch'u Sui-liang furnished the calligraphy.[35] The emperor thereby revived a tradition begun by the Later Han emperor Ming, who in A.D. 60 had the likenesses of twenty-eight famous generals and four other meritorious officials of his predecessor's reign placed in the Cloud Terrace (*yün-t'ai*) of the Southern Palace.[36]

[32]*CTS* 71.18; *HTS* 97.14b.

[33]*CTS* 77.1b, 65.12–13; *HTS* 89.10–10b; *THY* ch. 45, p. 801.

[34]*TCTC* ch. 196, p. 6186, note of Hu San-hsing.

[35]Sung Min-ch'iu (1019–79), *Ch'ang-an chih* [A Gazetteer of Ch'ang-an] (*Ching-hsün-t'ang ts'ung-shu* ed., ca. 1790), 6.3. The portraits and panegyrics were destroyed at some unknown date, but in 1090, during the reign of Sung Che-tsung, they were remade, with what fidelity to the originals we can only guess. The second eulogy to Wei Cheng still survives; see *WCLC* 53.

[36]See *TCTC* ch. 44, p. 1438.

It is said that T'ai-tsung would often wistfully remember his departed minister and visit the Ling-yen-ko to view Wei's portrait and ponder their relationship. On one such occasion he composed a "seven-word" poem, which he sent to Wei's family. It went like this:

A sturdy bamboo touched by frost; its fine qualities have been destroyed.
A T'ai star[a] fallen from its place; an excellent minister has died.
I can only conceal my tears on this Cloud Terrace,[b]
And in vain face the surviving image of a man who will be no more.[37]

Obviously, the intense grief T'ai-tsung exhibited upon hearing of Wei's death and during the period immediately afterward was partially a reaction elicited by the social demands of the court, and was thus contrived for public consumption. Yet it was also partially genuine. Despite the frequent antagonisms between them, the emperor had greatly benefited from Wei's long years of devoted service in numerous capacities, during which time he had, it would seem, developed a grudging admiration for Wei's frank and bold manner. He was aware that his court was filled with yes-men who never attempted to oppose him, as Wei had, even when the emperor committed the gravest errors of judgment. He knew, too, that no one would take Wei's place as his moral conscience, his human mirror.

The great show T'ai-tsung made over the memory of his late minister soon aroused the ire of Wei's enemies at court, who now charged that he had earlier formed a faction with two men he had recommended for official appointments, Hou Chün-chi and Tu Cheng-lun.[38] Hou, the conqueror of Kao-ch'ang, was beheaded in the fourth month of 643 after being charged with plotting rebellion along with the crown prince Ch'eng-ch'ien. Tu, a member of Ch'eng-ch'ien's staff, was first demoted to a post in the provinces for leaking the story that the emperor desired to dismiss the crown prince in favor of Li T'ai, and was demoted yet another time following the discovery of Ch'eng-ch'ien's plot. All this naturally reflected badly on Wei.

[a]The three T'ai stars of the Big Dipper correspond to the three dukes (*san-kung*), the highest offices (but largely honorific) in the T'ang bureaucracy.
[b]An illusion to the Cloud Terrace of Han Ming-ti.

---

[37]*WCKCL* 5.24b; *HL* 2.11b.
[38]*HTS* 97.15b. Whether these charges were true or not is difficult to determine. Ch'en Yin-k'o believes that Wei allied with powerful elements from the northeast (Tu Cheng-lun) and northwest (Hou Chün-chi) to create a formidable transregional faction; "Shan-tung

It was further alleged that Wei had saved copies of his remonstrances to the emperor and had shown them to his colleague Ch'u Sui-liang. Why this might have been considered offensive is suggested by the following incident. On one occasion, when a secretary of the Imperial Library requested permission to gather together all of the emperor's writings, T'ai-tsung refused and testily replied that if his own words had been of any benefit to the people they would already have been recorded by the historians, but if they had not, collecting them now was useless. He further observed that the great tyrant Sui Yang-ti had also made collections of his own writings.[39] Possibly, Wei hoped that Ch'u Sui-liang, who was famed as a master of calligraphy, would copy his remonstrances and thus give them a wide audience or, at least, preserve them for posterity. T'ai-tsung apparently viewed this as an act of lèse-majesté.

The accusations soon succeeded in turning T'ai-tsung against Wei, surely a most telling indication of the fragile nature of his loyalty to the dead man's memory. He cancelled the marriage of Wei Shu-yü to the Heng-shan Princess and even went so far as to order that Wei's gravestone be toppled from its place. At the time of Wei's death the emperor had bestowed the taxes of nine hundred households upon the minister's survivors. Now, the sources tell us, his "regard for [Wei's] family declined."[40]

For a few years afterwards Wei remained in disfavor at court, a state of affairs reflected in the following. Early in 644, when T'ai-tsung began seriously to consider attacking Koguryŏ, a move bitterly opposed by the remonstrating counselor Ch'u Sui-liang, the general Li Shih-chi came forward to support the emperor, saying, "Some time ago[41] when the Hsüeh-yen-t'o invaded, Your Majesty wanted to launch troops to chastise them. But Wei Cheng remonstrated and so you stopped, thus creating the present calamity. If we had earlier used Your Majesty's plan, the northern barbarians would have been pacified." T'ai-tsung then replied, "You are right. This really is Cheng's fault. We subse-

---

hao-chieh," 8–9.

[39] *CKCY* 7.7–7b; *TCTC* ch. 195, p. 6137.

[40] *CTS* 71.18b; *HTS* 97.15b.

[41] I.e., in 641. There is no record of Wei's protest against the T'ang attack on the Hsüeh-yen-t'o in the *WCKCL* or in either of his two biographies.

quently regretted it, but did not want to say anything for fear that it would block his other good plans."[42]

Despite vigorous protests from various quarters, T'ai-tsung went forward with his plans of conquest. Unfortunately, his summer campaign of 645 became bogged down in Liaotung and failed in its objective of quickly taking P'yŏngyang, the enemy's capital deep inside the Korean peninsula. In the early autumn the emperor called a retreat, but it was already too late: a great blizzard caught the T'ang forces by surprise, and many perished. All hopes of conquering Koguryŏ having been dashed and his army having been decimated by battle and natural catastrophe, T'ai-tsung now remembered Wei Cheng's prudent counsel. "If Wei Cheng were alive, he would not have allowed Us to do this," he observed miserably. He then ordered that a sacrifice be made to Wei and that his gravestone be restored, at the same time summoning Wei's wife and sons to his side, where they were generously rewarded.[43] Although the marriage between Wei Shu-yü and the Heng-shan Princess was never rescheduled, it is nevertheless clear that Wei Cheng had once more succeeded in bouncing back from ignominy to take his rightful place in the pantheon of T'ang worthies, where he was forever to remain.

[42] *TCTC* ch. 197, p. 6207.
[43] *HTS* 97.15b; *TCTC* ch. 198, p. 6230.

CHAPTER 8

Reflections in the Mirror: Wei Cheng's Thought

As the preceding chapters may have suggested, the corpus of Wei Cheng's extant writings is rather extensive: a considerable number of remonstrances and memorials, replies (*tui*) to simple queries or to questions of greater political or philosophical consequence posed by the emperor, minor literary works, poetry, biographical and topical treatises in the Liang, Ch'en, and Sui Standard Histories, and recorded dialogues at court with T'ai-tsung and fellow officials. The subject matter of these materials is quite heterogeneous. Nevertheless, they are all held together by certain unifying strands that comprise the core of Wei's political beliefs, and we might pause here to treat them at some length.

First, however, it may be useful to summarize some of the developments that had taken place in the realm of Chinese thought during the centuries immediately preceding Wei's time.[1] During the Han dynasty, classical studies had split into two broad "schools," the so-called New Text and Old Text, although members of each of these schools by no means agreed on all questions. The New Text School (*chin-wen chia*) was based on versions of the classics, some of which were allegedly set down from memory following the Ch'in burning of the books in 213 B.C. The Old Text School (*ku-wen chia*) was based on supposedly newly discovered classical texts written in an archaic script dating from the pre-Han period. Sharp distinctions between the two schools cannot always easily be made but, generally speaking, their philosophical beliefs divided as follows. The New Text School, of which Tung Chung-shu (ca. 179–ca. 104) is the most renowned exponent, placed a special emphasis

---

[1]The following discussion is based for the most part on P'i Hsi-jui, *Ching-hsüeh li-shih* [A History of Classical Learning] (1924; reprint, Hong Kong, 1961), pp. 101–219; Yang Hsiang-k'uei, "T'ang-Sung shih-tai ti ching-hsüeh ssu-hsiang" [Concepts of Classical Learning in the T'ang and Sung Dynasties], *Wen-shih-che* [Literature, History, and Philosophy] (1958, no. 5), pp. 7–16; Tjan Tjoe Som, *Po Hu T'ung*, 2 vols. (Leiden, 1949), 1:95–165; and Fung Yu-lan, *A History of Chinese Philosophy*, 2 vols. (Princeton, 1953), 2:7–167.

on the *Spring and Autumn Annals* as interpreted by the Kung Yang commentary and on the assumption that the *Annals* contained hidden meanings by which Confucius sought to convey his moralistic teachings. The thought of the Kung Yang commentary was heavily influenced by five elements and yin-yang cosmology and by prognostication and apocryphal texts (*ch'an-wei shu*) which, among other things, presumed the divinity of Confucius. The Old Text School arose essentially as a reaction to the New Text School. It favored the Tso commentary to the *Annals*, which was written with far less assumption of the principles of praise and blame than the New Texters saw in the *Annals*; purged Confucianism of much of its cosmological and supernatural beliefs; and leaned toward a more naturalistic view of the universe somewhat akin to that of Taoism. Its two best known exponents are Yang Hsiung (53 B.C.–A.D. 18) and Wang Ch'ung (27–ca.100). Toward the end of the Later Han there occurred a short-lived syncretism of Old Text and New Text ideas in the work of Cheng Hsüan (127–200), a syncretism that nevertheless minimized the five elements and yin-yang approach of the New Text School. In the post-Han period, the New Text School sank into rapid and almost complete oblivion.

The long-range trend, however, was for a continued division in Chinese thought, reinforced even further by the Period of Disunion, which created a gulf between North and South China not only in the political realm but in the philosophical as well. The school of Northern Learning (*pei-hsüeh*) followed for the most part the commentaries to the classics written by Cheng Hsüan and placed a heavy emphasis on such ritual texts as the *Record of Rites*. The school of Southern Learning (*nan-hsüeh*) represented a continuation of Old Text Confucianism heavily overlaid with *hsüan-hsüeh*, "dark learning" or Neo-Taoism, as interpreted most notably by Wang Pi (226–49). Both schools utilized the Tso commentary to the *Annals* but in differing interpretations. Over the years, however, whatever geographical distinction Northern and Southern Learning originally possessed gradually disappeared. What determined whether an individual subscribed to the ideas of one school over the other was personality, temperament, and philosophical and political outlook rather than, simply, geographical origin.

The Sui and T'ang reunifications of China brought with them an earnest attempt to reunify Chinese thought as well. The effort to create a new philosophical synthesis was most clearly revealed in the *Five Clas-*

sics with Orthodox Commentaries (Wu-ching cheng-i) in 170 (variant 180) *chüan,* compiled by imperial order between 638 and 653 under various supervisors.[2] The *Orthodox Commentaries,* which served as the basis for the popular *ming-ching* ("classics") examinations during the early T'ang, contains commentaries to the classics from both the schools of Northern and Southern Learning and thus effected, at least superficially, an amalgamation of Chinese thought under imperial auspices.

But this amalgam may not have been an accurate reflection of the philosophical attitudes of a majority of the seminal thinkers of the period. K'ung Ying-ta, the chief compiler of the *Orthodox Commentaries* and a northerner, appears to have favored scholars of the school of Southern Learning over those of their northern counterparts, and the definitive edition (*ting-pen*) of the Five Classics compiled early in T'ai-tsung's reign by Yen Shih-ku (a northerner, but a descendant of the southerner Yen Chih-t'ui) also more frequently employed southern versions of the texts,[3] all of which has prompted P'i Hsi-jui's somewhat hyperbolic remark that "Following the unification of classical studies there was Southern Learning but no Northern Learning."[4]

Where did Wei Cheng stand on the matter of Northern vs. Southern Learning? This is a difficult question to answer, given our still deficient understanding of the philosophical and, especially, the political content of the two schools, and also Wei Cheng's own distaste for pursuing questions of ideology divorced from their practical contexts. One of the rare instances in which Wei does comment on the problem is in the "Confucian scholars" section of the *Sui History,* where he very briefly traces differing interpretations of the classics employed by the two schools of thought during the Period of Disunion. Here he adopts a neutral position, merely noting that Northern and Southern Learning each had its own strong points and that thus each in its own way contributed to an understanding of classical doctrine.[5]

At the same time there appears to have been a strong early T'ang trend toward philosophical eclecticism that Wei also shared. The contents of the *Essentials of Government from Divers Books*—which Wei helped compile and which contains materials culled from schools of thought as

[2]See *THY* ch. 77, p. 1405, and *CTS* 73.16b.
[3]P'i Hsi-jui, *Ching-hsüeh li-shih,* pp. 176, 207.
[4]Ibid., p. 196.
[5]*SuiS* 75.1b.

varied as Confucianism, Taoism, Mohism, and Legalism—provide a good example of this eclecticism. Thus, while the doctrines of Confucius and Mencius constitute the core of Wei's thought, we also discover a rich overlay of elements from schools of Chinese philosophy that had acted upon and modified classical Confucianism all during the previous millenium.

BASIC PRINCIPLES OF GOOD GOVERNMENT

At the very basis of Wei's thought, around which all other elements in his political philosophy revolved, was the Confucian article of faith that good government would be achieved when a ruler's conduct had been set right and he became a moral exemplar for his people. The idea is an ancient one. In the *Analects* we read, "Master K'ung said, Ruling (*cheng*) is straightening (*cheng*). If you lead along a straight way, who will dare go by a crooked one?"[6] The *Mencius* (*Meng-tzu*) says, "Let the prince be benevolent, and all his acts will be benevolent. Let the prince be righteous, and all his acts will be righteous. Let the prince be correct, and everything will be correct. Once rectify the ruler, and the kingdom will be firmly settled."[7] By the time of the appearance of the *Great Learning* (*Ta-hsüeh*) and *Doctrine of the Mean* (*Chung-yung*) in the last centuries before our era, cultivation of the person (*hsiu-shen*) and rectification of the person (*cheng-shen*) were becoming fundamental themes in Confucianism.[8]

A corollary to this principle was that once the ruler had attained moral perfection the people would naturally emulate him, and in so doing be morally transformed themselves. This transformation, known as *chiao-hua*, was a basic Confucian goal. Happily, Wei Cheng argued early in Chen-kuan, T'ai-tsung had an excellent opportunity to transform all his subjects since they were now most susceptible to his moral influence. The emperor and one of his officials, Feng Te-i, had argued

---

[6] *Analects* 12.17; Arthur Waley, *Analects,* p. 167.

[7] *Mencius* 4.1; James Legge, *The Chinese Classics,* vol. 2, *The Works of Mencius,* pp. 310–11. On the theme of rectification of the ruler in Wei's writings, see Lung Shou-t'ang, "Wei Cheng chih cheng-chih ssu-hsiang" [Wei Cheng's Political Thought], *Hsiang-kang ta-hsüeh chung-wen hsüeh-hui hui-k'an* [Journal of the Chinese Literature Society, the Chinese University of Hong Kong] (1960), 46–47.

[8] See, for example, Legge, *The Chinese Classics,* vol. 1, *The Great Learning,* p. 359, "From the Son of Heaven down to the mass of the people, all must consider the cultivation of the person the root of *everything besides.*"

just the opposite: that after a long period of disorder, such as China had recently suffered, it would be a difficult task to change the people for the better. But Wei countered with the observation that after a long period of peace people tended to become arrogant and difficult to instruct; after a long period of chaos, what the people craved most was order, so that teaching them would be as easy as feeding the starving or giving water to the thirsty.[9]

Chiao-hua was not a concept that implied positive action; rather, according to the Confucians, the ruler had but to manifest his superior virtue and the people would automatically and voluntarily respond to his beneficent influence. For Wei, quiescence (*ching*) was the foundation of transformation.[10] The themes of folding one's hands yet accomplishing everything, quiescence, and good government by means of non-activity (*wu-wei erh chih*) that are so frequently encountered in Wei's writings are best known in their relationship to Taoism. Yet in *Analects* 13.6 Confucius says, "When a prince's personal conduct is correct, his government is effective without the issuing of orders," and *Analects* 15.4 actually contains the phrase *wu-wei erh chih*; thus the concept is by no means limited exclusively to classical Taoism.[11] As early as the Han dynasty, *wu-wei erh chih* had become a common theme of Confucianism and, as we have seen, occupied an important place as well in the thought of such essentially Confucian philosophers of the post-disunion period as Wang T'ung. Its employment by Wei thus appears to have been more a reflection of the existence of a Taoist pole in early T'ang Confucianism than an expression of his own deep commitment to Taoist ideology per se. Moreover, it was a powerful tool traditionally employed by bureaucrats who were attempting to restrict their ruler's scope of activity while at the same time seeking to enhance their own.[12]

Wei's use of the *wu-wei* theme was further intended to prod T'ai-tsung into making *wen* ("civil virtue") predominate over *wu* ("military

---

[9]*TCTC* ch. 193, p. 6084; *WCKCL* 3.2b–5; *CKCY* 1.16–17b. Feng Te-i's death shortly after T'ai-tsung came to power (*CTS* 63.3b; *HTS* 100.6) dates this episode early in Chen-kuan.

[10]*WCKCL* 3.2b.

[11]James Legge, *The Confucian Classics*, vol. 1, *Confucian Analects*, p. 266; H. G. Creel, "The Fa-chia: 'Legalists' or 'Administrators'?", in *Studies Presented to Tung Tso-pin on his Sixty-fifth Birthday, Bulletin of the Institute of History and Philology, Academia Sinica*, extra vol. 4 (Nankang, Taiwan, 1961), p. 614.

[12]See, for example, James T. C. Liu, "An Administrative Cycle in Chinese History: The Case of the Northern Sung Emperors," *Journal of Asian Studies*, 21 (1962), 143.

virtue") in his administration. The minister's repeated opposition to his emperor's military plans was based on the belief that nothing could be gained by warfare that could not be gained by moral suasion. It was for this reason, for example, that he called on the emperor not to send troops against the "barbarian" rebel Feng Ang, arguing that if Feng were treated with sincerity and trust, he would "by himself come to court."[13]

Wei's implacable hostility toward things military was also shown in his reaction to a martial dance performed at court during times of feasting and celebration. Entitled "The Prince of Ch'in Smashes the Ranks" (Ch'in-wang p'o-chen) and dating from the time of Li Shih-min's campaign against the rebel Liu Wu-chou early in Wu-te, it was performed to music in the Kuchean style by a company of 120 (alternately 128) men in full armor wielding halberds. At such times it is said that Wei would hang his head to indicate his displeasure at its military theme.[14]

Naturally, Wei's abhorrence of aggressive warfare had a very practical as well as an ideological basis. He was keenly aware that Yang-ti's abortive Koguryŏ campaigns had been a major factor in his demise and that warfare in general could weaken a state as easily as it could strengthen it, a view he neatly summed up in his commentary on the "Eastern Barbarians" (tung-i) section of the Sui History with an old saying, a rhymed couplet, which went: "Striving to broaden one's virtue leads to prosperity; striving to broaden one's territory leads to destruction" (wu kuang te che ch'ang; wu kuang ti che wang).[15] Wei must also have viewed any increased role of military officials in government with great alarm, since it would have served to undermine civil official preeminence.

Indeed, when the word "official" (kuan) appears in Wei's writings,

[13]WCKCL 1.8b.

[14]HTS 97.15; TCTC ch. 192, p. 6030, note of Hu San-hsing, ch. 194, p. 6101; THY ch. 33, p. 612; Hsiang Ta, T'ang-tai Ch'ang-an yü Hsi-yü wen-ming [T'ang Ch'ang-an and Western Regions Culture] (1933; reprint, Peking, 1957), p. 62. Cf. C. P. Fitzgerald's rather unconvincing thesis that Wei bowed his head because he was ashamed of his previous role under the crown prince Chien-ch'eng; Son of Heaven, p. 154. T'ai-tsung appears to have had the last laugh, though, by commanding that Wei Cheng and others furnish the verses to be sung in accompaniment to the Ch'in-wang p'o-chen dance music; WCKCL 4.15b–17.

[15]SuiS 81.17. This was an echo of themes in the Mo-tzu; see Burton Watson, Mo Tzu: Basic Writings (New York, 1963), pp. 54–55. More condemnations of warfare by Wei are found in SuiS 82.8b–9 and 83.18b–19.

we are always to understand it in the context of "civil official." The civil official, not his military counterpart, aided the ruler in achieving moral perfection. Good government came about only as a result of the cooperation between the ruler and his civil officials. As Wei once wrote to T'ai-tsung:

I have heard that the ruler is the head and his officials are the arms and legs. If they are well coordinated and of the same mind they will combine to form a [whole] body. If [the body] is formed but is incomplete, it will not yet constitute a whole man. Although the head is exalted, it still must depend on the arms and legs to form a [whole] body. [In the same way], even if a ruler is enlightened and wise, he must depend on his arms and legs [i.e., his officials] to bring about good government.[16]

How could the ruler's behavior best be rectified?—by his cheerful acceptance of remonstrance and advice from his officials, who would correct any errors of judgment he had made and ensure that he would never act in such a way as to jeopardize his rule. Early in Chen-kuan Wei observed:

Although the ruler is wise, he should still humbly accept [the opinions of other] men. Thereupon wise men will offer him their plans and brave men will exhaust their strength [on his behalf]. Yang-ti relied on his own talents and arrogantly used his own [ideas], so although he spoke of Yao and Shun, he acted like Chieh and Chou. Because he did not know this he was destroyed.[17]

Wei was fond of pointing out ways in which the sage-rulers of ancient times had made provision for remonstrance, such as the drum used by Yao and the wooden boards set up at the roadside by Shun.[18]

Because of the important place occupied by civil officials as administrators and as advisers to the throne, they naturally had to be chosen with the utmost care. The worth of an official, Wei observed in good Confucian fashion, was not merely related to his administrative capabilities. Equally or more important, he had to be of good moral fiber. As he once counseled T'ai-tsung:

Since ancient times the selection of officials has been a difficult task. Therefore, we examine their accomplishments and investigate their characters.

16 *WCKWC* ch. 1, pp. 10–11; also *CKCY* 3.4; *HL* 2.21b–22.
17 *TCTC* ch. 192, p. 6053.
18 *WCKWC* ch. 1, p. 16.

Today, if we seek a man [for office], we must first investigate his conduct, and only when we are certain that he is good will we employ him. If the man is unable to do his job well, it will only be because his talents and energy are not up to par and will cause no great harm. But if we mistakenly employ an evil man, if he is capable he will cause much harm. Only in times of disorder do we seek talent but pay no attention to conduct. In this time of great peace and plenty (*t'ai-p'ing*), before we employ anyone we must see to it that he possesses a combination of talent and good conduct.[19]

In the process of selection, the ruler had to advance the morally superior man (*chün-tzu*) and reject the petty man (*hsiao-jen*). At the same time, differentiating one from another was not an easy task, Wei warned, and the ruler had to learn not to allow the defects of worthy men and the merits of inferior men to delude him about their ultimate usefulness:

Petty men are not without their minor virtues and superior men are not without their minor faults. The minor faults of superior men are like flaws in white jade; the minor virtues of petty men are like the single cuts lead knives can make [before they must be rehoned]. The good workman does not attach any importance to the single cut a lead knife can make because its minor virtue is incapable of obliterating a multitude of defects. The good businessman does not reject white jade with flaws because its minor defects are insufficient to spoil its great beauty.[20]

A further cardinal rule of good government was that penal law and punishment should not be oppressive. According to the theory behind *chiao-hua*, if the ruler was able to provide a perfect moral model, laws and punishments designed to regulate the people would be entirely unnecessary. As Wei once put it:

One cannot serve the three-foot laws [in ancient times, the bamboo slips on which laws were written were three Chinese feet long] to constrain the people of the Four Seas and still seek to fold one's hands and rule by non-activity (*wu-wei*). Therefore, when the sage and wise rulers altered the customs and changed the habits [of the people], they did not depend on strict punishments and laws, only on benevolence and righteousness. . . . Benevolence and righteousness comprise the trunk of rule, punishments comprise the branches. Ruling with punishment is like driving horses with a whip. When the people have all been transformed no strict punishments are meted out. When horses have completely exhausted their energy no whips are used.

[19] *WCKCL* 3.15–15b.
[20] *WCKWC* ch. 1, p. 7.

Speaking like this, punishment cannot result in good rule. This is already clear.[21]

At the same time, Wei was also realistic (or Legalistic) enough to conclude that law and punishment were necessary, if evil, tools of a ruler whose morality was frequently imperfect. His preface to the "Biographies of Harsh Officials" (k'u-li chuan) in the Sui History notes that there are four ways through which a nation could be administered: the first, benevolence and righteousness; the second, restraint of the people by a ritual code; the third, law; the fourth, punishment. Benevolence and righteousness and restraint by ritual were the essentials, or "trunk"; law and punishment were the non-essentials, or "branches." But if law and punishment alone could not bring about chiao-hua, they might nevertheless ultimately aid its attainment: "Without the trunk [the tree] does not stand; without the branches it is incomplete."[22] Once having acknowledged the utility of these Legalist tools, Wei made certain to point out that they worked best during times of great disorder, such as in the Warring States period, but that during times of peace, such as China was experiencing during Chen-kuan, laws and punishments were best when they were moderate and compassionate.[23]

In much of Wei's thought there are echoes of Mencius' economic doctrines. Mencius had said, "If the seasons of husbandry be not interfered with, the grain will be more than can be eaten."[24] Like all Confucians, Wei believed in the primacy of agriculture over trade and industry. Once, upon hearing that a prefecture in Chien-nan (Szechuan) and an imperial atelier at the capital were manufacturing silk gauze, embroidered silk, and metallic baubles for the pleasure of the emperor, Wei wrote a remonstrance that well illustrates his views on economic priorities:

[Working with] gold, silver, pearls, and jade interferes with agriculture. Embroidering with metallic and colored threads harms a woman's work. "If one man does not till the soil, [someone in the empire] will suffer hunger. If one woman does not weave, [someone in the empire] will suffer

[21]Ibid., pp. 13–14.
[22]SuiS 74.1.
[23]See WCKCL 3.8, 3.21-21b, 4.3-3b; WCKWC ch. 1, pp. 13–17, ch. 2, pp. 24–25. Lung Shou-t'ang, "Wei Cheng," 56–57, discusses certain parallels between Wei Cheng's thought and Legalism.
[24]Mencius 1.1; Legge, The Chinese Classics, vol. 2, The Works of Mencius, p. 130.

cold."[25] Men of antiquity either cast these things into deep springs or burned them on the thoroughfares, but Your Majesty is fond of them. I cannot bear the shame of it.[26]

Thus, the state would flourish only when the ruler did not interfere with the agricultural labor of the peasantry by making excessive or unseasonal demands on them in order to wage war, construct palaces, manufacture useless articles of luxury, and the like.

As we have seen, Wei's anxiety about the economic consequences of T'ai-tsung's policies is evident in many of his memorials and remonstrances. He opposed the plan to conscript the *chung-nan* into the army because manpower for agricultural labor and corvée would thereby be reduced. He opposed the Feng and Shan sacrifices because China had not yet recovered from the economic dislocations of the late Sui period and the people, he felt, should not be obliged to support the pomp and ceremony the sacrifices required. It would be wrong, though, to assume that Wei's economic concerns stemmed solely from his deep compassion for the masses. Nor were they caused, as some Chinese Marxist historians would have us believe, merely by his fear of the consequences of peasant discontent, which, they say, he developed during his service under the late Sui rebels Yüan Pao-tsang and Li Mi. On the contrary, Wei ultimately viewed the Chinese economic order from the top downward and was always concerned foremost with the economic well-being of the central government and the dynasty in general. Although he held that the people should not be taxed oppressively, he argued even more vigorously that policies which tended to reduce total productivity and tax receipts (like the plan to conscript the *chung-nan*) and thereby weaken the central government were to be avoided.

Illustrating this point was Wei's response early in Chen-kuan to the emperor's plan to create a modified "feudal" (*feng-chien*) system by enfeoffing princes of the blood and selected court officials with territory in various parts of China.[27] Wei gave several reasons why he opposed the plan, but the most important of them were related to the effect it would have had on the central government and the bureaucracy: the people had not yet recovered from the Sui disorders and if they were

[25]From *HS* 24A.8b.
[26]*WCKCL* 1.27.
[27]For court discussions on the *feng-chien* system, see *THY* ch. 46, pp. 824–30.

placed under the administration of princes and officials on the fiefs, they would fear increased exactions on their wealth and labor and would abscond; if a large amount of territory were distributed as fiefs, the central government would be able to levy direct taxes only on a shrunken royal domain and would soon become impoverished; if government revenues fell, the great ministers and other bureaucrats, who were dependent on their cash and food stipends, would have no way to subsist.[28]

CONSOLIDATION THEMES

Even if a ruler followed all of Wei's ideas concerning the conduct of government discussed above, there was still the possibility that initial success might cause him to become less diligent and to slacken his efforts. In Wei's view, by far the greatest obstacle to a ruler's success was complacency. He thus liberally sprinkled his writings and speeches with three mottoes or principles drawn from the Chinese classics, by means of which he exhorted T'ai-tsung to maintain a constant vigilance over his administration. The first principle comes from the *Book of Odes* (it is also quoted twice in the *Tso-chuan*): "All are [successful] at first, But few prove themselves to be so at the last" (*mo pu yu ch'u, hsien k'o yu chung*).[29] The second is based on three passages in the *Book of History* and the *Tso-chuan* that are similar in meaning: (1) "Be careful for the end at the beginning" (*shen chung yu shih*), which Wei alters slightly to "Be careful at the end as you were in the beginning" (*shen chung ju shih*);[30] (2) "Be careful of the beginning and fearful of the end (*shen shih erh ching chung*); then in the end you will have no distress";[31] and (3) "He who at last, as at first, is careful as to whom and what he

[28]*WCKWC* ch. 1, pp. 26–27; *THY* ch. 46, pp. 826–27.

[29]Legge, *The Chinese Classics*, vol. 4, *The She King* (3.1), p. 505; vol. 5, *The Ch'un Ts'ew with the Tso Chuen*, Duke Hsüan, second year, p. 288, and Duke Hsiang, thirty-third year, p. 562, all slightly emended. For Wei Cheng's use of this phrase, see, for example, *CKCY* 6.6 and *HL* 2.32b.

[30]Legge, *The Chinese Classics*, vol. 3, *The Shoo King*, p. 211. For Wei Cheng's use of the phrase, see *TCTC* ch. 192, p. 6048. It is occasionally quoted by other of T'ai-tsung's officials, such as Yü Shih-nan (*CTS* 72.3b) and Chang Hsüan-su (*CTW* 148.8b), suggesting that it may have been part of the Confucian vocabulary of the time.

[31]Legge, *The Chinese Classics*, vol. 5, *The Ch'un Ts'ew with the Tso Chuen*, p. 517, slightly emended. It, in turn, was based on a passage in the *Book of History*: "To give heed to the beginning, think of the end;—the end will then be without distress" (*shen chüeh ch'u, wei chüeh chung; chung i pu k'un*); Legge, *The Shoo King*, p. 490. For Wei's use of the *shen shih erh ching chung* phrase, see *CKCY* 1.7.

follows is a truly intelligent sovereign" *(chung shih shen chüeh yu wei ming-ming hou)*.[32] The third principle, which Wei employed most often of the three, is also from the *Tso-chuan:* "In a position of security think of peril *(chü an ssu wei)*. If you think thus, you will make preparation against the danger, and with the preparation there will be no calamity."[33]

Wei appears to have been somewhat pessimistic concerning the ability of monarchs to avoid the dire consequences of complacency, as can be seen from the comments he made during a court debate that took place in 638. T'ai-tsung had inquired of his officials whether founding a dynasty or preserving it was more difficult. Fang Hsüan-ling had replied that when a dynasty was established all the contenders for the throne struggled violently for power; therefore the founding was more difficult. Wei, however, argued just the opposite. "From the time of the rulers of old, none failed to gain [the empire] by hardship or lose it by indolence. Preserving what has been gained is the more difficult."[34]

Some eight centuries before Wei Cheng's time, Lu Chia had cautioned his monarch, Han Kao-tsu, that although he had won the empire on horseback he could not rule it from horseback,[35] thereby inaugurating a great Confucian *cri de coeur*. Like Lu Chia, Wei appears to represent a recurrent type of official in Chinese history whose tenure of office comes soon after the founding of a dynasty. Such an official exhorts his prince to dismount from his horse of conquest and make civil rather than military virtue his central concern. He stresses that the overriding need of the regime is the preservation in the civil realm of the gains it had already won on the battlefield. He therefore advises extreme caution in the making of domestic and foreign policy with a view toward reinforcing the foundations of dynastic power. An analysis of Wei's role under T'ai-tsung suggests that he embodied many of the characteristics associated with what we might call the "consolidation minister."[36]

[32]Legge, *The Chinese Classics*, vol. 3, *The Shoo King*, p. 210.

[33]Ibid., vol. 5, *The Ch'un Ts'ew with the Tso Chuen*, p. 453. For Wei's use of this phrase and its variations, see *WCKCL* 3.17, 3.19, 4.5b, 4.21b; *CKCY* 10.11, 10.18b. See also its use by Wei's contemporaries Ts'en Wen-pen, *CKCY* 10.9, Chang Hsüan-su, *CTW* 148.12b, and even the Taoist magus Sun Ssu-mo, as quoted in Joseph Needham, *Clerks and Craftsmen in China and the West* (Cambridge, 1970), p. 345.

[34]*TCTC* ch. 195, p. 6140; also *WCKCL* 4.11b–12b; *HL* 1.22–22b; *CKCY* 1.3b–4. Cf. a similar episode in *TCTC* ch. 195, p. 6161, and *CKCY* 10.18–18b, 1.8b–9.

[35]*SC* 97.7–7b.

[36]Perhaps one might even extend this typology to include those officials appearing at the beginning of any reign who tend to stress the consolidation of gains achieved during the

Too many rulers had failed to consolidate their regimes before embarking upon various ill-conceived domestic and foreign ventures,
and as a consequence had been toppled from their thrones. Yet the
failures of past history were nevertheless useful, Wei believed, in that
they could be employed as mirrors which might be held up to guide the
rulers of the present. By early T'ang times the tradition of the mirror
image (which Sung Shen-tsung later employed in selecting a title for
Ssu-ma Kuang's magnum opus) was already more than a millenium
old. The *Book of Odes* contains what is perhaps the prototype in Chinese
literature of all mirror imagery: "The mirror of Yin is not far-distant;–
It is in the age of the [last] sovereign of Hsia."[37] Here, the evil conduct
of Chieh, "bad last" ruler of Hsia, is held up as a warning example to
the rulers of the Yin (Shang) dynasty. The passage from the *Book of
Odes* was one of Wei's favorites, and in his writings he made copious use
of both it and mirror imagery in general.[38]

The Civil Official as a Restraint on Imperial Power

In Wei's eyes the civil official served his prince as a human mirror
whose counsel reflected the collective wisdom of ages past. Knowing well
that civil officials had the potential to exert a strong restraining force on
untrammeled monarchical authority—the source of ruin for many a
dynasty—he was thus fiercely protective of their powers and prerogatives. A considerable number of episodes in the sources reveal how
strongly Wei resisted every move by T'ai-tsung to impinge upon the
prudential and administrative roles of his civil officials. In one such
case, the emperor sharply reprimanded Fang Hsüan-ling and Kao
Shih-lien for daring to raise inquiries concerning articles being manufactured for imperial use at ateliers located in the vicinity of the Hsüan-
wu Gate. When the two officials pleaded with the emperor for forgive-

---

previous administration over any expansionary ideas their own rulers might entertain.

[37] Legge, *The Chinese Classics*, vol. 4, *The She King*, p. 510, translates the character *chien*
as "beacon." On mirror imagery see also Achilles Fang, *The Chronicle of the Three Kingdoms*,
2 vols. (Cambridge, Mass., 1952, 1965), 1: xviii-xix.

[38] See, for example, *WCKCL* 3.20; *WCKWC* ch. 3, pp. 29, 30; *SuiS* 45.19b. Hung Mai
(1123–1202), *Jung-chai sui-pi* (Wan-yu wen-k'u ed., Shanghai, 1939), ch. 16, pp. 154–55,
demonstrates that Wei belonged to a whole group of Han and T'ang dynasty officials who
advised their rulers to regard former dynasties as mirrors. But whereas Han officials like Lu
Chia pointed to Ch'in Shih-huang-ti as their *bête noire*, Wei and his fellow T'ang officials
could make use of a minatory example much closer to them in time—Sui Yang-ti.

ness, Wei became outraged at their obsequious attitude and bravely stepped forward to speak out:

I do not understand why Your Majesty reprimands them, nor do I understand why Hsüan-ling and Shih-lien beg forgiveness. Since Hsüan-ling [and Shih-lien] are employed as high officials, they are Your Majesty's legs and arms and eyes and ears. If there is something being manufactured, how can they not be allowed to know about it? If you reprimand their inquiry, none of your officials will comprehend it.[39]

Another time several memorialists suggested that T'ai-tsung ought to receive all memorials directly from his officials rather than allow them to pass through regular bureaucratic channels. In this way, it was said, he would avoid concealment of facts. Wei saw in this yet another attempt to hack away at civil official participation in government. When asked his opinion of the suggestion, he sarcastically replied that if the memorialists were requesting that the emperor do away with his officials and personally deal with all the administrative trivia at court, then the emperor ought personally to deal with all provincial affairs as well![40]

In a similar vein, Wei was ever ready to protest any sign that the emperor was not treating his officials with the respect due their privileged status in government. "I have heard," he would often say, "that 'A ruler in employing his ministers should be guided solely by the prescriptions of ritual.' "[41] A case in point was his objection to the sentencing of the prefect (*ling*) of Ch'ang-an county, Wang Wen-k'ai, to thirty strokes of the rod because he did not order the official P'ei Chi to quit the capital after being dismissed and sent home by the emperor.

"P'ei Chi's affair deserved ten thousand deaths. Now Your Majesty, remembering his old merit, did not follow the letter of the law; you merely dismissed him from office and went no further than reducing his enfeoffment by half. But even people sentenced to banishment are given some time [in which to prepare to leave]. Why was this not even more true in the case of Chi, who was [only] dismissed and sent back home? The Ancients said: 'Advance men with propriety (*li*), and send them away with propriety.' I

[39]*CKCY* 2.43b; *TCTC* ch. 196, p. 6173; Wang Tang, *T'ang yü-lin*, ch. 1, p. 16.
[40]*WCKCL* 3.5–5b; *TCTC* ch. 195, p. 6163.
[41]*WCKCL* 2.22; *WCKWC* ch. 1, pp. 5, 20; *TCTC* ch. 199, p. 6160. The quote derives from *Analects* 3.19; Waley, *Analects*, p. 99.

think that Wen-k'ai did not incessantly force [Chi to leave] because he was aware of Your Majesty's gracious pardon and knew that Chi was a great official. Then, if we discuss the facts of this case, there has been no crime." T'ai-tsung replied, "When I ordered Chi to pay his respects to his ancestors [i.e., sent him home without additional punishment], was this not propriety?" He then pardoned Wen-k'ai and did not [further] inquire [into the matter].[42]

In several other of his remonstrances discussed in this study, Wei Cheng similarly argued that the emperor had to follow to the letter the rules of propriety governing his relations with his ministers. By such means he attempted to ensure that the emperor would not capriciously trample on official class prerogatives and that officials would not be left to suffer unaided the vagaries of imperial authority. It would be enlightening to know just how far Wei's own contributions to T'ang ritual were similarly aimed at tightening the screws on imperial freedom of action relative to the official class.

FOXES ON THE CITY WALLS, RATS ON THE ALTARS OF STATE

Although the emperor represented a formidable threat to official class power and prestige, he was merely one among several such threats at court; following close upon his heels came members of the imperial house and their relatives by marriage. We have already seen how Prince Li T'ai began demanding greater deference from court officials once he felt he had received T'ai-tsung's support and how Wei Cheng had opposed him. Sometime later, in 638, Wei once again had to defend members of the official class against the imperial princes. This year the president of the Board of Rites, Wang Kuei, memorialized that according to T'ang law, officials of the third rank and above, upon encountering princes of the first rank (sons or brothers of the emperor), were not required to dismount from their horses as a sign of respect, but that lately everyone was disregarding this rule. T'ai-tsung angrily exclaimed, "Will you all honor yourselves and denigrate my sons? This is improper and cannot be done!" Wei thereupon remonstrated that since antiquity princes of the first rank had always been inferior to officials of the third and above. As for the latter dismounting for the princes, "If we inquire of ancient precedent, then there is nothing that

[42]*WCKCL* 1.11b–12.

can serve as a model. To practice [dismounting] at the present time would naturally violate the laws of the state."[43] The emperor then accepted Wang Kuei's memorial.

Wei also did not have to be reminded that since Han times relatives by marriage of the imperial family (*wai-ch'i*) had energetically vied with court officials for imperial favor, on occasion even usurping power for their own houses. He was thus strongly anti-*wai-ch'i* in sentiment. In chapter 5 we saw that Wei protested against the sentencing of Hsüeh Jen-fang to one hundred strokes of the bamboo and dismissal from office for detaining the father of a concubine of an imperial prince for questioning. The remonstrance he wrote at the time reads in part as follows:

Foxes on the city walls and rats on the altars of state are all petty creatures, [but] because they rely on [these essential structures] getting rid of them is not easy. How much more is this the case with relatives by marriage and imperial princesses? In former ages they were all difficult to control, and since the Han and Chin dynasties they have been out of hand. By the middle of the Wu-te period most of them were already arrogant and indolent. Only when Your Majesty ascended the throne did they become respectful. In doing his duty Jen-fang was able to preserve the law for the sake of the state. How can you unreasonably mete him out a severe punishment in order to achieve the selfish ends of your relatives by marriage?[44]

Wei's preface to the *wai-ch'i* section in the *Sui History* similarly reveals his strong bias against that group.[45]

Eunuchs, because of their proximity to the throne, their historical propensity to appropriate power at the expense of other court groups, and the tendency of Chinese monarchs to use them as a counterweight to the regular bureaucracy, were yet another source of anxiety for Wei. Early in the T'ang, eunuchs were for the most part confined to the palace and the environs of the capital; there was as yet little sign that they would attain a dominant position in T'ang government or that they would manipulate the throne itself, as they did during much of the eighth and ninth centuries. But by the middle of Chen-kuan, eunuchs were already being assigned as messengers to the provinces and even beyond the frontier, thus provoking the resentment of regular bureau-

[43]Ibid. 2.6; see also *CKCY* 7.14–14b; *TCTC* ch. 195, p. 6135.
[44]*WCKCL* 2.4b; see also *CKCY* 2.42b–43; *THY* ch. 51, p. 886.
[45]*SuiS* 79.1–1b.

crats. Wei's hostile attitude toward the eunuchs is revealed by an event
that took place in 637. At this time a eunuch messenger on assignment
had gone to the Bureau for the Surveillance of the Frontier (ssu-men)
to obtain a passport required of all those venturing through one of the
twenty-six checkpoints along the border. A secretary of the Bureau,
probably with some malice, had delayed the request. The eunuch had
reported the matter to the throne, causing the immediate demotion of
the secretary to a provincial post. Angered that a mere eunuch had
precipitated the dismissal of a regular official, Wei quickly remonstrated:

It has always been difficult to treat the likes of eunuchs with any intimacy,
since they lightly make up stories and find it easy to provoke trouble. The
practice of employing them to travel alone as envoys to far-off places is unwise
and should not be broadened. [The matter] should receive your most
careful consideration.[46]

The emperor was persuaded to rescind his dismissal of the secretary,
and promised that from that time forward eunuchs would no longer be
employed as provincial envoys.[47]

Lastly, Wei blocked an attempt by still another rival power group,
the Buddhist clergy, to enhance its influence over the throne.
Memorialists, undoubtedly encouraged by the clergy itself, had suggested to the emperor that he daily receive a delegation of Buddhist
monks in private audience to aid him in his religious worship. It was
obvious to Wei that this was merely a ploy to allow the Buddhists a
hand in determining state policies, and he would have none of it:

Buddhism basically esteems purity in order to avoid worldly frivolities and
strife. Furthermore, religious and secular matters are unalike. Long ago
Shih Tao-an was the most eminent monk of the age. When Fu Yung-ku
[Fu Chien of the Former Ch'in, rg. 351–85] rode with him in the same carriage, Ch'üan I regarded it as improper. Shih Hui-lin [another monk] was
not without talent and refinement. When Sung Wen[-ti] [rg. 424–53] led
him up to the palace hall, Yen Yen-chih said: "As to this exalted position,
is it proper to cause a man maimed by punishment [i.e., the tonsure] to

[46]WCKCL 2.13; also CKCY 5.18b; TCTC ch. 195, p. 6158; THY ch. 65, p. 1132. WCKCL
2.23b contains a somewhat different version of the same episode. The incident is discussed
in J. K. Rideout, "The Rise of the Eunuchs during the T'ang Dynasty," Asia Major, n.s., 1
(1949), 58–59.
[47]CKCY 5.18b.

occupy it?" Now if Your Majesty wishes to honor a belief in Buddhism, why would it be necessary to receive the monks daily in separate audience?[48]

The proposal was quietly shelved. Yet Wei was no Han Yü, the great literatus-official of the late eighth–early ninth century renowned for his eloquent attack on Buddhist influence in Chinese society. Rather, he appears to have had no strong antipathy towards Buddhism per se and made no criticism of the routine Buddhist observances that filled court life. Indeed, when T'ai-tsung learned that kingdoms on the Korean peninsula had landed some Buddhist monks at a place in modern Shantung province and surmised that they were spying on China, Wei was quick to allay his fears.[49]

On Correct and Evil Officials

Officials were susceptible to erosion of their authority not only by the emperor and those court groups just discussed, but also by the more unscrupulous of their colleagues who were ever ready to further their own careers at the expense of others. In Wei's eyes the censor Ch'üan Wan-chi had been such a person.[50] So too, probably, was Wei Hung-chih, an obscure, low-ranking official who for some reason unspecified in the histories dared to criticize the chief ministers, thereby over-stepping his position and incurring Wei's wrath. In retaliation, Wei wrote a memorial in which he implied that Hung-chih had formed a faction (p'eng-tang),[51] a term that in Chinese politics generally bore a strong pejorative connotation. As we see in another of his memorials, according to Wei there were two types of associations of men at court, one good, the other bad. If men came together for a good purpose, they were called t'ung-te, or "united in virtue"; if they came together for an evil purpose, they were called p'eng-tang.[52] Interestingly, the distinction Wei makes here between the two types of associations precedes by four centuries Ou-yang Hsiu's famous essay "On Factions" (P'eng-tang lun), in which Ou-yang made the unorthodox proposal that his sovereign not indiscriminately label all factions bad, but rather dis-

[48] WCKCL 3.24–24b. See also HL 1.13b–14; THY ch. 47, p. 836. I am indebted to Professor Arthur F. Wright for his aid in this translation.
[49] WCKCL 4.23.
[50] See above, p. 152.
[51] WCKWC ch. 1, p. 7.
[52] Ibid., p. 8.

tinguish between factions composed of superior and petty men.[53] What Wei was implying in his own memorial, naturally, was that T'ai-tsung should discern who among his officials had merely "united in virtue" and who had formed actual factions, and that only the latter deserved punishment for deluding the throne and interfering with the policies of upright officials.

Of what modes of official behavior did Wei Cheng approve? As there was an ideal ruler who could serve as a moral exemplar for his people, so too was there an ideal official who could serve as a model for all men of his class. In a memorial written in 640, Wei described at length the qualities possessed by such an official, quoting from the description of the "six correct officials" (liu-cheng) by the Former Han scholar Liu Hsiang (ca. 79–ca. 8 B.C.):

Who are known as the liu-cheng?

The first: When sprouts have not yet stirred and signs have not yet been perceived, he alone clearly sees the possibilities of preservation and destruction and the essentials of success and failure, makes preparations against [destruction and failure] before they have appeared, and causes his ruler to excel and to occupy a glorious position. Such a one is a divinely inspired official (sheng-ch'en).

The second: With a humble mind he exhausts his ideas. Daily he offers good advice. He exhorts his ruler with propriety and righteousness; he advises his ruler with far-sighted plans. He accords with his ruler's excellences and corrects his evils. Such a one is an excellent official (liang-ch'en).

The third: He rises early and retires late. He is not remiss in recommending the worthy and repeatedly speaks about events of old to encourage his ruler. Such a one is a loyal official (chung-ch'en).

The fourth: He clearly ascertains [the roots of] success and failure. At an early time he prevents [failure] and corrects [faults]. He stops up the leaks [through which failure may flow] and cuts off their source. He turns misfortune into prosperity and in the end causes his ruler to be without anxiety. Such a one is a wise official (chih-ch'en).

The fifth: He protects civil virtue and serves the law. When he is employed as an official and exercises power, he does not accept presents, refuses emoluments, eschews gifts, and is frugal with food and drink. Such a one is a pure official (chen-ch'en).

The sixth: When the nation is in confusion and in chaos he does not

53See James T. C. Liu, Ou-yang Hsiu (Stanford, 1967), pp. 52–55.

flatter, but dares to oppose his ruler's stern countenance and to speak of his ruler's faults to his face. Such a one is an upright official (*chih-ch'en*).[54]

Obviously, Wei Cheng had taken the *liu-cheng* as a guide for his own official conduct.

At the same time Wei also quoted from Liu Hsiang's description of six types of "evil officials," the *liu-hsieh*. The ordinary official (*chü-ch'en*) thinks only of his office and is covetous of his salary. He goes with the times and has no fixed principles. The flattering official (*yü-ch'en*) says "good" to whatever his ruler says and "you may" to whatever his ruler proposes to do. He ascertains what his ruler likes and advances it in order to please him; he agrees with his improper conduct in order to make him happy, without taking account of future harm. The treacherous official (*chien-ch'en*) is inwardly designing but respectful on the surface. He watches his ruler's countenance and employs artful speech accordingly. He is jealous of worthy and capable men; he reveals the good points and hides the defects of those he wishes to recommend and reveals the faults and hides the good points of those he wishes to degrade. He causes his ruler to reward and punish unfairly and the ruler's orders to be disobeyed. The slandering official (*ch'an-ch'en*) has knowledge sufficient to hide his faults and eloquence sufficient for him to advise others. In the palace he separates flesh and blood and at court incites disturbances. The base official (*chien-ch'en*) monopolizes and usurps power and makes mountains out of molehills. He forms a faction with members of his own family to enrich his house. He alters the meaning of his ruler's orders to enhance his own position. The official who destroys the state (*wang-kuo chih ch'en*) fawns upon his ruler with artful talk. He beguiles his ruler into unrighteousness. He surrounds his ruler with a faction so as to hinder his right perception of things. He causes black and white, right and wrong to be undifferentiated. He causes the bad name of his ruler to be broadcast at home and abroad.[55] Thus, the wise ruler is one who can distinguish those among his officials who follow the path of the *liu-cheng* from those who follow the path of the *liu-hsieh*. Ultimately, good government depends on the ruler's under-

---

[54]*WCKWC* ch. 1, p. 9. The original text is found in Liu Hsiang, *Shuo-yüan* (*SPTK* ed., Shanghai, 1929), 2.1–2.

[55]*WCKWC* ch. 1, pp. 9–10; *Shuo-yüan* 2.2–3b.

standing of human nature—one of the most fundamental of all Confucian themes.

Indeed, herein lies a basic characteristic (basic flaw, some might argue) of Wei's thought: its almost complete lack of originality. Wei was not a seminal thinker, the creator of a new philosophical system. His extant writings and recorded speeches, mostly responses to practical problems besetting the conduct of his prince and the administration of government, do not concern themselves with purely ideological or doctrinal matters. Where Wei's ideas on politics, administration, interpersonal relations in government, and so on, do emerge, they represent for the most part a reworking of or a new emphasis on some rather venerable Confucian themes, both classical and post-classical. Wei's writings are predictable, often tedious, relieved from time to time only by the liveliness of his invective and the ingenuity of the devices that he used to provoke the emperor. If studies on Confucianism typically skip in time all the way from the Later Han dynasty up to the appearance of the celebrated Han Yü (768–824), precursor of the Neo-Confucian revival, it may well be with good reason. From the purely philosophical point of view at least, the intervening period appears to have been a wasteland, when no one save the much discredited Wang T'ung came forward to take up the great Sage's mantle. Yet even Wang T'ung was more imitator than innovator, content to expound upon the Way without expanding upon it.

Nevertheless, following the long Period of Disunion, which saw the eclipse of Confucianism by other, more vigorous philosophies, perhaps it was enough, as Wei did, to passionately proclaim the great principles of Confucianism everywhere throughout the halls of government. From the moment of his arrival at the Chen-kuan court, Wei lived and breathed Confucianism, stale as this Confucianism may seem to us in retrospect.[56] In the doctrines he so forcefully espoused, Wei saw the means of arresting the premature dynastic decay that had plagued China for the past several centuries. But Wei's intent was not merely to strengthen the power of the throne; rather it was to provide restraints

---

[56]Given the examples of both Wang T'ung and Wei Cheng, I cannot agree with the assertion that before the Sung "while there were Confucian scholars, there were virtually no Confucianists; that is, persons who adhered to the teachings of Confucius as a distinct creed which set them apart from others"; Wm. Theodore de Bary et al., *Sources of Chinese Tradition* (New York, 1960), p. 411.

on this power at the very moment he was seeking to increase the advisory and policy-making roles of the civil official. Wei's writings and speeches, and his political behavior in general, were designed to demonstrate to his colleagues (and their successors) how they might defend themselves against the throne and other court groups, how they might curb imperial excesses, and how they might wage the struggle to gain a paramount voice in decision making. More than anyone else during his time, Wei pointed to the power the civil official potentially could wield in government and more than anyone else he attempted to translate that potential into reality.

CHAPTER 9

Wei Cheng's Impact on T'ai-tsung and the Chen-kuan Period

If the sheer bulk of historical materials relating to a man were an accurate indicator of the power he controlled during his own lifetime, then Wei Cheng might well be labelled the most powerful official at T'ai-tsung's court. Sources dealing with T'ai-tsung's reign devote an unusually large amount of space to him. This is particularly true of Wu Ching's *Essentials of Government of the Chen-kuan Period,* some of whose sections are almost exclusively made up of Wei's memorials, remonstrances, and speeches. Wei also has the distinction of being the only Chen-kuan official to merit an entire biographical chapter to himself in both the T'ang Standard Histories; even the great statesmen Chang-sun Wu-chi and Fang Hsüan-ling were not so honored. The conclusion suggested by these bits of evidence is that Wei played an especially strong and salutary role during his time. Indeed, the twentieth-century Chinese scholar Sun Kuo-tung has called Wei the most influential of all T'ai-tsung's officials.[1]

The power of Wei's influence is attested to by various anecdotes. On one occasion, for example, the emperor was admiring a beautiful sparrow he had received as a gift and had set it on his arm. Seeing Wei Cheng approach, who he suspected would ridicule such frivolity, he hid the sparrow in his robes. The minister had many matters to discuss with his prince and it was some time before he left. By then the poor bird had suffocated.[2] Another time T'ai-tsung intended to go on an imperial progress to a region south of the capital, and full preparations had been made there for his arrival, but suddenly, he cancelled the trip. When Wei heard of the matter and inquired about it, T'ai-tsung

---

[1]"T'ang-tai san-sheng chih," 44.
[2]*HL* 2.33b; *TCTC* ch. 193, p. 6059; Wang Tang, *T'ang yü-lin,* ch. 3, p. 90.

meekly replied, "At first I really had that intention, but I feared your rebuke and so stopped midway."[3]

TACTICS AND STRATEGIES

How did Wei achieve such sway over his sovereign? For one thing, like all members of the scholar-official class, he well knew that if the ruler's power was in theory absolute, it was in reality quite susceptible to being influenced, manipulated, or even controlled by his subordinates. For another, he had at his disposal a vast arsenal of time-tested strategies, the stock-in-trade of all officials, by which he brought pressure to bear on his prince. Wei's great strength lay in the fact that he was able to employ these strategies, which involved both rhetorical arm-twisting and subtle coercion, much more successfully than most of his colleagues.

Sometimes Wei would simply launch a direct and blunt attack on T'ai-tsung by baldly outlining the faults of his administration and personal conduct. Other times he would raise the sad specter of the Sui and implore T'ai-tsung not to repeat the mistakes that had ruined that dynasty. Often, though, he would adopt a far more exquisite or devious approach, and on these occasions his effect on the emperor was usually all the more potent. For example, he would lard his proposals with historical precedents, especially Han precedents, since the early T'ang rulers hoped to establish as solid and long-lived an empire as had the Han. He would play upon T'ai-tsung's anxiety over the historical image he would transmit to posterity with repeated warnings that not to follow his advice was to risk destroying the emperor's good name forever. He would fulsomely praise T'ai-tsung's achievements even during times when the latter's virtue, by Wei's own high standards, was obviously deficient, in the hopes of dissolving imperial resistance to his proposals.[4] He would resort to gesture, such as hanging his head during performances of the *Ch'in-wang p'o-chen* dance, or to ridicule, as in the Chao-ling episode. He would artfully contrast T'ai-tsung's actions with those of his predecessors in order to censure him.

A good instance of this last tactic occurred late in 628 after T'ai-tsung had executed an official, Lu Tsu-shang, for first having accepted a new office and then having refused it on the pretext of illness. Later

---

[3] *WCKCL* 4.11; *HL* 1.22, 2.33b; *TCTC* ch. 193, p. 6059; Liu Su, *Ta-T'ang hsin-yü*, 9.6–6b.

[4] See, for example, *WCKCL* 3.21, 4.1b, 4.2b–3, 4.16b, 4.21–21b.

on the day of the execution, T'ai-tsung met with his officials. When
he chanced to inquire about the nature of Emperor Wen-hsüan (rg.
550–59) of the Northern Ch'i dynasty, Wei shrewdly replied:

Unusually tyrannical, but when arguing with others over principles, if he
knew his own to be crooked he was able to accord with theirs. I have heard
that during the [Northern] Ch'i, Wei K'ai was first employed as an administrator-in-chief (*ch'ang-shih*) of Ch'ing prefecture. It happened that he was
sent as an envoy to Liang. When he returned he was made an administrator-
in-chief of Kuang prefecture, but he did not go, and Yang Tsun-yen memorialized about it. Greatly angered, Emperor Wen-hsüan summoned and
reprimanded him. [Wei] K'ai replied, "First I was employed as an administrator-in-chief of the great border territory of Ch'ing prefecture. Now that
I have labored as an envoy and am even more without fault, I·have nevertheless received a post in a small prefecture. That is why I do not go."
[Emperor Wen-hsüan] then turned to [Yang] Tsun-yen, saying, "This man
is right." Consequently he pardoned him.

Thereupon, the sources say, T'ai-tsung shamefacedly had to concede
that he was inferior even to Emperor Wen-hsüan.[5]

Many years later, in 640, a deputy commander of the victorious
Chinese armies on the Kao-ch'ang campaign, Hsüeh Wan-chün, was
accused of having had illicit sexual relations with women of the conquered kingdom, to which charge he pleaded innocent. At his trial,
T'ai-tsung decided to confront Hsüeh with the very women with whom
he had allegedly committed the offense. But Wei Cheng stepped forward to remonstrate against this move, citing the great military renown
Hsüeh and his brothers enjoyed in the empire and the impropriety of
sending the women of a "destroyed state" to confront a Chinese general
before the entire court over so unsavory a matter as fornication. "If
[the accusation] is true then what you will have gained will be slight.
If it is false then what you will have lost will be great." Then Wei went
on to allude to two rulers out of China's remote past who had magnanimously pardoned men who had committed improprieties and who had
thereby reaped rewards for their compassion.

The first of these was Duke Mu of the Ch'in state, who, discovering
that a group of three hundred aborigines had just eaten a prize horse
of his that had run free, decided to pardon them because, as he put it,

[5]Ibid. 3.7–7b; see also *HL* 1.3–3b; *TCTC* ch. 193, p. 6058.

"A *chün-tzu* does not punish men just because of some animal." Instead he presented the offenders with jars of wine, observing that "I hear that to eat the flesh of a fine horse without drinking wine can harm a man." Later, the aborigines came to the Duke's aid in an attack on the state of Chin and with great valor repaid the gift of the horse and wine.[6]

The second, Prince Chuang of the state of Ch'u, once feasted his officials well into the night until all had become tipsy. Suddenly all the lanterns went out, and in the darkness one of the guests happened to tug on the robe of a concubine of the prince, who was nearby. The concubine then seized the chin-strap of the official's cap and informed the prince that an impropriety had been committed against her but that she had retrieved the chin-strap of the offender's cap so that he could easily be identified once the lanterns were again lit. The prince, however, was of another mind: "I served my guests wine and caused them to become intoxicated and impolite. How can I humiliate one of my own men merely to demonstrate the chastity of a concubine?" He then ordered all his guests to remove the chin-straps of their caps and only then allowed the lanterns to be relit. Sometime later, when the states of Ch'u and Chin made war against one another, the prince noticed that one of his men by means of extraordinary valor repeatedly led his forces to victory over the enemy. When the prince questioned him, the warrior revealed that he had been the guest whose chin-strap had been seized by the concubine, and that by exerting himself in Ch'u's victory over Chin he had repaid the prince's kindness.[7]

"Moreover," Wei continued, "[Prince] Chuang of Ch'u and [Duke] Mu of Ch'in were both barbarian Feudal Princes. They are ranked among the Five Hegemons and their fame has been handed down the ages. How much more is Your Majesty the ruler of an empire whose virtue is greater than that of a Yao or a Shun. If you act improperly, how will you be able to display [your good name] to posterity?"

The emperor was thus persuaded to adopt Wei's advice and let the matter drop.[8]

Superficially, at least, the effects of Wei's tactics on the emperor appear to have been considerable. Wei was often able to persuade his prince to reverse decisions he had already made or cancel plans he had

[6]The story originates in *SC* 5.12–12b and is repeated in Liu Hsiang's *Shuo-yüan* 6.7b–8.
[7]This story is told in Liu Hsiang, *Shuo-yüan* 6.8–8b.
[8]*WCKCL* 2.22–22b.

not yet carried out. Perhaps one of the most striking results of Wei's incessant pressure, seen most notably during the first decade of Chenkuan, was that T'ai-tsung began to parrot many of his minister's favorite mottoes in his own speeches. In 632, for example, when the official Yü Shih-nan praised T'ai-tsung in a work he wrote called *Wise and Virtuous Discourses* (*Sheng-te lun*), the latter demurred and observed:

Your estimate of me is too exalted. We do not presume to imitate the ancients, yet compared to [rulers of] recent times, We have somewhat surpassed them. You have only seen Our beginning, however, and do not yet know what Our conclusion will be. If We are able to be careful at the end as We were in the beginning (*shen chung ju shih*), then these discourses can be handed down [to later ages]. If not, then We fear that it will only cause later generations to laugh at you.⁹

At times both the emperor and Wei would declaim the same mottoes in an almost ritual fashion. Sample the following toasts at a feast in 631 attended by the emperor and his ministers:

T'ai-tsung: We hear that since ancient times emperors and kings were by no means always able to transform [the people]. If there was peace internally, there was disorder externally. Now the far-off barbarians have all submitted to Us, and the hundred grains are plenteous. Bandits are not active, and inside and outside [China] there is peace. We are delighted to have achieved this state of affairs, and so We happily drink with you. [But] all this has [not been brought about] by Our efforts alone; it is also by means of all of you that we mutually preserve and aid [the state]. However, "while in security do not forget destruction (*an pu wang wang*); during times of order do not forget disorder." Although We know that there are no problems today, We must also think of the future. If We are always able to do this, only then can it be esteemed.

Wei Cheng: . . . Now there is a great peace in the empire. If we are happy, it is because when Your Majesty is in a position of security you think of peril (*chü an ssu wei*) and are never indolent.

T'ai-tsung: The myriad affairs are important; how can We not think of them? You may inform the recorders (*ch'i-chü lang*) always to write on their tablets: "while in a position of security think of peril" (*chü an ssu wei*). If We do not think on it, then you must remind Us.¹⁰

Again the following year, at another banquet attended by the emperor and his high-ranking ministers, there was the following dialogue:

⁹*TCTC* ch. 194, p. 6098.
¹⁰*WCKCL* 4.21–21b; *HL* 1.27–27b.

T'ai-tsung: We and you together rule the empire. If China is now at peace and the four quarters are quiescent it is only because you have all exhausted your loyalty and sincerity and together have brought about the great achievement of peace and plenty. We are really delighted by it. But in security we must not forget peril (*an pu wang wei*). . . .

Wei Cheng: . . . I have heard that when drinking with Duke Huan [of Ch'i], Pao Shu-ya toasted him, saying, "I want you not to forget the time when you were in Chü, and Kuan Chung not to forget the time he was in Lu, and Ning Ch'i not to forget the time he fed the cows" [i.e., when they were all in straitened circumstances in earlier times]. When Your Majesty is in a position of security you think of peril (*chü an ssu wei*); in times of order you think of disorder. Your not forgetting these principles has already surpassed Shu-ya's wishes.[11]

It is significant, too, in an assessment of Wei's strength at court, that despite vicissitudes in his relationship with the throne, he was never once dismissed from office or degraded. This record is all the more startling when placed beside those of many other Chen-kuan officials, some of whom were greatly favored by T'ai-tsung, but who were nevertheless abruptly dismissed from their posts for some misdemeanor (e.g., Fang Hsüan-ling) or demoted and sent out to the provinces for various lengths of time (e.g., Kao Shih-lien).

The Politics of Morality and Its Limits

Having examined data supporting the traditional view concerning Wei's strong role under T'ai-tsung, it is now time to examine the other side of the question. It should be apparent by now that Wei's greatest influence on T'ai-tsung was exerted in the ethical as opposed to the strictly political realm (although it is not always easy to distinguish sharply between the two). Because of Wei's belief that the political and economic well-being of the state was ultimately dependent on the moral well-being of the ruler, he was always concerned above all with T'ai-tsung's moral health. By way of example, we might use his very first remonstrance to the throne late in 626, on which occasion he was concerned lest T'ai-tsung forfeit the people's trust and confidence by rescinding a tax reduction he had already announced for that year. Here, Wei was not interested in the welfare of the peasantry—who, had the tax reduction not gone into effect, would have had to pay increased

[11] *WCKCL* 3.8b–9; also *HL* 1.4–5.

taxes—so much as he was interested in the general principle that the ruler had to provide an example of good faith for his subjects.

This is not to say that Wei's concern never extended beyond the moral realm. Frequently he demonstrated some very practical concerns, such as the time he opposed the conscription of the *chung-nan* group because it would have reduced the tax yield and manpower reserve for corvée, or the time he opposed the Feng and Shan rites because of the poor economic state of the region surrounding Mount T'ai. Yet the majority of his remonstrances, memorials, and speeches to T'ai-tsung deal primarily with the latter's moral conduct and the means by which it and, hence, his rule could be improved.

It was precisely because Wei's influence extended chiefly over the moral realm that it was, in the last analysis, so circumscribed. For morality and practical politics, in China as elsewhere, seldom mix. Although the emperor frequently was willing to accept Wei's admonitions concerning relatively minor matters, such as the punishment of officials, the presentation to a daughter of an excessively large betrothal gift, the acceptance of inappropriate tribute gifts, and so on—matters governed by law or ritual—he was generally unwilling to allow Wei a decisive voice in determining the all-important decisions that fundamentally affected the throne or the T'ang house. In terms of practical results, Wei's remonstrances on major issues were frequently ineffective. Here it should be emphasized that the minister was completely powerless to prevent his sovereign from reaching some of the most momentous decisions of his reign: to destroy the Khanate of the Eastern Turks; to resettle the Turks inside China's borders; to establish a modified "feudal" (*feng-chien*) system for princes of the blood and high-ranking officials; to carry out the Feng and Shan sacrifices; to annex the kingdom of Kao-ch'ang. Not all of these decisions were actually implemented, but for reasons in no way related to Wei's opposition to them. It should be remembered, too, that shortly after Wei's death T'ai-tsung undertook his disastrous Koguryŏ campaigns despite his minister's repeated warnings against military adventurism.

To be sure, Wei was not the only official to suffer some diminution of influence over the emperor during the latter's second decade in power. Ch'u Sui-liang also bitterly but unsuccessfully opposed the annexation of Kao-ch'ang, and he, along with Fang Hsüan-ling and Chang-sun Wu-chi, vigorously spoke out against T'ai-tsung's Koguryŏ campaigns, but also to no avail. Yet these three, despite their occasional

differences of opinion with T'ai-tsung, at least commended themselves
to the emperor by virtue of their generally pragmatic and reasonable
approach to policy making. Wei Cheng, on the other hand, consumed
by a passionate belief in the moral efficacy of Confucianism in government and driven to preach his "sacred policies" at every opportunity,
merely frustrated and provoked the emperor. It was for this reason that
Wei, far more than his high-ranking colleagues, met with such a dis-
cernible decline in his real power at court.

As we have seen, though, Wei's career with T'ai-tsung is usually
depicted in the most glowing of terms as a major success story. Generation after generation of Confucian moralist-commentators and scholar-
officials have lauded him, and not without reason. For the Confucian
moralists, it was not important that Wei occasionally failed to persuade
T'ai-tsung not to carry out a given policy. What was important to them
was that he was the embodiment of Confucian learning and ethics, and
that he sought to exert a beneficent moral influence on his sovereign.
After all, Confucius himself had encountered little success in practical
politics, yet his ethical precepts had made him the most revered figure
in all China. The wielding of ethical power, not political power, was
what most concerned the Confucian moralists.

Wei was a hero as well to the scholar-officials. He had labored tire-
lessly to defend their powers and perquisites against imperial encroachment and had been an ardent advocate of the return of the civil official
after a long period of eclipse to a dominant position in government.
During the Period of Disunion political power had been wielded by
those with genealogical status or military might on their side, and the
Confucian ideal of the civil official whose authority derived not from
pedigree or arms but from moral rectitude and superior administrative
skill was seldom realized in practice. Strict Confucians were still seldom
found in the upper ranks of officialdom during the Sui, and even after
the establishment of the T'ang it was by no means certain that the
civil official ideal would prevail. As a case in point, had T'ai-tsung's
plan to recreate a feudal system actually been implemented, political
power in T'ang government might well have devolved on members or
relatives of the ruling house rather than on the civil bureaucracy.
Alternately, it might have reverted to the great landholding families
and entrenched clans that had monopolized politics during the Period
of Disunion.

Clearly, Wei Cheng helped to ensure the ascendancy of the civil official ideal during Chen-kuan. But it is also true that this ideal could never have triumphed had not the emperor himself wanted to strengthen the hands of his own bureaucrats at the expense of other loci of power in the empire, particularly, as we have seen in chapter 4, at the expense of the entrenched aristocratic lineages of the northeastern plain. To combat the great centrifugal power that these clans represented, T'ai-tsung looked to his own supporters, men who for the most part were descendants of minor official families. Since one of the reasons the emperor gave for his edict emending the *Compendium of Clans* was the wish "to honor the officials of the present court,"[12] it is clear that in the revised edition of the survey the families of high-ranking Chen-kuan civil officials, along with the imperial family and its relatives by marriage, also received appropriately augmented social ranks. By raising the prestige and social status of his high officials, the emperor hoped to create a new social elite in China to replace the four surnames and clans of similar reputations, one that at the same time would constitute a bedrock of support for his house. For very different reasons, then, Wei Cheng and T'ai-tsung were allies in the enterprise of enhancing official class prestige. Nevertheless, the result was what counted, and there was no doubt in the minds of later generations that during Chen-kuan Wei Cheng had been the strongest force in raising the position of the civil official class to unprecedented heights.

In the final analysis, then, Confucian commentators and scholar-officials acclaimed Wei because they approved both of his role as a moral crusader, despite its actual limitations, and of his efforts to increase the political credit of the civil bureaucrary. By applauding his free and fearless criticism of his monarch and his advocacy of civil official preeminence, they gave expression to the hope of achieving the same conditions in their own times. For them, Wei's career was vivid proof of their value to the ruler and a heady reminder of the power they might exercise in government. These were the men, after all, who wrote the histories and historical commentaries in China, and these were the men who shaped and broadcast Wei's hortatory image down the ages.

[12]*CKCY* 7.12; *THY* ch. 36, p. 664; *TCTC* ch. 195, p. 6136.

CHAPTER 10

Apotheosis, Myth, and Symbol: Wei Cheng's Image in Chinese History

At the end of the last chapter we spoke of Wei Cheng's image. Perhaps it would be more correct to refer to his image in the plural rather than the singular, since standing alongside the image shaped by Confucian historians are others shaped by popular literature and folk-religion. The Wei Cheng of history, as we have seen, is a model minister and critic nonpareil; the Wei Cheng of literature is a wily strategist and Taoist adept; the Wei Cheng of folk-religion is a spirit guardian of gates and doors. Although these various personae of Wei Cheng live in their separate worlds, they nevertheless all bear the unmistakable stamp of his personality and, as such, serve to accent his symbolic role in Chinese politics.

THE HISTORICAL IMAGE

Wei's historical image, essentially an idealization nourished over the centuries by sympathetic and admiring Confucians, was already taking shape during his lifetime. T'ai-tsung, for one, was wont to compare Wei with such luminaries as Kuan Chung and Chu-ko Liang.[1] Within half a century after Wei's death, memorials to the throne were already hailing his role as remonstrator and his contributions to the Chen-kuan period.[2] The work of the T'ang scholar Wang Fang-ch'ing, who late in the seventh century gathered together Wei's remonstrances and

[1] *CKCY* 2.6; *WCKCL* 5.18. The comparison between Wei Cheng and Kuan Chung is especially interesting, for their careers had numerous parallels. Kuan Chung (d. 645 B.C.) was tutor to the brother of Duke Huan of Ch'i (685–43 B.C.) and supported this brother in the Ch'i war of succession that erupted upon their father's death. Duke Huan killed his brother but forgave Kuan Chung and eventually made him his chief minister. It is not without significance that Duke Huan and Kuan Chung figure prominently in several discussions between T'ai-tsung and Wei Cheng.

[2] See, for example, the memorial of Ch'en Tzu-ang to Empress Wu, *HTS* 107.17b.

speeches and published them as the work now known as the *Recorded Remonstrances of Duke Wei of Cheng,* and Wu Ching, who early in the eighth century compiled the *Essentials of Government of the Chen-kuan Period,* served to exalt still further Wei's reputation as a model minister and to crystallize it for all time in the minds of educated Chinese. At least seven works devoted solely to Wei's remonstrances and other writings were compiled during the T'ang.[3] His fame was also celebrated in T'ang poetry and prose.[4]

Soon, like other great ministers before him, Wei became a historical exemplar whose deeds and words were deserving of invocation. Sometime late in the eighth century the general Li Sheng observed to his aides: "Wei Cheng excelled at straightforward remonstrance. I personally esteem him." When one of these aides disparagingly observed that Wei's crusading zeal perhaps befitted a civil official but was unsuited to a military man, Li replied: "You are mistaken. I have been given responsibilities both as a general and minister of state. If I know that the court has committed some error and do not speak out, then how could I be a minister!"[5] When the Later T'ang dynasty (923–37) official Feng Tao wished to encourage his ruler to remain vigilant over his administration, he did so with the following advice: "After the tenth year of Chen-kuan (636), the Minister Wei Cheng memorialized T'ang T'ai-tsung asking that all should be like the beginning of the Chen-kuan period. Now I also wish Your Majesty to think of the good things you did at the beginning of your reign. If Your Majesty would do so, then the empire would be fortunate indeed."[6] Similarly, the twelfth-century Sung official Ts'ai K'an lauded Wei's remonstrances to his emperor and suggested that if the latter wanted to emulate the success of the Chen-kuan period, he, like T'ai-tsung, should adopt the advice they contained.[7] In 1657, early in the Ch'ing dynasty, when the Hsün-chih emperor built a tomb for his late consort and visited it

[3]See *WCKCL, k'ao-cheng* section, 1–4b.

[4]See the short pieces by Ch'en Yen-po, P'ei Ta-chang, Kao Shih, and Tu Mu in Li Fang et al., comps., *Wen-yüan ying-hua* [The Flowers of the Garden of Letters], (982–87; reproduction of 1567–72 ed., Taipei, 1965), 180.6, 180.6b, 301.10b, and 307.6, respectively, and the *fu* by Huang T'ao in *CTW* 822.18–19b.

[5]*TCTC* ch. 232, p. 7483.

[6]Wang Gung-wu, "Feng Tao: An Essay on Confucian Loyalty," in *Confucian Personalities,* Arthur F. Wright and Denis Twitchett, eds. (Stanford, 1962), p. 137.

[7]Ts'ai K'an (fl. 1165–74), *Ting-chai chi* (n.p., 1897), 1.1.

frequently, one of his officials, Yao Wen-jan, remonstrated with him by recounting Wei's ridicule of T'ai-tsung for his construction of the Chao-ling and the emperor's subsequent destruction of the tower he had built to view the tomb.[8]

Nevertheless, Wei Cheng's example has not always been viewed so favorably. A few commentators have caviled at Wei's failure to prevent some of T'ai-tsung's more notable excesses, such as his construction of the Fei-shan Palace. Others have found fault with Wei for what they consider to have been his excessively practical approach to government, that is, his tendency to deal on a piecemeal basis with deficiencies in T'ai-tsung's conduct and administration as they arose rather than attempting to reform the emperor's very character by the power of Confucian moral principle.[9] The issue receiving the most attention from Wei's critics, though, has been the checkered pattern of his early political career—his frequently shifting allegiances and service to multiple masters that marked the period prior to the Hsüan-wu Gate incident. This criticism was especially strong after the rise of Neo-Confucianism and the premium it placed on the concept of loyalty.[10] The eleventh-century Sung commentator Fan Tsu-yü's criticism of Wei Cheng and Wang Kuei for serving T'ai-tsung even after he slew their former masters[11] is symptomatic of this new emphasis in Confucianism. Some centuries afterwards, Wei was still being excoriated by men like P'an Te-yü (1785–1839) for his divided allegiances and for what P'an viewed as his gross opportunism.[12] Yet it should be remembered that for the time in which Wei lived, a career under rulers of different houses, not to mention more than one ruler of a single house, was in no way extraordinary. During the politically chaotic Period of

[8]*Ch'ing-shih* [Ch'ing History] (Taipei, 1961), ch. 264, p. 3829.

[9]See the arguments of Chen Te-hsiu (1178–1235) in *CKCY* 2.8–8b, and of Lung Shou-t'ang, "Wei Cheng," 47.

[10]For an examination of the Neo-Confucian concept of loyalty and its effect on the historical image of one official, see Wang Gung-wu, "Feng Tao."

[11]Fan Tsu-yü (1041–98), *T'ang-chien* [The Mirror of T'ang] (*Ts'ung-shu chi-ch'eng* ed., Shanghai, 1936), ch. 2, pp. 13–14. Wei's and Wang's example, Fan maintains, cannot in any way be compared to that of Kuan Chung, who served Duke Huan of Ch'i even after he murdered his brother, Kuan Chung's former master. This was because, Fan points out, the brother, unlike Li Chien-ch'eng of the T'ang, was not heir to the throne. Cf. a casuistic solution to the problem of Wei Cheng's loyalty, using the Kuan Chung-Duke Huan of Ch'i analogue, offered by the late Ming scholar Wang Fu-chih in his *Tu T'ung-chien lun*, 20.11–12.

[12]See Chan Hok-lam, "Liu Chi (1311–75) and His Models: The Image-Building of a Chinese Imperial Adviser," *Oriens Extremus*, 15 (1968), 44–45.

Disunion, at least, service to multiple masters was not just a common occurrence but a necessary by-product of the age.[13] Of early T'ang officials, most had served the Sui and at least one or two rebel leaders before joining the T'ang. The emphasis on loyalty to a single ruler was largely Neo-Confucian in origin and did not overly concern the officials of the early T'ang.

Moreover, Confucius himself had once upheld the concept of service to more than one master, using by way of illustration the relationship between Kuan Chung and Duke Huan of Ch'i:

Tzu-kung said, I fear Kuan Chung was not Good. When Duke Huan put to death his brother Prince Chiu, Kuan Chung so far from dying on Chiu's behalf became Duke Huan's Prime Minister. The Master said, Through having Kuan Chung as his Minister, Duke Huan became a leader of the feudal princes, uniting and reducing to good order all that is under Heaven; so that even today the people are benefiting by what he then did for them. Were it not for Kuan Chung we might now be wearing our hair loose and folding our clothes to the left! We must not expect from him what ordinary men and women regard as "true constancy"—to go off and strangle oneself in a ditch or drain, and no one the wiser.[14]

By analogy, according to Confucius, Wei's substantial contributions to the early T'ang should have wiped away any odium attached to his transfer of loyalties.

Interestingly enough, no commentator appears to have raised the point that, in certain respects at least, other facets of Wei's personality and career violated Confucian criteria for the morally superior man. At the end of the Sui, Wei had been hungry for political position and had wandered across the countryside seeking office under rebel leaders. Upon entering Ch'ang-an with Li Mi at the end of 618, he had sought to ingratiate himself with Kao-tsu and within a short time had attracted attention to himself by means of his scheme to pacify the northeastern plain. Later, by attempting to thwart the political ambitions of Li Shih-min, he had tried to ensure that he would serve the crown prince Chien-ch'eng when the latter became emperor. In this respect, Wei was not in accord with Confucius' criteria for the morally superior man, who

[13]See Mao Han-kuang, *Liang-Chin Nan-pei-ch'ao shih-tsu cheng-chih chih yen-chiu* [Studies on Aristocratic Politics during the Two Chin and Northern and Southern Dynasties], 2 vols. (Taipei, 1966), 1: 300.

[14]*Analects* 14.18; Waley, *Analects*, p. 185.

"does not grieve that other people do not recognize his merits. His only anxiety is lest he should fail to recognize theirs." "He does not mind not being in office; all he minds about is whether he has the qualities that entitle him to office. He does not mind failing to get recognition; he is too busy doing the things that entitle him to recognition."[15] Similarly, once having attained a position of influence, Wei seems to have been loath to share it with certain other officials or power groups at court. Assuredly, part of the reason was that he was defending civil official preeminence. But it is also clear that he was jealously guarding his personal prestige and power and that this was one reason why he moved against officials, such as the architect Chiang Hsing-pen, who had become too influential with T'ai-tsung. We discover, therefore, that Wei's conduct not only failed to be in accord with certain Confucian criteria for good officials, but actually reflected behavior patterns which Confucius on one occasion outlined for small-minded officials: "Before they have got office, they think about nothing but how to get it; and when they have got it, all they care about is to avoid losing it. And so soon as they see themselves in the slightest danger of losing it, there is no length to which they will not go."[16] Wei Cheng's emulation of the Confucian model of the morally superior man and good official thus fell somewhat short of perfection.

Despite such flaws and the criticism of a relatively few detractors, Wei's name has generally evoked highly favorable responses from commentators who have emphasized his great courage, his ability to bring powerful moral suasion to bear on his prince, and his success in hurling devastating criticism at the throne. Most have agreed with the judgment of Wu Ching that since the two Han dynasties there was only one outstanding remonstrating official—Wei Cheng[17]—and with Wang Fu-chih (1619–92), who rated Wei equal to perhaps the most famous minister of them all, Chu-ko Liang.[18]

THE LITERARY IMAGE

Writers of popular literature, on the other hand, have not been much

[15]Analects 1.16 and 4.14; ibid., pp. 87, 104–05.
[16]Analects 17.15; ibid., p. 213.
[17]CKCY 2.8b.
[18]Wang Fu-chih, Sung-lun [Essays on the Sung] (reproduction of the Ch'uan-shan i-shu ed., Taipei, 1965), 6.1.

concerned with Wei's morality, for their aim has been not to improve morals but to entertain.[19] In pursuit of this goal they exaggerated aspects of Wei's personality and career—his youthful flirtation with Taoism particularly—and placed him in numerous situations that are historically untenable. In so doing, they created a far more lively and colorful portrait of Wei than is found in the histories.

Wei's literary image was already taking shape during the T'ang dynasty. The *Tales of the Hsiao and Hsiang Rivers (Hsiao-Hsiang lu)* narrates the story of how Wei, here portrayed as an ardent Taoist in his youth, did not believe in ghosts or spirits and how he was persuaded to change his mind. It tells of the time Wei set out on a journey to the top of Heng Mountain to visit some Taoist hermits. At the foot of the mountain, however, a great blizzard blew up, preventing his ascent. Before the youth there suddenly appeared a Taoist priest who invited him to take shelter in his home nearby. After warming themselves before a fire and fortifying themselves with drink, the two engaged in a lively discussion on Taoism, during which the priest raised the matter of ghosts and spirits. Wei vehemently denied their existence; the priest chided his guest for his disbelief but did not press the point. The next day, the weather having cleared, Wei continued his journey up the mountain with a present of wine from the priest and a letter addressed to one of the hermits on the mountaintop. On the road Wei chanced to look back at the house where he had spent the night, but in place of the house there was only a large grave. Reexamining the letter the priest had given him, he noticed that it now read, "To the spirit of Heng Mountain." In disgust Wei threw the letter to the ground. It thereupon turned into a mouse and scurried away. "From this time on," the story wryly concludes, "Cheng believed somewhat more in ghosts and spirits."[20]

By the time of the Sung and Yüan dynasties, numerous semi-historical popular stories and dramas dealing with the exciting and turbulent Sui-

[19]For a treatment of the literary images of various Chinese historical figures, see Robert Ruhlmann, "Traditional Heroes in Chinese Popular Fiction," in *The Confucian Persuasion,* Arthur F. Wright, ed. (Stanford, 1960), pp. 141–76.

[20]Quoted in Li Fang et al., comps., *T'ai-p'ing kuang-chi,* (977–78; Taipei, 1962), 327.41–41b. The entry is recorded as having been derived from the *Hsiao-Hsiang lu.* There are two works of T'ang date, both now largely lost, bearing this title: one in ten *chüan* by Liu Hsiang (*HTS* 59.20b and *SungS* 206.3) and one in ten *chüan* by Li Yin (*SungS* 206.2).

T'ang transition period were perpetuating Wei's popular literary image not only as a Taoist adept but also as a brilliant tactician. Like his historical image, Wei's popular image is largely an idealization— his disturbing record of service to the crown prince Chien-ch'eng, his efforts to prevent Li Shih-min from succeeding to the throne, and so on, are played down or ignored entirely. Conversely, from the moment of Wei's first meeting with Shih-min, he is shown to be the latter's unswerving ally. In one episode he even helps save his life. No longer is Wei the punctilious, humorless, stern moralist acclaimed by the Confucian image makers; he is now replaced by a rather jovial character, full of courage and cunning, who delights in disobeying his superiors.

In the *Romances of the Sui and T'ang (Sui-T'ang yen-i)*, some stories of which date to the Sung dynasty or earlier, Wei first appears as a former Taoist hermit who is now the keeper of a Taoist monastery.[21] Much later he reappears as an official on the staff of the rebel Li Mi. At this point in the story, Li Shih-min has taken a respite from his campaigns against rebels of the northeastern plain and has gone on a deer hunt that takes him dangerously close to Li Mi's headquarters. He is soon captured and sentenced to die by Li Mi, but Wei Cheng hurriedly intervenes, advising Li Mi that great calamity in the form of swift and powerful T'ang reprisals would result if Shih-min were executed and that it would be better instead to demand ransom for his life. Li Mi agrees, claps Shih-min into prison, and goes off on one of his numerous campaigns. Wei and the others who are left in charge of his camp now decide that Shih-min and not Li Mi is destined to win the empire. At Wei's instigation, they secretly visit Shih-min to declare their allegiance to him and eventually devise the means to set him free.[22]

Following Li Mi's defeat later in the novel, Wei reaches the T'ang capital at Ch'ang-an, whereupon emperor Kao-tsu orders him to serve not the crown prince Chien-ch'eng, as was historically the case, but rather Shih-min. This is a convenient plot device as it avoids tarnishing Wei in the eyes of the reader and provides a fitting fictional reward for his aid in securing Shih-min's freedom. Naturally, no details are given concerning Wei's masterminding of the crown prince's

[21]Ch'u Jen-hu, *Sui-T'ang yen-i* [Romances of the Sui and T'ang] (1695; Hong Kong, 1966), pp. 71ff.
[22]Ibid., pp. 391–93.

strategy against his brother. What is included, though, is Wei's speech to Shih-min following his victory at the Hsüan-wu Gate, since it is a good illustration of his courage before his superiors.[23]

Wei's final appearance in the *Romances of the Sui and T'ang*, like his first, emphasizes his Taoist background. Following the death of Empress Chang-sun, T'ai-tsung becomes seriously ill with melancholia. In the hope of curing him, Wei informs the emperor that he is in contact with a spirit of the nether world, named Ts'ui Chüeh, who can make him well again. Wei then writes a letter to Ts'ui, burns it in front of T'ai-tsung's sickbed, and informs the emperor that by the following morning he will be cured. At dawn the next day, T'ai-tsung awakes to see a lone sparrowhawk flying about his chamber with a slip of paper in his mouth. The bird vanishes shortly afterwards, leaving only the paper acknowledging that Wei's message had reached Ts'ui Chüeh. T'ai-tsung soon finds himself transported to the nether world, where he meets Ts'ui and other denizens, including his two slain brothers. Following other adventures, he awakes to find himself surrounded by his concubines and his son, the crown prince—he had been dreaming and is now completely cured. When Wei Cheng inquires if he had seen Ts'ui, the emperor relates to him the details of his dream.[24]

Wei's effort to set Shih-min free from jail, discussed previously in conjunction with the *Romances of the Sui and T'ang*, supplies a major plot for one drama dating from the Yüan or Ming period, called *Wei Cheng Changes the Order (Wei Cheng kai-chao feng-yün-hui)*, and is alluded to in at least two others.[25] In *Wei Cheng Changes the Order*, Wei and Hsü Mao-kung are left in charge of Li Mi's camp while the latter victoriously leads his men in battle against the general Meng Hai-kung. Soon, to celebrate his success over Meng, Li sends an order back to camp that all prisoners are to be released, all, that is, except Shih-min and his

[23]Ibid., pp. 407, 410, 522. At this point (p. 522), however, a bow is made to historical fact by informing the reader that when Wei first arrived in Ch'ang-an, because Chien-ch'eng's erudition was mediocre, Kao-tsu had appointed Wei to serve as his tutor.

[24]Ibid., pp. 533–36.

[25]The other two dramas are *Ch'ang-an-ch'eng ssu-ma t'ou T'ang* [In the city of Ch'ang-an Four Horses Surrender to the T'ang] and *Ch'eng Yao-chin fu-p'i lao-chün-t'ang* [Ch'eng Yao-chin Splits the Temple with an Axe]. The three plays, all anonymous, are found in *Ku-pen hsi-ch'ü ts'ung-k'an ssu-chi, Mai-wang-kuan ch'ao-chiao-pen ku-chin tsa-chü* (Peking, 1960). See *ts'e* 56.40b, 54.52b, and 56.16b, respectively.

comrade-in-arms Liu Wen-ching. But the crafty Wei Cheng, not to be thwarted in his plans for the T'ang hero, adds one stroke to the character *pu* ("do not") preceding the word "to release" on the order and makes it read *pen* ("be certain to"). He then uses the forged document to secure the freedom of Shih-min and Liu. While these plays frequently differ with the *Romances* concerning details of plot, their depiction of Wei's character is essentially the same. He is still a cunning and formidable strategist who, when necessary, opposes the will of his superiors. Performed throughout China until our own century, these dramas have provided many Chinese with their only, if largely fictional, knowledge of Wei Cheng's role in the founding of the T'ang.

THE FOLK-RELIGIOUS IMAGE

The origin of Wei's image as a door-god (*men-shen*) is shrouded in obscurity. The story that apparently gave rise to his cult, however, is contained in various sources. The most detailed treatment appears in the famous novel *A Record of a Journey to the West (Hsi-yu chi)* by the Ming dynasty author Wu Ch'eng-en (1500–82), which was in turn based largely on folk stories dating from the tenth century or even earlier. *A Record of a Journey to the West* treats the voyage of the Buddhist pilgrim Hsüan-tsang to India and back during the period 629–45. While based on historical fact, it is mainly composed of fantastic episodes, peopled by demons and spirits, that have provided the plots for countless Chinese plays and movies.

The novel narrates the following story concerning the origin of Wei's cult.[26] The Dragon King, a deity in charge of rainfall, makes a wager with a magician concerning the amount of rain to fall on Ch'ang-an at a certain hour on a certain day. Later, the Dragon King learns that his superior in Heaven, the Jade Emperor, has ordered that the rain fall exactly according to the magician's prediction. But being proud and avaricious, the Dragon King is unwilling to lose the wager and defies the Jade Emperor, causing it to rain less than the magician had said it would. As a consequence of his disobedience, the Jade Emperor decrees that the Dragon King is to be beheaded at noon the following day by

[26]Wu Ch'eng-en (1500–82), *Hsi-yu chi* [A Record of a Journey to the West] (Shanghai, 1921), ch. 10, pp. 1–21. There is a translation of this episode in Arthur Waley, *Monkey* (New York, 1958), chapter 10. See also Henri Doré, *Recherches sur les superstitions en Chine*, 18 vols. (Shanghai, 1911–38), 11: 976–78.

T'ang T'ai-tsung's minister Wei Cheng. In great fear, the Dragon King appears in human form to beg the T'ang ruler to prevent Wei Cheng from decapitating him. T'ai-tsung takes pity on him and grants his request.

Unfortunately, T'ai-tsung's plan to foil the execution by engaging Wei in a game of draughts at the noon hour the next day miscarries. Wei falls asleep in the midst of the game and sends his spirit to pursue and decapitate the Dragon King, whose head, still dripping blood, is soon carried into the palace. Thereafter, the Dragon King's spirit returns to haunt T'ai-tsung for seven successive nights, causing him to go without sleep and to become gravely ill. In desperation the emperor accepts a proposal that his generals Hsü Mao-kung and Yü-ch'ih Ching-te be assigned to guard the portals of the palace so that he might repose in peace. The strategem works, yet T'ai-tsung soon grows worried about the health of his two generals, who remain awake all night at their work. He therefore orders that portraits of the two be made and hung on the palace doors to guard him in their stead. For two or three days T'ai-tsung sleeps undisturbed, but at the end of this time a great commotion is heard at the back of the palace. When informed of this, Hsü Mao-kung suggests that Wei Cheng be assigned to guard the rear portals. After Wei takes up his position at the rear, the Dragon King's spirit does not return. On Taiwan it is still common to find portraits of Hsü Mao-kung, Yü-ch'ih Ching-te, and Wei Cheng painted on doors of Taoist temples, guarding them against evil spirits.

From the foregoing descriptions it will be noted that there are certain elements common to each of Wei's three images, whether it be the historical, where he is a peerless remonstrator and critic; the literary, where he disobeys Li Mi's order not to free Li Shih-min; or the folk-religious, where he defies T'ai-tsung's wishes that he not slay the Dragon King. In each we see him as perverse and noncompliant—a scrappy fighter battling forces stronger than himself—but whose ingenuity and justness of purpose always win the day.

WEI CHENG IN THE CULTURAL REVOLUTION

Despite Wei's transformation into such colorful personifications as Taoist adept and door-god, it is his historical image that has been most consistently nourished and perpetuated among educated Chinese. For Confucian scholars and bureaucrats alike, Wei as a symbol of moral crusading and political protest has been most relevant to their own lives and careers. Just how strong and tenacious this symbol has remained in our own time was recently demonstrated during the Cultural Revolution in the People's Republic of China.

The complex motives and ideological factors that gave rise to the Cultural Revolution need not be discussed here. Stated simply, the Cultural Revolution, launched about November 1965, appears to have been an attempt by Mao Tse-tung and his supporters to recapture the revolutionary ideals and fervor that had characterized the Chinese Communist revolution in the days preceding and immediately following the Communist takeover in 1949. It was also the means by which Mao, chairman of the Chinese Communist Party (CCP), hoped to purge from the party and high government positions those "revisionist" elements, especially the chairman of the Republic, Liu Shao-ch'i, who opposed his policies and teachings.

At the height of the purges, in the summer of 1966, Lu Ting-i, member of the CCP Central Committee, director of the CCP Propaganda Department, and minister of culture, was disgraced and removed from his posts. Lu and other members of the Propaganda Department and Ministry of Culture were accused of "carrying out a 'counter-revolutionary program for literature and art' that was opposed to the Mao Tse-tung line for literature and art."[27] A year later, more specific charges were brought against Lu in a full-page article in the government mouthpiece, The People's Daily (Jen-min jih-pao), headed "The publication of 'The Biography of Wei Cheng' reveals the anti-revolutionary face of Lu Ting-i."[28] According to the article, during 1962 "The Biography of Wei Cheng" was published by order of Lu Ting-i.[29] Lu assigned a special staff to put the biography into modern colloquial Chinese (pai-hua) and to add explanatory footnotes. "He gave them instructions on how the preface was to be written, personally cleared the manuscript, and sent assistants of his to the publishing house to press for the earliest possible publication of the book."[30]

[27]Asia Research Centre, The Great Cultural Revolution in China (Hong Kong, 1967), pp. 167–68.

[28]Jen-min jih-pao [The People's Daily], November 9, 1967.

[29]This is the New T'ang History biography. It appears as part of the Annotated and Explained Biographies of Statesmen of Successive Ages (Li-tai cheng-chih jen-wu chuan-chi i-chu) series, under the title Wei Cheng, annotated by Chao Wu (Peking, 1962).

[30]American Consulate-General of Hong Kong, Survey of the China Mainland Press, no. 4061

Why should this seemingly innocuous activity of Lu have led to his downfall? It was because Mao's supporters feared what Wei Cheng symbolized, a point soon made clear in the article:

"The Biography of Wei Cheng" portrays with enthusiasm how Wei Cheng served as an opposition to the emperor. The book's preface[31] (first draft) says: "Wei Cheng, a famous statesman of the early T'ang dynasty, was an outspoken man who dared to offend the emperor by thrusting advice on him." The book itself devotes a good deal of space to describing how Wei Cheng was "aspiring, daring and not afraid of offending T'ai-tsung by his advice," how "tenacious and upright" he was, how "vigorous and straight-forward." Lu Ting-i himself on many occasions spoke about Wei Cheng, saying: "Wei Cheng was a stubborn opposition to Emperor T'ai-tsung of the T'ang dynasty. His criticisms were very sharp. . . . At one meeting, he made a vicious attempt to stir up the audience by saying: "It still seems necessary to carry forward the spirit of Wei Cheng of the T'ang dynasty . . . why should we lag behind him?"

"It is now clear," the article adds, "that Lu Ting-i's concoction, 'The Biography of Wei Cheng,' was a poisonous shaft directed at Chairman Mao, the red sun in our hearts; it was a manifesto for stirring up a counter-revolutionary restoration."[32]

We also learn that during the period 1960 to 1962, Mao's enemies, the "capitalist roaders in the Party," were "stirring up gusts of evil wind," laying the groundwork for a take over by "China's Khrushchev," Liu Shao-ch'i, who is never mentioned by name. At a conference of the Central Committee of the Party in 1962, Liu advocated that an open

---

(November, 1967), p. 2, This is a partial translation of the *Jen-min jih-pao* article cited above. In quoting from this source in the present study, transliteration has been altered through-out to conform with standard Wade-Giles usage.

[31]I have not found this version of the preface in any copy of Chao Wu's *Wei Cheng* that I have examined.

[32]*Survey*, pp. 2–3. Lu Ting-i's invocation of Wei Cheng was not the only use of a historically venerated figure as a symbol of anti-Mao protest during the 1960s. In January of 1961, Wu Han, a scholar specializing in Ming dynasty history, who was also a member of the CCP Peking Municipal Committee and vice-mayor of Peking, published a historical drama entitled *Hai Jui's Dismissal (Hai Jui pa-kuan)*. (Recently translated by Clive Ansley, *The Heresy of Wu Han. His Play 'Hai Jui's Dismissal'; and Its Role in China's Cultural Revolution* [Toronto, 1971]). Its central message was that Hai Jui (1514–87) was an upright official who was wrongly dismissed from his post for criticizing his emperor, an obvious jibe at Mao's dismissal of the general P'eng Te-huai. A campaign to purge Wu Han was launched in November, 1965, when his play and others like it were branded "poisonous weeds"; see *The Great Cultural Revolution*, pp. 91–115, 187–88. The preface of the *Jen-min jih-pao* article on Lu Ting-i draws an analogy between Lu's "crime" and that of Wu Han.

opposition be allowed to form within the Party and among the people, at which time he was backed by Lu Ting-i, who averred that even ancient Chinese emperors like T'ang T'ai-tsung had allowed political opposition in the form of loyal officials like Wei Cheng. By raising the spectre of Wei Cheng and making him a symbol of open political opposition, Lu had, the article complains, resurrected a "1,300 year-old political corpse."[33]

If the great emperor T'ai-tsung had allowed political opposition, could Chairman Mao not fail to do the same? The article curtly dismisses the possibility:

Is it true that Wei Cheng was really Emperor T'ang T'ai-tsung's "stubborn opposition"? No. Both Wei Cheng and T'ai-tsung were feudal rulers who ruthlessly exploited and suppressed the peasants. Wei Cheng was simply a superior loyal servant of T'ai-tsung. His "loyal advice" was advice loyal to the feudal T'ang dynasty regime.[34]

Not only did Lu Ting-i attempt to popularize the concept of a "Wei Cheng spirit" of political opposition, he also went so far as to advocate that certain of Wei Cheng's policies be adopted by the CCP! At a Party meeting in May, 1962, Lu invoked Wei's consolidation themes: Wei's admonitions to T'ai-tsung against war, extravagance, excessive conscription of men for corvée, and his advice that quiescence brought about peace while hyperactivity brought about disorder. He even inquired, "Aren't we mobilizing too many people for unpaid labor?" Such themes, *The People's Daily* article indignantly concludes, were the same as those advocated by the Party revisionists in order to persuade China to put its arms in a storehouse so that they might usurp power and overthrow the dictatorship of the proletariat.[35]

The tragicomic Lu Ting-i affair serves to remind us that even in contemporary China the remote past can influence the present with startling impact. It attests to Wei Cheng's ability—given, perhaps, the inevitable persistence in China of ruler-bureaucratic tensions— to continue to inspire and motivate Chinese officials even in our own day. Most of all, it demonstrates the great success achieved by Wei Cheng's numerous image-builders down the ages. For despite the passing of more than a millenium, the rise and fall of dynasties, and, in

[33]*Survey*, p. 1.
[34]Ibid., p. 3.
[35]Ibid., pp. 5–6.

this century, the replacement of the imperial order by new forms of government, Wei Cheng's symbolic role as fearless critic, moral crusader, vigilant consolidator, and ardent champion of the bureaucratic cause seems to be as pertinent as ever.

A Statistical Comparison of High-level
Officialdom of the Sui and Early T'ang Periods

The following tables are based on data derived from Yamazaki Hiroshi, "Zuichō kanryō no seikaku" [The Character of Bureaucracy in the Sui Dynasty], *Tōkyō Kyōikudaigaku bungakubu kiyō,* 6 (1956), 15–17, 26–31; Yen Keng-wang, *T'ang p'u-shang-ch'eng-lang piao* [Tables of High Officials in the Department of Affairs of State during the T'ang Dynasty], 4 vols. (Taipei, 1956), 1:21–26; Wan Ssu-t'ung, "T'ang chiang-hsiang-ta-ch'en nien-piao" [Chronological Tables of High Officials, Chief Ministers, and Generals of the T'ang Dynasty], in *Erh-shih-wu shih pu-pien* [Supplements to the Twenty-five Standard Histories], 6 vols. (1937; reprint, Peking, 1957), 5:7217–21; and biographical sections in the *CTS* and *HTS*.

A. Heads[a] of the Three Departments with Direct Ancestors in
Officialdom during the Sui, Wu-te,[b] and Chen-kuan[c] periods.

Period	Total	Officials with Fathers and/or Grandfathers in Officialdom	%
Sui	18	18	100.0
Wu-te	10	10	100.0
Chen-kuan	17	15	88.0

[a]See above, p. 54, and p. 54, n. 5

[b]Up to T'ai-tsung's seizure of power in 6/626.

[c]Including the period from 6/626–12/626 and up to the accession of Kao-tsung in 5/649.

B. Presidents of the Six Boards with Direct Ancestors in Officialdom
during the Sui, Wu-te,[a] and Chen-kuan[b] periods.

Period	Total	Officials with Fathers and/or Grandfathers in Officialdom	%
Sui	46	41	89.0
Wu-te	17	14	82.3
Chen-kuan	35		
	(33)[c]	24	72.7

[a]Up to T'ai-tsung's seizure of power in 6/626.
[b]Including the period from 6/626–12/626 and up to the accession of Kao-tsung in 5/649.
[c]Of the 35 officials in this group, biographical information is available for only 33; the percentage figure is based on a total of 33 instead of 35.

C. One Hundred and Five[a] Early T'ang Dynasty Upper-level
Officials with Direct Ancestors in Officialdom

Period	Total	Father and/or Grandfather in Officialdom	No biography	Excluded or Unclear
Wu-te	34			
	(24)[b]	22 (91.7%)	7	3[c]
Chen-kuan	77			
	(58)[b]	42 (72.4%)	14	5[d]

[a]Since this number includes some officials who served both Kao-tsu and T'ai-tsung, the sum of the figures in the "total" column is greater than 105.
[b]Total figure minus the number of officials without biographies or whose ancestry in officialdom is not clear. Percentages are based on these figures rather than the total.
[c]This figure represents three imperial family members.
[d]This figure represents two imperial family members and three officials whose ancestry in officialdom is unclear.

D. Native Places of the Heads[a] of the Three Departments during
the Sui, Wu-te,[b] and Chen-kuan[c] Periods.

Period	Total	Northwest	Northeast	South
Sui	18	13 (72.2%)	4 (22.2%)	1 (5.6%)
Wu-te	10	4 (40.0%)	4 (40.0%)	2 (20.0%)
Chen-kuan	17	5 (29.5%)	8 (47.0%)	4 (23.5%)

Period	Northwest	Northeast and South
Sui	72.2%	27.8%
Wu-te	40.0%	60.0%
Chen-kuan	29.5%	70.5%

[a]See above, p. 54, and p. 54, n. 5.
[b]Up to T'ai-tsung's seizure of power in 6/626.
[c]Including the period from 6/626–12/626 and up to the accession of Kao-tsung in 5/649.

E. Native Places of the Presidents of the Six Boards during
the Sui, Wu-te,[a] and Chen-kuan[b] Periods.

Period	Total	Northwest	Northeast	South	Unclear
Sui	67	38 (56.7%)	28 (41.8%)	1 (1.5%)	0
Wu-te	17				
	(14)[c]	6 (42.9%)	7 (50.0%)	1 (7.1%)	3
Chen-kuan	35				
	(32)[c]	16 (50.0%)	14 (43.8%)	2 (6.2%)	3

Period	Northwest	Northeast and South
Sui	56.7%	43.3%
Wu-te	42.9%	57.1%
Chen-kuan	50.0%	50.0%

[a]Up to T'ai-tsung's seizure of power in 6/626.

[b]Including the period from 6/626–12/626 and up to the accession of Kao-tsung in 5/649.

[c]Percentages are based, not on grand totals, but on totals of officials with known and un-ambiguous geographical origins. These latter totals are given in ( ) in the table.

Major Sources Devoted to Wei Cheng and His Writings Used in This Study

A. The Filiation of the *Wei Cheng-kung chien-lu*

The *New T'ang History* "Monograph on Literature" (*i-wen chih*) lists seven works containing material devoted to Wei Cheng and his writings. The *Wei Cheng chi* in twenty *chüan*[1] and the *Wei Cheng chien-shih* in five *chüan*[2] are both listed without compilers. Five other works and their compilers are also listed: the *Wei Wen-chen ku-shih* in ten *chüan* by Wang Fang-ch'ing;[3] the *Wei Wen-chen ku-shih* in eight *chüan* by Chang Ta-yeh;[4] the *Wen-chen kung ku-shih* in six *chüan* by Liu Wei-chih;[5] the *Wen-chen kung shih-lu* in one *chüan* by Wang Fang-ch'ing;[6] and the *Wen-chen kung chuan-shih* in four *chüan* by Ching Po.[7] The *Sung-shih* "Monograph on Literature" lists three works on Wei Cheng: the *Wei Hsüan-ch'eng ku-shih* in three *chüan*, anonymous;[8] the *Wei Hsüan-ch'eng chuan* in one *chüan* by Wang Fang-ch'ing;[9] and the *Wei Hsüan-ch'eng li chung-chieh* in four *chüan*, anonymous.[10]

The above works have all been lost except for one by Wang Fang-ch'ing[11] now bearing the title *Wei Cheng-kung chien-lu (Recorded Remonstrances of Duke Wei of Cheng)* in five *chüan*. Wang Fang-ch'ing began his official career late in the reign of the third T'ang emperor, Kao-tsung (rg. 650–84), and under Empress Wu (rg. 684–705) served in several offices both in the provinces and the capital. For a time he was director of the Department of the Imperial

[1]*HTS* 60.10.
[2]Ibid. 59.2b.
[3]Ibid. 58.19b.
[4]Ibid. 58.14b.
[5]Ibid. 58.14.
[6]Ibid. 58.14b.
[7]Ibid. 58.14.
[8]*SungS* 203.20. Hsüan-ch'eng is Wei Cheng's *tzu*.
[9]Ibid. 203.18. This was probably identical to the *Wen-chen kung shih-lu* in one *chüan* listed above.
[10]Ibid. 207.14.
[11]Biographies: *CTS* 89.13–18b, and *HTS* 116.1–3.

Library (*lin-t'ai chien*) and compiled dynastic history (*kuo-shih*). He eventually rose to the post of tutor to the crown prince, the future Chung-tsung. Wang died in 702. The problem is, which of the works listed in the T'ang and Sung "Monographs on Literature" has come down to us as the *Wei Cheng-kung chien-lu*?

An anonymous *Wei Cheng chien-shih* in five *chüan* and a *Wei Cheng chien-lu* in five *chüan* by Wang Fang-ch'ing are listed as separate works in the *Yü-hai* of the Sung writer Wang Ying-lin.[12] The late Ch'ing scholar Wang Hsien-kung has suggested that although these two works were often confused by later scholars, the *Chien-shih* is the *Chien-shih* in five *chüan* listed anonymously in the T'ang "Monograph on Literature," and the *Chien-lu* is identical to the *Wei Wen-chen ku-shih* by Wang Fang-ch'ing also listed therein.[13] His view is based on that of the Sung scholar Ch'en Chen-sun, who maintained that Wang Fang-ch'ing's *Chien-lu* and his *Ku-shih* were one and the same.[14]

There is no mention of the *Wei Cheng-kung chien-lu* in either of Wang Fang-ch'ing's biographies. But from the title of Wang's office listed above his name on the title page, it is believed that he compiled the work sometime during Kao-tsung's reign.[15] Exactly what sources Wang used in the compilation is not known; in his preface, he merely notes that he "carefully examined the national records" (*kuo-tien*).[16]

The editors of the *General Catalogue of Collected Books in the Four Treasuries* (*Ssu-k'u ch'üan-shu tsung-mu*) praise the *Chien-lu* for its accuracy. They also note that Ssu-ma Kuang made copious use of it when writing about Wei Cheng in his *Comprehensive Mirror*.[17] Indeed, Ssu-ma Kuang quoted directly from Wang's work several times in his *K'ao-i*.[18]

Early in the period 1330–33, the Yüan scholar Chai Ssu-chung compiled an addition to Wang Fang-ch'ing's work called the *Wei Cheng-kung chien hsü-lu* (*Continued Recorded Remonstrances of Duke Wei of Cheng*) in two *chüan*; the work was printed between 1333 and 1335. By early Ming times, however, it had become extremely rare, prompting the scholar P'eng Nien to compile another *Hsü-lu* in one *chüan*. Ironically, while P'eng's work appears to have become lost, Chai's work was preserved for posterity in the *Yung-lo ta-tien*, which was completed early in the fifteenth century.[19]

A final and major addition to Wang Fang-ch'ing's *Wei Cheng-kung chien-lu*

---

[12]Wang ying-lin, *Yü-hai* 61.13b.
[13]*WCKCL*, the preface by Wang Hsien-kung, 1–1b.
[14]Ch'en Chen-sun, *Chih-chai shu-lu chieh-t'i*, ch. 5, p. 153.
[15]Ibid.; *SKCSTM* 57.6b.
[16]*Wei Cheng-kung chien-lu* (*Chi-fu ts'ung-shu* ed., 1879), preface, p. 1.
[17]*SKCSTM* 57.7.
[18]See, for example, *TCTC* ch. 192, p. 6039; ch. 193, p. 6060; ch. 194, p. 6094.
[19]*SKCSTM* 57.14b–15.

was made late in the Ch'ing dynasty by the brothers Wang Hsien-ch'ien (1842–1918) and Wang Hsien-kung,[20] who in 1883 at Changsha published five works on Wei. Four of these were by Hsien-kung: (1) the *Wei Cheng-kung chien-lu chiao-chu*, a fully annotated version of the *Wei Cheng-kung chien-lu* of Wang Fang-ch'ing; (2) a rearranged and occasionally annotated edition of Chai Ssu-chung's *Hsü-lu* bearing the identical title; (3) a chronological outline of Wei Cheng's life in one *chüan*, the *Wei Wen-chen kung nien-p'u*; and (4) the *Wei Wen-chen kung ku-shih shih-i* (*Collected Anecdotes Concerning Duke Wei of Cheng*) in three *chüan*, which was an attempt to gather together as much information as possible concerning Wei Cheng from the Standard Histories, encyclopedias, and other compendia. His brother Hsien-ch'ien contributed a critical and annotated comparison of Wei's biography in the *Old* and *New T'ang History* called the *Wei Cheng lieh-chuan Hsin-Chiu T'ang-shu ho-chu* (*Combined Notes to the Biography of Wei Cheng in the New and Old T'ang History*) in one *chüan*.

The *Wei Cheng-kung chien-lu* of Wang Fang-ch'ing is thus the earliest work on Wei Cheng to have survived, having been compiled not later than forty years after the minister's death. There are 129 sections containing Wei's remonstrances, his conversations with T'ai-tsung and other Chen-kuan officials, and some miscellaneous sections relating to his death and its aftermath, all with background material.[21] The *Hsü-lu* of Chai Ssu-chung, on the other hand, is of more limited value. As Wang Hsien-kung notes, it does not so much continue the Wang Fang-ch'ing work as duplicate many of its sections. Chai also drew upon episodes in the *Comprehensive Mirror* and the *Essentials of Government of the Chen-kuan Period*.[22] For its accuracy and scope, then, the *Wei Cheng-kung chien-lu* is unrivaled as a source for Wei Cheng's career under T'ang T'ai-tsung, and it, in the annotated version by Wang Hsien-kung, along with the *Wei Cheng-kung wen-chi* (see below), has provided the core of materials on Wei used in the present study.

B. The *Wei Cheng-kung wen-chi*

The most authoritative collection of Wei Cheng's extended prose writings (minus his remonstrances and *tui*) is found in the *Wei Cheng-kung wen-chi* (*Collected Prose of Duke Wei of Cheng*). The *Wen-chi*, in three *chüan*, was originally included in the *Chi-fu ts'ung-shu* (Tingchou, 1879–92), whose chief compiler

---

[20]For the biography of Wang Hsien-ch'ien, see *Ch'ing-shih*, ch. 481, pp. 5217–18. His younger brother, Hsien-kung, has no biography.

[21]*WCKCL*, "k'ao-cheng" section, 1. The work is usually recorded as containing 130 sections.

[22]See Wang's preface to the *WCKCL*, 1b.

was Wang Hao (1823–88).[23] Wang's *Wen-chi* was culled chiefly from Wei
Cheng's writings contained in *chüan* 139–41 of the *Ch'üan T'ang-wen* (*Complete T'ang Prose*), completed in 1814. However, Wang compared his own
materials with Wei's writings in other sources and corrected the texts accordingly, including fewer pieces in his collection than in the *Ch'üan T'ang-
wen* by omitting those also found in the *Wei Cheng-kung chien-lu*.[24]

[23]For the present study, the author has used a punctuated version of the *WCKWC* as it
originally appeared in the *Chi-fu ts'ung-shu, Ts'ung-shu chi-ch'eng* ed. (Shanghai, 1937).

[24]See Wang Hao's postscript, appended to the *Ts'ung-shu chi-ch'eng* edition of the *WCKWC*
and the *Wei Cheng-kung shih-chi*, p. 46.

Glossary

(Aspirated consonants follow their unaspirated equivalents.)

A-fang 阿房 pl.n.

An Lu-shan 安祿山 pr.n.

an pu wang wang 安不忘亡 "while in security do not forget destruction"

an pu wang wei 安不忘危 "in security we must not forget peril"

Chai Ssu-chung 翟思忠 pr.n.

chan-shih chu-pu 詹事主簿 superintendent of accounts in the household of the crown prince

ch'an-ch'en 讒臣 "slandering official"

ch'an-wei shu 讖緯書 prognostication and apocryphal texts

Chang Hsing-ch'eng 張行成 pr.n.

Chang Hsüan-su 張玄素 pr.n.

Chang Liang 張良 pr.n.

Chang-sun Empress 長孫皇后

Chang-sun, Wu-chi 長孫無忌 pr.n.

Chang Ta-yeh 張大業 pr.n.

Chang Yüeh 張說 pr.n.

Ch'ang-an 長安 pl.n.

Ch'ang-an-cheng ssu-ma t'ou T'ang 長安城四馬投唐 *In the City of Ch'ang-an Four Horses Surrender to the T'ang*

Ch'ang Ho 常何 pr.n.

Ch'ang-lin ping 長林兵 Ch'ang-lin Troops

ch'ang-shih 長史 administrator-in-chief

chao 詔 imperial edict

Chao-ling 昭陵 pl.n.

ch'ao-chang kuo-tien ts'an-i te-shih 朝章國典參議得失 designation

Ch'ao-ko 朝歌 pl.n.

Ch'ao Kung-wu 晁公武 pr.n.

che-ch'ung-fu 折衝府 Intrepid Militia

chen-ch'en 貞臣 "pure official"

Chen-kuan 貞觀 r.n.

Chen-kuan cheng-yao 貞觀政要 *Essentials of Government of the Chen-kuan Period*

Chen-kuan chih chih 貞觀之治 "the good rule of the Chen-kuan reign"

Chen Ti-erh 甄翟兒 pr.n.

Ch'en Chen-sun 陳振孫 pr.n.

Ch'en Hou-chu 陳後主 (emperor)

Ch'en Tzu-ang 陳子昂 pr.n.

Ch'en Yen-po 陳彥博 pr.n.

Ch'en Yin-k'o 陳寅恪 pr.n.

Cheng 鄭 s.

cheng 正 "ruling," "straightening"

Cheng Hsüan 鄭玄 pr.n.

Cheng-kuo-kung 鄭國公 Duke of Cheng principality

cheng-shen 正身 "rectification of the person"

cheng-shih 正史 Standard History

cheng-shih t'ang 政事堂 Hall of Government Affairs

Cheng T'ing 鄭頲 pr.n.

cheng tsai-hsiang 正宰相 regular chief ministers

ch'eng 丞 assistant to the deputy prefect

Ch'eng, King of Chou 周成王

Ch'eng Ta-ch'ang 程大昌 pr.n.

Ch'eng Yao-chin fu-p'i lao-chün-t'ang 程咬金

斧劈老君堂 *Ch'eng Yao-chin Splits the Temple with an Axe,*

Chi 籍 (ruler of Western Ch'u)

Chi 稷 pr.n.

Chi Pu 季布 pr.n.

chi-shih-chung 給事中 grand secretary of the Department of the Imperial Chancellery

chi-shih ts'an-chün 記室參軍 secretary

Chi-yu 季友 pr.n.

ch'i 啓 "communication from inferior to superior"

Ch'i, Prince of 齊王

ch'i-chü-chu 起居注 "diary of activity and repose"

ch'i-chü lang 起居郎 recorder

ch'i-chü she-jen 起居舍人 official charged with recording the actions of the ruler

Ch'i-shih 齊史 t.

Chiang Hsing-pen 姜行本 pr.n.

Chiang-nan 江南 pl.n.

Chiang-nan ho 江南河 canal

Chiang-tu 江都 pl.n.

chiao-hua 教化 moral transformation

Chieh 桀 ("bad last" ruler of the Hsia dynasty)

chien 監 Directorate

chien 鑑 "mirror," "beacon"

chien-ch'a yü-shih 監察御史 examining censor

chien-ch'en 奸臣 "treacherous official"

chien-ch'en 賤臣 "base official"

chien-chiao shih-chung 檢校侍中 acting president of the Department of the Imperial Chancellery

chien-i ta-fu 諫議大夫 remonstrating counselor

chien-kuan 諫官 remonstrating official

Chien-nan 劍南 pl.n.

ch'ien-niu pei-shen 千牛備身 palace guard

Ch'ien Ta-hsin 錢大昕 pr.n.

chih 志 monograph

chih-ch'en 智臣 "wise official"

chih-ch'en 直臣 "upright official"

chih ch'i-chü 知起居 official in charge of recording the deeds and actions of the emperor

chih men-hsia shih 知門下事 "in charge of the Department of the Imperial Chancellery"

chih-shu shih-yü-shih 治書侍御史 vice-president of the Censorate

ch'ih 敕 imperial order

Chin-shang shih-lu 今上實錄 t.

Chin-shang wang-yeh chi 今上王業集 *Record of the Kingly Enterprise of the Present Ruler*

chin-shih 進士 examination

Chin-shu 晉書 *Chin History*

Chin-wen chia 今文家 New Text School

Chin-yang 晉陽 pl.n.

chin-yüan 禁園 Forbidden Park

Ch'in, Prince of 秦王

Ch'in Shih-huang-ti 秦始皇帝 (emperor)

Ch'in-wang fu 秦王府 Prince of Ch'in Office

Ch'in-wang p'o-chen 秦王破陣 "The Prince of Ch'in Smashes the Ranks"

ching 靜 quiescence

ching-chi chih 經籍志 "Monograph on Literature"

Ching Po 敬播 pr.n.

ch'ing 情 "human factors"

Ch'ing-ho 清河 pl.n.

Chiu 糾 pr.n.

Chiu-ch'eng-kung li-ch'üan ming 九成宮醴泉銘 "Inscription on the Sweet Spring of the Chiu-ch'eng Palace"

Chiu-ch'eng Palace 九成宮 "Nine Perfections" Palace

Chiu T'ang-shu 舊唐書 *Old T'ang History*

Chiu-tzu 龜茲 Kucha

chou 州 prefecture

Chou, Duke of 周公

Chou 紂 ("bad last" ruler of the Shang)

Chu Hsi-tsu 朱希祖 pr.n.

Chu-ko Liang 諸葛亮 pr.n.

ch'u-chih ta-shih 黜陟大使 grand commissioner of promotion and demotion

Ch'u Sui-liang 褚遂良 pr.n.

Chu Tzu-she 朱子奢 pr.n.

Chuang, Prince of Ch'u 楚莊王

Ch'un-ch'iu 春秋 *Spring and Autumn Annals*

chung-ch'en 忠臣 "loyal official"

Chung Chün 終軍 pr.n.

chung-nan 中男 adolescent

chung shih shen chüeh yü wei ming-ming hou 終始慎厥與惟明明后 "He who at last, as at first, is careful as to whom and what he follows is a truly intelligent sovereign"

chung-shu ling 中書令 president of the Department of the Imperial Secretariat

chung-shu she-jen 中書舍人 grand secretary of the Department of the Imperial Secretariat

chung-shu sheng 中書省 Department of the Imperial Secretariat

Chung-shuo 中說 *Discourses on the Mean*

Chung-tsung 中宗 (emperor of the T'ang)

Chung-yung 中庸 *The Doctrine of the Mean*

Ch'ung-wen kuan 崇文館 College for the Veneration of Literature

Chü 莒 pl.n.

chü an ssu wei 居安思危 "while in a position of security, think of peril"

chü-ch'en 具臣 "ordinary official"

Chü-lu 鉅鹿 pl.n.

Ch'ü-ch'eng 曲城 pl.n.

Ch'ü Wen-t'ai 麴文泰 (King of Kao-ch'ang)

Ch'ü-yang 曲陽 pl.n.

chüan 卷 chapter

Ch'üan I 權翼 pr.n.

ch'üan-kuei 權貴 "powerful and esteemed"

Ch'üan Wan-chi 權萬紀 pr.n.

chün 軍 army

chün-ch'en 君臣 ruler-minister (relationship)

chün-fu 軍府 military district

chün-kung 郡公 duke of a commandery

chün-t'ien 均田 "equal-field" system

chün-tzu 君子 morally superior man

Ch'ün-shu cheng-yao 羣書政要 t.

Ch'ün-shu chih-yao 羣書治要 *Essentials of Government from Divers Books*

Ch'ün-shu li-yao 羣書理要 t.

Fan Tsu-yü 范祖禹 pr.n.

Fang Hsüan-ling 房玄齡 pr.n.

Fang-lin Gate 芳林門

Fei-shan Palace 飛山宮

Feng Ang 馮盎 pr.n.

feng-chien 封建 "feudal" system

Feng and Shan [rites] 封禪

Feng Tao 馮道 pr.n.

Feng Te-i 封德彝 pr.n.

Fu Chien 符堅 (ruler of the former Ch'in)

fu-chien 副監 assistant superintendent

Fu Yung-ku 符永固 pr.n.

Hai Jui 海瑞 pr.n.

Hai Jui pa-kuan 海瑞罷官 *Hai Jui's Dismissal*

Han Hsin 韓信 pr.n.

Han Ming-ti 漢明帝 (emperor)

Han Wu-ti 漢武帝 (emperor)

Han Yü 韓愈 pr.n.

hao-chieh 豪傑 local military elite

Heng mountain 恒山

Heng-shan Princess 衡山公主

Ho-fen 河汾 pl.n.

Ho-kuan-tzu 鶡冠子 "Feather-cap Master"

Ho-kuan-tzu 鶡冠子 t.

Ho-nan 河南 pl.n.

Ho-pei 河北 pl.n.

Ho-tung 河東 pl.n.

Hou-chu 後主 (emperor of the Ch'en dynasty)

Hou Chün-chi 侯君集 pr.n.

Hou Ying 侯嬴 pr.n.

Hsi-ho 西河 pl.n.

Hsi-yü 西域 Western Regions

Hsi-yu chi 西遊記 *A Record of a Journey to the West*

Hsia Ch'ü-yang 下曲陽 pl.n.

Hsiang 項 s.

Hsiang-po 項伯 pr.n.

Hsiang prefecture 相州

Hsiang-yang 襄陽 pl.n.

Hsiang Yü 項羽 pr.n.

Hsiao-Hsiang lu 瀟湘錄 *Tales of the Hsiao and Hsiang Rivers*

hsiao-jen 小人 petty man

Hsiao-ming 孝明帝 (emperor of the Northern Wei)

Hsiao Te-yen 蕭德言 pr.n.

Hsiao Yü 蕭瑀 pr.n.

Hsieh 契 pr.n.

Hsieh-li Qaghan 頡利可汗 (Turkish chieftain)

Hsüeh-yen-t'o 薛延陀 tr.n.

hsien 縣 county, subprefecture

Hsien, Duke of Chin 晉獻公

hsien-ling 縣令 subprefect

Hsien-ling 獻陵 pl.n.

hsien-ma 洗馬 librarian in the household of the crown prince

hsien-nan 縣男 baron of a county

Hsin-ch'eng Princess 新城公主

Hsin-li 新禮 *New Rites*

Hsin-lo 新羅 Silla

Hsin T'ang-shu 新唐書 *New T'ang History*

hsing-chün 行軍 armies-on-campaign

hsing-jen 行人 secretary-envoy

hsiu-shen 修身 "cultivation of the person"

hsiu-ts'ai 秀才 examination degree

hsü 序 introduction

Hsü Ching-tsung 許敬宗 pr.n.

Hsü Mao-kung 徐茂公 pr.n.

Hsü Shih-chi 徐世勣 pr.n.

Hsü Shih-hsü 許世緒 pr.n.

Hsüan-ch'eng 玄成 pr.n.

hsüan-hsüeh 玄學 "dark learning," Neo-Taoism

Hsüan-tsang 玄奘 pr.n.

Hsüan-tsung 玄宗 (emperor of the T'ang)

Hsüan-wu Gate 玄武門

I-ch'eng Princess 義成公主

I-ning 義寧 r.n.

i-ts'ang 義倉 relief granary

I Yin 伊尹 pr.n.

jen 仁 righteousness

jen-ch'ing 人情 human feelings

Jen-min jih-pao 人民日報 *The People's Daily*

Jen-shou Palace 仁壽宮

ju-lin chuan 儒林傳 "Biographies of Confucians"

Jung Chao-tsu 容肇祖 pr.n.

Jung-yang 滎陽 pl.n.

Kanei Yukitada 金井之忠 pr.n.

K'ai-huang 開皇 r.n.

K'ai-yüan 開元 r.n.

K'ang, King of Chou 周康王

Kao-ch'ang 高昌 pl.n.

Kao-chi-po 高雞伯 pl.n.

Kao Chün-ya 高君雅 pr.n.

Kao K'ai-tao 高開道 pr.n.

Kao Shih 高適 pr.n.

Kao Shih-lien 高士廉 pr.n.

Kao-tsu 高祖 (emperor of the Former Han)

Kao-tsu 高祖 (emperor of the T'ang)

Kao-tsu shih-lu 高祖實錄 *Kao-tsu Veritable Records*

Kao-tsung 高宗 (emperor of the T'ang)

Kao Yao 皋陶 pr.n.

K'ao-i 考異 *Investigations of Discrepancies*

Ku Chi-kuang 谷霽光 pr.n.

ku-wen chia 古文家 Old Text School

Ku Yin 顧胤 pr.n.

k'u-li chuan 酷吏傳 "Biographies of Harsh Officials"

kuan 官 "(civil) official"

Kuan Chung 管仲 pr.n.

Kuan-lung chi-t'uan 關隴集團 Kuan-lung bloc

Kuan Lung-feng 關龍逢 pr.n.

Kuan-nei 關內 pl.n.

Kuan-shu 管叔 pr.n.

Kuan-yu 關右 "to the right of the [T'ung] Pass"

kuang-lu-ch'ing 光錄卿 president of the Court of Imperial Banquets

Kuang-t'ung ch'ü 廣通渠 canal

Kuang-wu 光武 (emperor of the Later Han)

kung-ch'en 功臣 "meritorious official"

Kung-yang commentary 公羊傳

K'ung Ying-ta 孔穎達 pr.n.

Kuo 郭 s.

kuo-shih 國史 "dynastic history"

Kuo Shu 虢叔 pr.n.

kuo-tien 國典 "national records"

kuo-tzu chien 國子監 Directorate of the State University

kuo-tzu hsüeh 國子學 School of the Sons of State

Lao 撩 tr.n.

Lei-li 類禮 *Categorized Rites*

Lei Yung-chi 雷永吉 pr.n.

Li 李 s.

li 里 unit of distance, roughly one-third of a mile

li 禮 ritual, etiquette

Li Ch'eng-ch'ien 李承乾 pr.n.

Li Chi 李勣 pr.n.

Li-chi 禮記 *Record of Rites*

Li Chiao 李嶠 pr.n.

Li Chien-ch'eng 李建成 pr.n.

Li Chih 李治 pr.n.

Li Ching 李靖 pr.n.

Li Hsüan-pa 李玄霸 pr.n.

Li Hun 李渾 pr.n.

Li Jen-fa 李仁發 pr.n.

Li Kang 李綱 pr.n.

Li K'o 李克 pr.n.

Li Kuei 李軌 pr.n.

Li Mi 李密 pr.n.

li-pu shang-shu 吏部尚書 president of the Board of Civil Appointments

li-pu shang-shu 禮部尚書 president of the Board of Rites

Li Shen-t'ung 李神通 pr.n.

Li Sheng 李晟 pr.n.

Li Sheng 酈生 pr.n.

Li Shih-chi 李世勣 pr.n.

Li Shih-min 李世民 pr.n.

Li Shu-t'ung 李樹桐 pr.n.

Li Ssu 李斯 pr. n.

Li T'ai 李泰 pr. n.

Li wei 禮緯 t.

Li-yang 黎陽 pl.n.

Li Yin 李隱 pr.n.

Li Yüan 李淵 pr.n.

Li Yüan-chi 李元吉 pr.n.

Li Yüan-kuei 李元軌 pr.n.

liang-ch'en 良臣 "excellent official"

Liang-i Hall 兩義殿

Liang Shih-tu 梁師都 pr.n.

Liang Wu-ti 梁武帝 (emperor)

Liang Yüan-ti 梁元帝 (emperor)

Liao-ch'eng 聊城 pl.n.

lieh-chuan 列傳 "biographies"

Lieh-nü chuan-lüeh 列女傳畧 *Concise Biographies of Virtuous Women*

lin-t'ai chien 麟臺監 director of the Department of the Imperial Library

ling 令 prefect

ling 令 administrative law

Ling-hu Te-fen 令狐德棻 pr.n.

Ling-nan 嶺南 pl.n.

Ling-piao 嶺表 pl.n.

Ling-yen-ko 淩煙閣 pl.n.

liu-cheng 六正 "six correct officials"

Liu Chih-chi 劉知幾 pr.n.

Liu Hei-t'a 劉黑闥 pr.n.

Liu Hsiang 劉向 pr.n.

Liu Hsiang 柳祥 pr.n.

Liu Hsiao-chen 劉孝眞 pr.n.

liu-hsieh 六邪 "six evil officials"

liu-nei 流內 "within the current"

Liu P'an-sui 劉盼逐 pr.n.

Liu Pang 劉邦 pr.n.

Liu Pei 劉備 pr.n.

liu-pu 六部 Six Boards

Liu Shao-ch'i 劉少奇 pr.n.

liu-shou 留守 garrison commander

Liu Wei-chih 劉褘之 pr.n.

Liu Wen-ching 劉文靜 pr.n.

Liu Wu-chou 劉武周 pr.n.

Lo Ching 婁敬 pr.n.

Lo Hsiang-lin 羅香林 pr,n.

Lo I 羅藝 pr.n.

Lo-k'ou 洛口 pl.n.

Lu 魯 pl.n.

Lu Chia 陸賈 pr.n.

Lu-t'ai 鹿臺 "Deer Terrace"

Lu Ting-i 陸定一 pr.n.

Lu Tsu-shang 盧祖尚 pr.n.

lun 論 discussion

Lun-yü 論語 *Analects*

Lung-hsi 隴西 pl.n.

Lung-yu 隴右 pl.n.

lü 律 penal law

lü-hsüeh 律學 School of Law

Lü Pu 呂布 pr.n.

Lü Tsu-ch'ien 呂祖謙 pr.n.

Lü Wen 呂溫 pr.n.

Ma Chou 馬周 pr.n.

Ma-i commandery 馬邑郡

Mao Tse-tung 毛澤東 pr.n.

men-hsia sheng 門下省 Department of the Imperial Chancellery

men-shen 門神 door-god

min-pu shang-shu 民部尚書 president of the Board of Finance

ming-ching 明經 "classics" examination

ming-ju 明儒 "eminent Confucian"

Ming prefecture 洺州

Ming-t'ang 明堂 "Hall of Light"

Ming-te Palace 明德宮

mo pu yu ch'u, hsien k'o yu chung 靡不有初 鮮克有終 "All are [successful] at first, But few prove themselves to be so at the last"

Mou Jun-sun 牟潤孫 pr.n.

Mu, Duke of Ch'in 秦穆公

nan-hsüeh 南學 Southern Learning

Nan-yang 南陽 pl.n.

Nan-yüeh 南粵 pl.n.

Nei-huang county 內黃縣

nien tzu tsai tzu 念玆在玆 "Think on this, rest your mind on this"

Ning Ch'i 甯戚 pr.n.

Nunome Chōfū 布目潮渢 pr.n.

Ou-yang Hsiu 歐陽修 pr.n.

Ou-yang Hsün 歐陽詢 pr.n.

pa-tso 八座 Eight Seats

Pa-yeh-ku 拔野古 tr.n.

pai-hua 白話 modern colloquial Chinese

pai-kuan 百官 One Hundred Officials

Pan Ku 班固 pr.n.

Pan Piao 班彪 pr.n.

P'an-lung-t'ai pei 攀龍臺碑 t.

P'an Te-yü 潘德輿 pr.n.

Pao Shu-ya 鮑叔牙 pr.n.

pei-hsüeh 北學 Northern Learning

Pei-shih 北史 *Northern Dynasties History*

P'ei 裴 s.

P'ei Chi 裴寂 pr.n.

P'ei Ta-chang 裴大章 pr.n.

pen 本 "be certain to"

pen-kuan 本貫 native place

P'eng Nien 彭年 pr.n.

p'eng-tang 朋黨 faction

P'eng-tang lun 朋黨論 "On Factions"

P'eng Te-huai 彭德懷 pr.n.

Pi Kan 比干 pr.n.

pi-shu ch'eng 秘書丞 assistant in the Department of the Imperial Library

pi-shu chien 秘書監 director of the Imperial Library

P'i Hsi-jui 皮錫瑞 pr.n.

Pien Bridge 便橋

pien nien 編年 "chronicle"

pu 不 "do not"

pu-neng shu hsing-chi 不能著形迹 "incapable of displaying proper formal behavior"

P'u-chou fu 蒲州府 pl.n.

san-kung 三公 Three Dukes

san-sheng 三省 Three Departments

san-t'ai 三臺 (stars)

Shan-nan 山南 pl.n.

Shan prefecture 潭州

Shan prefecture 陝州

shan-tung 山東 "east of the mountains"

Shan-tung 山東 pl.n.

Shan-tung chi-t'uan 山東集團 Shan-tung bloc

Shan-tung hao-chieh 山東豪傑 Shantung military elite

Shan-tung tao ta-hsing-t'ai shang-shu ling 陝東道大行臺尚書令 president of the

Department of Affairs of State of the Shan-tung Circuit Grand Field Office

shang-ko 上閣 council chamber

Shang-lin 上林 pl.n.

shang-shu 尚書 president of a Board

shang-shu ling 尚書令 president of the Department of Affairs of State

shang-shu sheng 尚書省 Department of Affairs of State

shang-shu tso-ch'eng 尚書左丞 assistant to the left vice-president of the Department of Affairs of State

shang-shu tso-p'u-yeh 尚書左僕射 left vice-president of the Department of Affairs of State

shang-shu yu-ch'eng 尚書右丞 assistant to the right vice-president of the Department of Affairs of State

shang-shu yu-p'u-yeh 尚書右僕射 right vice-president of the Department of Affairs of State

shen 神 spirit

shen chüeh ch'u, wei chüeh chung; chung i pu k'un 慎厥初惟厥終終以不困 "To give heed to the beginning, think of the end;—the end will then be without distress"

shen chung ju shih 慎終如始 "Be careful at the end as you were in the beginning"

shen chung yu shih 慎終于始 "Be careful for the end at the beginning"

shen-fou pien'tung 沉浮變通 "Bob upon the waters and freely adapt to circumstances"

Shen Nung 神農 pr.n.

shen shih erh ching chung 慎始而敬絡 "Be careful of the beginning and fearful of the end"

sheng-ch'en 聖臣 "divinely inspired official"

sheng-te 盛德 "abundant virtue"

Sheng-te lun 聖德論 *Wise and Virtuous Discourses*

shih 使 commissioner

shih 石 dry measure

shih ching 詩經 *Book of Odes*

shih-chung 侍中 president of the Department of the Imperial Chancellery

Shih Hui-lin 釋惠琳 pr.n.

shih-kuan 史官 History Office

shih-lang 侍郎 vice-president of a Board

shih-lu 實錄 "veritable records"

Shih-pi Qaghan 始畢可汗 (Turkish chieftain)

Shih Tao-an 釋道安 pr.n.

Shih-tsu chih 氏族志 *Compendium of Clans*

Shih-t'ung 史通 *Conspectus of History*

Shih-wu ts'e 時務策 *Questions on Current Political Affairs*

shu-hsüeh 書學 School of Calligraphy

Shu-huai 述懷 "Setting Down Innermost Thoughts"

shu pu i shih 書不以實 "not written truthfully"

Shu-ya 叔牙 pr.n.

Shun 舜 pr.n.

ssu 司 Court

ssu-chen 四鎮 "Four Garrisons"

ssu-hao 四皓 Four Elders

ssu-hsing 四姓 "four surnames"

Ssu-k'u ch'üan-shu tsung-mu 四庫全書總目 *General Catalogue of Collected Books in the Four Treasuries*

ssu-k'ung 司空 director of public works

Ssu-ma Ch'ien 司馬遷 pr.n.

Ssu-ma Kuang 司馬光 pr.n.

Ssu-ma T'an 司馬談 pr.n.

Ssu-men 司門 Bureau for the Surveillance of the Frontier

ssu-men hsüeh 四門學 School of the Four Gates

ssu-t'u 司徒 director of instruction

Su-le 疏勒 Kashgar

Su Mien 蘇冕 pr.n.

Sui-ching lieh-chuan 隋靖列傳 t.

Sui Kao-tsu 隋高祖 (emperor)

Sui-shu 隋書 *Sui History*

Sui-T'ang t'ung-lu 隋唐通錄 t.

Sui-T'ang yen-i 隋唐演義 *Romances of the Sui and T'ang*

Sui Wen-ti 隋文帝 (emperor)

Sui Yang-ti 隋煬帝 (emperor)

Sui-yeh 碎葉 Toqmaq

Sun An-tsu 孫安祖 pr.n.

Sun Fu 孫甫 pr.n.

Sun Fu-chia 孫伏伽 pr.n.

Sun Kuo-tung 孫國棟 pr.n.

Sun Ssu-mo 孫思邈 pr.n.

Sung Che-tsung 宋哲宗 (emperor)

Sung Hsien 宋戚 pr.n.

Sung Shen-tsung 宋神宗 (emperor)

Sung Wen-ti 宋文帝 (emperor)

Ta-an Palace 大安宮

Ta-ch'eng-hsiang T'ang-wang kuan-shu chi 大丞相唐王官屬記 *Record of the Great Chancellor Prince of T'ang and His Officials*

ta-chiang-chün fu 大將軍府 Administration of the Grand General

ta-chih 大志 "driving ambition"

Ta-hsing-ch'eng 大興城 "Great Revival City"

Ta-hsüeh 大學 *Great Learning*

ta-ju 大儒 "great Confucian"

Ta-ming Palace 大明宮

Ta-T'ang ch'uang-yeh ch'i-chü-chu 大唐創業起居注 *Diary of the Founding of the Great T'ang Dynasty*

Ta-yeh 大業 r.n.

Ta-Yü mo 大禹謨 "The Counsels of the Great Yü"

Tai Chou 戴胄 pr.n.

Tai Sheng 戴聖 pr. n.

Tai-shih li 戴氏禮 t.

T'ai-chi Hall 太極殿

T'ai-hang mountains 太行山

t'ai-hsüeh 太學 Superior School

t'ai-p'ing 太平 "time of great peace and and plenty"

T'ai (mountain) 泰山

t'ai-shang huang 太上皇 "retired emperor"

t'ai-shou 太守 prefect

T'ai-tsung 太宗 (see T'ang T'ai-tsung)

T'ai-tsung shih-lu 太宗實錄 *T'ai-tsung Veritable Records*

t'ai-tzu t'ai-shih 太子太師 grand tutor to the crown prince

tang 黨 faction

T'ang Chien 唐儉 pr.n.

T'ang T'ai-tsung 唐太宗 (emperor)

tao 道 circuit, province

Tao-kuan nei po-shu fu 道觀內柏樹賦 "*Fu on a Cypress in a Taoist Monastery*"

tao-te 道德 "the Way and its power"

Tao-tsang 道藏, t.

T'ao T'ang 陶唐 pr.n.

t'e-chin 特進 honorary office

Ti-chu ming 砥柱銘 "Ti-chu Inscription"

tien-nei shao-chien 殿內少監 assistant director of the Department of Imperial Domestic Service

t'ien-ming 天命 Mandate of Heaven

T'ien-t'ai Mountains 天臺山

t'ien-ts'e fu 天策府 Office of Heavenly Strategy

t'ien-ts'e shang-chiang 天策上將 Supreme Commander of Heavenly Strategy

t'ien-tzu 天子 Son of Heaven

ting 丁 adult

ting-pen 定本 authoritative edition

tou 斗 dry measure

Tou Chien-te 竇建德 pr.n.

tsai-hsiang 宰相 chief minister

tsai-hsiang shih-hsi piao 宰相世系表 "Genealogical Table of Chief Ministers"

Ts'ai K'an 蔡戡 pr.n.

Ts'ai-shu 蔡叔 pr.n.

ts'an-yü ch'ao-cheng 參豫朝政 designation

Ts'ang-hai 滄海 pl.n.

Ts'e-fu yüan-kuei 册府元龜 *Storehouse of Documents of the Great Tortoise*

tsei 賊 "bandit"

Ts'en Chung-mien 岑仲勉 pr.n.

Ts'en Wen-pen 岑文本 pr.n.

Tso-chuan 左傳 Tso commentary

tso-kuang-lu ta-fu 左光祿大夫 honorary title

tso-shih-i 左拾遺 reminder of the left

tsu-yung-tiao 租庸調 triple tax

Ts'ui 崔 s.

Ts'ui Chüeh 崔珏 pr.n.

Ts'ui Shan-wei 崔善爲 pr.n.

tsung-heng 縱橫 Vertical and Horizontal Alliances

tsung-heng chih shuo 縱橫之說 theories of the Vertical and Horizontal Alliances (*Realpolitik*)

tsung-kuan 總管 commander-in-chief

tsung-kuan fu 總管府 administration of the commander-in-chief

tsung-lun 總論 general discussion

Tu Cheng-lun 杜正倫 pr.n.

Tu Fu-wei 杜伏威 pr.n.

Tu Ju-hui 杜如晦 pr.n.

Tu-ku 獨孤 s.

tu-tu 都督 governor-general

tu-tu fu 都督府 government-general

Tu Yen 杜淹 pr.n.

T'u-li Qaghan 突利可汗 (Turkish chieftain)

T'u-po 吐蕃 tr.n.

T'u-yü-hun 吐谷渾 tr.n.

T'un-liu 屯留 pl.n.

tui 對 replies

Tung Cho 董卓 pr.n.

Tung Chung-shu 董仲舒 pr.n.

tung-i 東夷 "Eastern Barbarians"

tung-tu 東都 Eastern Capital

T'ung-an Princess 同安公主

T'ung-chi ch'ü 通濟渠 canal

T'ung Pass 潼關

t'ung-te 同德 "united in virtue"

Tzu-chih t'ung-chien 資治通鑑 Comprehensive Mirror for Aid in Government

Tzu-ku chu-hou-wang shan-o lu 自古諸侯王善惡錄 A Record of Good and Evil of Feudal Princes and Rulers since Antiquity

Tzu-kung 子貢 pr.n.

Tzu-yu 子游 pr.n.

tzu yu chuan 自有傳 "He has his own biography"

Tz'u Li-chi 次禮記 t.

Tz'u prefecture 磁州

tz'u-shih 刺史 prefect

wai-ch'i 外戚 relatives by marriage of the imperial house

Wang Chi 王績 pr.n.

Wang Chih 王質 pr.n.

Wang Ch'ung 王充 pr.n.

Wang Fang-ch'ing 王方慶 pr.n.

Wang Fu-chih 王夫之 pr.n.

Wang Fu-chih 王福畤 pr.n.

Wang Hao 王灝 pr.n.

Wang Hsien-ch'ien 王先謙 pr.n.

Wang Hsien-kung 王先恭 pr.n.

Wang Kuei 王珪 pr.n.

wang-kuo chih ch'en 亡國之臣 "official who destroys the state"

Wang Pi 王弼 pr.n.

Wang Po 王勃 pr.n.

Wang Shih-ch'ung 王世充 pr.n.

Wang T'ung 王通 pr.n.

Wang T'ung-ling 王桐齡 pr.n.

Wang Wei 王威 pr.n.

Wang Wen-k'ai 王文楷 pr.n.

Wang Ying-lin 王應麟 pr.n.

wei 僞 "pretended"

Wei Chang-hsien 魏長賢 pr.n.

Wei Cheng 魏徵 pr.n.

Wei Cheng chi 魏徵集 t.

Wei Cheng chien-shih 魏徵諫事 t.

Wei Cheng kai-chao feng-yün-hui 魏徵改詔風雲會 *Wei Cheng Changes the Order*

Wei Cheng-kung chien hsü-lu 魏鄭公諫續錄 *Continued Recorded Remonstrances of Duke Wei of Cheng*

Wei Cheng-kung chien-lu 魏鄭公諫錄 *Recorded Remonstrances of Duke Wei of Cheng*

Wei Cheng-kung chien-lu chiao-chu 魏鄭公諫錄校注 t.

Wei Cheng-kung wen-chi 魏鄭公文集 *Collected Prose of Duke Wei of Cheng*

Wei Cheng lieh-chuan Hsin-Chiu T'ang-shu ho-chu 魏徵列傳新舊唐書合注 *Combined Notes to the Biography of Wei Cheng in the Old and New T'ang Histories*

Wei K'ai 魏愷 pr.n.

Wei commandery 魏郡.

Wei prefecture 魏州

Wei Hsüan-ch'eng chuan 魏玄成傳 t.

Wei Hsüan-ch'eng ku-shih 魏玄成故事 t.

Wei Hsüan-ch'eng li chung-chieh 魏玄成厲忠節 t.

Wei Hung-chih 韋宏質 pr. n.

Wei River 渭水

Wei Shou 魏收 pr.n.

Wei Shu 韋述 pr.n.

Wei-shu 魏書 *Northern Wei History*

Wei Shu-yü 魏叔玉 pr.n.

Wei-shui chih ch'ih 渭水之恥 "humiliation at the Wei River"

Wei Tan 魏澹 pr.n.

Wei T'ing 韋挺 pr.n.

Wei-tzu 微子 Viscount of Wei

wei-wei shao-ch'ing 衛尉少卿 vice-president of the Court of Imperial Insignia

Wei Wen-chen ku-shih 魏文貞故事 t.

Wei Wen-chen kung ku-shih shih-i 魏文貞公故事拾遺 t.

Wei Wen-chen kung nien-p'u 魏文貞年譜 t.

Wei Yen 魏彥 pr.n.

wen 文 "civil virtue"

Wen, King of Chou 周文王

Wen, Marquis of Chin 晉文侯

wen-chen 文貞 "refined and pure"

Wen-chen kung chuan-shih 文貞公傳事 t.

Wen-chen kung ku-shih 文貞公故事 t.

Wen-chen kung shih-lu 文貞公事錄 t.

Wen-chung-tzu 文中子 pr.n.

Wen-hsüan, 文宣 (emperor of the Northern Ch'i)

wen-hsüeh kuan 文學館 College of Literary Studies

Wen-ssu po-yao 文思博要 t.

Wen Ta-ya 溫大雅 pr.n.

Wen-tsung, 文宗 (emperor of the T'ang)

Wen Yen-po 溫彥博 pr.n.

wu 武 "military virtue"

Wu, King of Chou 周武王

Wu Ch'eng-en 吳承恩 pr.n.

Wu Ching 吳兢

Wu-ching cheng-i 五經正義 *Five Classics with Orthodox Commentaries*

Wu Han 吳哈 pr.n.

wu kuang te che ch'ang, wu kuang ti che wang 務廣德者昌務廣地者亡 "Striving to broaden one's virtue leads to prosperity; striving to broaden one's territory leads to destruction"

Wu Shih-huo 武士彠, pr.n.

Wu-tai-shih chih 五代史志 *Monographs of the Histories of the Five Dynasties*

Wu-te 武德 r.n.

wu-wei 無爲 non-activity

wu-wei erh chih 無爲而治 good government by means of non-activity

Wu-yang commandery 武陽郡

Ya-tan Ho-kan 厭怛紇于 pr.n.

Yang Ch'ing 楊慶 pr.n.

Yang Hsiung 楊雄 pr.n.

Yang Hsüan-kan 楊玄感 pr.n.

Yang Kung-jen 楊恭仁 pr.n.

Yang Tsun-yen 楊遵彥 pr.n.

Yang Wen-kan 楊文幹 pr.n.

Yang Yüan-sun 楊元孫 pr.n.

Yao 堯 pr.n.

Yao Wen-jan 姚文然 pr.n.

Yeh 鄴 capital of Eastern Wei and Northern Ch'i dynasties

Yen-ch'i 焉耆 Karashahr

Yen Chih-t'ui 顏之推 pr.n.

Yen Li-pen 閻立本 pr.n.

Yen Li-te 閻立德 pr.n.

Yen-men 雁門 pl.n.

Yen Shih-ku 顏師古 pr.n.

Yen Yen-chih 顏延之 pr.n.

ying-yang fu 鷹揚府 Sui militia organization

Yu, King of Chou 周幽王 pr.n.

yu ssu-fang chih chih 有四方之志 "had ambitions to conquer the empire,"

Yung-chi ch'ü 永濟渠 canal

Yung-hsing quarter 永興坊

Yung-lo ta-tien 永樂大典 t.

Yü 禹 pr.n.

Yü-ch'en 諛臣 "flattering official"

Yü-ch'ih Ching-te 尉遲敬德 pr.n.

Yü-hai 玉海 t.

Yü Shih-nan 虞世南 pr.n.

yü-shih ta-fu 御史大夫 president of the Censorate

yü-shih t'ai 御史臺 Censorate

Yü-t'ien 于闐 Khotan

Yü-wen Hua-chi 宇文化及 pr.n.

Yü-wen K'ai 宇文愷 pr.n.

Yü-wen Shih-chi 宇文士及 pr.n.

yüan-che 元澤 "primeval swamp"

Yüan-ching 元經 *Primal Classic*

Yüan-ho chün-hsien t'u-chih 元和郡縣圖志 t.

Yüan Hsing-ch'ung 元行沖 pr.n.

Yüan Kai-su-wen 淵蓋蘇文 pr.n.

Yüan Pao-tsang 元寶藏 pr.n.

yüan-shuai 元帥 commander-in-chief

Yüeh 粵 pl.n.

Yün-t'ai 雲臺 Cloud Terrace

Bibliography

I. Works written or compiled by Wei Cheng and major Chinese sources on Wei Cheng based on contemporary or near contemporary materials.

Ch'enS. *Ch'en-shu* 陳書 [Ch'en History]. 36 *chüan.* Compiled 629–36 by Yao Ssu-lien 姚思廉 et al. I-wen Photolithographic reproduction of the Ch'ien-lung Palace ed.

CKCY. *Chen-kuan cheng-yao* 貞觀政要 [Essentials of Government of the Chen-kuan Period]. 10 *chüan.* Compiled ca. 707–09 by Wu Ching 吳兢. *Ssu-pu pei-yao* 四部備要 ed.; Taipei, 1967.

CTS. *Chiu T'ang-shu* 舊唐書 [Old T'ang History]. 200 *chüan.* Compiled 940–45 by Liu Hsü 劉昫 et al. I-wen photolithographic reproduction of the Ch'ien-lung Palace ed.

CTShih. *Ch'üan T'ang-shih* 全唐詩 [Complete Poetry of the T'ang Dynasty]. 900 *chüan.* Compiled 1707 by Ts'ao Yin 曹寅 et al.

CTW. *Ch'üan T'ang-wen* 全唐文 [Complete Prose of the T'ang Dynasty]. 1000 *chüan.* Compiled by Tung Kao 董誥 et al., 1814. Taipei, 1965.

HL. *Wei Cheng-kung chien hsü-lu* 魏鄭公諫續錄 [Continued Recorded Remonstrances of Duke Wei of Cheng]. 2 *chüan.* Compiled ca. 1330–33 by Chai Ssu-chung 翟思忠. Edited and annotated by Wang Hsien-kung 王先恭. Changsha, 1883.

HTS. *Hsin T'ang-shu* 新唐書 [New T'ang History]. 225 *chüan.* Compiled 1043–60 by Ou-yang Hsiu 歐陽修 et al. I-wen photolithographic reproduction of the Ch'ien-lung Palace ed.

KSSI. *Wei Wen-chen kung ku-shih shih-i* 魏文貞公故事拾遺 [Recovered Anecdotes Concerning Duke Wei Wen-chen]. Compiled and annotated by Wang Hsien-kung 王先恭. Changsha. 1883.

LS. *Liang-shu* 梁書 [Liang History]. 56 *chüan.* Compiled 629–36 by Yao Ssu-lien 姚思廉 et al. I-wen photolithographic reproduction of the Ch'ien-lung Palace ed.

PCh'iS. *Pei Ch'i-shu* 北齊書 [Northern Ch'i History]. 50 *chüan.* Compiled 629–36 by Li Pai-yao 李百藥 et al. I-wen photolithographic reproduction of the Ch'ien-lung Palace ed.

SuiS.   Sui-shu 隋書 [Sui History]. 85 *chüan*. Compiled 629–36 by Wei Cheng 魏徵 et al. I-wen photolithographic reproduction of the Ch'ien-lung Palace ed.

TCTC.   Tzu-chih t'ung-chien 資治通鑑 [Comprehensive Mirror for Aid in Government]. 294 *chüan*. Compiled 1084 by Ssu-ma Kuang 司馬光. Taipei, 1962.

TFYK.   Ts'e-fu yüan-kuei 册府元龜 [Storehouse of Documents of the Great Tortoise]. 1000 *chüan*. Compiled 1005–13 by Wang Ch'in-jo 王欽若 et al. Reproduction of 1642 ed.; Taipei, 1967.

THY.   T'ang hui-yao 唐會要 [Collected Statutes of the T'ang Dynasty]. 100 *chüan*. Compiled 961 by Wang P'u 王溥. Taipei, 1963.

WCKCL.   Wei Cheng-kung chien-lu chiao-chu 魏鄭公諫錄校注 [Annotated Edition of the Recorded Remonstrances of Duke Wei of Cheng]. 5 *chüan*. Compiled prior to 702 by Wang Fang-ch'ing 王方慶 and annotated by Wang Hsien-kung 王先恭. Changsha, 1883.

WCKWC.   Wei Cheng-kung wen-chi 魏鄭公文集 [Collected Prose of Duke Wei of Cheng]. 3 *chüan*. Compiled 1879–92 by Wang Hao 王灝. *Ts'ung-shu chi-ch'eng* 叢書集成 ed.; Shanghai, 1937.

WCLC.   Wei Cheng lieh-chuan Hsin Chiu T'ang-shu ho-chu 魏徵列傳新舊唐書合注 [Combined Notes to the Biographies of Wei Cheng in the New and Old T'ang Histories]. Compiled and annotated by Wang Hsien-ch'ien 王先謙. Changsha, 1883.

Wei Cheng 魏徵. *Chiu-ch'eng-kung li-ch'üan ming* 九成宮醴泉銘 [Inscription on the Sweet Spring of the Chiu-ch'eng Palace]. 632. Reproduction of a stone rubbing of the original; Tokyo, 1966.

———, et al., comp. *Ch'ün-shu chih-yao* 羣書治要 [Essentials of Government from Divers Books]. 50 *chüan*. 631. *Ts'ung-shu chi-ch'eng* 叢書集成 ed.; Shanghai, 1936.

———, et al., comp. *Gunsho jiyō* 羣書治要 [Ch'ün-shu chih-yao]. 50 *chüan*. Tokyo, 1941.

Wei Cheng-kung chien-lu 魏鄭公諫錄 [Recorded Remonstrances of Duke Wei of Cheng]. 5 *chüan*. Compiled prior to 702 by Wang Fang-ch'ing 王方慶;
     a) *Chi-fu ts'ung-shu* 畿輔叢書 ed.; Tingchou, 1879–92.
     b) *Ts'ung-shu chi-ch'eng* 叢書集成 ed.; Shanghai, 1936.

Wei Cheng-kung shih-chi 魏鄭公詩集 [Collected Poetry of Duke Wei of Cheng]. *Ts'ung-shu chi-ch'eng* 叢書集成 ed.; Shanghai, 1937.

Wei Cheng-kung wen-chi 魏鄭公文集 [Collected Prose of Duke Wei of Cheng]. 3 *chüan*. Compiled by Wang Hao 王灝. *Chi-fu ts'ung-shu* 畿輔叢書 ed.; Tingchou, 1879–92.

Wei Wen-chen nien-p'u 魏文貞年譜 [Chronological Account of the Life of Duke Wei Wen-chen]. Compiled by Wang Hsien-kung 王先恭. Changsha, 1883.

WS.   *Wei-shu* 魏書 [Northern Wei History]. 114 *chüan*. Compiled 551–54 by
Wei Shou 魏收. I-wen photolithographic reproduction of the Ch'ien-
lung Palace ed.

II. Traditional Chinese Works

Chang T'ien-yü 張天雨. *Hsüan p'in-lu* 玄品錄 [Classified Record of Taoists].
5 *chüan*. In *Tao-tsang* 道藏 [The Taoist Repository]. Reproduction of
1445 ed.; Taipei, 1962.

Chao I 趙翼. *Nien-erh-shih cha-chi* 廿二史答記 [Detailed Notes on the Twenty-
two Histories]. 36 *chüan*. 1795. 2 vols., Taipei, 1965.

Ch'ao Kung-wu 晁公武 *Chao-te hsien-sheng chün-chai tu-shu chih* 昭德先生君齋
讀書志. 20 *chüan*. 1819 ed.

Ch'en Chen-sun 陳振孫. *Chih-chai shu-lu chieh-t'i* 直齋書錄解題 [Annotated
Catalogue of the Chih Library]. 22 *chüan*. ca. 1235. *Ts'ung-shu chi-ch'eng*
叢書集成 ed.; 1937.

Ch'eng Ta-ch'ang 程大昌. *K'ao-ku pien* 考古編 [Investigations of Antiquity].
10 *chüan*. 1181. *Ts'ung-shu chi-ch'eng* 叢書集成 ed.; Shanghai, 1939.

Ch'ing-shih 清史 [Ch'ing History]. 550 *chüan*. Taipei, 1961.

Chu I-tsun 朱彝尊 (1629–1709). *Ching-i k'ao* 經義考 [Examination of Interpretations of the Classics]. 300 *chüan*. Che-chiang shu-chü ed., 1897.

Ch'u Jen-hu 褚人穫. *Sui-T'ang yen-i* 隋唐演義 [Romances of the Sui and
T'ang]. 1695. Hong Kong, 1966.

Ch'un-ch'iu 春秋. See Legge, *The Chinese Classics*.

CYCCC.   *Ta-T'ang ch'uang-yeh ch'i-chü-chu* 大唐創業起居注 [Diary of the
Founding of the Great T'ang Dynasty]. 3 *chüan*. Compiled prior to 627
by Wen Ta-ya 溫大雅. *Chin-tai mi-shu* 津逮祕書 ed. of Mao Chin 毛晉,
1628–44.

Fan Tsu-yü 范祖禹 (1041–98). *T'ang-chien* 唐鑑 [The Mirror of T'ang].
24 *chüan*. *Ts'ung-shu chi-ch'eng* 叢書集成 ed.; Shanghai, 1936.

HS.   *Han-shu* 漢書 [Former Han History]. 100 *chüan*. Compiled 58–76 by
Pan Ku 班固. I-wen photolithographic reproduction of Ch'ien-lung
Palace ed.

Hung Mai 洪邁 (1123–1202). *Jung-chai sui-pi* 容齋隨筆. 5 *chüan*. Wan-yu
wen-k'u 萬有文庫 ed.; Shanghai, 1939.

Lao Ching-yüan 勞經原. "T'ang che-ch'ung fu k'ao" 唐折衝府考 [A Study
of the T'ang Intrepid Militia] 4 *chüan*. 1841. In *Erh-shih-wu shih pu-pien*
二十五史補編 [Supplements to the Twenty-five Standard Histories]. 6
vols.; 1937. Reprint, Peking, 1957. 6: 7593–7629.

Li Chi-fu 李吉甫, comp. *Yüan-ho chün-hsien t'u-chih* 元和郡縣圖志 [Geo-
graphical Gazetteer of Administrative Subdivisions of the Yüan-ho
Period]. 40 *chüan*. 813–15. Reproduction of *Chi-fu ts'ung-shu* 畿輔叢書
ed.; Taipei, 1965.

Li Fang 李昉 et al., comps. *T'ai-p'ing kuang-chi* 太平廣記. 500 *chüan*. 977–78. Taipei, 1962.

———, et al., comps. *T'ai-p'ing yü-lan* 太平御覽. 1000 *chüan*. 983. *SPTK* ed.; Taipei, 1967.

———, et al., comps. *Wen-yüan ying-hua* 文苑英華 [The Flowers of the Garden of Letters]. 1000 *chüan*. 982–87. Reproduction of 1567–72 ed.; Taipei, 1965.

Lin Pao 林寶. *Yüan-ho hsing-tsuan* 元和姓纂 [Compendium of Surnames of the Yüan-ho Period]. 18 *chüan*. Preface 813. Chin-ling shu-chü ed., 1880.

Lin T'ung 林侗. *T'ang Chao-ling shih-chi k'ao-lüeh* 唐昭陵石蹟考略 [A Brief Investigation of the Stone Records of the T'ang Chao-ling]. 5 *chüan*. 1697. *Ts'ung-shu chi-ch'eng* 叢書集成 ed.; Shanghai, 1939.

Liu Chih-chi 劉知幾. *Shih-t'ung* 史通 [Conspectus of History]. 20 *chüan*. 710. Shanghai, 1928.

Liu Hsiang 劉向 (ca. 79–ca. 8 B.C.). *Shuo-yüan* 說元. 20 *chüan*. *SPTK* ed.; Shanghai, 1929.

Liu Su 劉肅. *Ta-T'ang hsin-yü* 大唐新語 [New Anecdotes of the Great T'ang Dynasty]. 13 *chüan*. 807. *Pai-hai* 稗海 ed.; *Pai-pu ts'ung-shu chi-ch'eng* 百部叢書集成, Taipei, 1957.

Lun-yü 論語. See Legge, *The Chinese Classics*, and Waley, *The Analects of Confucius*.

Ma Tuan-lin 馬端臨, comp. *Wen-hsien t'ung-k'ao* 文獻通考 [Complete Examination of Documents and Compositions]. 348 *chüan*. Prior to 1319. Reproduction of 1748 ed.; Taipei, 1964.

Meng-tzu 孟子. See Legge, *The Chinese Classics*.

PS.   *Pei-shih* 北史 [Northern Dynasties History]. 100 *chüan*. Compiled 630–50 by Li Yen-shou 李延壽. I-wen photolithographic reproduction of the Ch'ien-lung Palace ed.

SC.   *Shih-chi* 史記 [Records of the Grand Historian]. 130 *chüan*. Compiled 104–87 B.C. by Ssu-ma Ch'ien 司馬遷. I-wen photolithographic reproduction of the Ch'ien-lung Palace ed.

Shih-ching 詩經. See Legge, *The Chinese Classics*.

Shu-ching 書經. See Legge, *The Chinese Classics*.

SKCSTM.   *Ssu-k'u ch'üan-shu tsung-mu* 四庫全書總目 [General Catalogue of Collected Books in the Four Treasuries]. 200 *chüan*. Compiled 1782 by Chi Yün 紀昀 et al. Taipei, 1964.

SPTK.   *Ssu-pu ts'ung-k'an* 四部叢刊. Shanghai, 1929.

Ssu-ma Kuang 司馬光. "Wen-chung-tzu pu-chuan" 文中子補傳 [Supplement to the Biography of Wen-chung-tzu]. In *Sung-wen chien* 宋文鑑 [Mirror of Sung Literature], Lü Tsu-ch'ien 呂祖謙, comp. 150 *chüan*. Wan-yu wen-k'u 萬有文庫 ed.; Shanghai, 1936.

Sun Fu 孫甫. *T'ang-shih lun-tuan* 唐史論斷 [Opinions on T'ang History]. 3 *chüan*. Preface 1052. *Ts'ung-shu chi-ch'eng* 叢書集成 ed.; Shanghai, 1939.

Sung Min-ch'iu 宋敏求 (1019–79). *Ch'ang-an chih* 長安志 [A Gazetteer of Ch'ang-an]. 20 *chüan*. *Ching-hsün-t'ang ts'ung-shu* 經訓堂叢書 ed., ca. 1790.

SungS. *Sung-shih* 宋史 [Sung History]. 496 *chüan*. Compiled 1343–45 by T'o T'o 脫脫 et al. I-wen photolithographic reproduction of the Ch'ien-lung Palace ed.

T'ang T'ai-tsung 唐太宗. *Ti-fan* 帝範 [Plan for an Emperor]. 2 *chüan*. 648. *Ts'ung-shu chi-ch'eng* 叢書集成 ed.; Shanghai, 1937.

Ts'ai K'an 蔡戡 (fl. 1165–74). *Ting-chai chi* 定齋集. 20 *chüan*. N.p., 1897.

Tso-chuan 左傳. See Legge, *The Chinese Classics*.

TTLT. *Ta-T'ang liu-tien* 大唐六典 [Six Canons of the Great T'ang Dynasty]. 30 *chüan*. Attributed to T'ang Hsüan-tsung 唐玄宗, compiled ca. 739. Reproduction of Konoe edition of 1724; Taipei, 1962.

Tu Yu 杜佑. *T'ung-tien* 通典 [Comprehensive Statutes]. 200 *chüan*. 801. Taipei, 1966.

Tuan Ch'eng-shih 段成式. *Yu-yang tsa-tsu* 西陽雄俎. 20 *chüan*. 853. *Ts'ung-shu chi-ch'eng* 叢書集成 ed.; Shanghai, 1937.

Wan Ssu-t'ung 萬斯同. "T'ang chiang-hsiang-ta-ch'en nien-piao" 唐將相大臣年表 [Chronological Tables of High Officials, Chief Ministers, and Generals of the T'ang Dynasty]. 3 *chüan*. In *Erh-shih-wu shih pu-pien* 二十五史補編 [Supplements to the Twenty-five Standard Histories]. 6 vols., 1937. Reprint, Peking, 1957. 5: 7217–21.

Wang Ch'ang 王昶, comp. *Chin-shih ts'ui-pien* 金石萃編 [Collected Essays on Bronze and Stone Monuments]. 160 *chüan*. 1805. Shanghai, 1921.

Wang Chih-ch'ang 汪之昌. *Ch'ing-hsüeh chai-chi* 青學齋集. 36 *chüan*. N.p., 1895.

Wang Fu-chih 王夫之 (1619–92). *Sung-lun* 宋論 [Essays on the Sung]. 15 *chüan*. Reproduction of the *Ch'uan-shan i-shu* 船山遺書 ed.; Taipei, 1965.

———. *Tu T'ung-chien lun* 讀通鑑論 [Essays on Reading the *Comprehensive Mirror*]. 30 *chüan*. Reproduction of the *Ch'uan-shan i-shu* 船山遺書 ed.; Taipei, 1965.

Wang Tang 王讜. *T'ang yü-lin* 唐語林 [A Forest of Anecdotes of the T'ang Dynasty]. 8 *chüan*. ca. 1100. Taipei, 1959.

Wang Ting-pao 王定保. *T'ang chih-yen* 唐摭言 [Collected Anecdotes of the T'ang Dynasty]. 15 *chüan*. ca. 955. Taipei, 1962.

Wang T'ung 王通 (584?–617). *Chung-shuo* 中說 [Discourses on the Mean]. 10 *chüan*. *SPTK* ed.; Shanghai, 1929.

Wang Ying-lin 王應麟 (1223–96). *T'ung-chien ti-li t'ung-i* 通鑑地理通釋 [Comprehensive Explanations of Geography in the *Comprehensive Mirror*].

14 *chüan*. *Chin-tai mi-shu* 津逮秘書 ed. of Mao Chin 毛晉, 1628–44.
Shanghai, 1922.

———, comp. *Yü-hai* 玉海 [The Sea of Jade]. 204 *chüan*. Che-chiang shu-chü
ed., 1883.

Wei Cheng kai-chao feng-yün-hui 魏徵改詔風雲會 [Wei Cheng Changes the
Order]. *Ku-pen hsi-ch'ü ts'ung-k'an ssu-chi, Mai-wang-kuan ch'ao-chiao-pen
ku-chin tsa-chü* 古本戲曲叢刊四集脈望館鈔校本古今雜劇 ed.; Peking,
1960.

Wei Shu 韋述 (d. 757). *Liang-ching hsin-chi* 兩京新記 [New Records of the
Two Capitals]. *Nan-ching cha-chi* 南菁札記 ed.; Taipei, 1963.

Wu Ch'eng-en 吳承恩 (1500–82). *Hsi-yu chi* 西遊記 [A Record of a Journey to
the West]. Shanghai, 1921.

Yao Hsüan 姚鉉 (968–1020), comp. *T'ang wen-ts'ui* 唐文粹. 100 *chüan*. *SPTK*
ed.; Shanghai, 1929.

III. Modern Chinese and Japanese Works

Adachi Kiroku 足立喜六. *Chōan shiseki no kenkyū* 長安史蹟の研究 [A Study of
Ch'ang-an Historical Remains]. Tokyo, 1933.

Chang Ch'ün 章群. *T'ang-shih* 唐史 [History of the T'ang Dynasty]. 2 vols.
Taipei, 1958 and 1965.

Chao Wu 趙武. *Wei Cheng* 魏徵. *Li-tai cheng-chih jen-wu chuan-chi i-chu* 歷代政
治人物傳記譯注 [Annotated and Explained Biographies of Statesmen
of Successive Ages] series. Peking, 1962.

Ch'en Ch'eng-chen 陳成眞. "Wei Cheng yü Chen-kuan chih chih" 魏徵與
貞觀之治 [Wei Cheng and the Chen-kuan chih chih]. M.A. thesis,
College of Chinese Culture (Chung-kuo wen-hua hsüeh-yüan), 1967.

———. "Wen-chung-tzu hsin-k'ao" 文中子新考 [A New Examination of
Wen-chung-tzu], *Ta-lu tsa-chih* 大陸雜誌 [The Continent], 36 (1968),
23–26.

Ch'en Yin-k'o 陳寅恪. "Chi T'ang-tai chih Li Wu Wei Yang hun-yin chi-
t'uan" 記唐代之李武韋楊婚姻集團 [The Li, Wu, Wei, and Yang
Marriage Blocs of the T'ang Dynasty], *Li-shih yen-chiu* 歷史研究, 1954,
no. 1, pp. 33–51.

———. "Lun Sui-mo T'ang-ch'u so-wei 'Shan-tung hao-chieh'" 論隋末
唐初所謂山東豪傑 [The So-called "Shan-tung hao-chieh" at the End of
the Sui and Beginning of the T'ang Dynasty], *Ling-nan hsüeh-pao* 嶺南
學報, 12 (1952), 1–14.

———. "Lun T'ang Kao-tsu ch'eng-ch'en yü T'u-chüeh shih" 論唐高祖
稱臣於突厥事 [On T'ang Kao-tsu Calling Himself a Subject of the
Turks], *Ling-nan hsüeh-pao* 嶺南學報, 11 (1951), 1–9.

———. *Sui-T'ang chih-tu yüan-yüan lüeh-lun kao* 隋唐制度淵源略論稿 [Draft

Outline of the Origin and Development of Sui and T'ang Institutions]. Chungking, 1944; Shanghai, 1946.

———. *T'ang-tai cheng-chih shih shu-lun kao* 唐代政治史述論稿 [Draft Narrative of the Political History of the T'ang Dynasty]. Chungking, 1944.

Ch'i Ch'en-chün 齊陳駿. "Shih-lun Sui ho T'ang-ch'u ti cheng-ch'üan" 試論隋和唐初的政權 [An Examination of Political Power during the Sui and Early T'ang], *Li-shih yen-chiu* 歷史研究, 1965, no. 1, pp. 103–22.

Chou I-liang 周一良. "Wei Shou chih shih-hsüeh" 魏收之史學 [Wei Shou's Historiography], *Yen-ching hsüeh-pao* 燕京學報, 18 (1935), 107–46.

Chou Tao-chi 周道濟. "T'ang-tai tsai-hsiang ming-ch'eng yü ch'i shih-ch'üan chih yen-pien" 唐代宰相名稱與其實權之演變 [Changes in the Names and Real Power of the Chief Ministers of the T'ang Dynasty], *Ta-lu tsa-chih* 大陸雜誌 [The Continent], 16 (1958), 103–11.

Chu Hsi-tsu 朱希祖. "Han-T'ang-Sung ch'i-chü-chu k'ao" 漢唐宋起居注考 [A Study of the Diaries of Activity and Repose of the Han, T'ang, and Sung Dynasties], *Kuo-hsüeh chi-k'an* 國學季刊 [Journal of Sinological Studies, Peking National University], 2 (1930), 629–40.

Fu Lo-ch'eng 傅樂成. "Hsüan-wu-men shih-pien chih yün-niang" 玄武門事變之醞釀 [Incidents that Led to the Hsüan-wu Gate Coup d'Etat], *Wen-shih-che hsüeh-pao* 文史哲學報 [Bulletin of the College of Arts, National Taiwan University], 8 (1958), 171–80.

Fujikawa Masakazu 藤川正數. "Tōdai (Jōkanki) fukuki kaisei ni okeru ni san no dōkō" 唐代(貞觀期)服紀改度における二三の動向 [Some Tendencies in the System of Clothing Regulations of the T'ang Dynasty (Chen-kuan Period)], *Hambun gakukai kaihō* 漢文學會會報 [Bulletin of the Chinese Literature Society], 17 (1957), 28–36.

Fukui Shigemasa 福井重雅. "Ō Tō sōgyō kikyochū kō" 大唐創業起居注考 [A Study of the Diary of the Founding of the T'ang Dynasty], *Shikan* 史觀, 63–64 (1961), 82–94.

Fukusawa Sōkichi 福澤宗吉. "Bungakukan gakushi ni tsuite" 文學館學士について [The Scholars of the Wen-hsüeh kuan], *Kumamoto Daigaku kyōikugakubu kiyō* 熊本大學教育學部紀要 [Memoirs of the Faculty of Education, Kumamoto University], 1 (1953), 35–41.

Harada Tanashige 原田種成. "Jōkan seiyō no seiritsu" 貞觀正要の成立 [The Formation of the *Chen-kuan cheng-yao*], *Shibun* 斯文, 22 (1958), 18–30.

———. *Jōkan seiyō teihon* 貞觀政要定本 [Authoritative Edition of the *Chen-kuan cheng-yao*]. Tokyo, 1962.

Hoshikawa Kiyotaka 星川清孝. "Gi Chō 'Jukkai' no shi to soji" 魏徵「述懷」の詩と楚辭 [Wei Cheng's "Shu-huai" and the Ch'u-tz'u], *Shibun* 斯文, 27 (1960), 12–27.

Hsiang Ta 向達. *T'ang-tai Ch'ang-an yü Hsi-yü wen-ming* 唐代長安與西域文明 [T'ang Ch'ang-an and Western Regions Culture]. 1933; reprint, Peking, 1957.

Hsiao Kung-ch'üan 蕭公權. *Chung-kuo cheng-chih ssu-hsiang shih* 中國政治思想史 [A History of Chinese Political Thought]. 2 vols. Chungking, 1945; Shanghai, 1946.

Ikeda On 池田溫. "Tōchō shizokushi no ichi kōsatsu—iwayuru Tonkō meizokushi zankan o megutte" 唐朝氏族志の一考察—いわゆる敦煌名族志殘卷をめぐって [A Study of the Compendia of Clans of the T'ang Dynasty with Special Reference to the *ming-tzu-chih* Remnants], *Hokkaidō Daigaku bungakubu kiyō* 北海道大學文學部紀要 [Annual Report on Cultural Science, Faculty of Letters, Hokkaido University], 13 (1965), 1–64.

Ise Sentarō 伊瀬仙太郎. *Chūgoku seiiki keieishi kenkyū* 中國西域經營史研究 [A Study of the History of China's Administration of the Western Regions]. 1955; 2nd ed., Tokyo, 1968.

Jen-min jih-pao 人民日報 [The People's Daily], November 9, 1967.

Jung Chao-tsu 容肇祖. "Mu-fang K'ung-tzu ti Wang T'ung" 摹仿孔子的王通 [Wang T'ung, Imitator of Confucius], *Ling-nan hsüeh-pao* 嶺南學報, 6 (1941), 1–16.

Kanno Dōmei 簡野道明. *Tōshisen shōsetsu* 唐詩選詳說 [Detailed Commentary on the Anthology of T'ang Poetry]. 2 vols. Tokyo, 1930.

Kao Pu-ying 高步瀛. *T'ang-Sung-wen chü-yao* 唐宋文舉要 [Selections from T'ang and Sung Literature]. 2 vols. Peking, 1963.

Ku Chi-kuang 谷霽光. "An-Shih luan ch'ien chih Ho-pei tao" 安史亂前之河北道 [Ho-pei *tao* Prior to the An-Shih Rebellions], *Yen-ching hsüeh-pao* 燕京學報, 19 (1936), 197–209.

"Kuan-yü Sui-T'ang shih yen-chiu chung ti i-ko li-lun wen-t'i" 關於隋唐史研究中的一個理論問題 [A Theoretical Problem in the Study of Sui and T'ang History]. *Li-shih yen-chiu* 歷史研究, 1958, no. 12, pp. 37–52.

Li Shu-t'ung 李樹桐. *T'ang-shih k'ao-pien* 唐史考辨 [An Examination of T'ang History]. Taipei, 1965.

———. "Tsai-pien T'ang Kao-tsu ch'eng-ch'en yü T'u-chüeh shih" 再辨唐高祖稱臣於突厥事 [A Further Examination of T'ang Kao-tsu Calling Himself A Subject of the Turks], *Ta-lu tsa-chih* 大陸雜誌 [The Continent], 37 (1968), 248–66.

Li T'ang 李唐. *T'ang T'ai-tsung* 唐太宗. Hong Kong, 1963.

Liu Po-chi 劉伯驥. *T'ang-tai cheng-chiao shih* 唐代政教史 [History of Politics and Education during the T'ang Dynasty]. Taipei, 1958.

Lo Hsiang-lin 羅香林. *T'ang-tai wen-hua shih* 唐代文化史 [A Cultural History of the T'ang Dynasty]. Taipei, 1955.

Lü Ssu-mien 呂思勉. *Sui-T'ang-Wu-tai shih* 隋唐五代史 [History of the Sui, T'ang, and Five Dynasties]. 2 vols. Shanghai, 1959.

Lung Shou-t'ang 龍壽鎧. "Wei Cheng chih cheng-chih ssu-hsiang" 魏徵之政治思想 [Wei Cheng's Political Thought]. *Hsiang-kang ta-hsüeh chung-wen hsüeh-hui hui-k'an* 香港大學中文學會會刊 [Journal of the Chinese Literature Society, the Chinese University of Hong Kong], 1960, 45–57.

Ma Ch'i-hua 馬起華. "Chen-kuan cheng-lun" 貞觀政論 [Commentary on the Politics of the Chen-kuan Period], *Kuo-li cheng-chih ta-hsüeh hsüeh-pao* 國立政治大學學報 [National Chengchi University Journal], 1 (1960), 243–93; 2 (1960), 359–99; 3 (1961), 373–400.

Mao Han-kuang 毛漢光. *Liang-Chin Nan-pei-ch'ao shih-tsu cheng-chih chih yen-chiu* 兩晉南北朝士族政治之研究 [Studies on Aristocratic Politics During the Two Chin and Northern and Southern Dynasties]. 2 vols. Taipei, 1966.

Maeno Naoaki 前野直彬 "Gi Chō—iki ni kanjita jinsei" 魏徵—意氣に感じた人生 [Wei Cheng—A Deeply Felt Life], *Rekishi to jimbutsu* 歷史と人物 [History and Historical Personalities], 11 (special expanded edition) (Nov. 1973), 82–93.

Matsui Shūichi 松井秀一. "Sokuten Bukō no yōritsu o megutte" 則天武後の擁立をめぐって [The Establishment of Empress Wu Tse-t'ien], *Hokudai shigaku* 北大史學 [Journal of the Historical Association of Hokkaido University], 11 (1966), 1–18.

———. "Tōdai zenki no kizoku" 唐代前期の貴族 [Aristocracy of the Early T'ang], *Rekishi kyōiku* 歷史教育 [The Teaching of History], 14 (May, 1966), 39–45.

Mou Jun-sun 牟潤孫. "T'ang-ch'u nan-pei hsüeh-jen lun-hsüeh chih i-ch'ü chi ch'i ying-hsiang" 唐初南北學人論學之異趣乃其影響 [The Differences of Academic Approach between the Northern and Southern Scholars in the Early T'ang Period and their Influence], *Hsiang-kang chung-wen ta-hsüeh Chung-kuo wen-hua yen-chiu-so hsüeh-pao* 香港中文大學中國文化研究所學報 [The Journal of the Institute of Chinese Studies of the Chinese University of Hong Kong], 1 (1968), 50–86.

Nunome Chōfū 布目潮渢. "Genmumon no hen" 玄武門の變 [The Hsüan-wu Gate Incident], *Ōsaka Daigaku kyōyōbu kenkyū shūroku* 大阪大學教養部研究集錄 [Researches of the Department of Education, Osaka University], 16 (1968), 17–51.

———. "Ri En shūdan no kōzō" 李淵集團の構造 [The Structure of Li Yüan's Organization], *Ritsumeikan bungaku* 立命館文學 [Ritsumeikan University Journal of Cultural Sciences], 243 (1965), 1–43.

———. "Tensaku jōshō, Sentōdō daikōdai shōshorei, Shin Ō Seimin—

sokuimae no Tō no Taisō 天策上將・陝東道大行臺尚書令・秦王世民— 即位前の唐の太宗 [Supreme Commander of Heavenly Strategy, President of the Department of Affairs of State of the Shan-tung Circuit Grand Field Office, the Prince of Ch'in, Shih-min—Prior to His Accession as T'ang T'ai-tsung], *Ritsumeikan bungaku* 立命館文學 [Ritsumeikan University Journal of Cultural Sciences], 255 (1966), 1–52.

———. "Tōchō sōgyōki no ichi kōsatsu" 唐朝創業期の一考察 [A Study of the Founding Period of the T'ang Dynasty], *Tōyōshi kenkyū* 東洋史研究 [The Journal of Oriental Researches], 25 (1966), 1–40.

———. "Yō Genkan no hanran" 楊玄感の叛亂 [The Revolt of Yang Hsüan-kan], *Ritsumeikan bungaku* 立命館文學 [Ritsumeikan University Journal of Cultural Sciences], 236 (1965), 1–30.

———. "Zuimatsu no hanranki ni okeru Ri Mitsu no dōkō" 隋末の叛亂期における李密の動向 [Li Mi's Rising in the Last Years of the Sui], *Shigaku zasshi* 史學雜誌 [Journal of Historical Studies], 74 (1965), 1–44.

Okazaki Fumio 岡崎文夫. "Gi Chō hyōden" 魏徵評傳 [Commentary on the Biography of Wei Cheng], *Rekishi to chiri* 歷史と地理 [History and Geography], 33 (1934), 9–16.

P'i Hsi-jui 皮錫瑞. *Ching-hsüeh li-shih* 經學歷史 [A History of Classical Learning]. 1924; reprint, Hong Kong, 1961.

Sa Meng-wu 薩孟武. *Chung-kuo cheng-chih ssu-hsiang shih* 中國政治思想史 [A History of Chinese Political Thought]. Taipei, 1969.

Seike Eizaburō 清家瑩三郎. *Tō no Taisō* 唐の太宗 [T'ang T'ai-tsung]. Tokyo, 1934.

Shih Chang-ju 石璋如. "Han-T'ang ti kuo-tu ling-mu yü chiang-yü" 漢唐的國都陵墓與疆域 [Capitals, Tombs, and Frontiers in the Han and T'ang], *Ta-lu tsa-chih* 大陸雜誌 [The Continent], 6 (1953), 243–50.

Sun Kuo-tung 孫國棟. "T'ang Chen-kuan Yung-hui chien tang-cheng ti shih-i" 唐貞觀永徽間黨爭的試釋 [An Explication of Factional Strife during the Period from Chen-kuan through Yung-hui of the T'ang], *Hsin-ya shu-yüan hsüeh-shu nien-k'an* 新亞書院學書年刊 [New Asia College Academic Annual], 7 (1965), 39–54.

———. "T'ang-tai san-sheng chih chih fa-chan yen-chiu" 唐代三省之制發展研究 [The Development of the Three Department System of the T'ang Dynasty], *Hsin-ya hsüeh-pao* 新亞學報 [New Asia Journal], 3 (1957), 17–121.

Takeda Ryūji 竹田龍兒. "Jōkan shizokushi no hensan ni kansuru ichi kōsatsu" 貞觀氏族志の編纂に關する一考察 [A Study of the Compilation of the Chen-kuan *Compendium of Clans*], *Shigaku* 史學, 25 (1952), 456–74.

T'ang Ch'ang-ju 唐長孺. *T'ang-shu ping-chih chien-cheng* 唐書兵志箋正 [Commentary on and Corrections to the Military Monograph of the New T'ang History]. Peking, 1962.

T'ang Ch'eng-yeh 湯承業. *Sui Wen-ti cheng-chih shih-kung chih yen-chiu* 隋文帝政治事功之研究 [The Political Achievements of Sui Wen-ti]. Taipei, 1967.

Ts'en Chung-mien 岑仲勉. "Chiao Chen-kuan shih-tsu-chih ts'an-chüan" 校貞觀氏族志殘卷 [A Collation of Remnants of the Chen-kuan *Compendium of clans*]. *Kuo-li Chung-shan ta-hsüeh yen-chiu-yüan wen-k'o yen-chiu-so li-shih-hsüeh-pu pien-chi* 國立中山大學研究院文科研究所歷史學部編輯 [Papers of the History Department of the Research Institute of the Graduate Faculty of Letters, National Sun Yat-sen University], 2 (1937), 315–30.

———. *Fu-ping chih-tu yen-chiu* 府兵制度研究 [A Study of the Militia System]. Shanghai, 1957.

———. *Hsi T'u-chüeh shih-liao pu-ch'üeh chi k'ao-cheng* 西突厥史料補闕及考證 [Supplementation and Verification of Historical Materials on the Western Turks]. Shanghai, 1958.

———. *Sui-T'ang shih* 隋唐史 [History of the Sui and T'ang Dynasties]. Peking, 1957.

———. *T'ang-shih yü-shen* 唐史餘瀋 [Marginalia on T'ang History]. Shanghai, 1960.

———. *Yüan-ho hsing-tsuan ssu-chiao-chi* 元和姓纂四校記 [A Fourfold Collation of the Compendium of Surnames of the Yüan-ho Period]. 3 vols. Shanghai, 1948.

Tsukiyama Chisaburō 築山治三郎. *Tōdai seiji seido no kenkyū* 唐代政治制度の研究 [Studies on the Governmental System of the T'ang Dynasty]. Osaka, 1967.

Wan Chün 萬鈞. *T'ang T'ai-tsung* 唐太宗. Shanghai, 1955.

Wang Li-chung 王立中. *Wen-chung-tzu chen-wei hui-k'ao* 文中子眞偽彙考 [Examination of the Truths and Falsehoods Surrounding Wen-chung-tzu]. Changsha, 1938.

Wang Ying-ling 汪吟龍. *Wen-chung-tzu k'ao-hsin-lu* 文中子考信錄 [Records Concerning the Existence of Wen-chung-tzu]. Shanghai, 1934.

Wu Che 吳澤. "Lun T'ang-tai ch'ien-ch'i t'ung-chih chieh-chi nei-pu tou-cheng yü chieh-chi tou-cheng" 論唐代前期統治階級內部鬥爭與階級鬥爭 [Class Conflict and Internal Conflict within the Ruling Class during the Early T'ang Dynasty], *Hsin chien-she* 新建設 (1962, no. 1). pp. 16–32.

Wu Che and Yüan Ying-kuang 吳澤·袁英光. "T'ang-ch'u cheng-ch'üan

yü cheng-cheng ti hsing wen-t'i" 唐初政權與政爭的性問題 [Problems Concerning the Characteristics of Political Power and Political Strife in the Early T'ang], *Li-shih yen-chiu* 歷史研究, 1964, no. 2, pp. 110–34.

Yamazaki Hiroshi 山崎宏. "Zuichō kanryō no seikaku" 隋朝官僚の性格 [The Character of Bureaucracy in the Sui Dynasty]. *Tōkyō Kyōikudaigaku bungakubu kiyō* 東京教育大學文學部紀要, 6 (1956), 1–59.

Yang Hsiang-k'uei 楊向奎. "T'ang-Sung shih-tai ti ching-hsüeh ssu-hsiang" 唐宋時代的經學思想 [Concepts of Classical Learning in the T'ang and Sung Dynasties], *Wen-shih-che* 文史哲 [Literature, History, and Philosophy], 1958, no. 5, pp. 7–16.

Yang Kuo-i 楊國宜. "Lüeh-lun 'Chen-kuan chih chih'" 略論「貞觀之治」[A Brief Discussion of the "Chen-kuan chih chih"], *Li-shih chiao-hsüeh* 歷史教學, 1961, no. 10, pp. 20–24.

Yen Keng-wang 嚴耕望. "Lun T'ang-tai shang-shu-sheng chih chih-ch'üan yü ti-wei" 論唐代尚書省之職權與地位 [On the Authority and Status of the Department of Affairs of State of the T'ang Dynasty], *Kuo-li chung-yang yen-chiu-yüan li-shih yü-yen yen-chiu-so chi-k'an* 國立中央研究院歷史語言研究所集刊 [Bulletin of the Institute of History and Philology, Academia Sinica], 24 (1953), 1–68.

———. *T'ang p'u-shang-ch'eng-lang piao* 唐僕尚丞郎表 [Tables of High Officials in the Department of Affairs of State during the T'ang Dynasty]. 4 vols. Taipei, 1956.

Yoshikawa Tadao 吉川忠夫. "Bunchūshi kō—toku ni Tōkōshi o tegakari toshite" 文中子考—とくに東皋子を手がかりとして [A Study of Wen-chung-tzu—with Special Reference to Tung-kao-tzu]. *Shirin* 史林, 53 (1970), 225–58.

Yüan Ting-chi 袁定基. *T'ang T'ai-tsung* 唐太宗. Peking, 1963.

IV. Works in Western Languages

American Consulate-General of Hong Kong. *Survey of the China Mainland Press.* No. 4061. November, 1967.

Ansley, Clive. *The Heresy of Wu Han. His Play 'Hai Jui's Dismissal'; and Its Role in China's Cultural Revolution.* Toronto, 1971.

Asia Research Centre. *The Great Cultural Revolution in China.* Hong Kong, 1967.

Balazs, Étienne. *Le traité economique du "Souei-chou."* Leiden, 1953.

———. *Le traité juridique du "Souei-chou."* Leiden, 1954.

———, "L'Oeuvre des Souei: L'Unification," in *Histoire et institutions de la Chine ancienne,* by Henri Maspero and Etienne Balazs, Paris, 1967.

Bingham, Woodbridge. *The Founding of the T'ang Dynasty: The Fall of Sui and the Rise of T'ang.* Baltimore, 1941.

————. "Li Shih-min's Coup in A.D. 626," *Journal of the American Oriental Society*, 70 (1950), 89–95, 259–271.

————. "The Rise of Li in a Ballad Prophecy," *Journal of the American Oriental Society*, 61 (1941), 272–80.

————. "Wen Ta-ya: The First Recorder of T'ang History," *Journal of the American Oriental Society*, 57 (1937), 368–74.

Chan Hok-lam. "Liu Chi (1311–75) and His Models: The Image-Building of a Chinese Imperial Adviser," *Oriens Extremus*, 15 (1968), 34–55.

Chavannes, Edouard. *Documents Sur les Tou-kiue (Turcs) Occidentaux*. Paris, 1900.

————. *Le T'ai chan*. Paris, 1910.

Ch'en Shou-yi. *Chinese Literature, A Historical Introduction*. New York, 1961.

Chen Tsu-lung. "On the 'Hot-Spring Inscription' Preserved by a Rubbing in the Bibliothèque Nationale at Paris," *T'oung Pao*, 46 (1958), 376–96.

Creel, H.G. "The Fa-chia: 'Legalists' or 'Administrators'?", in *Studies Presented to Tung Tso-pin on his Sixty-fifth Birthday, Bulletin of the Institute of History and Philology, Academia Sinica*, extra vol. 4, Nankang, Taiwan, 1961.

Crozier, Michel. *The Bureaucratic Phenomenon*. Chicago, 1964.

de Bary, Wm. Theodore, et al. *Sources of Chinese Tradition*. New York, 1960.

des Rotours, Robert. *Le traité des examens*. Paris, 1932.

————. "Les grands fonctionnaires des provinces en Chine sous les dynastie des T'ang," *T'oung Pao*, 25 (1927), 219–332.

————. *Traité des fonctionnaires et traité de l'armée*. 2 vols. Leiden, 1947.

Doré, Henri. *Recherches sur les superstitions en Chine*. 18 vols. Shanghai, 1911–38.

Downs, Anthony. *Inside Bureaucracy*. Boston, 1967.

Eisenstadt, S. N. "Political Struggle in Bureaucratic Societies," *World Politics*, 9 (1956–57), 15–37.

————. *The Political Systems of Empires*. Glencoe, Ill., 1963.

Elvin, Mark. *The Pattern of the Chinese Past*. Stanford, 1973.

Fang, Achilles. *The Chronicle of the Three Kingdoms*. 2 vols. Cambridge, Mass., 1952, 1965.

Feifel, Eugene. *Po Chü-i as a Censor*. The Hague, 1961.

Fitzgerald, C. P. *Son of Heaven: A Biography of Li Shih-min, Founder of the T'ang Dynasty*. Cambridge, 1933.

————. *The Empress Wu*, 1956. Reprint, London, 1968.

Fung Yu-lan. *A History of Chinese Philosophy*. 2 vols. Princeton, 1953.

Grousset, René. *L'Empire des steppes*. Paris, 1939.

Hervouet, Yves. *Un poète cour sous les Han: Sseu-ma Siang-ju*. Paris, 1964.

Hucker, Charles O. "Confucianism and the Chinese Censorial System," in *Confucianism in Action*, David S. Nivison and Arthur F. Wright, eds. Stanford, 1959.

————. *The Censorial System of Ming China*. Stanford, 1966.

Hung, William. "The T'ang Bureau of Historiography before 708," *Harvard Journal of Asiatic Studies,* 23 (1960–61), 93–107.

Kramers, R. P. "Conservatism and the Transmission of the Confucian Canon: A T'ang Scholar's Complaint," *Journal of Oriental Studies* (University of Hong Kong), 2 (1955), 119–32.

Legge, James. *The Chinese Classics*. 2nd ed. rev. 5 vols. Hong Kong, 1961. vol. 1, *Confucian Analects, The Great Learning. The Doctrine of the Mean;* vol. 2, *The Works of Mencius;* vol. 3, *The Shoo King;* vol, 4, *The She King;* vol. 5, *The Ch'un Ts'ew with the Tso Chuen.*

Levenson, Joseph. *Confucian China and Its Modern Fate*. Vol. 2, *The Problem of Monarchical Decay*. Berkeley, 1968.

Lewis, George Winston, "The Cheng-kuan cheng-yao: A Source for the Study of Early T'ang Government." M. A. thesis, University of Hong Kong, 1962.

Liu, James T. C. "An Administrative Cycle in Chinese History: The Case of the Northern Sung Emperors," *Journal of Asian Studies,* 21 (1962), 137–52.

————. *Ou-yang Hsiu*. Stanford, 1967.

Maurois, André. "The Ethics of Biography," in *Biography as an Art, Selected Criticism 1560–1960,* James L. Clifford, ed. New York, 1962.

Mote, F. W. "The Growth of Chinese Despotism: A Critique of Wittfogel's Theory of Oriental Despotism as Applied to China," *Oriens Extremus,* 8 (1961), 1–41.

Needham, Joseph. *Clerks and Craftsmen in China and the West*. Cambridge, 1970.

Pulleyblank, E. G. *The Background of the Rebellion of An Lu-shan*. London, 1955.

————. "The Tzyjyh Tongjiann Kaoyih and the Sources for the History of the Period 730–763," *Bulletin of the School of Oriental and African Studies,* 13 (1950–51), 448–73.

Rideout, J. K. "The Rise of the Eunuchs during the T'ang Dynasty," *Asia Major,* n.s. 1 (1949), 53–72.

Rogers, Michael C. *The Chronicle of Fu Chien: A Case of Exemplar History*. Berkeley, 1968.

Ruhlmann, Robert. "Traditional Heroes in Chinese Popular Fiction," in *The Confucian Persuasion*. Arthur F. Wright, ed. Stanford, 1960, pp. 141–76.

Sivin, Nathan. *Chinese Alchemy: Preliminary Studies*. Cambridge, Mass., 1968.

Soothill, William Edward. *The Hall of Light, A Study of Early Chinese Kingship*. London, 1951.

Tjan Tjoe Som. *Po Hu T'ung*. 2 vols. Leiden, 1949.

Twitchett, Denis. *Financial Administration Under the T'ang Dynasty*. 2nd ed. Cambridge, 1970.

––––. "Problems of Chinese Biography," in *Confucian Personalities*. Arthur F. Wright and Denis Twitchett, eds. Stanford, 1962.

Wang Gung-wu. "Feng Tao: An Essay on Confucian Loyalty," in *Confucian Personalities*. Arthur F. Wright and Denis Twitchett, eds. Stanford, 1962.

Waley, Arthur. *The Analects of Confucius*. New York, 1938.

––––. *Monkey*. New York, 1958.

Watson, Burton. *Mo-tzu: Basic Writings*, New York, 1963.

Wechsler, Howard J. "Kao-tsu the Founder" and "T'ai-tsung the Consolidator," in *The Cambridge History of China*. John K. Fairbank and Denis Twitchett, eds. (forthcoming).

––––. "Factionalism in Early T'ang Government," in *Perspectives on the T'ang*. Arthur F. Wright and Denis Twitchett, eds. New Haven, 1973.

Wright, Arthur F. "The Formation of Sui Ideology, 581–604," in *Chinese Thought and Institutions*. John K. Fairbank, ed. Chicago, 1957.

––––. "Sui Yang-ti: Personality and Stereotype," in *The Confucian Persuasion*. Arthur F. Wright, ed. Stanford, 1960.

––––. "The Sui Dynasty," in *The Cambridge History of China*. John K. Fairbank and Denis Twitchett, eds., (forthcoming).

––––. "T'ang T'ai-tsung and Buddhism," in *Perspectives on the T'ang*. Arthur F. Wright and Denis Twitchett, eds. New Haven, 1973.

Index